Controversial
Court Cases
in Connecticut
Part I

CONTROVERSIAL COURT CASES
in Connecticut
Part I

Regina Forker

LawFirst Publishing
The Connecticut Bar Association
New Britain, CT

2008

LawFirst Publishing
The Connecticut Bar Association

First published in 2008 by LawFirst Publishing
A division of the Connecticut Bar Association

Copyright © LawFirst Publishing, 2008
All rights reserved.

ISBN 0-9740069-9-8

Printed in the United States of America
14 13 12 11 10 09 08   1 2 3 4 5

Designed by: Jody L. Searing, Senior Graphic Designer
Edited by: Lewis K. Parker, Editor
              Emma L. Gormley, Associate Editor

Without limiting the rights under copyright reserved above, no part of this publication may be reproduced, stored in or introduced into a retrieval system, or transmitted, in any form or by any means (electronic, mechanical, photocopying, recording, or otherwise), without the prior written permission of both the copyright owner and the above publisher of this book.

The scanning, uploading, and distribution of this book via the Internet or via any other means without the permission of the publisher is illegal and punishable by law.

The Connecticut Bar Association
30 Bank Street
PO Box 350
New Britain, CT 06050-0350

Contents

Foreword		vii
Preface		xi
Acknowledgments		xiii
1	The Devil Comes to Connecticut: Connecticut Witch Trials in the Seventeenth Century	1
2	Teaching Tolerance: Prudence Crandall and Her School for "Young Ladies and Little Misses of Color"	34
3	A Mutinous Landing in Unsuspecting New Haven: The *Amistad* Trial	63
4	Privacy in the Bedroom: *Griswold v. Connecticut*	97
5	The Circus Comes to New Haven: The Trial of the Black Panthers	134
6	Desegregating Hartford Public Schools: *Sheff v. O'Neill*	174
Appendix A		215
Appendix B		227
Appendix C		231
Appendix D		305
Appendix E		347
Bibliography		361

Foreword

What makes a legal text canonical? This, after all, is the question that must be asked from the outset. We cannot simply mean notable cases. When we say the term canon, it presupposes authenticity or authority (as it does with scripture) or a significant work worthy of extensive study (as it does with literature), and we are really speaking about authorship in the first instance and reception in the second.

This book is about major cases. But with a bit of sleight-of-hand, this collection has been identified as "controversial cases." In a sense, then, this book describes trials that have challenged set norms, upset certain vested interests, or undercut the hegemony of received moral values. We are creating a kind of canon that makes us uncomfortable. But how is this true? No one would favor reinstating prosecution for sorcery, the shutting down of schools to teach African-American girls, the return of those who escaped slavery to be sold in slave markets, the bringing back of the government into the bedroom, divisive race-based criminal trials, or the reinstitution of segregation. Indeed, perhaps with the exception of the issue of how desegregation would be implemented, these trials would all be read by contemporaries with a comfortable sense of consensus. Nevertheless, these cases do tell us how the legal system responded in the past to political and cultural pressures, and the subsequent distortions created in the legal process.

Examining past legal controversies has two important purposes. First, it addresses the issue of the limits of tolerance—and reminds us how often these limits shift. In a classic study of New England deviance, *Wayward Puritans*, sociologist Kai Erikson describes the boundary tending function of legal sanctions. Not surprisingly, many of the cases in this volume deal with issues of gender and race. Both the witchcraft trials of the seventeenth century and *Griswold v. Connecticut*, which established a Constitutional right to use birth control in the twentieth century, may be analyzed through the lens of assertions of male control over gender relations. The trials of Prudence Crandall for teaching African Americans in the 1830s and the Hartford desegregation case, *Sheff v. O'Neill*, in our own time, are really bookend cases about the difficulties in achieving access to education despite social discrimination against racial groups. Both the

Amistad trial of kidnapped Africans who rose up against their captors, which was ultimately decided by the United States Supreme Court in 1841, and the trial of the New Haven Nine, the Black Panther murder trial, might be said to resurface the issue of what limits exist in justifying the use of violence in asserting claims for fundamental human rights.

But, secondly, these cases also have a thickly normative function. They warn us about how we as judges, lawyers, or the deliberative public might respond to controversial cases in our own time. The trial is not just a performative act, not just a forum for acting out divisive issues. It is a place to test our own notions of how legal norms respond within the crucible of significant contention. Almost all of the cases in this volume are, in some fashion, bad cases. Perhaps that is what makes them so important for us.

David Daube, a leading Roman legal historian, has written that bad cases can make good law. Yet it is remarkable how few important legal principles emerge from these trials. The *Amistad* case was important in tapping into a natural rights tradition separate from the Anglo-American tradition of common law; *Griswold* discovered a privacy right between the lines of the Constitutional text, but neither of these normative claims was fully unpacked in these cases. In other instances, the law is simply bad law. For all the window dressing of evidentiary standards, due process, and the close questioning of witnesses, there are no principles of legal thinking to be gained from the witchcraft prosecutions. The court's upholding of Connecticut's 1833 Black Law, which banned teaching non-resident African-American children, was questioned even in Prudence Crandall's own lifetime.

But it might be possible to recast our own legal psyches—the posture we take towards the interaction of law and society—by resorting to these histories. Perhaps we might think about how our legal decisions could be considered from the vantage point of a century in the future. Might the inequitable uses of law, that we today take for granted, some day become unthinkable? How do we allow social controversies to reshape legal norms? And, most importantly, what do such cases tell us about how to grapple with the failures of inherited legalism?

I am suggesting that the selection of notable legal controversies is really a canon of legal failure. But since this is a canon of sorts, we must ask ourselves the classic question of canonicity—how is it created? Religious communities have their sacred scriptures, literary scholars have their canon, and lawyers, legal scholars, and judges construct their own sense of what works remain essential legal cultural touchstones and what do not. The usual textual landscape for lawyers consists of statutes, treatises, and cases. Perhaps statutes do not serve as the heartland of the legal canon because their authorship is bound up with the political workings of legislatures. In common law jurisdictions, statutes are sometimes seen as expressive of public choice rather than more grounded legal thinking.

In the eighteenth-century, the notion of legal canon certainly would have been limited to treatises. Every educated lawyer would know his *Blackstone*. Indeed, when the United States became independent, perhaps the major project of the architects of a new American law was the publication of comprehensive treatises to replace *Blackstone*. James Wilson's lectures, delivered at the University of Pennsylvania in 1790, followed Blackstone's tradition of surveying the legal landscape in his lectures as Vinerian Professor at Oxford. Chancellor Kent's magisterial *Commentaries on American Law* (1826–1830) was a nod to Justinian's codex. Justice Joseph Story's many treatises on equity, conflict of laws, and commercial law served to create a tangible sense of a coherent American legalism.

With the transformation of legal education in the 1870s at Harvard, which was instituted by Christopher Columbus Langdell, case law became dominant in the minds of lawyers. The case book was intended as a Darwinian selection process. From the mass of cases—some well-decided, some not—came a canon of those ideal cases for teaching legal principles. The instructor's purpose was to relate one case to another, and ultimately to construct an ordered structure for legal rules. The canon—though this term was rarely used—applied to cases, not statutes or treatises.

A second canonical tradition emerged around popular didactic or moral literature—both low brow and high brow. *The Newgate Calendar*, subtitled *Malefactors' Bloody Literature*, allows the reader to vicariously experience rummaging through the seedy side of London's fog-filled embankments, brothels, and dens of thieves. First published in 1774 in five volumes, *The Newgate Calendar* included stories about such famous felons as Dick Turpin, John Wilkes, and Moll Cutpurse. Its ostensible purpose was didactic—the improvement of morals. But readers must have begun with a moral flaw or two to enjoy such salacious tales. At a presumably more elevated level, English *State Trials*, which covered cases of treason, seditious libel, piracy, and other offenses against the state, was published in various editions through the eighteenth century. The apotheosis of this work came with the publication of the most important edition, known as *Cobbett's Complete Collection of State Trials*, from 1809 to 1826 in 33 volumes. These two works set the boundaries of the permissible in pre-Reform era English culture. *The Newgate Calendar* described deviance in terms of crime—largely offenses against persons, and *State Trials* drew the limits of political activity—largely offenses against the governing order.

I have tried to suggest that the choice of controversial cases draws specifically upon lawyers' notions of canonicity, and, more specifically, both the casebook and collected trials traditions. As the heirs of Langdell, we might even accept one or two of the cases in this volume as canonical cases. But these are also didactic or moral cases in the tradition of the English collections discussed. What is striking—and what makes the choice of these trials so different from the case of the scriptural canon—is that all these cases were chosen because of a debate from *outside* the courtroom. We are, like the protagonists in *Controversial Court Cases in Connecticut, Part I*, insiders and outsiders at the same time.

                              Dr. Steven Wilf
                              Professor of Law
                              University of Connecticut School of Law

Preface

In thinking about the quiet, innocent state of Connecticut, one may think that nothing exciting ever really happens, that everyone drives a Volvo, that all children are educated at expensive private schools, and that those children turn into preppy, pretentious adults. One may even think that Greenwich and Fairfield represent the average Connecticut town, and that all Connecticut residents are Democrats that play golf and wear sweaters tied around their shoulders. The long list of controversial, even explosive cases that were in the running to be included in this book make it obvious that such stereotypes are untrue.

From its early beginnings as a colony and then as a state, Connecticut has dealt with controversy and strife in its courts. From the early witch trials to the ongoing case of *Sheff v. O'Neill*, Connecticut courts have yet to experience a lull in activity. While Massachusetts is famous for its witch trials in Salem, Connecticut certainly gave its "witches," or in many cases, innocent, but eccentric women, a run for their money; slavery was a worldwide problem, but it was in Connecticut where enslaved Africans went on trial for their freedom. One would think that the northern state of Connecticut would be progressive in the treatment of free African Americans, but the townspeople of the small, rural town of Canterbury made it clear whom they thought should and should not be educated when Prudence Crandall was put on trial. The Black Panthers originally hailed from California. The organization quickly gained popularity throughout the country; however it was in Connecticut where controversy arose and made national headlines. Milo Sheff was in fourth grade when he was chosen to be the face of Hartford's struggling schools; now, nearly 20 years after the lawsuit was filed, Hartford's schools remain much the same as when Milo attended them. The level of disparity between Connecticut's richest and poorest areas is overwhelming, with Greenwich and Fairfield on one end and Hartford, Bridgeport, and New Haven on the other. Unfortunately, that disproportion is all too apparent in Connecticut's education systems.

These cases represent the fact that we as a society are constantly surrounded by important and contentious issues. How we react to them and what we do with those reactions is what matters. This book may be a step in the right direction, making people aware of what our state's history has held, and what its future could hold.

Acknowledgments

There are a great number of people I want to thank for being part of this book and making it a reality. First, my editor, Lewis Parker, who came up with the idea and presented me with the opportunity to write a book while I was a 1L in law school, and all the staff at the Connecticut Bar Association who continually edited the book and put it together in order to get it published in time for the Annual Meeting deadline. I also want to thank the law firm of Brown Paindiris and Scott for giving me Fridays off last summer so I could actually write the book, and for always making sure I was still writing it. Thank you to my ever-busy law professor Steven Wilf for writing the foreword to this book.

All of the people and organizations who helped me with my research are greatly appreciated as well, including Lexis Nexis, for letting me use their vast resources to research the book, the Wethersfield Historical Society, Debra Avery, the Stamford Historical Society, the Huntington Library, the *Hartford News*, the Connecticut State Library, Yale's Gilder Lehrman Center for the Study of Slavery, the Prudence Crandall Museum, the New Haven Museum & Historical Society, Mystic Seaport, Planned Parenthood of Connecticut, the Yale Archives, Emory Douglas, Meres-Sia Gabri El, the Center for the Study of Political Graphics, the *Hartford Courant*, the Associated Press, the University of Connecticut Law Archives, Milo Sheff, the Connecticut Bar Foundation, and the University of Connecticut's Thomas J. Dodd Research Center. To all those whom I have inadvertently forgotten, I apologize and thank you as well.

I would also like to thank my family and friends for supporting me as I wrote this book, especially to Adam, for never reading a rough draft, but for dragging me away when I needed a break and for always supporting me in all that I do.

A special thanks to the Connecticut Bar Foundation for allowing me to access Catherine Roraback's taped interviews.

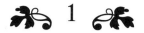

The Devil Comes to Connecticut
Connecticut Witch Trials in the Seventeenth Century

In seventeenth-century New England, witches were very real. That is, just about everyone was superstitious enough to believe that witches actually existed. Many people thought that Satan enticed ordinary people to the dark side, and that witches conspired with the Devil to wreak havoc on unsuspecting members of the community. Most New Englanders blamed witchcraft for causing all kinds of natural events ranging from flash floods to the death of babies to corn wilting on the stalks.

If you were thought to be a witch, chances are you were accused, tried, convicted—if you were tried at all—and put to death in Salem, Massachusetts, by hanging. No one convicted of being a witch in New England was ever burned at the stake, contrary to popular belief. Nineteen people were hung for allegedly practicing witchcraft in Salem, one was pressed to death with heavy stones, and at least five and as many as 13 died while waiting in jail (records conflict as to the correct number). Hundreds more were accused and jailed, had their property confiscated, and their lives ruined. The first Salem "witch trials" took place in 1692, but the first such trial in New England occurred long before the Salem panic in the quiet state of Connecticut in 1647.

The 1692 Salem Witch Panic involved a great many people, more than all the Connecticut trials combined, but it seems to have been an isolated incident. The Connecticut trials began long before, and lasted for some time after the Salem hysteria. In fact, the Salem trials seemed to have stirred things up again in Connecticut after a period of relative quiet. The

The trial of a seventeenth-century witch in Puritan America. Wood engraving 1892. *Courtesy of Photos.com.*

last witch trial that took place in New England was also in Connecticut when Winifred Benham and Winifred Benham, Jr. of Wallingford were tried and acquitted in 1697.

In 1647, Alse Young of Windsor, Connecticut, was hanged in Hartford's Meeting House Square where today the Old State House sits. From the records, it appears that Young was not only the first person in Connecticut to be executed for being a witch, but the first in America as well. Following Young's execution came a period of approximately 45 years during which people in Connecticut were accused of witchcraft and interaction with the Devil. The Connecticut witches all seem to have been given trials; how fair the trials were is up for debate. It also seems that Connecticut jurors and judges were apprehensive of sending these "witches" off to the gallows. There was often a lack of clear and convincing evidence that the "witches" did, in fact, dance with the Devil in the pale moonlight, or something to that effect. The witch "panics" in Connecticut did not yield quite so many dead as those in Salem. Approximately 37 people came under suspicion of being witches in Connecticut; approximately 11 were actually executed (it is unclear whether some went free or were executed and thus the number is not firm). This number can be compared to between 175 and 200 people under suspicion in Salem, with at least 20 executed in 1692.

The records regarding witch trials, convictions, and acquittals in Connecticut are scattered to say the least. Samuel Wyllys, Commissioner to the United Colonies in 1662, 1664, and 1667 and an assistant officer of the court until 1698, preserved much of the information that is available. The Wyllys papers contain transcripts of depositions presented at the witch trials, indictments of the witches, and the court's verdicts. The papers were passed on through Wyllys' family. They were eventually bought by the Connecticut State Librarian George Goddard on July 10, 1907, for $100. The originals are at Brown University and copies are housed at the Connecticut State Library. Other than Wyllys' collected papers, there seems to be no other comprehensive documentary history written while the trials were occurring. Years later, author and historian John Metcalf Taylor compiled a record of the Connecticut witches and their trials in his book *The Witchcraft Delusion in Colonial Connecticut*, published in 1908. Since then there have been multiple books, articles, and treatises published regarding the "other" (*i.e.*, non-Salem) witches.

THE LAW AGAINST WITCHES

Early in the colony's history, Connecticut lawmakers established a strict zero-tolerance policy for witchcraft. On December 1, 1642, the General Court in Hartford passed the first penal code—the Capitall Lawes Established by the Generall Court—that included 12 capital offenses, the second of which was for being a witch. "If any man or woman be a witch—that is, hath or consulteth with a familiar spirit—they shall be put to death." Even before this law was passed, the Colony of New Haven penned a similar law on April 26, 1636, citing particular Bible chapters and verses as its authority: "If any person be a witch, he or she shall be put to death, according to Exod. 22:18. Levit. 20:27. Deut.18:10–11."

The quoted Bible passages read as follows: Exodus 22:18 states, "Thou shalt not suffer a witch to live"; Leviticus 20:27 reads, "A man or woman who is a medium or spiritist among you must be put to death. You are to stone them; their blood will be on their own heads"; Deuteronomy 18:10–11 reads, "Let no one be found among you who sacrifices his son or daughter in the fire, who practices divination or sorcery, interprets omens, engages in witchcraft, or casts spells, or who is a medium or spiritist or who consults the dead."

The capital crime of being a witch disappeared in 1750 when the penal code was printed again and the crime was omitted.

GROUNDS FOR EXAMINATION OF A WITCH

Evidence against a person accused of being a witch was collected in three ways: (1) by a witch's own confession; (2) by searching the accused's body for "witch marks"; and (3) by the testimony and accusations of witchcraft. William Jones, deputy governor of Connecticut from 1692 to 1698, took notes from an unidentified document that spelled out specific grounds for examination of a witch. Jones' notes indicate that there were seven such grounds.

1. Notorious defamation by a common report of the people aground of suspicion;
2. If a fellow witch give testimony on his examination or death that such a person is a witch, but this is not sufficient for conviction or condemnation;
3. If after cursing, there follow death or at least mischief to a party;

4. If after quarreling or threatening a present mischief doth follow for party's devilishly disposed after cursing do use threatening and also is a great presumption against them;
5. If the party suspected be your son or daughter, the servant or familiar friend, near neighbors or old companion of a known or convicted witch, this also is a presumption, for witchcraft is an art that may be learned and conveyed from man to man and often it is falleth out that a witch dying leave some of the aforesaid heirs of her witchcraft;
6. If ye party suspected have ye devils mark for t'is thought when ye devil maketh his covenant with you he always leaves his mark behind him to know you for his own, if no evident reason can be given for such mark;
7. Lastly, if ye party examined be unconstant and contrary to himself in his answers.

Deputy Governor Jones also specified that conviction must be grounded on just and sufficient proofs. The proofs for conviction were of two sorts. Jones indicated that the red-hot iron test was considered less sufficient proof and used only in past times. Here is how this test worked: The accused party was to hold a red-hot iron in his or her hand. If the person was not hurt, he or she was cleared and considered innocent of witchcraft; if the person was hurt, he or she was convicted as a witch. According to Jones, this practice had been utterly condemned and no longer used. Also insufficient as proof was the testimony of a wizard who pretends to show the face of the witch in a "glass" or a mirror, for the "devil may represent a person innocent."

The water test was also used on occasion to determine whether a person was a witch. The water test was administered by tying the accused person's hands and feet together and dropping the person into a body of water. If the accused person bounced up and did not sink, the person was considered a witch because it was thought that the Devil was helping the person to stay afloat. If the person sank below the level of the water, the indication was that the Devil was not helping the person and the accused was proclaimed innocent.

This water test used to identify potential witches seems to have originated early in history and was first found to exist in the Code of Hammurabi, which was written in 1760 B.C. One translation interprets the Code to read: "If a man has placed an enchantment upon a man, and has not justified himself, he upon whom the enchantment is placed to the Holy River (Euphrates) shall go; into the Holy River he shall plunge. If

An illustration of the "water test." *Reproduced by permission of The Huntington Library, San Marino, California.*

the Holy River holds (drowns) him he who enchanted him shall take his house. If on the contrary, the man is safe and thus is innocent, the wizard loses his life, and his house."

Jones also noted that other forms of proof sufficient for conviction included the voluntary confessions of the suspected party. The testimony of two good and honest witnesses was also sufficient if their statements could prove one of three things: (1) that the accused person had invocated the Devil for help; (2) that the person had a "familiar spot" in any form of a visible creature such as a mouse or a cat; or (3) that upon oath the accused person had done an action or work with the Devil such as to show the face of a man in a mirror, used enchantments or spells, divined things to come, raised "tempests," or caused the form of a dead man to appear. This kind of testimony sufficiently proved that the accused person was a witch. And yet the author of the document copied by Jones warned jurors and courts not to condemn suspected persons on bare presumptions without good and sufficient proofs.

The "witch marks" Jones noted were commonly used to determine if a woman was a witch. According to Taylor in *The Witchcraft Delusion in Colonial Connecticut*, the courts in New England colonies referred to *Dalton's Country Justice*, a standard legal procedural authority that was commonly used in England. As instruction to the courts on how to find these marks and what they signified, the text stated that:

> These witches have ordinarily a familiar, or spirit which appeareth to them, sometimes in one shape and sometimes in another; as in the shape of a man, woman, boy, dog, cat, foal, hare, rat, toad, etc...And besides their sucking the Devil leaveth other marks upon their body, sometimes like a blue or red spot, like a flea-biting, sometimes the flesh sunk in and hollow. And these Devil's marks be invisible, and being pricked will not bleed, and be often in their secretest parts, and therefore require a diligent and careful search. These first two are main points to discover and convict those witches.

Although Jones didn't publish the document, "Grounds for Examination of a Witch," until 1692, earlier courts still required a strong connection between the accused person and the Devil, and would not convict based on mere presumptions.

THE FIRST WITCHES TO BE HANGED

ALSE YOUNG

According to early records, the first "witch" to be executed in Connecticut is said to be Alse (Alice) Young of Windsor, although almost no records as to her charges, trial, or conviction were either created or survived. What is left of her is an entry in Governor John Winthrop's journal from the spring of 1647. "One ____ of Windsor arraigned and executed for a witch." The blank indicated Winthrop was unaware of her name. It was not until 1908 that a researcher solved the mystery; he found a diary entry by Matthew Grant, a Windsor town clerk, who noted that on "May 26, 1647: Alse Young was hanged." Alse Young is not mentioned in any other court records. Nobody knows what she did to be branded a witch, or what evidence was brought against her. That she was indeed put to death as a witch seems to be confirmed by the fact that John Young, a Windsor landholder thought to be either her husband or father, left Windsor in 1649.

According to historians it would have been "most natural that he and his family should leave Windsor" due to the embarrassment that would ensue upon finding out that Alse was accused of being a witch. Some accounts suggest that Alse had a daughter named Alice Young Beamon who was accused of witchcraft some 30 years later in Springfield, Massachusetts.

And so the first Connecticut "witch" was hanged.

Mary Johnson

Alse Young was the first witch to be brought to trial and hanged, if indeed, she was given a trial before her death, but she was certainly not the last. Mary Johnson of Wethersfield was found guilty of being a witch in 1648, and was the first of the Wethersfield witches to be brought to trial.

Mary Johnson was the first person in New England to confess she was a witch. With Mary's own confession of her dastardly deeds with the Devil, the standards for conviction were eliminated and she was found guilty and sentenced to death. According to Mary, the Devil helped her with her chores when she asked him, sweeping ashes from the hearth, fetching the hogs, making them run around for her amusement. She confessed she made a pact with the Devil, "committed uncleanness" with men and devils, and had also murdered a child.

Governor Edward Hopkins conducted the trial that sentenced Mary to death. The magistrates were Thomas Wells of Wethersfield, Henry Wolcott of Windsor, and John Webster and John Cullick of Hartford. Her twelve-man jury included William Gibbens, John Talcott, William Wadsworth, and Andrew Bacon of Hartford; Samuel Smith, Nathanial Dickerson, Thomas Coleman, and John Deming of Wethersfield; Henry Clark, Matthew Allyn, William Phelps, and John More of Windsor. The records from the Particular Court of Connecticut note that on December 7, 1648, the jury found "the bill of indictment against Mary Johnson, that by her own confession she is guilty of familiarity with the Devil." While no details have survived regarding her execution, it seems certain she was hanged. The May 21, 1650 record of the General Court indicates that the prison-keeper's charges of six pounds, 10 shillings for her imprisonment were allowed and ordered to be paid "out of her estate." While awaiting her death, Mary bore a child in jail. It is possible her execution was postponed due to her pregnancy. According to the Colonial Records of Connecticut, the child was bound to Nathanial Rescew, the jailer's son, until he reached the age of 21. Mary paid Rescew 15 pounds in exchange for the promise that he would "meinteine and well educate her sonne."

The Carringtons

Several more people accused of being witches were brought to trial and hung in Connecticut from 1633 to 1654. Husband and wife John and Joan Carrington were indicted on February 20, 1651, at the Particular Court in Hartford. Their indictment read, "John Carrington thou art indicted by the name of John Carrington of Wethersfield, carpenter, that not having the fear of god before thine eyes thou hast entertained familiarity with Satan, the great enemy of God and mankind, and by his help has done works above the course of nature for which, both according to the law of God and the established law of this commonwealth, thou deservest to die." Joan Carrington's indictment read the same.

They were found guilty and sentenced to death on March 6, 1651. Little record of their trial remains and it is not known why they were convicted as witches. Their jury—composed of Mr. Phelps, Tailecoat, Hollister, Milton, White, Leawis, Smith, Pratt, More, Griswold, Harte, and Judd—found them guilty. The same group of magistrates that presided over Mary Johnson's case heard the Carringtons case as well.

Goodwife Bassett

Goodwife Bassett of Stratford, whose first name was not recorded, was charged with witchcraft in 1651, and based on her confession, was found guilty and hanged. (Goodwife was another word for Mrs., and was often shortened to Goody.) It is believed that just before she was put to death she indicated that another witch, most likely Goodwife Knapp, was operating in the Stratford/Fairfield area.

Goodwife Knapp

According to Taylor's history, Goodwife Knapp's case was "one of the most notable of the witchcraft cases. It stands among the early instances of the infliction of the death penalty in Connecticut." It is believed that Goody Knapp was a woman of "good repute," not an outcast in any way. She became "suspicioned" by her neighbors in Fairfield, and that set the ball rolling. Rumors that Knapp was a witch flew around town, and she was soon served with a formal indictment. While awaiting her trial, she was kept in the house of correction and while there was urged to "discover" more witches, but she was reluctant to do so. She was told that if she gave the names of other witches, her life would be spared. Goodwife Baldwin claimed that Knapp said, "There is a woman in town who is a witch and will be hanged within a twelve month and would confess herself a witch and clear her that she was none." Knapp denied ever making this statement, but Goodwife Staples may well have been the woman Knapp was referring to, if Knapp did indeed make such a statement.

Knapp was found guilty at her trial and executed in 1653. The whole town came out to watch her hang. After she was dead, a number of women examined her body for a witch's teat or Devil's mark. At the examination, Goodwife Staples proclaimed that "If these be the marks of a witch, I am one. These be no witch's teats, but such as I myself have, and other women, and so have you if you search yourself." Goodwife Odill, present at Knapp's post-mortem examination, told Staples that "No honest woman had such." Susan Lockwood, also present, said that "If I had such, I would be hanged and deserve it." Things did not go well for Staples after she made that statement.

Goodwife Staples

Rodger Ludlow, the lieutenant governor and a neighbor of Staples, told the Reverend and Mrs. Davenport that Staples was certainly a witch and also a liar who "went on in a tract of lying." Word spread quickly and Staples' husband Thomas brought a slander suit against Ludlow. Ludlow called witnesses to testify that Goody Knapp, right before she was hanged, told him that Staples was a witch. Many witnesses were called who spoke against Staples, attesting to her witch-like behavior. Hester Ward testified that Staples told her of two Indian gods she had that were going to make her rich. Several witnesses including Bethia Brundish and Deborah Lockwood testified that Goody Staples had, on several occasions, insisted that Goody Knapp was not a witch. Reverend John Davenport spoke in favor of Staples, and as a minister, it is likely he would have commanded the respect of the court. Davenport testified that he believed what Ludlow said was "utterly untrue and spoken out of malice." Others testified that Ludlow repeatedly called Staples a liar. Goodwife Gould of Fairfield testified that, in a church debate with Mr. Ludlow, Goody Staples had asked him to give just one example of a lie she had told. Mr. Ludlow replied that he "need not mention particulars, for she had gone on in a tract of lying." Goody Whitlocke of Fairfield testified that she too was present when a group of women searched Goody Knapp for witch's teats and shared Goody Staples' view that the teats were not there. "Several of the women said they could find none," she said at trial.

Staples' husband prevailed in his defamation suit and Ludlow was fined 15 pounds—10 for reparation of his wife's name and five for his "trouble and charge" in prosecuting his complaint against her accuser. The court could "see no cause to lay any blemish of a witch upon Goodwife Staples, but must judge that Mr. Ludlow hath done her wrong." This was not the end of the road for Staples though. She was indicted, tried, and acquitted for witchcraft again in 1692 with her daughter and granddaughter Mary and Hannah Harvey, during what would become known as the "Hartford Panic."

Lydia Gilbert

On October 3, 1651, Henry Styles of Windsor was killed during militia training exercises when Thomas Allyn accidentally discharged his musket. Allyn was indicted in December and pled guilty. The jury found it to be a "homicide by misadventure." He was fined 20 pounds for his "sinful neglect and careless carriage," and was forced to pay 10 pounds security for his good behavior in the future.

Allyn was not the only one charged in connection with Stiles' death though. On November 28, 1654 at the Particular Court in Hartford, Lydia Gilbert was indicted "for not having the fear of god before thy eyes, thou hast of late years or still dost give entertainment to Satan, the great enemy of God and mankind and by his help hast killed the body of Henry Styles, besides other witchcrafts for which according to the law of God and the established law of this commonwealth, thou deservests to die."

Styles was a boarder in Gilbert's home and he owed her money. Other than this evidence, nothing else is known of their relationship that would connect her to his death. The jury found Lydia guilty of witchcraft and sentenced her to death. Though there is no record of it, it is believed that Gilbert was hanged. Her death did not end the witchcraft legacy in her family, however. Katherine Harrison, believed to be either Lydia's daughter or her niece, was accused of witchcraft just a few years later in 1668.

ACQUITTAL FOR LACK OF SUFFICIENT PROOF

From about 1654 until 1661, most witches brought to trial in Connecticut were acquitted for lack of concrete evidence.

Elizabeth Godman

Elizabeth Godman was a servant in the house of the New Haven Deputy Governor Stephen Goodyear. Godman owned property herself, but she was a single woman and single women and widows were not allowed to live alone because New England laws stipulated that women must be under "family governance," so she lived with the Goodyears. Stephen Goodyear managed Godman's financial affairs. After awhile, Godman became estranged from the Goodyear family. She also was observed making rude remarks to neighbors and strange events such as sudden illnesses and weird noises seemed to occur whenever she was around. In May of 1653 after New Haven's minister gave a sermon on witchcraft, Goodwife Larremore and some others accused Godman of practicing the black arts. Instead of being brought to trial for being a witch, Godman brought suit against her accusers, saying that they had "given out speeches that made folks think she was a witch." Godman made complaints of Mr. and Mrs. Goodyear, Mr. and Mrs. Hooke (Mr. Hooke was New Haven's minister), Mrs. Bishop, Mrs. Atwater, Hannah and Elizabeth Lamberton, and Mary Miles.

In 1653, Governor Theophilus Eaton began a series of hearings. Mr. Hooke testified that he had reason for his suspicions of Elizabeth Godman. He testified she would "often be speaking about witches and rather justify them than condemned them; she said why do they provoke them, why do they not let them come into the church." Another suspicious thing about her, Hooke testified, "is that she could tell Mrs. Atwater had figs in her pocket when she saw none of them."

Hannah and Elizabeth Lamberton were spying on Godman one day, and they testified that they observed that she "lies as if somebody was sucking her, and upon that she [Godman] arose and said, 'Yes, yes, so there is.'" The girls claimed that Godman threatened Hannah and that two days after, Hannah began having fits in which she was pinched, heard a hideous noise, and was "in a strange manner, sweating and burning, and some time cold and full of pain."

Godman's strategy of pouncing on her accusers before they could pounce on her seems to have backfired. Based on the testimony made against her, the court decided that her "carriage and confession rendered her suspicious of witchcraft." They admonished her that "if further proof come, these passages will not be forgotten."

Soon after the trial, Godman was called again to court on August 7, 1655, for witchcraft and the "doing of strange things." More evidence was brought against her and the testimony that had surfaced at the earlier proceeding was admitted as well. Mr. Ball testified that Godman came into his yard one day to see their calf, which was tied to a post in their lot. When Elizabeth came near it, "the calf ran away with that post as if it had been a feather." Ball said he tied it up again; this time to a rail. On a different occasion, Godman came into their yard and looked at the calf "and it set a running and drew the rail after it till it came to a fence...in the winter the calf died." Goodwife Thorpe testified that after she refused to sell Godman a chicken, one by one, all the chickens on her farm died.

The court decided, based on the most recent testimony and the testimony from the previous case, that Godman "be committed to prison, there to abide the courts pleasure, but because the matter is of weight, and the crime whereof she is suspected capital, therefore she is to answer it at the Court of Magistrates in October next."

In October 1655, Godman went again before the court and was told that "she by her own confession remains under suspicion for witchcraft." Though she had brought "diverse persons to the court that they might say something to clear her, and much time was spent in hearing them, but to little purpose, the grounds of suspicion remaining full as strong as before and she found full of lying..." The court decided, however, that the evidence "is not sufficient as yet to take away her life, yet the suspicions are clear and many." She was instructed not to bother her neighbors and that if she did, she would go back to prison. She also had to pay 50 pounds to the court as security for her continuing good behavior.

Elizabeth Godman went to live with the family of Thomas Johnson in New Haven, and there she stayed until her death on October 9, 1660.

NICHOLAS BAYLEY AND HIS WIFE

On July 3, 1665, Nicholas Bayley and his wife (whose first name has not been recorded) came before the court in New Haven where they were accused of "sundry things...that doth render them both, but especially the woman, very suspicious in point of witchcraft." The charges were that Goody Bayley used lewd language when speaking about boars and sows in front of some neighbors; she was also accused of lying to Thomas Barnes, telling him that if he would mow a day for Mr. Gilbert, he would pay him one pound of wool, though Gilbert had never agreed to such a bargain. Goody Bayley confessed to these and other similar doings in court. The court decided that they were "not fit to live among such neighbors, and therefore the sentence of the court is, that betwixt this and the next court, they must consider of a way how to remove themselves to some other place, or give sufficient security to the court's satisfaction for their good behavior and pay the fine for lying, which is ten shillings." The Bayleys delayed leaving New Haven and repeatedly returned to court, apologizing for not paying a security for their behavior, and assuring the court that they would soon be gone. Eventually, the Bayleys left and no other records of them have been found to date.

николай AND MARGARET JENNINGS

At Hartford Court on September 5, 1661, the indictment against Nicholas and Margaret Jennings read: "Thou hast entertained familiarity with Satan, the great enemy of God and mankind, and by his help has done works above the course of nature, to the loss of lives of several persons, and in particular, the wife of Reynolds Marvin with the child of Balthazar deWolfe, with other sorceries for which, according to the law of God and the established laws of the common wealth thou deservest to die." They both pled "not guilty" to the charges.

Nicholas and Margaret were considered guilty, but not to what amounts to today's "beyond a reasonable doubt standard" and thus their lives were spared. According to the records of the Particular Court, the jury could not come to a decision the day of the trial and they were allowed to continue the case until the court reconvened in Hartford on October 9, 1661. Still the court failed to reach a unanimous verdict for either party and announced that a "major part" of the jury found Nicholas guilty of the indictment, while the rest only "strongly suspects it that he is guilty." As for Margaret, only "some of them find her guilty," and "the rest strongly suspect her to be guilty of the indictment."

THE HARTFORD "PANIC"

The year 1662 saw a flurry of witch trials throughout Connecticut—sometimes referred to as "The Great Hartford Witch Panic." "Panic," however, may be an overstatement because these witch trials only amounted to 11 accusations, though three, possibly four, people were killed as a result. There were two main sources of the Panic: Ann Cole, who became "possessed" by the devil, and eight-year-old Elizabeth Kelly who suddenly fell ill and died.

Elizabeth Kelly

It all started in Hartford when Elizabeth Kelly began complaining of stomach cramps after being in the company of Goody Ayres, a neighbor of "checkered reputation." Ayres had visited the family and together they ate hot broth out of a boiling pot. Ayres convinced Elizabeth to drink it before waiting for it to cool down, hence the stomach pains. Kelly's father treated her with angelica root powder, a remedy usually used for infections and purification of the blood. Soon after receiving the medicine, Elizabeth began screaming and having fits during which she claimed that Goody Ayres was upon her, choking her, and pricking her with pins. She called for her father to chop off Ayres' head with an axe. Elizabeth's fits and pains continued over the next few days. Goody Ayres, along with Goodwife Whaples and Rebecca Greensmith, visited the girl. Ayres told Elizabeth she would give her a piece of fine lace if she stopped talking badly about her. A few days later, just days after the fits began, Elizabeth died. Her last words were "Goody Ayres chokes me."

Goody Ayres

A six-man jury was appointed to hear the case against Goody Ayres that was brought by Elizabeth's family. Dr. Thomas Rossiter of Windsor performed the earliest recorded autopsy in America on Elizabeth. Rossiter seemed to have been unaware of the effects of rigor mortis as he found the bruised body, and large quantity of seemingly fresh blood that remained, to be quite unusual; his report stated that he found the condition of the body to be preternatural. Goody Ayres was also asked to handle the body before witnesses. Legend had it that a dead body would bleed afresh if touched by its murderer. When Ayres touched the body it "purged a little from the mouth," and their suspicions were confirmed. What observers probably saw was the body having postmortem spasms in which limbs move or twitch, a condition that commonly occurs after death. The bruising and remaining blood are easily explained as the effects of livor mortis, or the settling of blood in the body. This is apt to cause a reddish-purple skin discoloration; since the heart is no longer pumping blood, the blood cells fall due to gravity, creating pools of blood within the corpse.

Several neighbors also testified against Ayres at trial. Goody Burr and her son, Samuel, testified that Goody Ayres had once told them that while she lived in London, a suitor came to call on her. She agreed to go out with him, but after looking down at his feet and seeing hooves, she realized he was the Devil and refused to go with him. Joseph Marsh testified that he heard Ayres talk to Elizabeth before she died, coercing her to promise not to speak out against her anymore.

Ayres' husband testified on behalf of his wife and accused Rebecca Greensmith and Mary and Andrew Sanford of witchcraft. Rebecca testified at the Ayres trial, confessing to being a witch and conversing with the Devil, and implicated her own husband. She was then thrown into prison.

The water test was applied to both Goody Ayres and her husband, William, to ascertain whether they were witches. Both failed the test after they did not sink to the bottom. The test then confirmed their status as witches. Sensing that they would soon be executed for causing Elizabeth's death, Ayres and her husband fled Hartford, leaving behind their eight-year-old son.

Ayres' flight did not end the witch panic, but instead fanned the flames. The Ayres trial frightened the people of Hartford, and in 1662 and 1663 several more people were indicted as witches for having "familiarity with Satan."

Mary Sanford

In 1662, Mary Sanford and her husband, Andrew, were indicted for witchcraft. Mary was found guilty and probably hanged, but her husband was allowed to move to Milford where he remarried. At the Hartford Particular Court on June 13, 1662, before a grand jury composed of William Wadsworth, Thomas Wells, Benjamin Nubery, Joseph Fitch, William Pitkins, James Steel, William Heyden, John Bissell, Sam Wells, John Kilburn, Anthony Howkins, and Benedict Alvard, Mary Sanford was indicted and found guilty. Her indictment read "Thou hast entertained familiarity with Satan, the great enemy of God and mankind and by his help has acted and also hast come to the knowledge of secrets in a preternatural way beyond the ordinary course of nature to the great disturbance of several members of this commonwealth for which according to the law of God and the established law of this colony, thou deservest to die."

Ann Cole

Ann Cole, the daughter of God-fearing John Cole, lived next to the Greensmiths in Wethersfield. In 1662, Ann began speaking around town in a Dutch accent, though she had never been exposed to such a dialect.

These strange occurrences were believed to have been caused by the Devil who, "making use of her lips," held a discourse for a considerable time. Cole also seemed to be suffering from what seem to be epileptic-like fits or seizures in which her body violently contorted and she lost control of her movements. It was believed this was the Devil possessing her. The town came together in the meetinghouse for a day of fasting and prayer for Ann. During this meeting, Ann cried out against both Elizabeth Seager and Rebecca Greensmith, declaring them both to be witches. Greensmith was already in jail for having been deemed a witch at the Goody Ayres trial. Rebecca was put on trial, along with her husband, Nathaniel. Seager and Rebecca were both administered the water test; they did not sink and so they failed, proving their existence as witches.

THE GREENSMITHS

Mr. and Mrs. Greensmith were indicted at Particular Court in Hartford on December 30, 1662, before Magistrates Mr. Wyllys, Mr. Treat, Mr. Wolcott, Mr. Clark, and Secretary John Allyn. Their jury consisted of Edward Griswold, Walter Filer, James Ensigne, Mr. Olmstead, Sam Boreman, Goodman Winterton, John Cowles, Sam Marshall, Sam Hale, Nathan Willet, John Hart, John Wadsworth, and Robert Webster. On January 8, 1663, the jury found Nathaniel guilty of the indictment, and Rebecca confessed in open court that she was guilty.

Rebecca said she confessed at trial because, when her deposition was being taken, she felt as though her "flesh were being pulled from her bones." She said the Devil had appeared to her in the form of a deer and that he had frequent use of her body. She claimed she had not yet sealed a pact with him, but they had planned to formalize such a pact at Christmas, a holiday the Devil loved. Her testimony also heavily implicated her own husband; she claimed that he could lift the weight of two men, and that wild animals, possibly the Devil in disguise, were not afraid of him and often followed him around. Rebecca testified that

> I have seen logs that my husband hath brought home in his cart that I wondered at it that he could get them into the cart being a man of little body and weak to my apprehension and the logs were such that I thought two men such as he could not have done it.

She also testified that her husband asked her to keep quiet about him in court. "That my husband on Friday night last when I came to prison told me that now thou hast confessed against thyself, let me alone and say nothing of me and I will be good unto thy children."

When asked why she spoke out against her own husband, she said it was "out of love to my husband's soul, and it is much against my will that I am now necessitated to speak against my husband. I desire that the Lord would open his heart to own and speak the truth." Rebecca also confirmed stories that she, along with Goodwives Seager, Barnes, and Ayres, met in the woods to dance with the Devil.

Nathaniel Greensmith did not confess to anything, but because he had a history of theft and battery, he was not looked at favorably by the court.

In 1663, the Greensmiths and Barnes were convicted; they were hung on January 25, 1663, at Gallows Hill where Trinity College now stands. Historians call it a "logical place" for a hanging as it was able to provide an excellent view to a large number of people. The Greensmiths were the last people to be executed as witches in Connecticut. It is said that as soon as they were executed, Ann Cole became well again. As an observer reported, "After one of the witches was hanged, the maid was well."

Once the Greensmiths were hanged, their house reverted to the state. Ironically, the man who bought the house married Ann Cole. She was able to live out the rest of her days in that house because she had sent the Greensmiths to the gallows.

Mary Barnes

At Particular Court on January 6, 1662, the same day the Greensmiths were convicted, Mary Barnes and Elizabeth Seager were indicted. In Rebecca Greensmith's confession, she had implicated these women as witches. Barnes was found guilty of the indictment, but Seager was not. No records exist as to why one was guilty and the other was innocent, nor have any charges of witchcraft against Barnes survived. Though Seager lived through this round of accusations, she would soon find herself in court again, denying testimony that she was a witch.

Elizabeth Seager

On July 2, 1663, and again on June 26, 1665, Elizabeth Seager was indicted for "not having the fear of God before thine eyes thou has entertained familiarity with Satan the great enemy of God and mankind, and by his help hast acted things in a preternatural way beyond the ordinary course of nature, as also for that thou has committed adultery, and hast spoken blasphemy against God, contrary to the laws of God." She pled "not guilty" to the charges and her case went to the jury. In both cases, the jury found her guilty, but sentencing was delayed.

Seager's jury convicted her for the first time on July 2, 1663. Jury member Walt Tyler set out some of the reasons for her conviction. They concluded that she had "intimate familiarity, with such as had been witches, viz. Goody Sanford and Goody Ayres." In addition, in court she openly denied having any familiarity with the other witches, but she later confessed that she was very close to them. When asked about her water test, she said the "Devil that caused me to come here can keep me up."

During the trial in 1665, multiple neighbors testified against Seager. Mrs. Miggat stated that Seager came up to her one day and said, "God was naught, God was naught, it was very good to be a witch and desired her to be one, she should not need fear going to hell, for she should not burn in the fire." Miggat also testified that Seager came to her home in the middle of the night while she was in bed with her husband, whom Miggat could not wake while Seager was there. She claimed Seager slapped her on the face and then went away. Another neighbor, Goodwife Garrett, testified that after making "a cheese better than ordinary," while Goodwife Seager was in Garrett's barn husking corn, the cheese became full of maggots. She threw the cheese into the fire, at which time a scream came from Seager in the barn. "Seager came into the house, cried out she was full of pain, and sat wringing of her body and crying out what do I ail what do I ail." Goodman Garrett confirmed his wife's testimony. Goodman and Goodwife Garrett both testified that Seager told them she would send the Devil to tell them she was no witch. When asked why she would use the Devil to do this, Seager said, "Because Satan knew she was no witch."

A jury again found Seager guilty on June 26, 1665, for familiarity with Satan, but again her sentencing was delayed. On May 18, 1666, she was set free at a special session of the Court of Assistants. "This court considering the verdict of the jury and finding that it doth not legally answer the indictment do therefore discharge and set her free from further suffering or imprisonment." After the third time around, Seager decided Connecticut was not the right place for her and emigrated to Rhode Island.

THE "PANIC" IN SOUTHERN CONNECTICUT

Elizabeth Clawson and Mercy Disborough

The Southern Panic began when Daniel Wescot, the town selectman of Stamford, made a complaint against a servant girl he employed, Katherine Branch, who suddenly began having violent fits. He was worried that she was bewitched by witchcraft. According to Wescot's deposition, Katherine's fits caused her to "put out her tongue to a great extent I conceive beyond nature, and I put her tongue into her mouth again and then I looked in her mouth and could see no tongue but as if it were a lump of flesh down her throat and this of ten times."

On May 27, 1692, hearings began at the Court of Inquiry in Stamford. Nathan Gold and John Burr of Fairfield and Jonathan Selleck and Jonathan Bell of Stamford presided over the hearings.

Wescot continued to testify about the strange things Katherine had done. "She had been in a field gathering herbs when she was seized with pinching and pricking at her breast." He also said that Katherine spoke of seeing a cat who spoke to her multiple times; she said the cat promised her "fine things." She also had fits at night during which she would cry out "a witch, a witch," over and over again.

When Katherine was questioned before the court, she testified that she had met an old woman with two firebrands in her forehead. She claimed the old woman was Goody Clawson and accused Clawson of being a witch. She also accused Mary and Hannah Harvey, Mary Staples, Goody Miller, and Mercy Disborough of practicing witchcraft.

Wescot was so concerned with Katherine's behavior that he asked the town midwife, Sarah Bates, for help. Bates was the closest thing to a doctor the town had. Bates was unable to determine what was wrong with Katherine, but believed the illness "might be from some natural cause," and thus suggested that they burn feathers under her nose to take care of the fits. This was done, but by the next morning Katherine's condition remained unchanged. Wescot told Bates that he was convinced the girl was bewitched. After he said this, according to Bates, "the girl turned her head away from the Wescots, as to hide it in her pillow, and laughed."

Abigail Wescot, Daniel's wife, was not as convinced as her husband that Katherine was possessed or afflicted by witchcraft. Wescot's niece, Lidia Penior, testified that she heard her aunt say that Katherine was a "lying girl, that not anybody could believe one word what she said...and that she did not believe that Mercy nor Goody Miller nor Hannah nor any of those women was any more witches than she was."

Elizabeth Clawson was brought before the court and asked if she had been involved in afflicting Katherine Branch with witchcraft. She emphatically denied any involvement, and also denied that she was a witch. She did admit that there had been strained relations between her and the Wescots for a number of years, specifically between her and Abigail. The disagreement began some nine years prior over the weight of spun flax. Some hypothesize that Katherine took it upon herself to accuse a woman who was at odds with her master in order to gain their support in her accusations.

Daniel Wescot testified against Clawson, saying that she "took occasion upon any frivolous matter to be angry and pick a quarrel with both myself and wife."

Several other neighbors also testified against Clawson, confirming that Katherine suffered from terrible fits. Several testified in favor of Clawson as well. Elezer Slawson, a near neighbor of Goody Clawson, testified that he "did always observe her to be a woman for peace and to counsel for peace, and when she hath had provocations from her neighbors would answer and say we must live in peace for we are neighbors and would never to my observation give threatening words nor did I look at her as one given to malice."

A search of Elizabeth's body for witch's marks was ordered on May 28, 1662, the day of the hearings. Mary Ambler, Sarah Finch, Bethiah Wood, Sarah Trehearn, and Martha Homes were "faithfully sworn, narrowly and truly to inspect and search her body, whether any suspicious signs or marks, did appear that were not common or that were preternatural." The women searched her and "with one voice return their answer that they found nothing save a wart on one of her arms."

Having also been accused of being a witch by Katherine Branch, Mercy Disborough was brought before the court on May 28, 1662. Mercy denied being involved with Branch and also denied that she was a witch. She testified that she never saw or knew of the girl before and that "she never heard there was such a person in the world before now." Upon seeing Mercy in the courtroom, Katherine "fell down into a fit."

The same women who searched Clawson for witch marks also searched Mercy, though her results were not as favorable. The women came back and said that they "all unanimously agree, consent and affirm, that they found a teat or like one in her privy parts, at least an inch long which is not common in other women, and for which they can give no natural reason for."

The court was adjourned for the time being and Mercy and Elizabeth were placed in the Fairfield jail. Throughout the next month, additional testimony was given in preparation for the trial to be held in September. Mercy was brought back on June 2, 1692. Several people testified against her. Thomas Bennett testified that he lost several calves after a run-in with Mercy where she told him she would make him "as bare as a bird's tail." Henry Grey testified that after a deal between him and the Disboroughs to buy one of his calves went bad, the calf was soon found dead in a swamp. Ann Godfrey testified that when she went to Mercy's house one day, Mercy told her that she was "praying to her God." Ann asked Mercy who her god was; Mercy "told her that her God was the Devil." Joseph Stirg and Benjamin Dunning, men who kept watch over Mercy at the jail testified that she had said, "If she were hanged she would not be hanged alone."

On June 4, 1692, a group of 76 people from Stamford, including several elected officials, came together with a signed a petition attesting that Goody Clawson was not a witch. The document read:

> Our neighbor, Stephen Clawson, having desired us whose names are under written, seeing there is such a report of his wife raised by some among us, that we would speak what we know concerning his said wife and her behavior among us for so many years now know all whom it may concern that we do declare that since we have known our said neighbor goodwife Clawson we have not known her to be of a contentious frame nor given to use threatening words or to act maliciously towards her neighbors but hath been civil and orderly towards others in her conversation and not to be a busybody in other means concerns. Given under our hands in Stamford, 4th June 1692.

On September 14, 1692, the trial of Goody Clawson and Mercy Disborough was held at a Court of Oyer and Terminer in Fairfield. Governor Robert Treat, Deputy Governor William Jones, Major Nathan Gold, John Allyn, Andre Leet, Captain John Burr, William Pitkin, and Captain Moses Mansfield presided over the trial. Lieutenant James Bennett and Mr. Eliphalet Hill were appointed attorneys on behalf of the Sovereign King and Queen to prosecute Elizabeth Clawson and Mercy Disborough.

Mercy requested that she be given the water test to prove that she was innocent of being a witch. Both Elizabeth and Mercy were given the test on September 15, 1692, and they both failed. Abram Adams and Jonathan Squires testified that "when Elizabeth Clawson was bound hand and foot and put into the water she swam like a cork and Joseph Stirg labored to press her into the water and she buoyed up like a cork." After Mercy was put into the water, "she swam upon it."

The women were both indicted and accused of afflicting and doing harm in a preternatural way to the body of their Majesties' subjects by the instigation of the Devil. The women were once again searched for witch marks. Elizabeth was found to have no marks, and Mercy's mark that was discovered earlier had shrunk, but a new mark had appeared.

Katherine Branch came to court and testified that

> some time this last summer she saw and felt Goodwife Clawson and Mercy Disborough afflict her not together but apart by scratching pinching and wringing her body and further said that Goodwife Clawson was the first that did afflict her and afterwards Mercy Disborough.

The jury was unable to come to a verdict regarding the two women. The court decided that the women should be "kept in safe custody till a return may be made to the General Court for farther direction what shall be done in this matter." The court indicated that the "gentleman of the jury are also to be ready when farther called by direction of the General Court to perfect their verdict." The court said they would allow the attorneys for their Majesties to "find farther testimony they may have liberty to make farther use of them when the court shall meet again."

The court ordered everyone to reconvene on October 13, 1692. The jury declared Mercy Disborough guilty according to the indictment of familiarity with Satan. The court sent the jury back to reconsider their verdict and upon coming back "they saw no reason to alter their verdict but do find her guilty as before." The court then approved their verdict and the governor sentenced her to death.

The jury found Elizabeth Clawson not guilty according to the indictment. The court approved the verdict and granted her freedom, but required her to pay her "just fees and prison charges for the time she was imprisoned."

Just days after Mercy was pronounced guilty, a group of supporters gathered and submitted a petition regarding the fact that one of the jurors from the September trial was not in attendance at the October trial; a substitute was appointed who had not been there in September. The petition argued that the conviction should be overturned due to the illegal substitution.

Three magistrates were assigned to deal with the issue—Samuel Wyllys, William Pitkin, and Nathaniel Stanley—and Mercy's execution was postponed. Six months after being given the case, the three magistrates finally submitted a report in May 1693 in which they agreed with

> Our neighbour Stephen Clason haueing desired us whose names
> are under writen: seing there is such a report of his wife: vais=
> =ing sume among us: that we would speak what we know conser
> ning his said wife and her behauiour among us for so many yeers
> now know ow whome it may conserne that we doe declare that
> since we haue known our said neighbour: goodwife clason we
> haue not known her to be of a contentious frome nor giuen to
> use threatning words or to act maliciously towards her neighbour
> but hath bene siuil and orderly towards others in her conuersa
> and not to be a busy body in other mens conserns:
> giuen under our hands in stanford: 4 June: 1692:

Abraham Ambler
Mary   Ambler
    her mark
Dinidth Snoffield
Samuell finch
Sara finch
    her mark
Samuell finch Juner
Joseph Finney
Mary finey
Abraham finch
John finch
Beniamin finch
Susanah Green
    her mark
Joseph Garsons
Elisabeth Garsons
    her mark
Zacheriah Dibboll
Sori her mark
Samuel Hait
Hanah Hait
    her mark
Edw: Clason Jener
Jonas Holly
Elisabeth E holly

Obadiah Steuens
Deborah Steuens
Isac finch
Samuell Newman
Abraham finch Ju
Samuell homes
Steuen Homs
Martha Homs
    her mark
Jonathan Bell sen
Susana Bell
Jonas Garly
Cory Clason
John Smith
and his wife
Thomas newman
Mary   newman
    her mark
Joseph Garnsy
Joseph Steuenes
Sarah   Steueneys
    her mark

(above and facing page) A June 4, 1692, petition indicating that Goody Clawson was not a witch, signed by 76 people of Stamford. *Reproduced with permission of The Stamford Historical Society.*

Moses Knap   Samuell hardy
and his [wife?]   Rebeck X hardy
                              her mark
Joseph Browne
                           anye A hendy
John Criddy   her mark

John Scofield   John [Scott?]
John Finch   hanagatt
Benjamin [hair]   Stephen Bishop

hannah [hay]   mercy ^ Bishop
[yet her] [David?]   her mark
                           Samuell Dean
Joseph Harris   Ann Dean
hanna B [farris]   John Dean
  her mark
                           Abigall Dean

       John pettit   S John Auston
Elizabeth E [ceman?]   hannah H Auston
  her mark   her mark
[edg] P poneger
  her ^ mark
hana well
  hur mark
Richard Scofield

John Knap
Caleb Knap
John [Bates?]
Samuell bates
Sarah bates
Samuell [Crust?]

the petitioners and found that the substitution was illegal. "One man altered, the jury is altered," they reported. They also went beyond their charge and decided that the evidence presented was not "sufficiently convictive of witchcraft" and thus Mercy should not have been found guilty in the first place.

The General Court followed the recommendations of the three magistrates and eventually acquitted Mercy and released her. What Mercy did the day of her release and with the rest of her life has been lost to history.

AFTER THE PANICS

Though Hartford's "panic" had come and gone and the last of the Connecticut witches were hung, the state was not yet free from superstition, and several more trials were held.

KATHERINE HARRISON

Though she was not hanged, much controversy surrounded Katherine Harrison of Wethersfield. She was not well-liked by her neighbors, and the dislike festered until it culminated in her being accused of practicing witchcraft and having "familiarity with the Devil." She was first brought to court in October of 1668 and indicted for witchcraft.

Katherine had a long list of complaints against her. Thomas Bracey claimed that she and a man named James Wakeley appeared by his bedside one night and afflicted and pinched him "as if his flesh had been pulled from his bones." Neighbor Thomas Whaples called her a notorious liar, a Sabbath breaker, and that Rebecca Greensmith said, before her own condemnation, that Katherine was a witch. Alexander Keeny and Samuel Hurlbert said that back in England she was possibly a prostitute that followed the army around. Mary Hale testified that she saw Katherine's apparition in the form of a big black dog with Katherine's head hovering over her bed, sitting on her legs and chest, and preventing her from breathing.

According to Elizabeth Smith, Katherine spun too much flax for one woman and was much too strong for her own good. "Time and again she flaunted her knowledge of many matters that were in future time to be accomplished." Elizabeth, a fellow servant who worked with Katherine at John Cullick's house in Hartford, wanted to marry a young man named Chapman. The two decided to marry without telling or getting permission from their employers, which was against the law at the time. The law read,

"No person under government of parents, master, guardian or such like may entertain a motion to marriage without the knowledge or consent of their masters." Cullick was dead set against the marriage. Katherine "predicted" that Elizabeth would not marry Chapman; she said that Elizabeth would wed a young man named Simon instead (Simon was the name of another servant who worked with the girls). Surprisingly, the marriage to Chapman fell through and Elizabeth eventually wed a man named Simon.

After her indictment, Katherine submitted a rebuttal to the court on October 6, 1668, and even offered to take the water test to prove that she was not a witch. She complained that the townspeople had been harassing her. "May it please this honored court, to have patience with me a little; having none to complain to, but the fathers of the commonwealth...I am bold to present you with these few lines, as a relation of the wrongs that I suffer." One of her oxen was badly injured and left on her doorstep, a cow's back was broken, her brands on heifers and pigs were cut out and replaced with another's brand, a heifer was stuck with a knife and wounded to death, a cow's hind leg was cut off, a horse wounded, a steer's back was broke, and 30 poles of hops were spoiled, among other atrocities. "I hope they will be looked upon, by this honored court according to their nature and judged according to their demerit, that so your poor suppliant may find some redress."

Throughout October of 1668, more depositions were taken to be used as evidence against Katherine. William Warren testified that not only was Katherine a fortune teller, she admitted to it and had told him his fortune by looking at his hands. Rebecca Smith, a seventy-five-year-old woman, testified that Katherine had wanted a black hat of Goody Gilbert's but Gilbert refused to sell it to Katherine. After the refusal whenever Gilbert wore the hat, her "head and shoulders was much afflicted; after the cap being pulled off, Goody Gilbert said she was well...After being afflicted several times, it was suspected to be by witchcraft." Gilbert then burned the hat. John Wells testified that his body became frozen when he stumbled upon Katherine milking a cow that was not hers. Richard Montague testified that somehow Katherine had recovered an entire swarm of bees that had escaped from a neighboring plot of land. "Katherine neither went nor used any lawful means to fetch the said bees," he testified.

John Graves, a neighbor of Harrison's, tied his cows near the border of their adjoining lands so they could graze. "In a little time the oxen as affrighted fell to running and ran with such violence that he judgeth that the force and speed of their running make the yoke so tied fly above six foot high to his best discerning." According to Graves, the cows were used to being tied in such a way and had never run away as they did when they were near the Harrison property.

Katherine was acquitted the first time around, but it was not the end of her career as a "witch." On May 11, 1669, Katherine was again summoned into the Court of Assistants in Hartford on suspicion of witchcraft. On May 25, she was indicted with the following charges: "Thou has had familiarity with Satan…and by his help hast acted things beyond and beside the ordinary course of nature, and hast thereby hurt the bodies of diverse of the subjects of our sovereign lord, the King for which by the law of God and of this corporation thou oughtest die."

She pled not guilty and the trial was heard before a jury of 12 men, none from Wethersfield. The jury was unable to come to a decision quickly, and the case was continued until the court reconvened in October. Katherine went back to Wethersfield, and 38 of her closest friends petitioned the court to lock her away until the jury made their decision. Odd things began happening upon Katherine's release, and the townspeople feared the "dreadful displeasure of the Almighty God" at allowing her to be free.

Katherine somehow managed to remain free between trials, but returned to Hartford on October 12, 1669, when the court reconvened and the jury found her guilty. Instead of issuing a death sentence, the court dismissed the jury and called together a panel of ministers to advise the court as to what they should do. The court wanted to know what could be considered legal proof, for they had many witnesses testify to similar, but not identical, observations about Katherine. The ministers said that a plurality of witnesses must testify to "one and ye same individual fact; and without such a plurality there can be no legal evidence of it." They cited John 8:17, which says the testimony of two men is true.

The court also wanted to know whether fortune telling or discerning secrets are evidence of familiarity with the Devil. The ministers found that "Those things, whether past, present, or to come, which are indeed secret—that is, which cannot be known by human skill in arts or strength of reason arguing from the course of nature—nor are made known by divine revelation…must needs be known (if at all) by information from the Devil.…Hence communication of such things, in way of divination… seems to us to argue familiarity with the Devil."

In May 1670, a special session of the Court of Assistants was held in Hartford. After the court reviewed the trial and the minister's opinions, they reversed Katherine's conviction. They could not "concur with them so as to sentence her to death." She was essentially banished from Wethersfield as a condition of her acquittal for "her own safety and contentment of the people who are her neighbors." She moved to New York where her history of witchcraft followed her, though she was eventually left to live in peace. Katherine was the last woman to be called a witch in Wethersfield.

THE WITCHES' CONTINUING CONTROVERSY

Though Katherine Harrison's trial was one of the last for witches in Connecticut, the witches' legacy continues. Mary Sanford, a witch put to death during the great Hartford Panic, seems to be calling from the grave. Debra Avery, an eighth-generation descendent of Sanford, along with others, has called for the state to exonerate her ancestor.

Avery, who is home schooling her fourteen-year-old daughter, Addie, decided to make this call for exoneration an independent study project. After doing all the research, Addie decided to meet with several state representatives about exonerating the people who had been accused and executed for witchcraft. In 2007, Addie drafted language for the bill based on Salem's exoneration legislation.

"We are seeking *exoneration* for all 11 convicted witches in the Connecticut Colony," Avery said. "We're still debating on whether or not to include the three others who were convicted and then reprieved. A pardon would not be what we can seek because a pardon releases a convicted person from the punishment. Those we seek to exonerate received their punishments."

The Averys have come up with several theories surrounding their ancestor's death, including reasons for why Mary was executed and her husband was released. The Averys reasoned that on occasion, married couples accused of witchcraft would strike a deal where one parent would take the blame for both in an effort to ensure the children had at least one parent to care for them. "Is that what she was doing?" Avery wondered.

Because there are so few details regarding Mary's death, the Averys have theorized that the Sanfords could have been targeted as some form of political retribution. Andrew Sanford was a "chimney viewer," a position similar to today's building inspector. The Averys speculate that perhaps a certain inspection didn't turn out quite right, and the Sanfords were targeted because of it.

There are no records of the burial for any of the executed witches, and because they were convicted of dealing with the Devil, they were probably refused a Christian burial. Many members of the Sanford family were buried in Hartford's Center Cemetery, and Debra thinks there is a possibility that Mary was secretly buried there. Several unmarked graves are believed to be those of blacks or condemned witches. Renovations to the cemetery called

Commemorative bricks remembering Alse Young and Mary Sanford located in the Ancient Burial Ground at Center Church in Hartford. © *Regina Forker*.

for fundraising and Debra recently purchased a brick inscribed with Mary's name. "Mary Sanford, June 13, 1662, Our Grandmother." Debra and Addie's work has caught the attention of more than just Connecticut pagans wishing to have the witches exonerated; the *Wall Street Journal* picked up their story as well.

Connecticut State Representative Michael Lawlor (D-East Haven) heard through the media about the push to officially pardon the witches. He thought it would be an interesting topic to bring up at the Judiciary Committee for which he is the chair. He said that there are plans for hearings to be conducted in 2008 and hopes the witches will soon be pardoned.

According to Connecticut's Board of Pardons and Paroles, there is currently no procedure for such a posthumous pardon, but the ability to create such a procedure and allow the pardon is solely within the province of the General Assembly.

Also involved in the push to exonerate the witches is Anthony Griego, a retired police officer from New Haven, and a practicing pagan. Though Griego is not related to any of those executed or accused, he became involved with the cause mainly because he believes the witches were falsely executed.

"Several years ago I wrote to the Mayor of Windsor, home town of Alse Young, in the hopes of generating interest for her. No response," he said. Since then Griego has written to several others about the pardons, but he said there didn't seem to be much interest. Still, he is optimistic about the bill Lawlor plans to propose in the legislature.

"I believe that based on the information that our group supplies, Representative Michael Lawlor will in fact be successful in getting a bill passed pardoning all those who were executed for the crime of Witchcraft." Avery expressed the same optimism. "We don't feel it will be objected to since it won't cost any money," she said.

Griego also made it clear that the group was not looking for the state to pay the ancestors of these witches. "It is important to us to clear their names but not to open avenues for financial restitution," he said.

Griego is part of the "group of interested people who hope to get pardons for 11 people executed in Connecticut for witchcraft." This group organized itself after state historian Walter Woodward gave a lecture on witchcraft at the University of Connecticut's Torrington campus in 2005. According to Griego, "Most of the people there were interested in the lecture for the history, but there were also many other pagans and witches present." It was at this lecture that Avery asked Woodward whether anyone had sought to have the witches pardoned. After the lecture, several attendees got together and started talking about pardons and that "got the ball rolling," he said.

"At this time we have no formal name nor do we hold regular meetings, although this is subject to change," Griego said.

The Averys are against formalizing the group. "Addie is determined to keep this an informal group of interested people who have come forward to support the legislation," Debra said. "Tony has indicated he thinks we should be a formal group, but we feel that we don't need to beat the drums to make this happen."

The group organized a memorial service in Hartford's Barnard Park on May 26, 2007, to mark the 360th anniversary of Alse Young's 1647 execution. Griego was responsible for presenting what is known of Young's history at the memorial. The names of the 11 executed people were read at the memorial and a bell tolled for each. For each of the executed witches there was a white rose laid at the base of a tree; a twelfth rose was laid to remember the children of those executed. A hangman's noose dangled above the roses.

May 26th, 2007. Addie Avery, descendant of Mary Sanford, speaking at the 360th commemoration of Alse Young's hanging at Barnard Park in Hartford. Avery's mother, Debra Avery, is in the background. © *Andy Hart, The Hartford News.*

Several states have pardoned those accused of witchcraft in the seventeenth and eighteenth centuries. Massachusetts began pardoning the witches soon after they were accused. On January 15, 1697, Governor William Phips declared a day of repentance and all witchcraft convictions were repealed. In 1711, restitution was made to the victims' families. In August of 1957 the General Court of Massachusetts issued a resolution finding that those executed for witchcraft in 1692 may have been illegally tried, convicted, and sentenced; the court also declared its belief that witchcraft trials were shocking and the result of a wave of popular hysterical fear of the Devil in the community. In 2001, the 1957 resolution was updated with additional names. The year 2007 marked the 315th anniversary of the Salem witch trials and Salem Mayor Stanley Usovicz stated that it would have been a good time for the city of Salem to issue an official declaration pardoning all those affected by the witch panic. However, the pardon was not enacted.

Virginia Governor Timothy M. Kaine pardoned Grace Sherwood on July 10, 2006, who on July 10, 1706 was the only person in Virginia to be convicted as a witch after failing the water test. Governor Kaine's pardon was in the form of a letter to the mayor of Virginia Beach, the town where Sherwood was tried. Kaine also declared July 10 to be Grace Sherwood Day.

When all was said and done, the witch trials in Connecticut left 11 people dead. Were they really witches? Common sense seems to tell us, of course not. But why were these people indicted and convicted by their peers? Why were their peers so willing to testify against them? Did some of the accused women suffer from epilepsy that caused them to have fits, leaving their neighbors to think the Devil possessed them? That's what some scientists have argued; others say that the accused people were actually exposed to some sort of fungus that acted as a hallucinogen, hence their confessions of dancing with the Devil. Some of the witches' victims are believed to have died not because they were bewitched, but because they had pneumonia. And today we realize that many of the events attributed to witchcraft, such as flash floods or droughts, were only natural phenomena. Whatever the cause and whatever the real reasons, the witch hysteria seems to have died out in Connecticut, at least for now.

See Appendix A for more information about Connecticut's witchcraft trials.

Teaching Tolerance

Prudence Crandall and Her School for "Young Ladies and Little Misses of Color"

Thirty years before the people of the United States went to war with each other over the institution of slavery, Prudence Crandall fought her own personal war in Connecticut. The Quaker teacher wanted the freedom to teach whom she wanted and to give young black girls the opportunity to be educated. Hers was a major battle in the fight against inequality, and although she decided to close her school, her actions made great headway for those who continued the fight after her.

Prudence Crandall came from modest beginnings. Her father, Pardon Crandall, married Esther Carpenter when Esther was 15 years old. Esther's father, Hezekiah Carpenter, allowed his daughter to marry Crandall only on the condition that the couple would live nearby. Hezekiah built the Crandalls a house next to his own house in Hopkinton, Rhode Island, so that he could keep watch over the couple, and it was in this house that Pardon and Esther's four children were born. On September 3, 1803, Esther gave birth to Prudence. Hardworking and frugal, her Quaker family taught the values of a plain and simple life.

Prudence's future controversial endeavors would not be a new phenomenon in her family. As far back as 1651, members of the Crandall clan were getting themselves into disputes. John Crandall, an Anabaptist, was arrested in Boston over a disagreement regarding the proper procedure for baptism. Following his banishment, he left Massachusetts and ventured to Rhode Island to join Roger Williams and several other Anabaptists where he helped establish the settlement of Westerly, of which Hopkinton grew to be an offshoot.

In 1813, just weeks after Esther gave birth to Hannah Almira, the Crandalls' fourth child, the family packed up and moved to Connecticut. Esther's protective father had just died, and Pardon was eager to start a life of his own without his father-in-law watching over his shoulder. They settled into a large red farm house near Canterbury. A pocket of Quakers had settled there and in other nearby towns. The Crandalls lived a prosperous, happy life in Canterbury. Pardon farmed during the summer and took turns in the winters with other fathers teaching at the local school when no schoolmaster was available; he was also the village overseer of the poor and the poor house, which was built in 1828.

Prudence began her education at the Friends' Boarding School in Providence, a Quaker nursery school established in 1784; it is still in operation today as the Moses Brown School. Prudence was sent away to boarding school; her parents planned for her to have a proper Quaker education, and so she was sent to Providence. The school was progressive for its time, ensuring that both boys and girls were admitted, offering scholarships to poor children, and admitting students of varied religious backgrounds. She was instructed in a more diverse selection of subjects than she would have encountered had she gone to a more local school. Her education included arithmetic, rhetoric, grammar, Latin, and the sciences. Though the school offered a great deal educationally, it was still a Quaker school, and Quaker beliefs included the idea that "plain clothes, plain speech, and plain manners were the rule." It is thought that Prudence may have begun her teaching career at the Friends' Boarding School when she was an older student by acting as a teacher's aide or apprentice.

In 1830, Prudence left Providence and returned to Connecticut to begin teaching on her own. She briefly taught at a school in Lisbon, Connecticut, and then became a boarding school teacher at a school in Plainfield, near Canterbury. It was in 1831 that the people of Canterbury decided they needed a school for their daughters in order to avoid sending them away to private boarding schools across the state and around New England. A boarding school in their town would also lift Canterbury up a notch, both socially and politically. State Attorney Andrew T. Judson, a supporter of the school, was all too pleased to help get it off the ground. Judson had his sights set on being the state's next governor, and thought the school would elevate him, and Canterbury, to a new level.

Canterbury residents were not partial to buying their wares and sending their children abroad. They preferred to keep things in-house and local. A committee of the Temperance Society, of which Prudence and her sister-in-law belonged, urged residents to remain local in order to promote Canterbury businesses. The Society report stated, "The first step to be taken is for each and all of our citizens to manifest by their example their determination to encourage our own citizens by purchasing their domestic productions of the manufacturers and mechanics in our town in preference to going broad for the articles or encouraging foreigners to bring articles to us." Itinerant peddlers and gypsies were not well-liked and not welcomed, the people tried to keep their relations with outsiders to a minimum. Other forms of incentive were introduced to encourage home production. For example, a reward of $15 was offered by the Temperance Society to "the person who produces the greatest quantity of silk on a single farm."

Creating a local school so that Canterbury girls could be well-educated close to home fit well into Canterbury's pro-local scheme. Sending their daughters off to Mrs. Values Boarding School in Hartford, Miss Hyde & Miss Sigourney's school in Norwich, the Catherine Beecher School for Young Ladies in Hartford (Catherine Beecher was Harriet Beecher Stowe's sister), or Miss Pierce's School for Young Ladies in Plainfield would clearly go against Canterbury's goal of promoting local businesses.

A SCHOOL FOR THE YOUNG MISSES OF CANTERBURY

It is not clear whether it was Prudence or a group of Canterbury citizens who first came up with the idea to start a school in Canterbury, but either way, Prudence became involved and things moved ahead quickly. A group of prominent and wealthy Canterbury men became the school's oversight committee, known as its "Board of Visitors." Its members included Judson; Dr. Andrew Harris, a leading Canterbury physician and mentor to Prudence's brother Reuben; Daniel Frost, an attorney and active temperance promoter; Rufus Adams, Justice of the Peace; Samuel L. Hough, an axe manufacturer who provided Prudence with a $1,500 loan to buy the $2,000 house where the school was to be located; William Kinne, secretary of the Congregational Church; Daniel Packer, a state senator; and Reverend Dennis Platt, Canterbury's Congregational minister who served as chairman of the board.

Prudence bought the house in order to have a place to run the school. That she bought it herself was unusual for the time. Almost no women owned their own real estate. If women did purchase property, it legally became their husbands' property once they married. The house that Prudence bought, which was really a mansion, was the Paine house; it had become available after its owner, Luther Paine, was found dead in the backyard while he was in the middle of chopping wood.

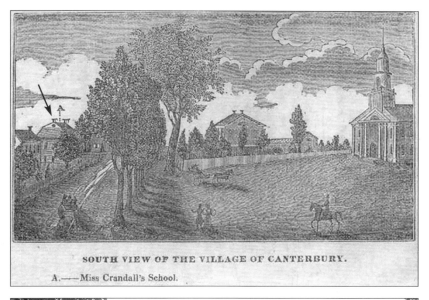

(top) Drawing with Prudence's house pointed out. *Image courtesy of Yale's Gilder Lehrman Center for the Study of Slavery http://www.yale.edu/glc/.*

(bottom) The Prudence Crandall house today. © *Regina Forker.*

The school's first pupils were the daughters of the Board of Visitors, and the board's goal was to use their contacts to encourage more students from the area to attend the school. Advertisements for the school were published in several newspapers, including the *Brooklyn Advertiser*. The following announcement appeared in the *Brooklyn Advertiser*:

> Miss Crandall has lately opened a boarding school exclusively for females, at the Village of Canterbury and will teach the following branches, viz, reading, writing, arithmetic, English grammar, geography, ancient and modern together with delineating maps, history, natural and moral philosophy, chemistry and astronomy.
>
> There will be no vacation during the year, therefore, scholars can enter or leave at any time without interruption.
>
> Books and stationary will be furnished at wholesale price if wanted.
>
> The terms of tuition for 12 weeks per term are as follows: "For English studies—$3.00. Board, including washing in the family of the instructress $1.50 per week.
>
> Every scholar of the family is required to attend public worship, somewhere, on the Sabbath.
>
> In connection with the school, Mr. Andrew Cutler, A.M. will deliver a course of chemical lectures during the coming winter, commencing on Tuesday evening, the 15th day of the present month.
>
> The Board of Visitors recommend to the public patronage of Miss Crandall's school and cheerfully add that she has already acquired a high reputation as an instructress and the assiduity and attention which she devotes to the health and morals of her pupils, renders her school a suitable place for education.

Classes began in November 1831. The pupils attending the new school included Sarah Adams, Eliza and Phoebe Hough, Amy Baldwin, Frances Ensworth, Frances and Sarah Coit, Hannah Pearl, and Mary Clark. Several of the girls, aged eight to 18, lived too far away to travel each day to the school and they boarded in the house with Prudence. Stephen Coit, a neighbor of Prudence's and a local store owner, bartered with Prudence in order to pay part of his daughters' tuition. Prudence traded education for supplies from Coit's store.

The school's oversight committee, the Board of Visitors, visited the school on January 20, 1832 and they were pleased with what they saw. They published the following notice in the *Norwich Courier* on March 31, 1832:

> CANTERBURY
> Female Boarding School
> Prudence Crandall, Principal
> To the public she presents her grateful acknowledgments for the generous patronage hitherto received and respectfully solicits continuance of the same.
> The location of the school possesses many natural advantages and is surrounded with good society.
> Young ladies and little misses will be furnished with every accommodation to spend their time usefully and agreeably at this institution. The school is regularly organized and now open for the reception of scholars....
> At a meeting of the Board of Visitors of the Canterbury Female Boarding School on January 20, 1832.
> Resolved unanimously: that the first quarterly examination of this school has given entire satisfaction to the Board of Visitors.
> Resolved that the Chairman and Secretary sign these resolutions and present the same to Miss Crandall.
> Dennis Platt, Chairman
> Andrew T. Judson, Secretary
> Canterbury March 10, 1832

About the time that Prudence opened her school, she converted from her staid and somber Quaker faith that she had been taught as a youth to a more robust form of Baptist. Her brother, Reuben, who remained a staunch Quaker, disapproved of her switch, finding it appalling that she had been baptized a Baptist by full-scale immersion in the Quinebaug River. After joining the Packerville Baptist Church in 1830, Prudence's Quaker brethren disowned her. Though Quakers generally promoted the education of young girls, the fact that Quakers believed that women should be restrained from speaking out or taking action against what they thought was wrong turned Prudence away from Quaker ideology. She would often leave the girls in the care of her sister, Almira, to attend meetings with Baptist ministers in nearby towns. She was known to occasionally rent a chaise carriage from Stephen Coit and drive to hear revivalists speak. At least one time, Prudence rented a carriage from Coit and took a few of her students along with her to a meeting at the Packerville Baptist Church.

Portrait of Prudence Crandall painted by Carl Henry in 1981 from the original commissioned by her supporters in 1834. *Courtesy of the Prudence Crandall Museum, administered by the Commission on Culture and Tourism, State of Connecticut.*

THE NEW HAVEN SCHOOL FOR BLACK MEN

Before Prudence and the Canterbury town elite even thought about opening a school, a similar idea for a school was being developed in New Haven. On October 1, 1831, an editorial in the *New Haven Palladium* stated: "We will inform [our readers] that we mean, without any jesting, to say there has been an attempt, a serious attempt, to get up an institution in this place for the education of colored men."

The idea for a "Negro college" in New Haven was initiated by Reverend Simeon Jocelyn, a white minister preaching to a black congregation. Jocelyn was the founding pastor of the African-American congregation that became Dixwell Avenue Congregational Church. He garnered the support of William Lloyd Garrison, publisher of an important abolitionist newspaper, *The Liberator*, and Arthur Tappan, an abolitionist with ample financial resources; both of these men would also play key roles in assisting Prudence in starting and keeping open her school for young black women. Arthur Tappan, along with his brother, Lewis, bought land for the school in the southern section of New Haven and agreed to use $1,000 to start a fundraising effort to build the school. Together, the three men developed a plan for the school and presented it in June of 1831 at the annual Convention of the Free People of Colour in Philadelphia. Their plan called for a school that would allow its black students to "cultivate habits of industry and obtain a useful mechanical or agricultural profession, while pursuing classical studies." The school would be operated by a group of trustees made up of three white and four black people. The convention unanimously approved the plan and the men returned to New Haven and began to take action.

William Lloyd Garrison started speaking about the school to gather support, and it was through speaking—or rather his inability to speak—that he gained the attention of Samuel May, a Unitarian minister from Massachusetts who would become another key player in Prudence's affairs. Garrison was often unable to find halls and churches that were willing to allow him to present abolitionists views and especially the plans for a school for black men because the idea for such a school was met with disdain. Seeking an available space in order to give a speech, Garrison placed an advertisement in a newspaper; May answered the ad, offering to allow Garrison to speak at his Unitarian church in Brooklyn, Connecticut.

It was around this time that the national stir about slavery began. On August 21, 1831, Nat Turner, a slave in Southampton, Virginia, gathered up fellow slaves on the plantation where he worked and proceeded to murder the plantation owner and his entire family. The band of slaves continued their killing spree for two days; and before it all ended, 55 people had been killed. Turner went into hiding, but he was found two months later and hanged on November 11.

Nat Turner's rebellion caused a tidal wave of fear to sweep across the country, and New Haven was not unaffected. The events in Virginia did not bode well for New Haven's attempt at a school for blacks. Panic broke out across the country and innocent blacks were tortured and killed; a flurry of state laws were passed to quash the education or progress of blacks because it was believed that Nat Turner had garnered his inspiration to kill the whites from verses in the Bible, which he was able to read himself. Because he often preached to his fellow slaves, he became known as "The Prophet." From then on, literate blacks were considered a threat to public safety. There was a very slim chance that a school with the primary purpose to educate blacks would ever come to fruition.

Public sentiment regarding the school was disapproving and hostile. Jocelyn presented his idea of the school on September 7, 1831, at his church, the Center Church on the Green. An editorial in the *Connecticut Journal* dated September 9, 1831, read, "The location of a college of blacks here [in New Haven] would be totally ruinous to the city...whose certain effect will be to lower the town's public morals—to drive from our city its female schools—its throngs of summer visitors—and to stop the vital stream of the city, the influx of young men to Yale College."

Dennis Kimberly, New Haven's mayor, called a meeting for September 10 at City Hall to deal with the issue of the school for blacks. A short note in a New Haven newspaper on September 10 announced the town meeting and urged townspeople to reject the "Negro college." The newspaper stated:

> If it is necessary to have an African College in Connecticut, may the projectors of it, on mature consideration, conclude to locate it in the town of Cornwall...Cornwall possesses many advantages for such an institution, over other places; and it is not among the least of them, that the ladies of that town readily give themselves, better for worse, and worse for better, to the colored gentlemen. This and other considerations may have a strong tendency to draw the proposed College to that town. We hope, therefore, that our citizens will act with coolness on this subject.

The *New Haven Advertiser* noted in its next issue that City Hall was packed for the meeting. Tappan later recalled that "The opposers of the measure rallied in strong force and were vociferous in opposition. Several of them belonged to the legal profession, and by their inflammatory speeches, added greatly to the excitement." Before the meeting, Mayor Kimberly had formed a committee of 13 men, a "who's who" of the New Haven political and educational elite, to offer resolutions against starting the training school. The committee presented two resolutions. The first resolution argued that if a "Negro college" was built in New Haven, it would cause harm to Yale College and other schools in the area. The second resolution basically was an argument against the abolition of slavery. It read:

> RESOLVED...that the propagation of sentiments favorable to the immediate emancipation of slaves in disregard of the civil institutions of the States in which they belong, and as auxiliary thereto the contemporaneous founding of Colleges for educating colored people, is unwarrantable and dangerous interference with the internal concerns of other States, and ought to be discouraged.

With the loud shouts of the huge crowd attending the meeting echoing in his ears, Jocelyn found himself virtually alone against this mass of people. Hundreds and hundreds of people whom he knew as neighbors were now voicing their stand against founding the college as he had proposed. By a vote of 700 to 4, with Jocelyn being one of the dissenters, the school proposal was blocked. The vote in New Haven on that hot afternoon ended any chance to start a college for black men. It would take over 20 more years for the vision of a school for black men to become reality.

CANTERBURY'S FIRST BLACK STUDENT

Back in Canterbury, Prudence's school for young ladies was up and running. She was soon exposed to what Garrison was writing in *The Liberator* via William Harris, the head of one of the few free black families in Canterbury at the time. Slavery had never been as prevalent in Connecticut as it was in other, especially southern, states due to the lack of large plantations for slaves to work on (most enslaved people in Connecticut were used as domestic workers or as laborers on small farms with one or two slaves to a household); although slavery wasn't abolished in Connecticut until 1848, slavery as an institution had been slowly dying out for some time in Connecticut before Prudence established her school. William Harris acted as an agent for *The Liberator*, a volunteer who helped distribute the newspaper around the country. Harris' son, William, was engaged to Mariah Davis, who acted as a "family assistant," as Prudence liked to call the servants at the school. Prudence saw Mariah's copy of the paper and the articles in it moved her. *The Liberator* advanced the idea that blacks needed an education in order to be on a level footing with their white counterparts; it also renounced slavery as a sin. Prudence looked at *The Liberator* as a confirmation of what she already knew to be true. When she finished her chores, Mariah would sit in on Prudence's classes, and

Sarah Harris, William's daughter, who was also a "family assistant" at the school, looked on, wanting to join the classes as a formal student.

History is not clear on whether it was Sarah who initially asked Prudence to be part of the school or whether Prudence offered the opportunity to Sarah. Regardless of who initiated the proposition, Sarah entered the school as a student in the fall of 1832 and the controversy began to stir. Prudence had contemplated the consequences of her actions before giving Sarah permission to become a student, and she was quoted in the *Windham County Advertiser* in 1833 as saying, "Her repeated solicitations were more than my feelings could resist and I told her if I was injured on her account I would bear it—she might enter as one of my pupils." Prudence was aware that there would be some opposition to Sarah's admittance to the school; just how much, however, she seemed to have underestimated. While thinking about whether or not to admit Sarah, Prudence turned to the Bible for guidance, especially to Ecclesiastes 4:1 where she read, "So I returned, and considered all the oppressions that are done under the sun; and behold the tears of such as were oppressed, and they had no comforter: and on the side of their oppressors there was power, but they had no comforter." Prudence took the passage as a sign—she would be able to help the oppressed by admitting Sarah as a student, and her decision was made.

Initially there was no real problem because no formal announcement had been made of Sarah's admittance. It was only after a few days had passed that the girls began to go home to their parents and tell them that a black girl had joined their ranks. It was the parents who began to get angry. In an 1869 letter to Ellen Larned, the Windham County historian, Prudence, recalling earlier events, explained, "The wife of an Episcopal clergyman who lived in the village told me that if I continued that colored girl in my school it could not be sustained. I replied to her, that it might sink, then, for I should not turn her out!" After being approached by several Canterbury citizens, Prudence decided to make a bold move. In her letter to Ellen Larned, she said "I made up my mind that if it were possible I would teach colored girls exclusively."

A SCHOOL EXCLUSIVELY FOR BLACK GIRLS

On February 24, 1833, Prudence told her white students as of April 1, the start of the next term, she would be accepting black girls exclusively. On February 25, three members of the Board of Visitors, Daniel Frost, Andrew Harris, and Rufus Adams, as well as a local merchant, Richard

Fenner, went to visit Prudence regarding her announcement. Prudence was visited by another group of prominent Canterbury citizens on March 1. Both groups cautioned her to revoke her plan, urging her to continue schooling the white girls of Canterbury, and only the white girls. They expressed concern that the blacks would feel they deserved equality once the school was changed to cater directly to them and that the black students may become dangerous. The location of the school, on Canterbury's town green, was a concern for Prudence's affluent neighbors; the last thing they wanted was a school for blacks across the street from their stately homes. They asked whether Prudence had considered the embarrassment she would cause at the Congregational church if she arrived with a group of black girls on Sunday. To their concerns, Prudence reportedly replied, "Moses had a black wife!"

On March 2, 1833, Prudence confirmed her convictions when an ad ran in *The Liberator* announcing the opening of her school for Young Ladies and Little Misses of Color.

On March 9, a town meeting was called to order to discuss the impending doom of Canterbury. Because Prudence was a woman, it would not have been appropriate for her to attend such a meeting, let alone speak at it, so Samuel May and Arnold Buffum went as her attorneys on her behalf. Prudence sent with them a letter of introduction, instructing the moderator of the meeting to allow them to speak for her. They were authorized to reach some sort of reasonable settlement so that the school could continue operating; the letter indicated that Prudence was willing to sell the house back to Canterbury and move to a more remote location. May's records of the meeting indicate that it was well attended. The meeting was held at the town Meeting House, which could hold up to 1,000 people. May later recalled that the Meeting House was "filled to its utmost capacity, and with difficulty we passed up the side aisle into the wall pew next to the deacon's seat in which sat the moderator."

Buffum and May did not receive a warm welcome. May's records indicate that before the two men were even given a chance to speak, "a series of Resolutions were laid before the meeting, in which were set forth the discourage and damage that would be brought upon the town if a school for colored girls should be set up there, protesting emphatically against the impending evil and appointing of the civil authority and selectmen a committee to wait upon 'The person contemplating the establishment of said school…point out to her the injurious effects, incalculable evils, resulting from such an establishment within the town, persuade her if possible to abandon the project.'" Rufus Adams, a member of the Board of Visitors, introduced this resolution. May recorded that Adams' malice, or superficial observation.

HIGH SCHOOL FOR YOUNG COLORED LADIES AND MISSES.

It is with a rush of pleasurable emotions that we insert, in another column, the advertisement of Miss P. CRANDALL, (a white lady) of Canterbury, Connecticut, for a High School for young colored Ladies and Misses. This is a seasonable auxiliary to the contemplated Manual Labor School for Colored Youth. An interview with Miss C. has satisfied us that she richly deserves the patronage and confidence of the people of color; and we doubt not they will give her both. The following extract from a letter, received by us from a highly respectable gentleman, contains all that need be said in her favor:

'Miss C. has, for a number of years, been principal of a high school for the education of Females, and has earned great credit to herself and school, as well for her peculiar qualifications in conducting it, as for her untiring zeal for the improvement of those entrusted to her charge. Miss C. possessing naturally a great share of the excellent virtue, viz. *Philanthropy*, has been provoked by the benevolent exertions of the day towards ameliorating the condition of the wretched suffering African, in this country, and to cast her mite into the treasury; and, sir, for myself, I have no doubt, knowing as I do her rare qualifications and firmness of purpose, that she would prove a most valuable auxiliary to the African cause.'

In making the alteration in her School, Miss C. runs a great risk; but let her manifest inflexible courage and perseverance, and she will be sustained triumphantly. Reproach and persecution may assail her, at the commencement, but they will soon expire. Her terms are very low—the branches which she proposes to teach are various—she has a large and commodious house—and the village of Canterbury is central and pleasant.

The advertisement in *The Liberator* announcing the opening of Prudence's school for young colored Ladies and Misses. *Image courtesy of Yale's Gilder Lehrman Center for the Study of Slavery http://www.yale.edu/glc/.*

speech "grossly misrepresented what Miss C. had done, her sentiments and purpose and threw out several mean and low insinuations against the motives of those who were encouraging her enterprise." Immediately after Adams' outcry against the school came Andrew Judson and his similar impassioned plea. According to May, Judson declared that "having a school for nigger girls so near him was insupportable." Judson's house was next to Prudence's; he was concerned not only for the value of his property, but the real estate value for property throughout the town. His tirade sang out against Prudence, spoke of a conspiracy, belittled her actions, and called for the people of Canterbury to be "roused by every consideration of self-preservation, as well as self-respect to prevent the accomplishment of the design."

Not only was the color of their skin a problem, the black students' wealth and financial situation became a problem for Canterbury citizens as well. The tuition was not being decreased for the black students and it was outrageous to the whites in Canterbury that there were black families that could afford such steep tuition. Acknowledging that these people of an inferior race could afford the school was unacceptable, and such an idea was not only insulting, but also frightening. As Judson would soon privately indicate to May, white residents in Canterbury were not willing to allow blacks to become equal with them in any sense.

When May and Buffum indicated to the moderator their wish to be heard, Judson then accused them of insulting the town by interfering with business that was not their own. In an account of the meeting to *The Liberator* in 1833, May said, "Gentleman sprang to their feet in hot displeasure; and with fists doubled in our faces roughly admonished us that if we opened our lips there, they would inflict upon us the utmost penalty of the law if not a more immediate vengeance."

"Thus forbidden to speak, we of course sat in silence and let the waves of invective and abuse dash over us. But we sat thus only until we heard the moderator say 'This meeting is adjourned.'" At that point, the two spoke up, knowing they could not be held in contempt if the meeting was over. "I sprang to the seat on which I had been sitting and cried out 'Men of Canterbury, I have a word for you. Hear me!'" The two men spoke as quickly as possible, urging those who stayed to listen that Prudence meant no harm to the town by starting this school. They were soon removed from the building when the church trustee ordered them all out, though they stayed to speak with those who would listen outside on the green. May and Buffum had agreed with Prudence beforehand that they would not return to her home after the meeting, not wishing to draw any attention to the house.

A few days after the meeting, Sam Hough, another member of the Board of Visitors, came to Prudence's home to formally read her the resolutions introduced at the meeting:

> Whereas it hath been publicly announced that a school is to be opened in this town on the first Monday in April next, using the Language of the advertisement, 'for young ladies and little misses of color' or in other words for the people of color, the obvious tendency of which would be to collect within the town of Canterbury large numbers of persons from other states, whose character and habits might be various and unknown to us, thereby rendering insecure, the persons, properties, and reputations of our citizens. Under such circumstances, our silence might be construed into an approbation of the project.
>
> Thereupon resolved—that the location of a school for the people of color at any place within the limits of this town for the admission of persons of foreign jurisdictions meets with our unqualified disapprobation and it is to be understood that the inhabitants of Canterbury protest against it in the most earnest manner.
>
> Resolved—that a committee be now appointed, to be composed of the Civil Authority and Selectmen, who shall make known to the person contemplating the establishment of said school, the sentiments and objections entertained by this meeting, in reference to said school, pointing out to her, the injurious effects and incalculable evils resulting from such an establishment within the town and to persuade her to abolish the project.

Prudence was not especially upset by the reading of the resolution and continued to receive girls from around the Northeast in preparation for their first day of school in April. She only noted her regret that the people of Canterbury did not understand what she was doing.

Garrison, however, was outraged at the meeting and the resolutions that came from it. In the March 16 issue of *The Liberator*, he published a scathing report of what had happened, printing the "names of the principal disturbers in black—black as the infamy which will attach to them as long as there is any recollection of the wrongs of the colored race."

Prudence was not supportive of Garrison's tactics and told him so in a letter. "Permit me to entreat you to handle the people of Canterbury with all the mildness possible, as everything severe tends merely to heighten the flame of malignity among them." Garrison was unable to contain his biting commentary and continued to write in opposition to how Canterbury was reacting to Prudence and her school.

Judson approached May independently in order to persuade him against supporting Prudence's plan. The two men had known each other professionally before this incident. Judson made it clear that the town would not merely allow Prudence to relocate her school to another area, or even another town. Their opposition to the school went beyond real estate value and Canterbury's preference for locals—it was embedded in a hostile and prejudiced mind-set regarding black people generally.

"The colored people can never rise from their menial condition in our country; they ought not to be permitted to rise here," Judson told May. "They are an inferior race of beings, and never can or ought to be recognized as the equals of the whites...The condition of the colored population can never be essentially improved on this continent." He also informed May that they would be pursuing the passage of a state law prohibiting such a school from being open.

THE BIRTH OF THE "BLACK LAW"

April 1, 1833, came as if there had been no opposition; Prudence opened her school for young ladies and little misses of color as planned. William Lloyd Garrison said of Prudence, "Miss Crandall is as undaunted as if she had a whole world on her side. She has opened her school and is resolved to persevere."

The day the school was opened, townspeople held another meeting. Prudence showed no sign of backing down; she was obviously audacious even in the light of their previous actions. Realizing that Prudence was fearless and fully intended to establish the school, the residents of Canterbury felt a new plan of attack was necessary. It was at this meeting that the idea for the "black law" was publicized. Those at the meeting voted to petition the Connecticut General Assembly for "some law by which the introduction of foreign blacks, might be regulated in a proper degree by the feelings and wishes of the inhabitants of the town."

In the meantime, they attempted to use existing laws to remove the black students, or at least scare them away. The town selectmen of Connecticut had the authority to instruct "any person not an inhabitant of this state, to depart such town." The law authorized towns to avoid spending their resources on poor migrants who had decided to settle there. The penalty for not complying with the instructions was a fine of $1.67 per week until the migrants left, a hefty sum considering tuition at Prudence's school was only $3 per term. The girls were considered by the town to be migrants and Canterbury Sheriff Roger Coit came to the school on April 13 to serve seventeen-year-old Ann Eliza Hammond with such a warning. Hammond was a black girl who had arrived from Providence to attend the school. May offered to pay a $1,000 bond, not only for Hammond but for all the girls at the school from out of state, ensuring that the town would not be responsible for them in any way, but his offer was denied.

Although Coit's harsh action did not scare Prudence, it did have the intended effect on potential students. By April 9, 1833, Prudence had only one boarder, Hammond, and one day scholar, Sarah Harris. She urged Jocelyn in a letter to "encourage those that are coming to come immediately." In a letter from Prudence to Mr. Jocelyn dated April 17, she stated that another boarder had joined her school.

According to Kazimiera Kozlowski, curator of the Prudence Crandall Museum, teachers like Prudence would have left detailed records of who attended the school in a given semester, and what courses and subjects were taught. Prudence was unable to do this with her black students due to all the consequences of admitting them. People visited the school regularly when it was primarily for white girls, but now neighbors and townspeople were coming to protest her choice of students. There are, therefore, no concrete records as to who attended the school or what life was like while it was a school for black girls. What is known about those who attended has been gleaned from court records because many of Prudence's students were called to testify at her trial.

The townspeople soon took other measures to ensure that the school would fail. At an informal meeting held at the town Masonic lodge, the town shopkeepers agreed not to sell Prudence or her students anything they might need. With Canterbury's policy against foreign peddlers, this agreement would ensure that Prudence could not obtain the supplies she needed for the school to remain open. The one man who held out, surprisingly, was Stephen Coit, the same man whose daughters were no longer able to attend Prudence's school. According to a letter from Prudence to Simeon Jocelyn, Coit told the rest of the merchants in town that "if anyone wished to buy of him he would sell to them."

Throughout the next month, Judson did not sit idle waiting for the Assembly to pass his law. He collected more than 900 signatures on a petition that called for Prudence's school to be done away with. In April he went to the Assembly and informed the members of the "horrors" that Canterbury was being forced to deal with. Among Judson's comments, he stated:

> The establishment or rendezvous falsely denominated a school was designed by its projectors as the theatre, as the place to

promulgate their disgusting doctrines of amalgamation and their pernicious sentiments of subverting the union. These pupils are to be congregated here from all quarters under the pretense of educating them but really to scatter fire brands, arrows and death among brethren of our own blood.

Judson's presentation was not heard alone, but in tandem with letters of support from Prudence's father, Pardon. In one letter to the legislature, he wrote:

Instead of the leading men of Canterbury coming forward to encourage or assist to enlighten the ignorant or elevate the deprived people of color, they have called together a number of town meetings and passed resolutions to do all in their power to destroy this institution. I entreat the members of the Assembly when acting on this petition to remember those self evident truths that all mankind are created free and equal, that they are endowed with inalienable rights of which no man nor any set of men have any right to deprive them....My request is that you will not pass any act which will curtail or destroy any of the rights of free people of this state or other states whether they are white or black.

Before addressing his concerns in a letter to the legislature, Pardon sent a letter to the townspeople in an attempt to convince them to back down regarding the school. He wrote, "You are actuated by the same spirit that lighted up the fires of Smithfield that banished Roger Williams, the Quakers and Baptists from Boston, and particularly the actors in the Salem Witchcraft when they tried to kill the Devil who they imagined appeared to their inhabitants in the form of a Black man with his black Book. I once more entreat you to stop in your mad career before we are ruined." His warning went unheeded.

On May 6, 1833, Judson presented the Connecticut General Assembly with the petition and urged them to pass legislation that would force the school to shut its doors.

State Senator Phillip Pearl of Hampton was assigned as committee chair to evaluate Judson's petition. Pearl's daughter had attended Prudence's school when it was an all-white school. Not surprisingly, Pearl approved of the legislation. In his report to the General Assembly, Pearl stated, "The immense evils which such a mass of colored population would gather within this state when it has become their place of resort from other states and countries, would impose on our people burdens."

He also added, "Colored people in the midst of a white population… are an appalling source of crime and pauperism."

Just weeks after Judson's oration before the legislature, the Assembly signed the Black Law into effect on May 24, 1833. The purpose of the law was to prevent the establishment of a school for blacks who were not residents of Connecticut as well as to prevent the boarding and education of such persons. The penalty was a $100 fine for the first offense, $200 for the second, and double penalty for each successive offense.

The passage of the Black Law was celebrated back in Canterbury where residents shot rifles into the air, lit bonfires, and rang the bells in the Congregational church. Reaction to the law did not stop in Canterbury, however; it faced staunch criticism and opposition from New York newspapers as well as a protest petition against the law that was brought to the Connecticut legislature. The petition called for immediate repeal of the law, but the petition went unheeded.

Two weeks after the law was passed, Judson and Rufus Adams took it upon themselves to extend the law to anyone who supported Prudence in any way. They drove to Pardon's farm to tell him that if he had any further contact with his daughter he would be fined $100 and that it would double each time he visited her. They claimed the same applied to Prudence's mother, Esther, as well as to May and Prudence's other supporters. As for Prudence, if she received any of her supporters as visitors, she would be treated as a common criminal, arrested, and imprisoned in jail.

By this time Prudence had approximately 13 students. Her supporters were still advertising the school and urging people to send their daughters, but the response was not great. According to Prudence, the school was entering "weary, weary days." Prudence and the girls were beginning to see some rowdiness from the town; Prudence noted that "troops of boys" would follow her and the girls around wherever they went, blowing horns and beating drums. In addition to the pesky boys, Canterbury's leading men launched their legal attack. Two weeks after the law was passed, two Canterbury gentlemen came to inquire whether she had any non-resident students at the time; Prudence politely invited them in and introduced them to the girls. On June 27, Deputy Sheriff George Cady came to tell both Prudence and her sister, Almira, that they were under arrest in violation of the law and escorted them to their arraignment at the home of Chauncery Bacon (the nearest jail to Canterbury was several miles away in Brooklyn and local magistrates were often called upon to hold court in their own home when necessary). Rufus Adams read the complaint against her that had been brought by a parent of one of the girls who was no longer eligible to attend Prudence's school because she was white.

A HEROINE IS CREATED

Prudence's bail was set for $150; her sister was released because of her status as a minor, which prevented her from standing trial. Prudence informed her jailers that she did not have the money to pay the bond, a response that her opposition had contemplated. Knowing that Prudence was to be taken into custody, Judson had contacted May, who had already been more than willing to post a $1,000 bond on behalf of the black students. Judson's plan was for May to post Prudence's bond, but May and Prudence vowed not to fall into that trap. May inquired of Judson whether there were not Canterbury men who would pay the bond. Judson insisted that as her friend, May should be the person to pay it. May replied that he was too good a friend of Prudence's to relieve her enemies of their present embarrassment and refused to pay it.

Prudence was escorted by Sheriff Coit to the Brooklyn jail as people watched from the side of the road. May met Prudence's entourage at the jail and assured her he had the money to pay her bond if she did not want to enter the jail; she replied that her only concern was that they would not put her in jail. There was a commotion because the only cell within the jail was rumored to have been last occupied by Oliver Watkins, a criminal convicted of strangling his wife, in the days before Watkins had been put to death. In all actuality, Prudence spent the night in the more spacious debtors' cell where Watkins did not stay, but would only have received friends and clergy there in his final days. Coit remarked to May before locking up Prudence that it would be a "damn shame" and "eternal disgrace" to put Prudence within the cell. May agreed with Coit, urging him to drop the charges so that she would be set free, but the sheriff refused, remarking "We don't want any more niggers coming among us." According to May's written recollections, he previously arranged with the jailer to put the room "in as nice order as possible, and permitted me to substitute, for the bedstead and mattress, fresh and clean ones from my own house." Prudence spent the night in jail to prove her point. The next day at 4:00 p.m., her bail was posted by George Benson, one of her supporters, and she was set free.

As planned, Prudence's stint in jail did not go unnoticed. Rumors about her incarceration flew about the town, and local and national newspapers picked up the story. When she returned to the school, she was joined by additional students, and according to a visiting journalist, the number was up to 19 by this time. Prudence urged the girls not to "indulge in any angry feelings towards our adversaries," and they continued to ignore the events going on around them.

Soon after Prudence was released, small attacks on her, the girls, and the house began. The first incident was a rock thrown into a parlor window, smashing it to pieces. Prudence proceeded to display the rock on the mantelpiece and showed it to visitors. The broken window was to be the first of many such incidents. Her well, which supplied the school with its water, was, according to May, "defiled with the most offensive filth, and her neighbors refused her and the thirsty ones about her even a cup of cold water, leaving them to depend for that essential element upon the scanty supplies that could be brought from her father's farm." The local doctor also refused, on two occasions, to treat the girls as well as Crandall's entire family. More rocks were thrown at the house, and eggs were soon added to the mix.

It was at around this time that Arthur Tappan came into the picture to assess the situation. He wrote a letter to May in which he said, "Consider me your banker. Spare no necessary expense...See to it that this great case shall be thoroughly tried, cost what it may."

Because state and local newspapers had adopted the habit of printing accusations and misrepresentations regarding Prudence and her students, but failing to allow her or her representatives to respond, Tappan decided that Prudence's "obvious" solution was to start a newspaper as soon as possible. They were able to get their hands on a recently abandoned press in Brooklyn and there *The Unionist* was created—the first issue was put out on August 1, 1833—and for the next two years it was published every Thursday. *The Unionist* provided a forum for people on both sides of the black school debate, and a response to Prudence's jailing by Judson and Adams appeared in its second issue.

THE FIRST TRIAL

Prudence's trial took place on August 22, 1833, presided over by the Honorable Joseph Eaton and held in Brooklyn, Connecticut, the Windham County seat. May commented that the trial was ironically held "within a stone's throw of the house where lived and died General Israel Putnam, who, with his compatriots of 1776, periled his life in defense of the self-evident truth that all men were created equal."

Prudence was charged with instructing and boarding non-Connecticut residents without consent of the civil authority and selectmen of Canterbury. For conviction, the prosecution need only prove that Prudence engaged in one of these activities, either boarding or instructing. The indictments of both counts were practically identical, reading "with force and arms" she had received girls into her school; and with "force and arms" she had instructed certain colored girls, who were not inhabitants of the state, without having first obtained in writing, permission to do so as required by the law under which she was prosecuted.

Financed by Tappan, May hired three of Connecticut's finest lawyers to represent Prudence. William Wolcott Ellsworth, Calvin Goddard, and Henry Strong acted as Prudence's counsel, and all of them were opposed to the Black Law. Ellsworth was the son of Oliver Ellsworth, second Chief Justice of the U.S. Supreme Court; his other claim to fame was that he was married to Noah Webster's daughter. Opposing counsel consisted of Judson, Ichabod Bulkley, and Chauncey Fitch Cleveland, though at the last minute, due to an illness, Cleveland was replaced by Jonathan Welch.

Judson made the first opening statement, and according to May's recollections, "endeavored to keep out of sight the most odious features of the law which had been disobeyed by Miss Crandall." May said that Judson urged the court that it was only a "wise precaution" to keep out of the state such an "injurious kind of population," arguing it was not fair or safe to allow Prudence to invite foreigners to come into Connecticut without the permission of state or local officials. "If it were not for such protection as the law in question had provided, the Southerners might free all their slaves, and send them to Connecticut instead of Liberia, which would be overwhelming," Judson said. "Why should a man be educated who could not be a freeman?" he asked.

May recalled that Judson's assertions were "vigorously assailed by Mr. Ellsworth and Mr. Strong, and shown to be untenable by a great array of facts adduced from the history of our own country...the force of which was palpable."

One week prior to trial, Deputy Sherriff Cady issued summonses to Prudence's students so that they could testify that Prudence had, in fact, both boarded and taught them, and to testify that they were not, nor ever had been, residents of Connecticut. The girls were worried about the summons and Prudence was upset as well. Because she intended to confess to breaking the law, she did not see a need for the girls to be brought into the ordeal. As a result, she closed the door in Cady's face.

The prosecution succeeded in summoning the girls and called several as witnesses. The defense argued that the girls could not be compelled to testify about things that might implicate them in a crime, but the judge allowed them to be called. Ann Peterson and Catherine Ann Weldon from New York and Ann Eliza Hammond from Providence all appeared before the court. The prosecution's effort was fruitless, however, as the girls refused to answer any questions once they took the stand.

In addition to bringing the students as witnesses, the prosecution brought several people to the stand who had visited the school while it was operating as a school for black girls; none, however, could recall seeing Prudence engaged in teaching them. Asahel Bacon and Ebenezer Sanger both testified that they had gone to visit Miss Crandall's school and that Prudence had told them where the girls were from. It was not until Mary Benson testified to seeing Prudence teaching arithmetic and geography that the prosecution's case was sealed.

More than a dozen witnesses were called in order to testify against Prudence and the trial lasted two days. Prudence's students were not the only ones unwilling to testify against her. Reverend Levi Kneeland of the Packerville Baptist Church spent a night in jail before agreeing to be a witness.

Both Strong and Ellsworth contributed to the closing argument for Prudence. They did not deny that Prudence's school was run exclusively for blacks, but they charged the jury not with the task of determining whether Prudence broke the law, but whether it was a Constitutional law. They urged the jury to find that it, in fact, violated Article IV, Section 2 of the Constitution, the privileges and immunities clause, because it denied blacks the privileges and immunities of the several states. The counselors urged the jury to find that because blacks were citizens just as whites were, the law violated their rights as citizens when it prohibited blacks from other states to come to Connecticut for the purpose of getting an education.

Closing argument for the prosecution was again made by Judson. He reiterated the fact that towns should be able to choose who is allowed to become inhabitants, and thus, it was neither safe nor fair to allow Prudence to go about as she pleased, inviting strange foreigners in without asking permission. He also argued that the power to regulate a school is within the confines of the state's power and not the federal government. He responded to Strong and Ellsworth's Constitutional claim by explaining that the word "citizen," as used in the Constitution, did not include non-white persons and thus the privileges and immunities clause did not apply to them. "It is quite immaterial how that term...may be understood in common parlance at the present day. The real question is what the framers of the Constitution meant when they said in such concise and emphatic language, 'the citizens of each State shall be entitled to equal privileges and immunities of citizens of the several states?'"

According to May, the judge's charge to the jury was somewhat "timid" and he told them it was his opinion that "the law was constitutional and obligatory on the people of the state."

With the judge's charge given, the jury, consisting of 12 white men, retired to deliberate and was gone for several hours. They returned only to tell the court they had been unable to come to a unanimous decision. May said the jury stated to the court that there was "no probability they should ever agree." Seven were for conviction and five were for acquittal. The members of the jury were initially sent back to deliberate again, but the third time they informed the court that they could come to no decision, and they were finally discharged.

Normally what would have happened under these circumstances is that the trial would have been continued until the next term of the Windham County Court, which was in December. The prosecution, unable to wait that long, began a new case against Prudence.

THE SECOND TRIAL

The new case was to be tried before the Connecticut Supreme Court on October 3, 1833, with Judge David Daggett presiding. Daggett, who had been appointed Chief Justice of Connecticut's Supreme Court in 1832, was a well-known politician and attorney regarded to be hostile toward black people (he had been one of those who spoke out in opposition to the "Negro college" at New Haven's infamous Town Meeting on September 10, 1831), as well as, according to May, a "strenuous advocate of the Black Law." Daggett had been the only professor of law at Yale College (also one of the co-founders of the Yale Law School), the mayor of New Haven for two terms, and a former U.S. Senator. Sitting with Daggett as associate judges were Clark Bissell and Thomas Williams.

May, who had assumed the case would not be heard again until December, had left the area to visit friends in Boston and, due to previously scheduled speaking engagements, was unable to return in order to attend the second trial. May noted in a diary that he "could only write and instruct the counsel of Miss Crandall, in case a verdict should be obtained against her, to carry the cause up to the Court of Errors." Prudence was arrested for the second time on September 26, but two sympathetic supporters posted her bond to keep her out of jail. Given only six days' notice of the new trial, Prudence and her counsel were caught off guard.

Prudence entered a plea of "not guilty" and each side put forth the same arguments they had presented in the first trial, but this time the judge had more than a "timid" set of instructions for the jury. Though May was not there, he recounted that Daggett "delivered an elaborate and able charge, insisting upon the constitutionality of the law." Daggett is said to have insisted the jury put aside their feelings regarding the popularity of the Black Law. It was his opinion, he told the jury, that "to call slaves, Indians or free blacks 'citizens,'…would be a perversion of the term as it was used in the United States Constitution. Such persons were not styled as citizen when the Constitution fixed the basis for representation as 'free persons' and excluded indentured servants and Indians." Not surprisingly, the jury quickly came back with a verdict of guilty.

Prudence's counsel immediately filed a bill of exceptions as well as an appeal to the Court of Errors. They claimed that the superior court had no jurisdiction over the matter and that the particular information submitted in the formal charge was insufficient. The appeal was granted, which prevented Prudence from being sentenced. The appeal was scheduled to be heard before the Supreme Court of Errors in Brooklyn in July of 1834.

The ensuing months were busy for all involved. Prudence accepted a proposal of marriage from Calvin Philleo, a match that would prove to be less than satisfactory for her. Prudence's case had caused other occurrences besides marriage proposals; race riots broke out across the Northeast in New York, Philadelphia, and even Norwich, Connecticut, though they were not directly connected with Prudence and her school.

THE FINAL TRIAL

On July 18, 1834, in Brooklyn, Connecticut, Prudence Crandall's last trial began, though she chose not to be there. Again, the same arguments by both sides were made. Ellsworth and Goddard put forth their Constitutional claim, and Judson reiterated that blacks were not citizens and thus the Constitution didn't apply to them. In his argument, Judson exclaimed that if the law were declared unconstitutional, the "consequences will inevitably destroy the government itself, and this American nation—this nation of white men, may be taken from us, and given to the African race!"

While it wasn't a decisive victory, Prudence's conviction was overturned when Judge Williams, who sat previously as Daggett's associate judge, issued the court's judgment. The judges were unwilling to overturn Daggett's decision, but recognized the conviction's technical defect. The reasons were based on the technical point raised in Prudence's appeal— the court found that there was an "insufficiency of information." In the original warrant for her arrest, Prudence had been charged with "harboring and boarding colored persons, not inhabitants of this state, without license, for the purpose of being instructed." Judge Williams interpreted this charge to imply that the boarding house had no license, but not that the school did not have a license. Since the purpose of the law was to regulate unlicensed schools, the omission in the warrant was a "fatal flaw," as Williams put it.

The court specifically avoided the Constitutional issue by stating that it "did not decide either of the points presented by counsel," *i.e.*, whether the law was Constitutional and whether blacks were citizens. The issue of black citizenship was to go unresolved for another 20 years until the U.S. Supreme Court decided *Scott v. Sanford* in 1857.

THE LAST STRAW

Though she had prevailed and was able to continue operating her school, the townspeople's treatment of Prudence and her students grew worse by the day. She found a dead cat with its throat slit, hanging by its neck on her gate. Someone set fire to the corner of her home, but because it was started where the wood was somewhat decayed, the house was saved from going up in flames. Upon finding the blaze, she did receive help from the town in putting it out. Their assistance is not likely to have

The burning of schools dedicated to educating blacks became common. *Courtesy of the Prudence Crandall Museum, administered by the Commission on Culture and Tourism, State of Connecticut.*

stemmed from the kindness in their hearts; a fire in one house would surely spread to the others close by on the green. Prudence was also unable to find anyone to marry her and Philleo. The new pastor of the Canterbury Congregational church received an anonymous donation the day of the would-be nuptials. The condition attached was that the pastor not perform their marriage. The marriage debacle occurred on August 12. On September 9, 1834, the harassment got out of control.

"Midnight ruffians" as they were described by Garrison in *The Liberator*, awoke Prudence, her new husband, and about 20 students when they broke into the house armed with pipes and clubs, breaking more than 90 window panes. They ransacked the first floor, leaving it virtually uninhabitable.

It was at this point that Prudence feared not only for her life, but for the lives of her students as well. The drastic attack called for drastic measures, and Prudence decided to close the school. Her decision was supported by her husband, her father, and even Samuel May, who had fought with her every step of the way to keep it open. In having to tell the students the school was to be closed, May said, "The words almost blistered my lips. My bosom glowed with indignation. I felt ashamed of Canterbury, ashamed of Connecticut, ashamed of my country, ashamed of my color."

An advertisement regarding the incidents ran on September 11, 1834, in both *The Unionist* and *The Liberator*. It was placed by Prudence's husband, inquiring about those who had ransacked the house. An award of $50 was offered, but no response was ever received. The ad also announced the closing of the school. "Human endurance has its bounds, and the requirements of duty have theirs…it appears that another cowardly attack has been made upon Miss Crandall's (now Mrs. Philleo's) dwelling, by some midnight ruffians in Canterbury, and that it has been deemed advisable to abandon the school in that heathenish village, and to let ANDREW T. JUDSON and his associates, with the whole State of Connecticut, have all the infamy and guilty which attach to the violent suppression of so praiseworthy an institution. *O, tempora! O, mores!*" In addition to the reward and closing proclamation, the final aspect of Calvin Philleo's ad was to announce the house was officially for sale.

Since they had married two months earlier, Calvin Philleo was legally entitled to do what he wished with his wife's property, including being able to sell it, without her consent. The house was sold on November 15, 1834, for $2,000—the same amount Prudence had paid for it three years earlier. Prudence's signature appeared on the deed transferring the property.

In the words of Samuel May, "Thus ended the generous, disinterested, philanthropic, Christian enterprise of Prudence Crandall."

LIFE AFTER CANTERBURY

After the school closed and the house sold, Prudence, Calvin, and Calvin's two children moved to Troy Grove, Illinois. Calvin died in 1874 when he was 87 years old. It is unclear whether it was Calvin's death or Prudence's inability to cope with him any longer that caused Prudence to make her way at age 73 to Elk Grove, Kansas, where her brother Hezekiah had become a farmer. Her marriage to Calvin had been unhappy almost from the start. "…my husband opposed me, more than anyone," she said. "He would not let me read the books that he himself read, but I did read them. I read all sides and searched for the truth, whether it was in science, religion, or humanity." When she reached Kansas, Prudence lived in a small house full of books and continued to be an educator; she ran a school for local children from her home. She also continued to give lectures on social justice, especially on temperance and women's rights.

In an article that appeared in a Topeka, Kansas, newspaper in 1885, Prudence stated:

> My humble dwelling is situated in one of the most beautiful spots on earth. The aspirations of my soul to benefit the colored race were never greater than at the present time. I hope to live long enough to see a college built on this old farm, into which can be admitted all the classes of the human family, without regard to sex or color…I want professorships of the highest order…You see that my wants are so many, and so great, that I have no time to waste, no time to spend in grief…I only need to mourn over my own misdeeds and shortcomings, which are many.

Samuel Clemens read about Prudence's living conditions and offered to start a campaign to buy back her house in Canterbury for her. Prudence declined the offer, saying that she preferred to live in Kansas. Instead, she wrote to Clemens and asked him for his photograph and a copy of his most recent book, *The Innocents Abroad*.

On April 2, 1886, almost 53 years exactly from when the school for black girls was first opened, Prudence was informed that the Connecticut General Assembly had voted to pay her a $400-a-year pension for the rest of her life. When she heard the news she reportedly said that, "I shall never plead poverty…My plea will be for justice…When a state has falsely imprisoned an innocent citizen and passed unconstitutional laws by which they are harassed and property destroyed it is right they should compensate the abused…I feel that it is a duty I owe myself and also to the State to ask for redress for such slander and abuse as I have received at their hands." The petition to grant her the pension bore 112 signatures, the first of which was Thomas G. Clarke, nephew of Andrew Judson.

In 1995, the Connecticut General Assembly passed yet another Act concerning the fate of Prudence Crandall. This time, however, the Act declared Prudence Crandall to be Connecticut's state heroine.

Though Prudence was forced to close her school, it was not before she made major waves in the debate over equality. She blazed a path that would make it easier for others to follow in her footsteps. In the paramount decision of *Brown v. Board of Education* in 1954, the arguments made by William Ellsworth and Henry Goddard at Prudence's trial were cited in argument before the U.S. Supreme Court; the Court decided in that case that the "separate but equal" treatment of black students in public schools was unconstitutional.

Notice of Prudence Crandall's death on January 28, 1890, made national news, and her obituary in the *Cleveland Gazette* read as follows:

> THE RECENT death in Kansas of Prudence Crandall Philleo recalls an incident in her life which is of singular interest to Afro-Americans. In 1833 she started a school for colored children in Canterbury, Ct. Her school-house was mobbed and she arrested and thrown into jail, it being a crime at that time to conduct a school for colored people. Of late years she has lived in Kansas, and for the past few years has received a pension of $400, voted her by the Connecticut Legislature. Another old *friend* of the race gone.

Prudence Crandall Philleo Remembered, Cleveland Gazette, February 8, 1890. *Ohio Historical Center Archives Library.*

See Appendix B for more information on Prudence Crandall.

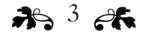

A Mutinous Landing in Unsuspecting New Haven
The *Amistad* Trial

In August 1839, cities in New York and Connecticut along the Long Island Sound were abuzz with rumors of a mysterious ship that had been sighted numerous times, her sails torn and flapping in the wind, flying no flag, and more importantly, full of Africans. Was it the mythical *Flying Dutchman*, full of dead sailors doomed to sail until the end of time, or were its passengers real-life pirates, going village by village, pillaging and killing all in their path? The ship was actually *La Amistad*, a Spanish ship tattered from her long, arduous journey from Cuba. She would soon arrive and dock in New York's Long Island Sound, where she would then be taken against her will to New Haven, Connecticut. The landing in New Haven would prove to be one of the most controversial moorings ever made in quiet, little Connecticut.

THE SLAVE TRADE

The excursion that eventually landed in New Haven began thousands of miles away in the African village of Mani in the European settlement of Sierra Leone. There lived Sengbe Pieh, more widely known as Joseph Cinqué, who made his living as a rice farmer. Knowing how to cultivate and harvest rice was a valuable skill that slave traders knew southern American farmers would appreciate when buying their slaves. On his way to his rice fields one morning, Cinqué was surrounded by a large group of other Africans. They fought and struggled with Cinqué, but did not kill him; instead, they bound him up and brought him to the island of Lomboko where he remained for more than a month. Several factors could cause a person to be captured by slave traders; on occasion, those who were slow in paying their debts would be captured by those to whom they owed money; their sale to slave traders would more than pay off their debts. Breaking tribal laws could also cause you to be sacrificed to the slave dealers. Often, however, capture would be the result of random raids initiated by Europeans to find as many strong men as possible to sell on their next leg of the triangular journey traveled by slavers.

The slave trade thrived on a route that formed a triangle on the map. Ships would depart from either the United States or Europe, laden with rum and beautiful fabrics. The traders would sail to Africa where they would exchange the products for new slaves. After acquiring as many slaves as their ships could hold, they would travel to Cuba. Here, the slaves would be traded for raw materials such as sugar cane and cotton, which would be transported back to either the United States or Europe; there the raw materials would be transformed to the finished products such as rum and silk, and the process would begin all over again.

The ships were massive and designed specifically to hold as many slaves as possible; capacity was usually 300 to 400 slaves per ship. Each deck had only between three and four feet of space between the floor and the ceiling. While the slaves were on board, they would lie side by side, chained together with almost no room to move. The smell of human waste would soon become unbearable. Though there were large open tubs for the captives to use, because it was usually impossible to get up, most of them relieved themselves were they lay. When they went up to eat, their quarters were cleaned with water and vinegar. The vessels were not meant to last long though; the rotting stench would soon become ingrained into the ship. After four or five voyages transporting slaves, the ships would often be abandoned.

The ships were heavily guarded at all times because the captives usually greatly outnumbered the ship's crew; usually the captives' hands, feet, and necks would be chained. When the slaves were allowed to come up from below deck, they were fed just enough to keep them alive. Disease spread like wildfire and usually at least a third of the passengers did not complete the journey. Because their cargo was so valuable, ship crews were vigilant about monitoring the Africans for disease; at the first sign of symptoms, an affected slave would be thrown overboard to avoid having the illness spread.

The Africans who captured Cinqué were hired by Europeans to catch other Africans to sell them into slavery. It was a dangerous profession because usually the very people hired to catch slaves would be sold into slavery themselves. Historians have questioned why the Africans did not band together to stop the slave trade as they were all affected and they clearly outnumbered those coming into their country to capture them. It may have been because the warring villages chose to continue the practice for practical reasons; not only were the villages able to dispose of their enemies once and for all, but they earned a large profit in the process. Greed overpowered human dignity and morals.

While at Lomboko, Pedro Blanco, the wealthy and notorious slave dealer who controlled the island, decided to purchase Cinqué, along with several others after examining them to ensure that they were strong and healthy. The inspection was carried out not only so that the slave trader would be able to sell the Africans for a good price, but also to make sure they were strong enough to survive the long journey from Africa to Cuba.

In 1839, even though it had been outlawed in most of the world, the slave trade was still widespread, especially along the triangular route between Africa, Cuba, America, and Europe. British antislavery cruisers patrolled African waters to stop slaves from being smuggled out of areas along the African coast. Even the United States, though it allowed slavery, had prohibited the importation of more slaves from Africa.

On March 2, 1807, the U.S. Congress had passed "an Act to prohibit the importation of slaves into any port or place within the jurisdiction of the United States, from and after the first day of January, in the year of our Lord one thousand eight hundred and eight." The language of the Act read, "Be it enacted by the Senate and House of Representatives of the United States of America in Congress assembled, That from and after the first day of January, one thousand eight hundred and eight, it shall not be lawful to import or bring into the United States or the territories thereof from any foreign kingdom, place, or country, any negro, mulatto, or person of colour, with intent to hold, sell, or dispose of such negro, mulatto, or person of colour, as a slave, or to be held to service or labour." The Act also provided for the forfeiture of vessels used specifically for slave trading as well as penalties for not complying with the Act. If you were caught bringing slaves into the United States, you would be charged with a high misdemeanor—the fine would range from $5,000 to $20,000, your ship would be forfeited to the government, and you would have no right or claim to the people you were transporting. Anyone smuggling people from other countries and transporting them to the United States to sell them into slavery "shall suffer imprisonment for not more than ten years nor less than five years, and be fined not exceeding ten thousand dollars, nor less than one thousand dollars."

Great Britain outlawed slavery in 1787 and had since entered into several treaties with nations throughout the world, ensuring that other nations also stopped importing slaves from Africa. Spain had entered into a similar agreement in 1817 though Spain did not outlaw the practice of slavery for those already in the country. While laws were in place all over the world prohibiting the importation of slaves from Africa, there were still people willing to break the law, thus keeping slave traders such as Blanco in business, and a very profitable business at that.

Cinqué and the several hundred other captured Africans were taken on a two-month journey from Sierra Leone to Havana, Cuba, where they were to be displayed for sale in the streets. Several days before landing in Cuba, the slaves were ordered to be released from their chains, bathed, fed, and given fresh clothes. No one in Cuba would want to buy a dirty, sickly slave who had just come from a ship's hold. Once the captain had sighted land, the ship was forced to wait until nightfall to enter the port since they were operating in violation of the 1817 treaty. British antislavery ships were known to patrol the waters. Once night fell, the slaves were unloaded into a number of warehouses where they remained for two weeks. Here they regained their strength, became re-accustomed to sunlight, and were allowed to exercise. When they were marched into town

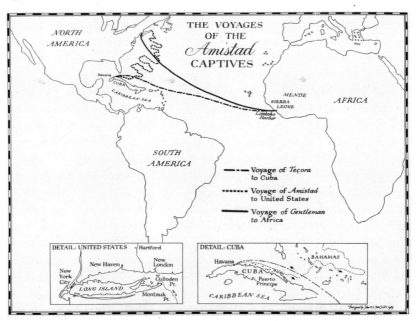

Voyages of the *Amistad* captives. Map by John O. C. McCrillis, © 1989. *The New Haven Museum & Historical Society.*

from the warehouses, it seemed as though the slaves had already been on the island for some time, making them more valuable in the eyes of those who would buy them.

Cinqué, along with 48 others who had survived the journey from Africa, were bought by a slave trader named Jose Ruiz for $450 apiece. Ruiz took possession of the slaves on June 28, 1839. After securing passports for each of them indicating that they were "ladinos," or Spanish subjects who had been living on the island of Cuba for some time, he had them loaded onto the infamous *La Amistad*, which ironically is the Spanish word for "friendship." The ship then set sail for what should have been a two-day journey to Puerto Principe, Cuba.

Already on board was the *Amistad's* captain, Ramon Ferrer and his crew: his two slaves, Antonio and Celestino; and two other sailors, Manuel Pagilla and Yacinto. The ship's cargo included the 49 newly purchased slaves, jewelry, cloth, machetes, and other manufactured goods that Ruiz would later claim was worth $40,000. Slave trader Pedro Montes chose the *Amistad* to transport his cargo as well; Montes had purchased four African children in Cuba.

MUTINY

The makeup of the ship was ripe for mutiny. There were 53 slaves versus seven crew members. Though the slaves were periodically allowed to come up and walk around on deck unchained, they were never allowed to be unchained all at once and they were heavily guarded at all times. Severe storms had thrown the ship off course and it was taking longer to get to their destination than expected. The delay not only put a strain on supplies, causing the captives' food and water to be strictly rationed, but it also gave the captives time to examine their surroundings and make a plan. As their journey progressed, the captives kept their eyes open for tools they could use to break free. Before long they found that boxes of machetes were on board. Burna, one of the African captives, was a blacksmith by trade. On the third night of the journey, July 1, 1839, as all the crew slept, Burna was able to open the shackles with a nail Cinqué had found; one by one, each man freed himself and soon they were ready to fight for their freedom.

The first Africans to be free went straight for the machetes and began handing them out. Cinqué moved ahead first, taking three other captives with him. They went above deck and soon encountered the man steering the ship; his screams quickly awoke the rest of the crew. Captain Ferrer, assuming the strict rationing had caused the slaves to revolt in hunger, cried "Throw some bread at them!" thinking it would alleviate the problem. The battle was quick and violent; Captain Ferrer killed one African and injured two others before he himself was killed. He was struck many times with machetes, but eventually died after several captives strangled him with their bare hands. The captives also killed Ferrer's slave, Celestino; Celestino had been the ship's cook and had tormented the captives, leading them to believe that they would be eaten. The dead bodies were dumped overboard. The two other sailors, making up a good part of the *Amistad's* crew, quickly lowered themselves into a small boat as soon as the scuffle began and rowed away as fast as they could, though the *Amistad* was at least 20 miles from shore at that point. The fate of the sailors is still unknown. Because they had been attacked, accounts of the events would probably have appeared in newspapers had they made it ashore. The most likely scenario is that they drowned at sea.

Ruiz surrendered, but Montes tried to hide after being injured; he was eventually found and tied up with Ruiz. The Africans needed to keep them alive because they did not know how to operate the ship. Their goal was to sail the ship back to Africa, and they needed the Spaniards to do it for them. Ruiz and Montes realized that their only hope for survival was to steer the ship toward the United States where they hoped the captives would be recognized as their property. Sailing to Africa would surely mean death for them. The two made plans to sail east by day, so the Africans believed they were heading toward Africa, then north by

The Mutiny on the *Amistad* by Hale Woodruff, oil on canvas, © 1940. *The New Haven Museum & Historical Society.*

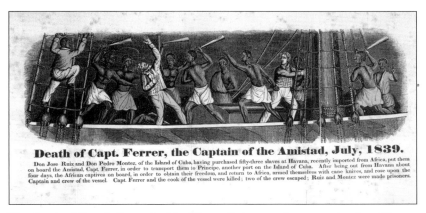

The Death of Captain Ferrer, by John Warner Barber, woodcut engraving from The History of the Amistad Captives, © 1840, printed in New Haven, Connecticut. *The New Haven Museum & Historical Society.*

night, so that they slowly but surely sailed into United States' waters. Their zigzagged journey would take almost two months on a ship prepared for a two-day journey.

Upon taking control of the ship, the Africans broke open the boxes of goods aboard, finding that the exotic cloths made good clothes. Approaching ships were greeted by Africans dressed in silk and brandishing machetes; most backed away quickly, thinking they'd encountered a band of pirates.

DROPPING ANCHOR ON THE "HIGH SEAS"

The supplies on board soon dwindled to nothing, as the Africans were unable to barter with passing ships for necessary items like water. Several Africans, in an act of desperate thirst, died after drinking bottles of medicine that were stored in the ship. They were soon forced to drop anchor and go ashore to attempt to get supplies. On August 25, they anchored the ship off Long Island, New York, which allowed Cinqué, Burna, and Grabeau to row to shore. They successfully purchased two dogs, a bottle of gin, and some sweet potatoes, an efficient use of the Spanish doubloons they had found on the ship. They were able to learn that there were no slaves in this part of the world, and that there were no Spaniards either. The same day that they planned to get on their way, they were apprehended by the *USS Washington*. Lieutenant Thomas Gedney ordered that

La Amistad, Artist unknown, watercolor on paper, © 1840. *The New Haven Museum & Historical Society.*

the schooner be seized and greedily escorted the ship to New London, Connecticut. The reason for not bringing the Africans ashore in Long Island was that slavery was outlawed in New York, but not in Connecticut. Gedney was hoping to claim the slaves as his own cargo and make a nice profit on his fortunate discovery.

Federal district judge Andrew T. Judson, a noted anti-abolitionist (see the chapter on Prudence Crandall), was notified of the ship's arrival by New Haven Marshall Norris Willcox, and Judson immediately left Canterbury for New London. Upon arrival in New London, Judson boarded the ship to conduct an investigation. Ruiz and Montes informed Judson that they had been lawfully transporting Spanish slaves when the slaves had mutinied and killed the captain; they claimed that the slaves, as well as everything on board, was Spanish property and asked that it be delivered to the Spanish consul in Boston. Judson's examination of the legal documents on board seemed to corroborate their story as the slaves all had authentic-looking Spanish passports. According to an article in the *New York Journal of Commerce* on September 2, 1839:

> Several bundles of letters were produced, saved from the *Amistad*, and such as were unsealed read. The contents being simply commercial can be of no interest to the reader. Among the papers

were two licenses from the Governor of Havana, Gen. Ezpelata, one for three slaves, owned by Pedro Montes, one of the men saved, and 40 owned by Senor Don Jose Ruiz, the other that has escaped, allowing the said slaves to be transported to Principe, and commanding said owners to report their arrival to the territorial Judge of the district, in which Principe is situated. A license was found permitting Pedro Montes, a merchant of Principe, to proceed to Matanzas, and transact business, which was endorsed by the Governor of Havana, and the officer of the port. Regular passports were produced, allowing the passengers to proceed to their destination. A license was found permitting Selestino Ferrers, a mulatto, owned by Captain Ramon Ferrers, and employed as a cook, to proceed on the voyage. Other licenses for each sailor were produced and read, all of which were regularly signed, and endorsed by the proper authorities.

The captives, unable to communicate with anyone who spoke English, were defenseless against Montes' and Ruiz's false representations. Judson denied delivery of the goods to the Spanish consul; instead, he decided to hold the slaves for the time being. He wanted them to go before the circuit court convening in Hartford on September 17, 1839; there the issue of property would be decided along with whether the slaves should be tried for murder and mutiny. Under Judson's direction, the slaves were transported to New Haven where they would be held at the jail.

Soon after they were transported to the jail, another suit was filed, this time by Gedney who claimed that he, as salvager of the ship, was the rightful owner of one-third the value of both the slaves and the goods aboard the ship. For saving Ruiz and Montes from total financial loss, Gedney felt he should be generously compensated.

PREPARING FOR TRIAL

While the captives waited in jail, abolitionists in the area got to work. They raised awareness and raised money; they felt this was just the thing they needed to spread their abolition movement across the country. Lewis Tappan and Simeon Jocelyn, both integral players in helping Prudence Crandall start and maintain her school for black girls, as well as Joshua Leavitt, were named as the heads of The *Amistad* Committee. They quickly began putting together a legal defense team for the captives, generating as much publicity as possible. To raise money for their cause, curious people were charged a fee to look at the captives while they waited for trial in jail.

The central issue soon became whether the Africans were free men or slaves. It was obvious they were not Spanish citizens—none of them recognized the names indicated on their Spanish passports, and none of them spoke the Spanish language. The abolitionists quickly spread the message that the captives were free men who should have been guaranteed freedom, liberty, and the right to return to their homes in Africa.

The captives' lawyers included Attorneys Roger Sherman Baldwin of New Haven, and Seth Staples and Theodore Sedgwick of New York. They would later convince John Quincy Adams, former president, and then-Congressman, to join them and speak on their behalf before the Supreme Court. Prosecuting the case was U.S. District Attorney W.S. Holabird, who was under orders from President Martin Van Buren to dismiss the case sooner rather than later, drawing as little attention to it as possible, and remove the case and the captives to Cuba.

The case was actually quite complicated. Not only were the captives facing charges of mutiny and murder, Gedney wanted part of the goods onboard the ship. Captain Henry Green, who encountered the ship even before Gedney, made a claim for the value as well. Ruiz and Montes wanted the slaves they had purchased. Merchants in Cuba also wanted to be reimbursed for the goods that they would never see again. Spain wanted the slaves extradited for trial. Finally, Captain Ferrer's family wanted both the *Amistad* returned as well as his slave, Antonio.

Recent research done by Michael Zeuske of the University of Cologne in Germany may shed new light on Captain Ferrer. According to Zeuske's research of documents in Havana, Ferrer may have owned another slave ship, *La Bella Antonia*, further implicating him in the established slave trading network. Zeuske noted that this new fact could mean that, "Ferrer was a central—and wealthy—cog in a criminal network of slave traders and their merchant partners."

On September 6, 1839, Spanish Ambassador Don Angel Calderon De La Barca wrote a letter to Secretary of State John Forsyth with a list of requests:

> *1st. That the vessel be immediately delivered up to her owner, together with every article found on board at the time of her capture by the Washington, without any payment being exacted on the score of salvage, nor any charges made, than those specified in the treaty of 1795, article 1st.*
>
> *2d. That it be declared that no tribunal in the United States has the right to institute proceedings against, or to impose penalties upon, the subjects of Spain, for crimes committed on board a Spanish vessel, and in the waters of the Spanish territory.*

3d. That the negroes be conveyed to Havana, or be placed at the disposal of the proper authorities in that part of Her Majesty's dominions, in order to their being tried by the Spanish laws which they have violated; and that, in the mean time, they be kept in safe custody, in order to prevent their evasion.

4th. That if, in consequence of the intervention of the authorities of Connecticut, there should be any delay in the desired delivery of the vessel and the slaves, the owners both of the latter and of the former be indemnified for the injury that any accrue to them.

Forsyth responded on September 16, informing Calderon that his letter had been immediately forwarded to President Van Buren and that "no time will be needlessly lost, after his decision upon the demand it prefers shall have reached me, in communicating to you his views upon the subject."

On September 14, 1839, a few days before the trial was to start, the captives were removed from New Haven and transported to Hartford. According to an article published in the *Colored American*, on September 28, 1839, "The public hotels at Hartford were filled [with] strangers, who were principally attracted [by] the novelty of the case."

THE AFRICANS' FIRST COURT APPEARANCE

On the day of the circuit court trial, Justice Smith Thompson did not appear, as he was "occupied with other duties," according to the *Colored American* article. The next day, the first order of business was for the Africans' counsel to submit to the court a writ of habeus corpus for the three female child captives that had no part in the uprising. This would require formal charges to be brought against them or that they would be excused from being eyewitnesses. The strategy was to use the girls to introduce the argument that there was no legal basis for holding them, and then expand that line of reasoning to the rest of the African captives. By showing that the captives were *people* and not *property*, they could prove that their fundamental rights were violated, and thus should be released as free men. The defense gave the court and opposing counsel a day to review and respond to the writ.

"On the 19th the children were brought into court; they appeared to be in great affliction, and wept exceedingly," an article in the *Colored American* stated. It was on this day that the issue of the habeas corpus writ was discussed at length in court.

For three days, representatives from both sides tried to convince the judge to look at the issues from their point of view. According to a September 23 article by Lewis Tappan in the *New York Commercial Advertiser*, "Mr. Baldwin...made a powerful argument against the claims of Senors Ruiz and Montez to take out any process from the District Court, for the arrest and detention of the negroes, as slaves; and against the power of the District Court to issue any such process. The negroes were in the state of Connecticut, and entitled to their freedom. The District Court had no power over them—much less any power to hold them as slaves."

According to the *Colored American*, "Mr. Baldwin's masterly speech was two hours and a half in length. He spoke with great severity of the conduct of Lieutenant Gedney in claiming salvage for the 'meritorious service' of aiding the Spanish gentlemen in reducing persons found free to a state of helpless bondage."

The *Commercial Advertiser* article continued, "Mr. Staples then went on...with exceeding force contending that the Africans, even by the law of Spain, were free, the moment they arrived at Havana—in proof of which he read a decree issued by the King of Spain in 1817, prohibiting the importation of slaves, and another decree, confirming it, issued by the Queen Regent in 1838."

Baldwin and Staples concluded their arguments, and counsel representing the United States was then heard. According to the *Commercial Advertiser*, "Mr. Holabird, the district attorney, followed with a very lame attempt to sustain the libel he had filed on behalf of the United States government."

The article continued: "Mr. Hungerford, of counsel for the Spaniards, followed with a long and highly ingenious speech, in which he contended that the Africans were the property of Senors Montez and Ruiz; that property in slaves was recognized by the laws of Spain and of the United States; that there was no proof that these negroes had been imported into Cuba from Africa, and had not been born slaves in the island; and finally that the Courts and the government of the United States were bound by the treaty with Spain, which provides for the mutual delivery of vessels and property, coming into the ports of either nation by stress of weather or other necessity."

After the attorneys concluded, witnesses were called to attest that the girls spoke no Spanish, only dialects of African, indicating they could not reasonably have been slaves in Cuba. According to court records, John Ferry, a native of Gallina, Africa, was one of those witnesses. Ferry had been brought from Africa to the West Indies as a slave when he was 11 or

12 years old and he still "retained a knowledge of his mother tongue." He testified that he had "seen and conversed with the three girls, and found that they spoke the Gallina language and no other; and from their speech and appearance, he was satisfied that they were native Africans, and very recently from that country."

Thompson was placed in a difficult position; on the one hand, President Van Buren had indicated on several occasions that he wanted the matter to be disposed of quickly and quietly as not to ruffle relations with Spain; on the other hand, it seemed as though these captives were not the murderous slaves Ruiz and Montes claimed them to be. In deciding the habeus issue, Thompson would, in effect, decide other integral issues interwoven through the case. In the court records Thompson was quoted as saying, "However abhorrent it may be to keep these persons in prison, or to view them in the light of property, and however desirous the court might be that they should all be set at liberty, they must not permit their private feelings to govern them in deciding upon the case before them."

THOMPSON'S CIRCUIT COURT DECISION

Three days after the trial began, Judge Thompson decided that the circuit court had no jurisdiction over the criminal charges since the events took place on a Spanish ship, in Spanish waters, and thus were not punishable by U.S. law. He did not decide whether the slaves were property or free men, but instead left the issue open for the district court. He did find, however, that the district court had jurisdiction over the issues of property and salvage because the ship was found on the high seas.

While the Africans had made it through their first trial seemingly unscathed with no prejudicial or permanent rulings made against them, the civil case pending against the captives regarding salvage and property was still ahead. It was scheduled to begin on November 19, 1839, and would be heard by Judson in district court.

WAITING FOR THE NEXT TRIAL

In the time between the two trials, there were several occurrences of note. The two teams of lawyers were instructed by Judson to determine exactly where Gedney had picked up the slaves in order to determine whether this case should even be heard in a Connecticut court. The location would have a profound impact on the outcome of the case.

Also, on October 17, Ruiz and Montes, having left Connecticut, were arrested at their New York City hotel and put in jail for false imprisonment, and assault and battery. The arrests were initiated by Lewis Tappan; he felt that the civil suits against the Spaniards were necessary in order for the captives to tell their story in court. The Africans claimed $3,000 in damages against Ruiz and Montes. According to an October 18, 1839 article in the *New York Commercial Advertiser*, Tappan's objective "probably is more to bring about another discussion of the legal questions involved in this affair, than to make any actual recovery of damages." To obtain the arrest warrants, Cinqué and Fuliwa, another captive, gave depositions in New Haven on October 7, 1839, with the help of interpreter James Covey. Cinqué's deposition, as printed in the *Commercial Advertiser* was as follows:

> Singweh, a colored man, deposeth and saith, that he was born at Mani, a town in Jopoa, in the Mendi country in Africa, and that his king Mahe Katumbo resided at Kwommendi, the capital of Jopoa, in said Mendi country; that he was sold by Birmaja, son of Shaka, king of Gendumah, in the Fai country, to a Spaniard, about six moons ago; that he was brought from Lowboka in a vessel with two masts; that he was landed at a village one day from Havana, where he was kept 5 days, then taken to another village, nearer Havana, where he was kept 5 days more; that he was taken thence by night on foot through Havana to the vessel which brought him from Havana; that he was driven by force and put on board said vessel; that they sailed the next morning; that by night his hands were confined by irons; that on board said vessel he had not half enough to eat and drink, only two potatoes and one plantain twice a day, and half a tea-cup of water morning and evening; that he was beaten on the head by the cook in presence of Pipi, who claims to be his owner, and Montez; and he was told one morning after breakfast that the white men would eat him when they landed.

The bail for Ruiz and Montes was set at $1,000 each. Ruiz staunchly refused to post his bail, hoping it would help his plight and earn him sympathy from the general public. Montes paid his fee as quickly as he could and set sail for Cuba immediately, never to be heard from in the United States again. Tappan's intended effect quickly came to fruition; their arrests were applauded by abolitionists, and anti-abolitionists across the country were enraged. *The Richmond Enquirer* insisted that the abolitionists working the *Amistad* trial should be placed in "lunatic asylums." The *New Orleans Times Picayune* accused the abolitionists of "going to all lengths to screen the black murderers from the consequences of their crimes." Some anti-abolitionists even hinted that the *Amistad* trial could be the start of a civil war.

JUDSON RETURNS: THE DISTRICT COURT PROCEEDINGS

In addition to the numerous claims filed by Spain, Ruiz, Montes, and others, the Africans filed a plea in abatement, attempting to get the case thrown out. A plea in abatement is a response by the defendant that does not dispute the plaintiff's claim but objects to its form or the time or place where it is asserted. The Africans argued that Gedney had illegally taken them out of the jurisdiction of New York, and thus, because the case could not be properly heard in Connecticut, they must be set free.

Several witnesses testified before the court when it reconvened on November 19, including Henry Green. He gave a description of the events the day he encountered the Africans on Long Island. He testified that "[Sinques] came up and asked, does this country make slaves. I answered no. Any Spanish here? No. Sinques then whistled, waved his hand over his head, and they all ran from the sand and shouted. There were four of us present, and 18 or 20 of the blacks—might be more. We were alarmed and ran to our wagons for our guns—they then ran up to us—shook hands—gave us their guns, a knife, a hat, 2 guns and handkerchief." Lieutenant Richard Meade of the *USS Washington* also testified as to the location of the ship when they found her.

At the conclusion of the proceedings on the 19th, the court agreed to adjourn until January. The prosecution was unable to remain in Hartford due to prior engagements, and James Covey, a key witness and interpreter for the defense in New York, was too ill to travel to Hartford at the moment. The next trial date was set for January 7, 1840. One last deposition, however, was taken the next day by Judson; Dr. Richard R. Madden, who had to return to Great Britain before the trial would reconvene in January, was deposed so his testimony could be heard in court.

On November 20, Judson held a private meeting at the City Hotel in Hartford with Dr. Madden. Madden had lived in Havana for over three years as a British official. He attested to the fact that between 20,000 and 25,000 slaves were brought to the island of Cuba from Africa each year. He spoke of the $10 a head "tax" paid to Cuban officials who turned a blind eye to the importation since it became illegal in 1820. He also testified that he had seen these particular captives in Havana and that they had most definitely just come from Africa. Somehow, Madden's testimony was leaked to the press and the Cuban slave trade quickly gained notoriety and disfavor with the public.

In a letter published in *New York Journal of Commerce* on November 19, 1839, John Quincy Adams, who would play a large role in the Africans' defense before the Supreme Court, detailed what happened to them since being captured in their homes and how he felt about their treatment thus far:

> The Africans of the *Amistad* were cast upon our coast in a condition perhaps as calamitous as could befall human beings, not by their own will—not with any intention hostile or predatory on their part, not even by the act of God as in the case of shipwreck, but by their own ignorance of navigation and the deception of one of their oppressors whom they had overpowered, and whose life they had spared to enable them by his knowledge of navigation to reach their native land.
>
> They knew nothing of the Constitution, laws or language of the country upon which they were thus thrown, and accused as pirates and murderers, claimed as slaves of the very men who were their captives, they were deprived even of the faculty of speech in their own defense. This condition was sorely calamitous; it claimed from the humanity of a civilized nation compassion;—it claimed from brotherly love of a Christian land sympathy;—it claimed from a Republic professing reverence for the rights of man justice—and what have we done?

In the months between the trials, both sides worked to strengthen their case. The Van Buren administration also made plans to smooth the whole thing over as election time was growing close and the Spanish government was becoming more annoyed by the day. On January 2, 1840, Secretary of State John Forsyth issued a memorandum to the Secretary of the Navy to take the captives into their control once the trial was complete in order to transport them to Cuba before any appeals could be made. The *USS Grampus* was dispatched to New Haven for that purpose. The order read as follows:

> *The vessel destined to convey the negroes of the Amistad to Cuba, to be ordered to anchor off the port of New Haven, Connecticut, as early as the*

> 10th of January next, and be in readiness to receive said negroes from the marshal of the United States, and proceed with them to the Havana, under instructions to be hereafter transmitted.
>
> Lieutenants Gedney and Meade to be ordered to hold themselves in readiness to proceed in the same vessel, for the purpose of affording their testimony in any proceedings that may be ordered by the authorities of Cuba in the matter.
>
> These orders should be given with special instructions that they are not to be communicated to any one.

January 7, 1840 arrived and the court reconvened in a courtroom packed to the limits with interested onlookers. The Africans again argued that the court had no jurisdiction because the captives were people and not property.

One of the first witnesses to testify was James Covey, the African who had been living in New Haven and served as an interpreter for the captives. Covey gave his opinion that it was virtually impossible that the Africans had lived in Cuba since none of them spoke any Spanish. His choppy testimony indicated that he was able to speak with them, he knew where they were from because they spoke of familiar landmarks; he also confirmed their story of being taken from their village to Lomboko and sold as slaves in Havana because the same thing had happened to him:

> *All these Africans were from Africa. Never saw them until now. I could talk with them. They appeared glad because they could speak the same language. I could understand all but [two or three]. They say they from Lumboko [three moons]. They all have Mendie names, and their names all mean something. Carbe means bone. Kimbo means cricket. They speak of rivers which I know--said they sailed from Lumboko. 2 or 3 speak different language from the others, the Timone (Tim-ma-ni) Language. Rivers spoken of, these run through the Vi Country. I learned to speak English at Siere Leone. Was put on board a Man of War one year and 1/2. They all agree as to where they sailed from. I have no doubt they are Africans. I have been in this country 6 months; came in a British Man of War, have lived in this town (New Haven) 4 months with Mr. Bishop.*

Covey's testimony provided an affirmation that the Africans' story of capture and captivity was not only plausible, but very likely.

Yale Professor Josiah Gibbs came to testify on January 8 regarding the term "ladinos" and why it was so important to the case. Before he could go into detail, however, counsel for Gedney objected. In response to the objection, to the surprise of the court, Judson declared that he was "fully convinced that the men were recently from Africa, and it was idle to deny it." This declaration was a major victory for the abolitionists; in one swift move, Judson had declared that the captives were not slaves, and thus not property. This had the effect of dissolving the claims of Ruiz and Montes and denied the United States from returning the captives to the Spanish government as property.

Cinqué was the next to testify and it seemed his testimony was the most anticipated by the crowd. Cinqué told of his journey, beginning in Mende where he was initially captured, and ending in Connecticut where he remained a prisoner:

> In vessel that brought us to Havana we were chained—hand and feet together [Here Cinqué sat down on floor and held his hands together and showed how they were manacled.] On board the Schooner *Amistad*...the cook told us they carry us to some place and kill and eat us. We were beaten.

The Trial of the Amistad Captives by Hale Woodruff, oil on canvas, © 1940. *The New Haven Museum & Historical Society*.

Fuliwa, the captive whose deposition had been used to arrest Ruiz and Montes, also testified on January 8, confirming Cinqué's story. He detailed the harsh treatment the captives had received on the *Amistad*:

> We all sailed from Lomboko in same vessel, all but the three little girls Teme, Kane Mahgru, and Carli. They natives of same country. Three moons to Havana, 10 nights at Havana; all kept in [house] together. one potato and 2 plantains to eat in Schooner - I was whipped, and Kimbo for stealing water. Sailors whipped...Cook told us they'd kill and eat us...The Captain killed one black man, before he was killed. Sinqua killed cook because cook said he was going to kill them and eat them. Killed Captain after he killed African.

After the captives testified, the prosecution brought Antonio, Captain Ferrer's slave, to testify before the court. The prosecution hoped that his testimony would outweigh that of the captives. Antonio identified Cinqué as one of the leaders of the mutiny and claimed that he saw Cinqué kill the captain with a machete. Antonio also testified that the *Amistad* regularly made such trips carrying slaves, and that Ruiz had used the *Amistad* before to transport slaves he had bought in Havana.

The trial was brought to a close on Friday, January 10. Judson adjourned the court and indicated he would have a decision by Monday.

JUDSON'S SURPRISING OPINION

On Monday, January 13, 1840, Judson opened the session by denying the defense's plea in abatement and confirmed that the court had jurisdiction over the matter. He found that because the seizure did not occur in a harbor, port, bay, or river, and based on the dictionary definition of "open seas" and prior case law regarding the definition, where Gedney had located the *Amistad* was on the high seas and not solely within the jurisdiction New York. "If this schooner had been within a known Port—a harbour—or bay, like Sag Harbour—Gardner Bay or Black Rock Harbour the aspect of this case would have been materially changed," Judson stated. "But this seizure was in fact made, beyond low water mark—where the tide ebbs and flows—in 4 fathom water, many miles from any known Port or harbour. The place of seizure was therefore in the open ocean where the dominion of the winds and the waves prevail without check or control."

Judson also rejected Green's claims for salvage because they had not rendered a "meritorious service" necessary for a claim of salvage. He did, however, find that Gedney, having rescued the goods "in a perilous condition" was entitled to one-third their value after the ship and its contents were sold; the slaves, however, were not part of the cargo as they were people and not property. Judson reiterated the facts that the Africans had been brought into Cuba in violation of anti-slave trade laws and treaty obligations, were not Spanish citizens, and mutinied only to regain their freedom.

Judson stated that "It is decreed, that the said Africans now in the Custody of said Marshall and libelled and claimed as aforesaid (excepting Antonio Ferrer) be delivered to the President of the United States by the Marshal of the District of Connecticut to be by him transported to Africa in pursuance of the Law of Congress passed March 3rd 1819 entitled 'An act in addition to the acts prohibiting the Slave trade.'" Antonio Ferrer, having been born in Cuba, was to be returned to his owners there.

Judson's decision came as a great surprise to many people because he was well known for having played an integral part in shutting down Prudence Crandall's school for young black girls. As a known anti-abolitionist, it was a true testament to the impartiality of the judicial system that Judson was able to put aside his personal feelings and make an unbiased ruling.

Having learned of the court's decision, the captain of the *Grampus* maneuvered his ship out of the port of New Haven. The *Hartford Courant* published the following on February 10, 1840:

> We are informed by a gentleman from New Haven that a short time previous to the trial of the Africans of the *Amistad*, before the U.S. District Court at New Haven, Judge Judson presiding, Martin Van Buren addressed a letter to the Judge recommending and urging him to order the Africans to be taken back to Havana in a government vessel, to be sold there as slaves—and that about the same time the U.S. schooner *Grampus* was ordered to New Haven for the purpose of receiving them. The schooner, we learned from several sources, arrived at New Haven about the time of the trial under 'sealed orders' and, after learning the decision of the court again, 'made off.' The letter of the President, recommending that these poor unfortunate Africans be sent into perpetual bondage, is said to contain statements disgraceful to the high station of its author, and which, were they published, would excite the indignation of every Republican freeman in the land. What will the friends of liberty say to this? Surely Martin Van Buren is playing the part of a tyrant with a high hand—else why this tampering with our courts of justice, this Executive usurpation, and this heartless violation of the inalienable rights of man? Of the truth of the above there is no doubt, and we leave the unprincipled author of such a proceeding in the hands of a just and high-minded People.

The administration's actions were not well received by the people who had come to feel sorry for the African captives.

The Act that Judson invoked to place the slaves in the care of the president stated in relevant part that it was "illegal to import any black individual from a foreign country with intent to hold him as a slave." It seems Judson's application of the law was a stretch as Ruiz and Montes never intended to bring the captives to the United States as slaves, but ended up in this country due to unforeseen circumstances.

The abolitionists were wary of the plan to have the slaves put in the care of the president. They did not trust that Van Buren would, in fact, have the slaves returned to Africa, and even if they were transported there, there was still a risk they would be kidnapped again. They were also not pleased with the fact that Judson declined to clearly state that the Africans were people who had the right to enjoy the same rights as whites. The decision, however, was a step in the right direction. The consensus throughout the defense team was that an appeal would not be pursued; the Africans had been through enough, and their main goal was to get home. They would however, remain in the fight if the prosecution filed an appeal, which they did.

IMMEDIATE APPEAL

The appeal was immediately filed by the United States in the circuit court. An appeal was also filed by Jose Antonio Tellincas and the House of Aspa & Laca, the Spanish owners of the *Amistad*, who filed a salvage claim for all material cargo and objecting to the fact that Gedney was granted a third of their goods.

The circuit court heard the case in April 1840. The Africans' first step was to move to dismiss the appeal. Their motion was denied by Justice Thompson, the same judge who had decided that the circuit court did not have jurisdiction over the claims of murder, piracy, and mutiny in September 1839.

In order to have the case continue up the judicial ladder, Thompson issued a pro forma decree upholding Judson's decision. The decree essentially agreed with all of Judson's findings without having to go through another full trial. The appeal filed by the owners of the *Amistad* was reserved for decision by the U.S. Supreme Court. Immediately after hearing news of the pro forma decree, the United States issued another appeal, this time to the Supreme Court, asking the Court to review the decision made by Judson. The case was set to be heard by the Court in their January 1841 session.

PREPARING FOR THE SUPREME COURT

Before the Supreme Court convened to hear the case, District Attorney Holabird filed a motion in circuit court on September 17, 1840, to have the ship and its contents sold:

The Subscriber would respectfully represent that the Schooner Amistad, and the goods which were found on board of her when she was brought within the jurisdiction of this Court and particularly described in the libel of Thomas R. Gedney & others, and in the apprisal of the same, and now in the custody of the Marshall of this District, the United States being claimants of the same and set forth in their Libel, are in a perishable and ruinous condition: said Schooner needing extensive and immediate repairs, to keep her afloat, and said goods constant attention, to preserve them from a total loss, and unless said Schooner and said goods are disposed of, they will soon be of no avail to any one—Therefore the Subscriber would pray your Honor to order a sale of said Schooner and said goods.

The court agreed and ordered the ship and its contents to be sold at public auction to the highest bidder in New London on October 15, 1840. Advertisements for the auction were ordered to be placed in the *New York Journal of Commerce* and the *New London Gazette & Advertiser*. The ship sold for $245, even though she had been valued at $600. According to an item in the *Intelligencer* on October 27, 1840 announcing the sale of the ship and its goods, the remaining goods included:

[l]ow-priced British prints and ginghams, a few pieces linen drills, bed ticking, cotton handkerchiefs, muslins, and threads, etc. Many of the cases had been broken open by the negroes, and several hundred yards of the linen goods were cut up into pieces of from one to ten yards. There were also one or two cases partly filled with toys, and one or more with saddles and saddler's trimmings—a quantity of sole leather and calf skins, and about two hundred boxes of vermicelli; of the latter article many of the boxes had been broken open and their contents scattered about, and among the others sad havoc had been made by mice. One hundred and forty boxes of that which was in the best condition sold for four and a quarter cents the pound. About twenty boxes of castile soap sold at between nine and ten cents the pound. The sole leather, of which there were about sixty sides, sold at from sixteen to twenty and a half cents per pound; and of the remaining articles of cargo, consisting of one or two cases of looking glasses, a small invoice of glass and crockery ware, etc., we are told that they sold for about their true value under the circumstances. A lot of castings, designed for cane mills, sold at $3 and 1/2 per cwt.

Together, the goods sold for $6,196.14. The total proceeds, in the amount of $6,441.14, were kept by the clerk of court, Charles Ingersoll, until the Supreme Court made a decision as to the salvage claims.

The African captives were certainly not being forgotten between trials. Not only did the auction draw attention to the cause, but a display at Peale's Museum and Portrait Gallery in New York also tended to publicize the Africans and their plight. As advertised in the *New York Commercial Advertiser* on June 16, 1840:

> *The thrilling and unprecedented events connected with the capture of the Amistad, which have excited so much public attention, not only in this country, but throughout the civilized countries of Europe, furnishes a subject of uncommon interest. The exhibition gives the accurate likeness of 29 of the Africans, in wax figures. These are not fancy pieces, but executed from casts, or moulds, taken from the faces of the Africans, by S. Moulthrop, of New Haven—by means of this process, a perfect exhibition of the form of each face, embracing every wrinkle, is given. In the exhibition is seen a striking representation of the Death of Capt. Ramon Ferrer, the Spanish Captain of the Amistad.*

For 25 cents, an adult could not only see the wax figures of the *Amistad* captives, but also hear a piano recital by Mr. S. W. Bassford, and fancy glass working during the day and evening by Mr. Owens; for 12½ cents they could bring their children along too.

Before the Supreme Court heard the arguments, counsel for both sides went through some changes. Tappan, working tirelessly for the Africans' cause, approached several prominent lawyers to join their team and present oral arguments before the Supreme Court. Their chances for winning in the Supreme Court seemed to be rather slim—five justices were southerners and not likely to be open to the idea of affording Africans the same rights as whites. Tappan first approached Daniel Webster, an experienced orator before the Supreme Court, but Webster declined the offer, noting he did not wish to "continue or extend his practice in that Court." Webster told Tappan that the legal team already in place was a fine one, and that his help would not be required. Webster's interest in becoming president may also have played a key role in his decision; taking a firm stance in support of the abolitionists would not gain him much southern support. Tappan, unsatisfied with Webster's response, turned to another well-known lawyer, Rufus Choate of Boston. Choate also declined due to his ailing health, prior commitments, and late notice. He too did not want to get involved with the abolitionists cause; he felt the issue of slavery was dangerously close to splitting the country in two. Tappan's third request was to former president and current senator, seventy-three-year-old John Quincy Adams, a known abolitionist who was openly passionate about equality and freedom. Though he had not appeared before the Supreme Court in over three decades, Adams reluctantly agreed to act as co-counsel and deliver closing arguments.

Also added to the attorney roster was U.S. Attorney General Henry D. Gilpin, who was to present arguments on behalf of the United States. The Van Buren administration had played a large role in the progression of the *Amistad* case thus far, but Van Buren lost to William Harrison in the election of 1840. Harrison would not be inaugurated, however, until March 3, 1841, and so Van Buren was able to maintain some influence on the remaining leg of the *Amistad* trial.

THE AFRICANS APPEAR BEFORE THE U.S. SUPREME COURT

On February 22, 1841, the justices of the Supreme Court of the United States began hearing oral arguments. When a case goes before the Supreme Court, no witnesses are called to testify, and no evidence is formally introduced. Oral arguments are made by both sides, interspersed with questions from the justices. After closing arguments, the Court deliberates, usually for a period of months, and then releases the decision. Attorney Gilpin was the first to be heard. The main thrust of his argument was that the Africans had to be returned to Cuba. He argued that they were legally being transported as slaves from Cuba and that the United States had no authority to question the legal sufficiency of the passports and other documents aboard the ship. He relied on treaties requiring the United States to return vessels found or rescued by the United States, along with their cargo, to their home ports.

Gilpin, after speaking for two hours, was followed by Roger Sherman Baldwin who had continued as part of the Africans' legal team. Baldwin began with a recreation of the events, starting with Cinqué being captured in Africa. Baldwin then went on to attack all of Gilpin's major points. He insisted that the United States did, in fact, have a right to question the legality of the documents produced by Ruiz and Montes regarding the *Amistad* and its cargo. He then addressed the treaties cited by Gilpin and reminded the court that before anything was to be returned, sufficient proof of ownership had to first be established. No such proof was offered by Ruiz or Montes that the captives had in fact already been slaves in Cuba. Baldwin also attacked the fact that the executive and the United States had no real interest in the matter since they had no property at stake, and could not enslave free men without violating the Constitution. Since the Africans landed in New York where slavery is illegal, and they were never slaves to begin with, the Africans were free upon landing in New York. If the United States was to send them back to Cuba as slaves, they would, in effect, be forcing the institution of slavery upon free men, something the government was prohibited from doing.

Baldwin stated:

> The recently imported Africans of the *Amistad*, if they were ever slaves, which is denied, were in the actual condition of freedom when they came within the jurisdictional limits of the State of New York. They came there without any wrongful act on the part of any officer or citizen of the United States. They were in a State where, not only no law existed to make them slaves, but where, by an express statute, all persons, except fugitives, etc., from a sister State, are declared to be free. They were under the protection of the laws of a State which, in this language of the Supreme Court in the case of *Miln vs. the City of New York*, 11 Peters, 139, 'has the same undeniable and unlimited jurisdiction over all persons and things within its territorial limits, as any foreign nation, when that jurisdiction is not surrendered or restrained by the Constitution of the United States.'

Baldwin occupied the Court for the remainder of the opening day, and continued when the Court reconvened the next morning. On February 24, 1841, John Adams took the floor and delivered an impassioned oration on behalf of the Africans. Adams' appearance before the Court had been delayed by a few days due to the death of a close friend. He began:

> In rising to address this Court as one of its attorneys and counselors, regularly admitted at a great distance of time, I feel that an apology might well be expected where I shall perhaps be more likely to exhibit at once the infirmities of age and the inexperience of youth, than to render those services to the individuals whose lives and liberties are at the disposal of this Court which I would most earnestly desire to render. But as I am unwilling to employ one moment of the time of the Court in anything that regards my own personal situation, I shall reserve what few observations I may think necessary to offer as an apology till the close of my argument on the merits of the question.
>
> I therefore proceed immediately to say that, in a consideration of this case, I derive, in the distress I feel both for myself and my clients, consolation from two sources—first, that the rights of my clients to their lives and liberties have already been defended by my learned friend and colleague in so able and complete a

manner as leaves me scarcely anything to say, and I feel that such full justice has been done to their interests, that any fault or imperfection of mine will merely be attributed to its true cause; and secondly, I derive consolation from the thought that this Court is a Court of JUSTICE. And in saying so very trivial a thing, I should not on any other occasion, perhaps, be warranted in asking the Court to consider what justice is.

For the next four hours, Adams reinforced and supplemented Baldwin's arguments. For example, he argued that the treaty cited by Gilpin in his argument was meant to apply to ships in distress, but only in wartime, a factor that was certainly missing in the case of the *Amistad*. Adams then went into detail regarding the president and his administration's multiple acts of inappropriate interference with the case. He discussed incriminating letters, originating from the office of the president, which ordered the *Grampus* to stand by to return the captives to Cuba before the Africans would be able to file an appeal. He spoke about Secretary of State John Forsyth's communications regarding the *Amistad* trial as well. According to Adams, Forsyth had told Holabird that there was no basis for any court in America to have jurisdiction over the case since the offenses occurred on a ship belonging to another nation; Adams then claimed that Forsyth instructed Holabird to hunt for treaty provisions requiring the United States to return the ship to the country where she came from, preferably "before our court sits."

Adams also spoke about the fact that there was evidence that the captives' passports had been altered before being given to Congress for examination. The original passports had indicated that the Africans were "ladinos," meaning they had been slaves in Cuba for some time; the documents given to Congress had the words "sound negroes" in the place of "ladinos," materially changing the meaning of the documents. Adams said to the Court:

> The whole of my argument to show that the appeal should be dismissed, is founded on an averment that the proceedings on the part of the United States are all wrongful from the beginning. The first act, of seizing the vessel, and these men, by an officer of the navy, was a wrong. The forcible arrest of these men, or a part of them, on the soil of New York, was a wrong. After the vessel was brought into the jurisdiction of the District Court of Connecticut, the men were first seized and imprisoned under a criminal process for murder and piracy on the high seas. Then

they were libeled by Lieut. Gedney, as property, and salvage claimed on them, and under that process were taken into the custody of the marshal as property. Then they were claimed by Ruiz and Montes and again taken into custody by the court.

And that was just the first day. Adams was not entirely pleased with his performance, but was feeling more confident the next morning. At 11:00 a.m., the justices entered the courtroom to inform the parties that Justice Barbour had died and the proceedings would be delayed until the following Monday, March 1.

On March 1, Adams spent another three-and-a-half hours reinforcing the wrongs done by the Van Buren Administration and repeatedly called for the Court to deliver justice to the African captives. The Washington correspondent for the *Colored American* gave this description of Adams' argument:

> *Of course you will not expect me to give you a sketch of a seven hours' speech, in a letter of this nature. Suffice it to say, that he took the ground that no law was applicable to the case of his clients, save that contained in our Declaration of Independence, two copies of which always hung in that room; that they had gained their Independence, and we had no right to interfere with them, nor the Spanish Government the right to demand them of us; that those who caused the arrest of Montez and Ruiz, though by some denominated fanatics, were, in his opinion, friends of human kind, friends of human liberty, unwilling to see forty of their fellow beings deprived of their liberty, and burnt at the stake, without an effort to save them; that the ghosts of the sixteen victims of Montea, sent by his ill treatment to premature graves, would pass by his couch in his dying hour, at which fearful sight he would exclaim, 'O! how will they press upon my soul tomorrow!' that the conduct of our Government, during the whole progress of this Amistad business, had been partial, unjust, despotic, and outrages; that he felt ashamed to have it said, that the country to which he belonged was thus disgraced by such management on the part of its Executive and his Attorney General; and that the time was, when the United States Government sympathized with the victims of the slave traders, and not with those traders themselves.*

When Adams was finished, Gilpin was allowed to make his closing arguments. For three hours he addressed the arguments of Baldwin and Adams, reinforcing his belief that the United States had every right to give Spain back her property; he also defended the Van Buren administration's interference in the case, as it was the duty of the executive to execute treaties.

The United States. App.ts } On appeal from the Circuit
42.   vs   } Court of the United States for
The Libellants & Claimants of the } the District of Connecticut.
Schooner Amistad, her tackle   } This Cause came on to be
apparel and furniture together } heard on the transcript of the re-
with her Cargo, and the Africans } cord from the Circuit Court of
mentioned and described in the } the United States for the Dis-
several Libels and Claims.   } trict of Connecticut and was ar-
                                  gued by Counsel. On considera-
tion whereof, It is the opinion of this Court that there is error in that
part of the decree of the Circuit Court affirming the decree of
the District Court which ordered the said Negroes to be delivered
to the President of the United States to be transported to Africa in
pursuance of the Act of Congress of the 3d of March 1819; and that
as to that part it ought to be reversed; and in all other respects
that the said decree of the Circuit Court ought to be affirmed. It is
therefore ordered adjudged and decreed by this Court that the decree
of the said Circuit Court be and the same is hereby affirmed except
as to the part aforesaid, and as to that part, that it be reversed;
and that the cause be remanded to the Circuit Court with directions to enter in lieu of that part a decree that the said Negroes be and are hereby declared to be free and that they
be dismissed from the custody of the Court and be discharged
from the suit and go thereof quit without day.
                                          March 9. 1841.

Opinion of the Supreme Court in *United States v. The Amistad*, March 9, 1841.
National Archives and Records Administration, Records of the Supreme Court of the United States.

THE FINAL VERDICT

The Court then deliberated for eight days. On March 9, the decision of the almost unanimous Court was read by Justice Story; only Justice Baldwin dissented with the outcome, but he chose not to write an opinion. The Court had come to the conclusion that the district court correctly dealt with the salvage and property claims of Gedney, finding his seizure was "highly meritorious" and the one-third rate was of "sound discretion" by the district court. The Court stated that the main issue that they were forced to decide was whether the Africans were the property of Ruiz and Montez. The Court found that the United States failed to prove they were, in fact, property, and thus, the Africans were free.

"This court having fully heard the parties appearing, with their proofs, do find, that the respondents, severally answering as aforesaid, are each of them natives of Africa, and were born free, and ever since have been, and still of right are free, and not slaves..." Justice Story said in his opinion. Because they were "natives of Africa...kidnapped....and unlawfully transported to Cuba, in violation of the laws and treaties of Spain..." Ruiz and Montes did not have any claim to them as property. As free individuals, they were not subject to any treaties of Spain. The Court found but one error in the District Court's decision, and that was in Judson's application of the congressional order placing the slaves under the care of the executive. Because the order applied only to Africans brought into the United States for the purpose of being held as slaves, and the Africans on the *Amistad* were free at the time they reached the United States, the order did not apply to them.

> It is admitted and proved, in this case, that these negroes are natives of Africa, and recently imported into Cuba. Their domicile of origin is, consequently, the place of their birth, in Africa. And the presumption of law is, always, that the domicile of origin is retained, until the change is proved.
>
> Upon the whole, our opinion is, that the decree of the circuit court, affirming that of the district court, ought to be affirmed, except so far as it directs the negroes to be delivered to the president, to be transported to Africa, in pursuance of the act of the 3d of March 1819; and as to this, it ought to be reversed: and that the said negroes be declared to be free, and be dismissed from the custody of the court, and go without delay.

The Court's decision gave the Africans full and unequivocal freedom; the executive would no longer have the power to send them back to Africa. Now they would be free to go of their own accord.

JOURNEY HOME

It had been almost two years since the Africans had been taken from their homes and placed into captivity. Their arduous journey in the fight for their freedom was finally over. The only thing left was to get them back home—but their lives would never be the same. Once they were released from prison, the Africans were taken to the home of an abolitionist in Farmington, Connecticut. There they spent their time making arts and crafts to sell in order to raise money for their voyage. Cinqué also did his part in order to raise money; he published the following letter in the *African Repository & Colonial Journal* on October 5, 1841:

> *FARMINGTON, CONN., OCT. 5, 1841.*
>
> *You have done a great deal for us. Now we want to go home, very much, very soon. As soon as you can send us. We want to land at no other place but Sierra Leone. When we get to Sierra Leone we get home we find a good place for our teachers, and then we tell our parents, come and see them. We want plenty of calicoes, not cut, and plenty of cloth for men's clothes—for pantaloons, coats and vests—not cut. For we think we wear 'Merica dress as long as we live, and we want our friends who come to live with us to wear 'Merica dress too. And we want plenty to give our friends and have them; give us elephant teeth, palm oil, camwood, and other things to send you to 'Merica. We will take good care of our teachers, we will not leave them. When we are in Mendi we never hear such a thing as men taken away and carried to Cuba, and then return home again. The first thing we tell them will be that the great God bring us back. We tell them all about 'Merica. We tell them about God and how Jesus Christ, his only beloved Son, came down to die for us, and we tell them to believe, for this your son was lost before now, and is found, for not any thing make him found but God. Now we want you to give your children to us—give to the teachers to try teach them. We will try to teach them to pray, and not to pray to anything but God.*
>
> *Some wicked people here laugh at Mr. TAPPAN and all our committee for spending so much for Mendi people. They say we are like dogs without any home. But if you will send us home you will see whether we be dogs or not. We want to see no more snow. We no say this place no good, but we*

afraid of cold. Cold catch us all the time. We have a great many friends here and we love them just as we love our brethren.

We want to go very soon, and go to no place but Sierra Leone.
Your friend,
CINQUÉ.

The Africans also went on a publicity tour of sorts, speaking and appearing at various churches and abolitionist groups around the Northeast to raise money. The *Amistad* Committee's plan was to keep the Africans here for several years in order to spread the word about the horrors of slavery, promote the abolitionist movement, and raise money for the cause. After six months of parading around, it was obvious the Africans wanted to return to their homes. It wasn't until one of the Africans, a man named Foni, committed suicide that the committee seriously started making preparations for their journey. As a Mende, Foni believed that his soul would live on Mendi country after his death, and he felt the only way he would ever see his home again was to kill himself.

The Return to Africa of the Amistad Captives by Hale Woodruff, oil on canvas, © 1940. *The New Haven Museum & Historical Society.*

On November 25, 1841, the remaining Africans boarded the *Gentleman*, and set sail for Sierra Leone. Along with them went five missionaries who intended to establish a Christian settlement there. Almost two months later, on January 15, 1842, the ship landed unscathed in Freeport, Sierra Leone, with 35 of the original 53 Africans.

The plan was for the Africans to stay with the missionaries and get the mission up and running. Upon landing in Africa though, many of the former captives deserted, going off to look for what remained of their families and friends. Most found that everything they had cherished was gone; their families had either moved on, died, or had been sold into slavery themselves. For some time, Cinqué stayed on to help the missionaries, but one night he left without telling anyone. He found that his own family had disappeared; he never reunited with them again. Cinqué was the last of the *Amistad* captives to have any contact with the missionaries. He returned to the mission in 1879 before he died, and was buried among the original missionaries.

Portrait of Cinque by Nathaniel Jocelyn, oil on canvas, © 1840. *The New Haven Museum & Historical Society.*

SPAIN'S CONTINUING BATTLE

Once the captives had been returned to Africa, Spain was forced to face reality and understand she would not be getting the captives back. As compensation for the loss, Spain requested money for the captives and the ship from the U.S. Congress. Some sympathetic southern Congressmen joined together and introduced a bill that would pay Spain $50,000 for the

The *Freedom Schooner Amistad*, a re-creation of the original ship, *La Amistad*, as it left Long Wharf Pier in New Haven to begin its 18-month Atlantic Freedom Tour retracing the infamous slave industry triangle on June 21, 2007. © *Regina Forker*.

The *Freedom Schooner Amistad* at its home port in Mystic Seaport. © *Regina Forker*.

losses. John Quincy Adams was virulently opposed to the bill, and led the opposition to its passage; he indicated that to pass such a bill would be an insult to the Supreme Court of the United States. The bill did not pass the first time around. With each new president came a similar request to compensate Spain, but every time it was denied. When Abraham Lincoln took office, the last such request was made and denied. Spain was never compensated for the ship or the captives.

Though their mission in Sierra Leone did not work out quite as planned, the American Missionary Association continued its work educating blacks. Through the years, the organization was able to raise enough money and awareness to start and run numerous universities geared toward the education of blacks, most of them in the South. Their schools include Atlanta University, founded in 1865; Fisk University, founded in 1866; Talladega College, founded in 1867; and Howard University, founded in 1867.

The Africans taken captive on the Amistad may not have started the Civil War, nor did they set all Africans free, but they did have an impact on how the country viewed the practice of slavery, as well as Africans in general. While their lives were forever changed, not necessarily for the better, their impact on slavery and on the United States in general was far-reaching and monumental.

See Appendix C for the U.S. Supreme Court decision in the *Amistad* case.

4

Privacy in the Bedroom
Griswold v. Connecticut

The case of *Griswold v. Connecticut* was not one that materialized quickly out of thin air; it was preceded by a multitude of cases involving the issues of privacy and birth control, and the battle had been raging long before Estelle Griswold came into the picture. For over 100 years on countless occasions, legal activists had been trying to overturn the law Estelle Griswold violated in 1961. One could say that the case could trace its beginnings back to 1873 when Anthony Comstock became obsessed with indulgence and sin, and decided to turn that obsession into a plea to the U.S. Congress. His actions would have a serious effect on the citizens of this country, especially those in Connecticut, who would be unable to undo his actions for an entire century. In addition to the Connecticut and federal Comstock Acts, multiple cases were heard before *Griswold* that would lay a foundation for what was to come.

THE FEDERAL COMSTOCK ACT

Anthony Comstock, who was born in rural New Canaan, Connecticut, in 1844, was a man who became fascinated with the sin he saw all around him. As a young man living in New York City, he felt he was constantly surrounded by sex, obscenity, gambling, prostitution, alcohol, and excessiveness in general. Raised as a devout Catholic, he decided to do something about what he regarded as the filth that he observed, and in 1873 began lobbying Congress to put a stop to the obscenity. He presented Congress with the Comstock Act, the goal of which was to protect American morality.

After working as a clerk in a store, Comstock served as a Union infantry soldier in the Civil War from 1863 to 1865. Once completing his service, he returned to New York City and found employment as a sales clerk. He made a connection with the Young Men's Christian Association and devoted much of his time working for the organization. By 1873, he had created the New York Society for the Suppression of Vice and was well on his way to influencing the containment of obscenity in America.

Comstock found an ally in Clinton Merriam, a New York Republican who was a member of the House of Representatives during the 42nd Congress in the early 1870s. Merriam introduced Comstock's legislation on March 1, 1873, supporting it wholeheartedly. "The purposes of this bill are so clearly in the public interests of morality and humanity that I trust it will receive the unanimous voice of the Congress," Merriam stated in his address to the House. He read aloud a letter from Comstock, outlining the strides that Comstock had made during the first year in which he began hunting down obscene objects like birth control, obscene literature, and their creators.

In the letter, Comstock boasted that he had already collected, "[o]bscene photographs, stereoscopic and other pictures, more than 182,000; obscene books and pamphlets, more than 5 tons...sheets of impure songs, catalogues, and handbills, etc., more than 21,000...obscene and immoral rubber articles, over 30,000..." Comstock urged Congress to pass the law so that he might prevent even more such "rubber goods," also known as condoms, from being sent through the mail, which he was powerless to confiscate. Even Comstock did not have the power to tamper with the U.S. mail.

Just two days after Merriam introduced the legislation, on March 3, 1873, "An Act for the Suppression of Trade in, and Circulation of, Obscene Literature and Articles of immoral Use," (sic) was passed by the House and Senate and became federal law.

The Act read:

> *[b]e it enacted by the Senate and House of Representatives of the United States of America in Congress assembled, That whoever, within the District of Columbia or any of the Territories of the United States, or other place within the exclusive jurisdiction of the United States, shall sell, or lend, or give away, or in any manner exhibit, or shall offer to sell, or shall otherwise publish in any manner, or shall have in his possession, for any such purpose*

or purposes, any obscene book, pamphlet, paper, writing, advertisement, circular, print, picture, drawing or other representation, figure, or image on or of paper or other material, or any cast, instrument, or other article of immoral nature, or any drug or medicine, or any article whatever, for the prevention of contraception, or for causing unlawful abortion, or shall advertise the same for sale, or shall write or print, or cause to be written or printed, any card, circular, book, pamphlet, advertisement or notice of any kind, stating when, where, how, or of whom, or by what means, any of the articles in the section hereinbefore mentioned, can be purchased or obtained, or shall manufacture, draw, or print, or in any wise make any of such articles, shall be deemed guilty of a misdemeanor, and, on conviction thereof in any court of the United States…he shall be imprisoned at hard labor in the penitentiary for not less than six months nor more than five years for each offense, or fined not less than one hundred dollars nor more than two thousand dollars, with costs of court.

This law was absolutely clear. It determined as "obscene" all printed information regarding birth control, as well as all tangible objects facilitating birth control. It also forbade the use of the mail to send or transport such materials. The penalty for using the mail to send such things was hard labor in the penitentiary for not more than 10 years and a fine of not more than $5,000, or both, at the discretion of the judge. Anyone who was found to knowingly aid or abet someone involved in violation of using the mail for such a purpose would also be found guilty of a misdemeanor and face the same punishment.

The law quickly came to be known as "The Comstock Law," due to the name of its initiator; all such acts of obscenity and the like soon came to be known as "Comstockery," a term coined by George Bernard Shaw. The dictionary defines "Comstockery" as "overzealous moral censorship of the fine arts and literature, often mistaking outspokenly honest works for salacious ones"—a perfect description of Comstock and his mission.

Even before Congress passed the law, Comstock had founded the New York Society for the Suppression of Vice, with the support of the Young Men's Christian Association (YMCA). Serving as director of the society, Comstock was able to carry out his ministry of protecting morality. Once the federal law was passed, Comstock was able to increase his ability to stop immorality; he was appointed as a U.S. Post Office censor, whose sole purpose was to go through the mail, searching for obscene materials. Comstock made sure that any sex education materials including medical texts on abortion and conception and any artwork that featured nudity was banned from the mail. In addition to his duty of inspecting the mail, Comstock was given the added responsibility of arresting those in violation of the newly enacted law. His police powers as a censor included the right to carry a weapon, and from March to December 1873, Comstock made over 50 arrests, 20 of which resulted in conviction. By 1914, his career in destroying vice was winding down and he noted in his annual report that over the years he had brought 3,697 people to trial, with 2,740 pleading guilty or being convicted.

THE CONNECTICUT ANTI-OBSCENITY LAW

Soon after the passage of the federal Comstock Act, the states began to follow suit, passing their own versions of the Act with the goal of preventing immorality and obscenity among their residents. Over the next few years, 24 states passed similar laws. Connecticut was one such state, but thanks to the amendments drawn up by Bridgeport representative, circus magnate Phineas T. Barnum, Connecticut's version of the law, passed in 1879, was probably the most stringent and restrictive in the country. Barnum's contribution was to add language prohibiting not just the distribution of contraceptives, but the "use" of them as well. In Connecticut, married couples were prohibited from using birth control and could be arrested, sentenced, and imprisoned for a year in jail for this offense.

TESTING THE LIMITS

In staunch opposition to Comstock and his law, Margaret Sanger, a pro-birth control and women's rights activist, began publishing a monthly magazine in New York appropriately entitled *The Woman Rebel*, which contained information about birth control, family planning, and contraception. This publication actually coined the term "birth control." In 1914, when she was indicted for publishing "obscenity," she fled the country and spent a year abroad rather than face the charges. She returned to the United States in 1915. On October 16, 1916, 43 years after the federal Comstock law was passed, Sanger and her sister, Ethel Byrne, opened the nation's first public birth control clinic in Brooklyn, New York. Sanger's clinic lasted a full nine days before police shut it down, but not before she was able to provide advice and information to scores of women for a ten-cent fee; on the first day that the clinic opened, 45 women waited in line to make their appointments. No doctors were onsite at the clinic, nor were any contraceptives actually distributed. Sanger and her sister were

An undated photo of Margaret Sanger. *Library of Congress, Prints & Photographs Division, LC-DIG-ggbain-20859.*

arrested for operating a clinic that distributed obscene information. They were freed from jail after posting a $500 bond. Within a few weeks, Sanger once again opened the clinic, but was quickly rearrested for "maintaining a public nuisance."

At Ethel Byrne's trial, her lawyer argued that New York's Comstock Law allowed the distribution of birth control information only in case of medical need and kept poor women from choosing the size of their families. The court found Byrne guilty and sentenced her to a month at the workhouse on Blackwell's Island. In prison, Byrne went on a hunger strike and was forcibly fed brandy, milk, and eggs. In support of Sanger and Byrne, the National Birth Control League held a rally at Carnegie Hall in which thousands of people came to hear Sanger speak. The rally raised enough money to provide a legal defense for Sanger. In return for getting her weakened sister released from prison, Sanger promised the New York governor that she would not reopen the clinic. In January 1917, Sanger's trial took place at the Court of Special Sessions in Brooklyn. Sanger was found guilty; the judge agreed to suspend her sentence if she promised not to reopen her clinic. Sanger refused, saying "I cannot promise to obey a law I do not respect." Sanger served a month in the penitentiary for women in Queens, New York.

Sanger's next steps were to establish the *Birth Control Review*, a journal on the subject of contraception and sexuality, organize the American Birth Control League (later to become the national Planned Parenthood organization), and write two books on the subject of contraception. Sanger's goals for the American Birth Control League were to educate the public about women's health, advocate repeal of the Comstock laws, sponsor medical research, and provide advice to women about birth control.

New York was not the only state where protests against the Comstock laws were gathering steam. Activists in Connecticut soon came together to call for an amendment or even repeal of the state law prohibiting obscenity. Specifically the bill, introduced by State Representative Samuel Sisisky, provided that "the giving of information or advice or medicine or articles for prevention of contraception by a doctor or nurse shall not be a violation" of the 1879 statute. The amendment was introduced to the state legislature in 1923 and a hearing to discuss it was scheduled. Sanger herself showed up in Hartford to rally a crowd of more than 800 people at Parson's Theatre before the legislative hearing on the amendment; she addressed the Connecticut legislature as well. Representatives of the Roman Catholic Church, including Auxiliary Bishop John Murray of Hartford, also came before the legislature, but not to support Sanger and her views; in fact, Murray spoke directly against Sanger. The Church urged the legislature to maintain the law as it existed in order to protect morality. Despite the fact that Sanger's beliefs garnered popularity with some people in Connecticut, the legislature ignored the call for reform and declined to amend or change the law at all. Many Connecticut citizens, even those who attended the rally, did not agree that birth control should be provided by doctors. One question asked of Sanger at the rally was, "Isn't birth control murder?" The *Hartford Courant*, in reporting the rally, indicated that the overall response to Sanger's ideas was "mixed," saying, "Many were not in accord with her contentions." A letter to the editor signed "An Old-Fashioned Mother in South Coventry," printed in the *Courant* on February 18, 1923, read in part: "Mrs. Sanger appears to be among those who believe first of all in absolute personal comfort and gratification which is becoming the ruination of our race. Legalizing the methods which she advocates means simplifying matters for illicit relations between men and women, making easier the way of the transgressor." The writer suggested that instead of legalizing birth control, "why not compel every married couple to support at least six children, either of their own or of other normal parentage, where said couple are financially able."

From 1923 to 1963, 29 bills were introduced to the Connecticut legislature for the purpose of amending or repealing the anticontraception law. Over and over again, contraception advocates lobbied the legislature to come to their senses and do away with the stringent and overbearing terms of the law. Between 1923 and 1935, a bill was proposed at every single session of the legislature, and every single time it was rejected in favor of leaving the law as it was. The Democratic-controlled legislature was very pro-Catholic, which translated into very anti-contraception.

Feeling overwhelmed and discouraged, Connecticut advocates laid to rest their unsuccessful strategy of lobbying. Activists finally decided to openly ignore the law. Birth control clinics opened in major cities throughout Connecticut in 1935. The first such clinic was the Maternal Health Clinic, started in Hartford in 1935. Sanger's Birth Control League soon established a Connecticut chapter, and the organization played a large role in launching more clinics around the state. Across the nation, other such clinics were popping up, many of them supported by public funds.

In 1936, this flagrant disregard for the law was brought to the attention of the courts. Margaret Sanger had a package of contraceptives sent to her through the mail from a Japanese doctor in an attempt to flout and test the law. The package was confiscated by the postal service, but Sanger had another package sent, this time to a licensed physician, Dr. Hannah Stone. Dr. Stone, not coincidentally, also served as the director of the Birth Control Research Bureau that Sanger had started in New York.

Sanger's goal in sending the contraceptives to the doctor was to create a test case; Sanger could not imagine that the courts would be able to uphold that the law could limit a doctor from giving patients a product that could save lives, and she was right.

The United States brought suit against "a package containing 120 vaginal pessaries more or less, alleged to be imported contrary to Section 305(a) of the Tariff Act of 1930," in *United States v. One Package* in 1936. The New York District Court agreed with Dr. Stone's argument that she could not be prevented from importing articles that would be used to keep patients healthy and alive; the federal government, however, appealed the decision to the U.S. Second Circuit Court of Appeals. On December 7, 1936, the Second Circuit affirmed the ruling of the district court and the encouraging result was celebrated by contraceptive advocates across the country. The language of the Second Circuit's decision clearly spelled out a medical exception to the federal Comstock Act. The court found that the Act was not designed to "prevent the importation, sale, or carriage by mail of things which might intelligently be employed by conscientious and competent physicians for the purpose of saving life or promoting the well being of their patients." Morris Ernst, Sanger's lawyer in the matter, heralded the decision as the "end of birth control laws." The court decision now allowed doctors to legally mail birth control devices to patients across the country.

THE WATERBURY CLINIC

The decision in *One Package* left birth control advocates wanting more. They had been given a judicial opinion confirming the notion that doctors could not be held back when it came to saving their patients' lives, but what they did not have was a law providing some sort of doctor's exception, or even better, a repeal of the archaic law completely. It is ironic that the original Comstock Act, as written in 1873, contained such a doctor's exception. It was successfully erased by Senator William Buckingham, a Republican from Connecticut, before the bill passed in the Senate. His amendment repealing the exception was virtually a non-issue as very little, if any, time was afforded to its discussion on the floor before Congress passed the bill into law.

After the decision in *One Package*, which seemingly provided a solution to getting around the Comstock Act, the Connecticut Birth Control League focused its efforts on opening more clinics. The predominantly Catholic city of Waterbury was chosen as the site for the next such clinic and space in the Chase Dispensary at Waterbury Hospital was obtained. The agreement with the hospital made it clear that the clinic was not a division of the hospital, the hospital was not responsible for what went on inside the clinic, and the clinic was not to use hospital supplies. Two doctors joined the league and acted as onsite practitioners. The clinic was not a simple walk-in operation where any woman could go to get contraceptives. In order to be seen at the clinic, her physician must have referred a woman there strictly for health reasons.

At a meeting in August 1939, members of the Connecticut Birth Control League discussed the success of their Waterbury clinic. The next day an article in the *Waterbury Democrat* titled "Birth Control Clinic Is Operating in City," was the story that would have the effect of shutting down the clinic. After seeing the article, Waterbury representatives of the Catholic Church quickly came up with a plan of attack. In a publicly released resolution against the Waterbury clinic, the Catholic Clergy Association of Waterbury stated:

> [I]t has been brought to our attention that a so-called birth control clinic, sometimes called a maternal health center, is existing in Waterbury...Resolved, that this association go on record as being unalterably opposed to the existence of such a clinic in our city and we hereby urge our Catholic people to avoid contact with it and we hereby publicly call the attention of the public prosecutors to its existence and demand that they investigate and if necessary prosecute to the full extent of the law.

The resolution was read the next Sunday in every Catholic church pulpit around Waterbury. William Fitzgerald, a Catholic parishioner and state's attorney from Waterbury, heard the Church's cry for help. Understanding that his predecessor had been recently dismissed for lack of prosecution against gambling violators, Fitzgerald considered it his duty to complete a full investigation of the clinic to ensure it was not operating outside the confines of the 1879 anticontraception law.

Fitzgerald was quickly able to obtain a warrant allowing the county deputy sheriff and a detective to search the clinic. After spending less than an hour searching the clinic, they took several boxes of items with them.

Fitzgerald's next step was to decide whom to charge with violation of the statute; he decided that the violators were the two physicians employed at the clinic, Roger B. Nelson and William A. Goodrich, as well as the founder and director of the clinic, Clara Lee McTernan, who, as it turned out, was also Fitzgerald's next door neighbor with whom he was on good terms.

The Connecticut Birth Control League soon hired Attorney J. Warren Upson to represent the defendants in the case of *State v. Nelson*. All three defendants pled not guilty to the charges of violating the abetting provisions of the 1879 anticontraception statute by providing birth control counseling and devices to at least six women. Upson's main argument was that the provision of the statute under which they had been charged violated both the federal Constitution and the Connecticut constitution. Upson filed a demurrer in which he admitted the facts as alleged by the state, but protested against the charges because of their unconstitutionality.

Judge Kenneth Wynne of the Connecticut Superior Court agreed with Upson's reasoning and effectively ruled that the 1879 anticontraception statute violated the U.S. Constitution. Wynne opined that physicians in Connecticut should have the option to give medical advice to their patients as they saw fit, even if that meant advising and prescribing the use of contraceptives. He stated in his opinion, "[i]s a doctor to be prosecuted as a criminal for doing something that is sound and right in the best tenets and traditions of a high calling dedicated and devoted to health? Should he be forced to practice furtively and in stealth rather than give up what his conscience and his honest professional judgment dictate?"

Also at issue in the case was whether the "obscene materials" confiscated during the raid conducted at the clinic should be destroyed or returned to their owners. This matter was heard by Judge Frank McEvoy, who decided that the raid was legally justified and that the materials should be condemned and destroyed.

Both decisions were quickly appealed to the Connecticut Supreme Court of Errors, Connecticut's highest court. Arguments were heard on January 4, 1940. In deference to the legislature, the court found that, "Any intention on the part of the Legislature to allow such an exception as would advantage the present defendants is negatived not only by the absolute language used originally and preserved ever since but also, signally, by its repeated and recent refusals to inject an exception."

Noting that similar laws had been unsuccessfully challenged previously in other jurisdictions, as well as numerous times before the Connecticut legislature, the court declined to find the law unconstitutional. Unfortunately for Upson and the CBCL, a similar case had just been tried in Massachusetts. *Commonwealth v. Gardner* came before the Massachusetts courts because Massachusetts had a similarly harsh anticontraception statute on the books. That case was decided in favor of maintaining the law as the legislature passed it. The defendants in *Gardner* tried to appeal the case to the U.S. Supreme Court, but they were denied certiorari for lack of a federal question. The Connecticut

Supreme Court interpreted that denial as "confirming the constitutionality of the Massachusetts statute...and, as already indicated, we regard the issues here as essentially analogous." The court's decision may also have been swayed by the three amicus (or friend of the court) briefs, filed on behalf of the state by Massachusetts attorneys who worked on the *Gardner* case.

What had seemed like a victory for the pro-contraceptive movement soon turned out to be a defeat. The highest court in the state had found that the legislature—and only the legislature—was the appropriate body to decide how public safety and morals should be protected and to what extent. Those who had been fighting on behalf of privacy and the right to use contraception were tired and disheartened; some lost interest and gave up. Those who were still in the fight decided it would be best to go back to the legislature and plead their case again.

ANOTHER TEST CASE TO COMBAT THE LAW

The Connecticut Birth Control League and the national Birth Control Federation changed their name to Planned Parenthood in the early 1940s. The change was meant to alert the public that their movement was not just about supplying condoms to unmarried women in order to promote promiscuity, but that their mission was to aid families in planning when they wanted to have children.

The Planned Parenthood League of Connecticut led the way in introducing a bill to the legislature twice a year from 1941 to 1963. In every session, without fail, the measure calling for a physician's exception was denied. In addition to bringing amended bills before the legislature, the Connecticut activists put their energy into finding another test case, similar to that of *Nelson*, but this time they found a private physician who had already prescribed contraceptives to patients whose lives would have been jeopardized if they had become pregnant. Warren Upson, the attorney used in *Nelson*, was unwilling to go ahead with further litigation regarding contraceptives, so he was replaced by New Haven attorney Frederick Wiggin.

Wiggin found the perfect test case in New Haven doctor Wilder Tileston. Dr. Tileston had already treated three women who had serious health problems that would be exacerbated, if not lethal, if they were to become pregnant. The three women were to be known as Jane Doe, Mary Roe, and Sarah Hoe. Wiggin made the first move—instead of waiting for Tileston to be charged with breaking the law, he filed a complaint in New Haven Superior Court.

While the complaint was being filed, the Connecticut legislature was debating the latest anticontraception reform bill. The bill passed without problem in the Republican-led House of Representatives, but was once again soundly defeated in the predominantly Democratic and Catholic Senate.

While the legislature was debating, Wiggin was negotiating. He agreed with New Haven state's attorney Abraham S. Ullman that they would not request a trial and the issue would go straight to the state supreme court. The superior court had the three women evaluated by independent physicians to determine their health status. The court physician's determinations were in line with Tileston's findings—pregnancy would be extremely harmful, if not deadly, to the three women.

The parties argued their application of the law to the Connecticut Supreme Court on February 4, 1942, and based their argument on a set of mutually agreed upon facts submitted to the court. Wiggin, in an effort to deliver a professional and respectable argument, was able to keep the audience to a minimum, discouraging Planned Parenthood members from attending and drawing attention to themselves. The court would not regard protestors favorably. The *Gardner* case out of Massachusetts that had been used as the persuasive precedent in *One Package* had been recently distinguished, and the Massachusetts Supreme Court had found that a woman's health exception was implicit within the statute, meaning doctors could prescribe contraceptives for women whose health would be at risk in the event of a pregnancy. Interpreting the Massachusetts law to be analogous to Connecticut's, Wiggin argued that Connecticut's statute also had embedded in it a provision concerning an exception for the health of a woman.

The court made its decision within four months, and putting aside Wiggin's arguments, noted again that the legislature, being the proper body to create such an exception, had repeatedly declined to do so. Thus, the court's role was to defer to the legislature's decision in keeping the anticontraception statute on the books as written. The majority opinion, written by Justice Arthur Ells stated, "[w]hen the legislature expresses the will of the people in a statutory enactment the language of which is plain and unambiguous, the law must stand unless it is clearly unconstitutional or unless it is plain that the legislature must have intended an exception which it did not express."

The court's decision was a close one, with two of the five justices dissenting, similar to the outcome in *Nelson*. In this case, however, Justice Christopher Avery, who was also one of two dissenters in *Nelson*, put his opinion on paper. Noting the fact that the statute was passed without any debate regarding a physicians' exception, Justice Avery stated:

> It is difficult to believe that the legislature in 1879, in passing the present statute as part of an act concerning offenses against decency, morality, and humanity, contemplated such a situation or that the law would be given such a construction. A proper respect for the legislature forbids an interpretation which would work such a result and be so contrary to human nature. A reasonable construction of the statute, considering its history and the circumstance under which it was enacted, requires that it be so interpreted as to permit duly licensed physicians to prescribe to married women contraceptive devices and information necessary to prevent conception when in the judgment of the physician conception would imperil the life or health of the patient.

With the dissent's opinion firmly down on paper, Tileston and birth control advocates were encouraged. They took steps to appeal the decision to the U.S. Supreme Court, the only avenue left to pursue since the case had been heard in Connecticut's highest court in the first instance. Almost exactly one year after the case was argued before the Connecticut Supreme Court, on January 13 and 14, 1943, Morris Ernst, the attorney who represented Margaret Sanger in the Second Circuit *One Package* case, and current chief attorney for the Planned Parenthood Federation of America, argued on behalf of Dr. Tileston before the U.S. Supreme Court.

The fatal flaw in the *Tileston* case was that Tileston's life was not the one in danger—the main thrust of their argument was that the statute violated the Fourteenth Amendment's guarantee that the states cannot deprive any person of life, liberty, or property without due process of law. Because the women whose lives were at risk were not the plaintiffs, the Court was unable to afford Tileston standing in the matter, meaning he was not the proper party to be bringing such a claim. A *per curiam*, or unsigned opinion issued by the Court as a whole, stated, "There is no allegation or proof that appellant's life is in danger. His patients are not parties to this proceeding and there is no basis on which we can say that he has standing to secure an adjudication of his patients' constitutional right to life, which they do not assert in their own behalf."

The outcome in *Tileston* was another major letdown for Planned Parenthood and other contraception advocates. They refused to give up the fight however, and returned to petitioning the legislature for an amendment to the law. At each legislative session for the next 10 years a bill was introduced, and each year it was defeated. Since 1923, advocates had been hammering away at the Connecticut legislature in hope of creating an amendment that would allow physicians to prescribe contraceptives for their at-risk patients. After almost 30 years of defeat, Connecticut advocates decided a new strategy was necessary in order to accomplish their goals.

IN COMES ESTELLE GRISWOLD

Estelle Griswold had led a full life before she became entwined in what would be one of the most influential and monumental Supreme Court cases in American history. As a student at Hartford High, "Stelle," as she was known, was often reprimanded for playing hooky, but performed so well academically that she skipped two grades. After Estelle Trebert graduated from high school, being unable to afford to go to college, she left for Paris to pursue her dreams of being a singer. She came back to the United States and in 1927 married fellow Hartford High graduate, Richard Griswold. They started their life together in New York City where she was a singer on the radio. In 1945, the Griswolds left for Europe to work for the United Nations and Christian Relief Agencies in the wake of World War II. While her husband was stationed in Berlin, Estelle's work took her all over the world. She went first to London, then to Holland, Germany, and even Argentina. Due to family illnesses, they both returned home in the early 1950s.

By 1953, Estelle and her husband, now an Episcopal minister, were living on Trumbull Street in New Haven. She was the executive secretary for the New Haven Human Relations Council, but it was an unpaid position, which she could not sustain for much longer. Coincidentally, she struck up a conversation with Jennie Heiser, fundraiser for the Planned Parenthood League of Connecticut, which happened to be located on Trumbull Street as well. Estelle knew virtually nothing about birth control because she was unable to have children of her own, but after a few weeks of interviews and meetings with the board, she accepted the position at $5,000 per year as executive director of the Planned Parenthood League of Connecticut in December 1953.

In taking over management of the organization, Estelle's goal was to make sure that the organization was serving the needs of the women in the community. Their first step was not to open a clinic of their own in the area, but to arrange appointments and transportation to a clinic run by Planned Parenthood of Eastern Westchester in Port Chester, New York, where such clinics were legal. For two years this operation continued, though it took a lot of effort without a lot of payoff.

In addition to the trips between New York and Connecticut, the Connecticut Planned Parenthood funded an infertility clinic at Yale, and Estelle continued to organize lobbying efforts in hopes of having the Connecticut legislature amend or repeal the anticontraception statute. In 1957, she enlisted the help of Dr. Charles Lee Buxton, who would eventually become an integral player in the *Griswold* case. Buxton, an avid supporter of contraception rights, ran the Yale clinic funded by Planned Parenthood, and was willing to help Estelle's cause by testifying at the legislative hearings in support of an amendment allowing a physician's exception. Buxton spoke about the tragic patients that he had treated who had died or fallen seriously ill due to unwanted pregnancies. Doctors in opposition to contraception and family planning methods also testified before the legislature; it was their opinion that birth control measures were harmful to children born to mothers who used it, and that birth control in general promoted promiscuity and was detrimental to society's moral attitudes. Buxton felt that what he heard from the other doctors at the hearing was outrageous, and left even more determined to take proactive steps to change the archaic law.

Estelle's next endeavor would be to bring another test case before the courts, but this time avoiding the fatal mistake of not using the patients as plaintiffs. In 1961, she was able to enlist the help of Dr. Buxton once again. He was willing to prescribe birth control for health reasons to several women who agreed to serve as plaintiffs in the case. Pauline and Paul Poe, Harold and Hannah Hoe, and Jane Doe were the pseudonyms of the patients recruited by Buxton; the attorneys in the case went to great lengths to keep the patients' identities confidential.

Pauline Poe had already given birth to three children, all of whom had significant problems, and none lived to be more than a few weeks old. Not surprisingly, she did not want to go through another pregnancy. Harold and Hannah Hoe were a married couple whose blood types would result in significant birth defects to any children they would have. Jane Doe had just had serious complications in her last pregnancy, resulting in her giving birth to a stillborn; she did not wish to become pregnant again.

Recruited for the challenge were two New Haven attorneys, Fowler Harper and Catherine Roraback. Their job was to bring a case that would be adjudicated in the courts. They would both play an integral part in the *Griswold* case as well.

Fowler Harper had passed the bar in 1921 before finishing his third year of law school at the Ohio Northern College of Law in Ada, Ohio.

Instead of becoming an attorney after he graduated, he decided to coach football at Wilmington College in Ohio where the team had gone three years without winning a game. After Coach Harper stepped in, the Quakers won 16 out of the 20 games they played under his direction. After coaching, he worked as a professor at law schools around the nation. In the 1930s, Harper became involved with the FDR administration and was appointed general counsel to the Federal Security Agency. In 1947, he joined the faculty of the Yale Law School, and held the position until his death in 1965.

Catherine Roraback was born and raised in Brooklyn, New York. She graduated from Yale Law School in 1948—she was the only female to be sworn into the Connecticut Bar that year. That same year she helped found the Connecticut Civil Liberties Union. After graduation, she stayed in Connecticut, practicing in New Haven, where she focused mainly on civil and criminal matters. Because Harper was not admitted to the Connecticut Bar, he contacted Roraback to help with the pending case. The two had met 15 years earlier in Washington, D.C. when they were both working there. Harper's invitation showed his deep respect for Roraback and her abilities as an attorney, especially because his goal from the start was to have the case proceed to the U.S. Supreme Court.

Harper and Dr. Buxton met at a cocktail party thrown by Estelle in 1961; though it is likely they already knew each other or had at least met on other occasions. It was at this party that the pair formulated the plan to get the next test case off the ground. Roraback later said during an interview, "I've always said that it was her martinis, which...were some of the strongest that you've ever seen, [that] probably was the beginning of the Griswold case."[1]

They knew they needed several test patients willing to participate, which could prove to be a real obstacle. Since contraceptives were so controversial to begin with, the prospect of having one's name and story used for such a case that would virtually announce to the world that you were trying to use contraceptives, would not prove to be a selling point. Buxton signed on to be the first test plaintiff, and was on the hunt for several couples willing to participate. In a May 2004 interview, Roraback said "...we always had married women or married clients in these [contraceptive] cases. You couldn't have talked about a single, unmarried person having the right to use birth control in Connecticut in 1958. As a matter of fact, National Planned Parenthood, even in its clinics in New York, only served people who said they were married."[2]

When Buxton found three women willing to take part in the case, he called Harper. Harper had been in contact with a student at Yale who was in a relationship, not yet married, and did not yet want children. He and his girlfriend were told they would have to go to New York in order to get contraceptives, and decided that they too would be willing to participate in the case, and even though they were not married, were accepted as plaintiffs. With the main obstacle of obtaining plaintiffs out of the way, things moved ahead quickly.

Harper developed the case strategy and decided that their first move would be to request a declaratory judgment stating clearly and unequivocally that the 1879 anticontraception statute was unconstitutional. Expecting that to fail, Harper's next step was to bring it to the appeals court, and then up the line to the U.S. Supreme Court.

THE NEXT TEST

Even though they had several different couples participating in the case and a separate complaint was filed for each, all the matters were consolidated and one main action was brought, in *Poe v. Ullman*. Ab Ullman, the state's attorney in New Haven, had already been involved with the contraception battle. In 1958, Roraback had brought a motion for a declaratory judgment to superior court in New Haven, essentially asking that the law that prevented these couples from obtaining contraception to save their lives, from their physicians no less, was unconstitutional in that it prevented them from exercising their right to life and liberty. "These people [the plaintiffs] have the right to be allowed to continue normal marital relations without being inhibited by the state," Roraback had argued. She stated that the 1879 law was unconstitutional and void because "A statute which by its very terms may inhibit the most personal relationships of marriage is itself unreasonable." The state's response was to file a demurrer, essentially agreeing with Roraback's facts in that the women were in precarious situations regarding pregnancy, and that it was true the law prevented their doctor from prescribing contraceptives. The main thrust of the state's argument, however, was that based on recent precedent, namely *Nelson* and *Tileston*, which dealt with almost precisely the same issues, the courts had found the law to be constitutional, and thus their motion for declaratory judgment should be dismissed.

Superior Court Judge Frank Healy sustained the state's demurrer, thus accepting Roraback's allegations, but ruled in favor of Ullman based on the fact that courts had already looked into the issues and found the law to be constitutional. Roraback quickly appealed this judgment to the Connecticut Supreme Court, the next stepping stone on the way to the U.S. Supreme Court.

While preparing for the state supreme court, Roraback was confronted by national Planned Parenthood attorneys, including Morris Ernst. They criticized Roraback's legal theories and tactics, and wanted more say in the handling of the matter; the national branch saw the problem in Connecticut as one of grave importance, and they were uncomfortable with the prospect of losing this battle again. Eventually the two teams of lawyers came to a middle ground, and the national Planned Parenthood attorneys settled on writing an amicus brief, arguing on behalf of Roraback's position, which would be submitted to the Connecticut Supreme Court for consideration.

Arguments before the state's highest court were heard on October 7, 1959. Things seemed to be looking up because the court was headed by Chief Justice Raymond E. Baldwin, a Republican who had previously favored creating a more lenient contraception statute while serving as a state legislator. Following their streak of bad luck, however, in this particular case Baldwin was not persuaded by Roraback's arguments and neither was the rest of the court. Adhering to *stare decisis*, or letting the previous decisions stand, the court announced its opinion on December 22, 1959, deciding that the 1879 anticontraception statute was in fact constitutional because it dealt with an issue that was within the state's power to regulate in order to protect the health and safety of the people.

The court noted in its opinion that:

> Courts cannot write legislation by judicial decree; this is particularly so when the legislature has refused to rewrite the existing legislation. The *Nelson* and *Tileston* decisions cannot be overruled by any attempt to reconstruct the statutes...We cannot say that the legislature, in weighing the considerations for and against an exception legalizing contraceptive measures in cases such as the ones before us, could not reasonably conclude that, despite the occasional hardship which might result, the greater good would be served by leaving the statutes as they are.

Even though a favorable decision by the Connecticut Supreme Court would have been appreciated, the main goal of the litigation was to reach the U.S. Supreme Court, and so the Connecticut court's decision was not the end of the line for Planned Parenthood. Now that they were dealing with a federal appeal, Harper was able to take a more active role in the next phase of the case, seeing as his lack of admittance to the Connecticut Bar would no longer be an issue. They quickly filed an appeal and briefs urging the Supreme Court to consider their case; the next step was to wait to see if at least four justices on the U.S. Supreme Court agreed to hear their case. The "Rule of Four" has been a longstanding tradition within the U.S. Supreme Court—as long as at least four justices vote to hear a case, it will be accepted; if less than four justices wish to hear it, the appeal will be automatically denied.

In Harper's brief to the Court, his main argument became that these citizens must be afforded their privacy. Harper argued that such a right was implicitly found within the Constitution via a person's right to life and liberty—the right and choice to use contraception was a private one, and a couple's private choice to do so should be left as such. Harper also noted the fact that several prominent public interest groups were interested in the case and more than willing to file amicus curiae briefs in support of these contentions.

On May 20, 1960, the case passed the "Rule of Four" test when five justices voted to hear the case; Chief Justice Earl Warren, along with Justices William Douglas, John Harlan, William Brennan, and Potter Stewart were interested in hearing the merits of the contraception case. Three justices voted not to hear the case and Justice Frankfurter chose not to vote at all; it was later learned that Frankfurter had served as an unofficial legal advisor to Planned Parenthood in the past and he felt there was a conflict of interest. Ironically, in the end, Frankfurter was the one who authored the Court's majority opinion. The vote to hear the case was a major step forward in the battle to recognize marital and personal privacy and allow contraception.

ROUND ONE IN THE U.S. SUPREME COURT

Harper filed his official brief outlining the relevant law and legal arguments in September of 1960. In preparation for oral argument, the justices' law clerks review the briefs submitted by the parties, then outline and analyze the arguments in a memorandum for the justices. One of the clerks, who often play a significant behind-the-scenes role in drafting opinions for the justices, felt that while there was a valid argument for the concept of marital privacy, the fact that the law had not been used to prosecute anyone, except in *Nelson* where the charges were essentially dismissed, and because the law was not likely to be enforced any time soon, the case was unsound and not ripe. In order for a case to be heard, there must be an actual problem to be dealt with—the issue must be ripe. Another flaw had presented itself that would not bode well for the contraception advocates.

Oral arguments before the Supreme Court were heard on March 1, 1961; Harper opened the day before all nine justices. Each side was allotted an hour and a half, and grudgingly, Harper yielded some of his time to a national Planned Parenthood representative, Harriet Pilpel. Ray Cannon, Connecticut assistant attorney general, represented Ullman. Both presentations were riddled with questions from the justices, making it difficult to gauge for which party the justices would rule.

The case, which stemmed from a small group of Connecticut citizens, drew national attention following oral argument at the Supreme Court. An article in *Time* magazine, published on March 10, 1961, made a mockery of the outdated law. "Late every night in Connecticut, lights go out in the cities and towns, and citizens by tens of thousands proceed zestfully to break the law." The article also noted in a footnote that, "[i]n forbidding the use of contraceptive devices, Connecticut is unique among the 50 states, and the laughingstock of all of them."

The flaw noted by one of the clerks would prove to be fatal for *Poe et al. v. Ullman*. The decision, released on June 19, 1961, indicated that a plurality of the justices agreed with the fact that the case was not properly before the Court at that time since there had been no enforcement of the statute; without enforcement of the statute causing some unconstitutional result, the Court felt it was powerless to do anything. Since Article III of the Constitution required that all cases brought before the Court embody a real "case and controversy," the lack of a concrete controversy in this case resulted in the Court's affirmation of the Connecticut Supreme Court's decision. Once again, the fight for privacy and contraception failed before the courts.

In the majority opinion, written by Justice Felix Frankfurter, the Court stated that:

> [a]ppellants' complaints in these declaratory judgment proceedings do not clearly, and certainly do not in terms, allege that appellee Ullman threatens to prosecute them for use of, or for giving advice concerning, contraceptive devices. The allegations are merely that, in the course of his public duty, he intends to prosecute any offenses against Connecticut law, and that he claims that use of and advice concerning contraceptives would constitute offenses. The lack of immediacy of the threat described by these allegations might alone raise serious questions of non-justiciability of appellants' claims.

Though a plurality ruled in favor of affirming the Connecticut Supreme Court, there was no strong majority consensus; a concurrence and two dissents were noted as well. Justice Brennan concurred in the decision, and wrote a separate opinion to indicate he thought the case could only be properly brought if and when a birth control clinic was opened and prosecuted under the statute. He stated that "The true controversy in this case is over the opening of birth-control clinics on a large scale...It will be time enough to decide the constitutional questions urged upon us when, if ever, that real controversy flares up again." Brennan was practically inviting Planned Parenthood to open up a clinic in Connecticut, make sure it was noticed, and that its operators were arrested and prosecuted under the 1879 statute.

Justice Douglas, in his dissenting opinion, expressed his frustration over the majority's assurance that based on an implied understanding and "tacit agreement," the law would never be enforced. "No lawyer, I think, would advise his clients to rely on that 'tacit agreement,'" he said. "What are these people—doctor and patients—to do? Flout the law and go to prison? Violate the law surreptitiously and hope they will not be caught? By today's decision we leave them no other alternatives." Douglas found that the right of a doctor to prescribe for his patient, treatment that will maintain their health, to be implicit in both the First and Fourteenth Amendments of the Constitution. He also noted that the right to privacy between a man and a woman, in the privacy of their marital bed, was off limits to regulation by the state. Justice Douglas stated:

> The regulation as applied in this case touches the relationship between man and wife. It reaches into the intimacies of the marriage relationship. If we imagine a regime of full enforcement of the law in the manner of an Anthony Comstock, we would reach the point where search warrants issued and officers appeared in bedrooms to find out what went on. It is said that this is not that case. And so it is not. But when the State makes "use" a crime and applies the criminal sanction to man and wife, the State has entered the innermost sanctum of the home. If it can make this law, it can enforce it. And proof of its violation necessarily involves an inquiry into the relations between man and wife. That is an invasion of the privacy that is implicit in a free society.
> ...
> [c]an there be any doubt that a Bill of Rights that in time of peace bars soldiers from being quartered in a home 'without the consent of the Owner' should also bar the police from investigating the intimacies of the marriage relation? The idea of allowing the State that leeway is congenial only to a totalitarian regime.

Also dissenting from the majority opinion was Justice Harlan. Harlan had trouble with the court's reasoning for dismissing the opinion, noting that previously the court had decided cases that were much less ripe; he found the circumstances in *Poe* to represent a true controversy. "This is not a feigned, hypothetical, friendly or colorable suit such as discloses a want of a truly adversary contest," he said. Harlan's biggest problem with the plurality's dismissal of the appeal was the fact that the plaintiffs right to privacy was on the line:

> [T]he most substantial claim which these married persons press is their right to enjoy the privacy of their marital relations free of the enquiry of the criminal law, whether it be in a prosecution of them or of a doctor whom they have consulted. And I cannot agree that their enjoyment of this privacy is not substantially impinged upon, when they are told that if they use contraceptives, indeed whether they do so or not, the only thing which stands between them and being forced to render criminal account of their marital privacy is the whim of the prosecutor.

Agreeing with Douglas, Harlan also found that the right to privacy stemmed from the Fourteenth Amendment to the Constitution. "I consider that this Connecticut legislation, as construed to apply to these appellants, violates the Fourteenth Amendment. I believe that a statute making it a criminal offense for *married couples* to use contraceptives is an intolerable and unjustifiable invasion of privacy in the conduct of the most intimate concerns of an individual's personal life." (Emphasis in original). Notably, in his dissent, Harlan condoned the prohibition of other private activities, namely "adultery, homosexuality and the like."

> In sum, even though the State has determined that the use of contraceptives is as iniquitous as any act of extra-marital sexual immorality, the intrusion of the whole machinery of the criminal law into the very heart of marital privacy, requiring husband and wife to render account before a criminal tribunal of their uses of that intimacy, is surely a very different thing indeed from punishing those who establish intimacies which the law has always forbidden and which can have no claim to social protection.
>
> Though undoubtedly the States are and should be left free to reflect a wide variety of policies, and should be allowed broad scope in experimenting with various means of promoting those policies, I must agree with Mr. Justice Jackson that '[t]here are

limits to the extent to which a legislatively represented majority may conduct…experiments at the expense of the dignity and personality' of the individual. *Skinner v. Oklahoma*. In this instance these limits are, in my view, reached and passed."

Also dissenting from the plurality was Justice Potter Stewart, who chose only to note, "[f]or the reasons so convincingly advanced by both Mr. Justice Douglas and Mr. Justice Harlan, I join them in dissenting from the dismissal of these appeals."

And so the battle again was lost, though some progress was made. There was no solid majority that voted to dismiss, only a plurality, and the dissents were strong and duly noted on the record. Refusing to give up and determined to see the law changed, the Planned Parenthood team regrouped and reformulated yet another plan to pursue their goals.

THE FINAL PHASE: OPENING THE CLINIC

With the loss at the U.S. Supreme Court, the Planned Parenthood team found themselves at the drawing board yet again. Taking the advice of Justice Brennan, they set in motion a plan to open a clinic in New Haven with a main purpose to distribute contraceptives. Just one day after the Poe decision was announced, on June 20, 1961, Estelle announced plans to open such a clinic via a news reporter with whom she shared their plans, noting that they would welcome prosecution by the state if they saw it as a violation of the law, even though the U.S. Supreme Court had found there was a "tacit agreement" not to prosecute under the statute. Their goal was to force the state to charge them with violating the statute so that they could begin the legal journey to the U.S. Supreme Court yet again.

Estelle's goal was to have the clinic up and running by October 1, 1961, and she went about leasing an appropriate space. They found a location around the street from their old headquarters in New Haven. Coincidentally, the new building at 79 Trumbull Street had been the site of the Connecticut Birth Control League headquarters some 30 years earlier. Though it was not possible to have the clinic operating full-time to start, they would provide services for two hours a day, three days a week. Four doctors and other employees volunteered their time to make the clinic a reality. Even though they were opening the clinic without regard for the 1879 law, they still limited the patients they would admit to married women, and unmarried women only if referred there by clergy for a pre-marital diaphragm fitting. Approximately 10 to 15 calls for appointments came in each week.

Though the October deadline came and went, it was not long after that the clinic was fully operational. The first 10 appointments were held on November 1, and the following day Estelle held a press conference announcing the clinic's success. It was here that she said that she hoped someone would complain so that the state's attorney would have no choice but to charge him or her with violating the 1879 contraceptive law. Not only were they distributing contraceptives, but also married couples were going home and using them.

A local citizen doing his civic duty soon moved along the plans for prosecution; within days of its opening, James Morris, an employee of a local New Haven business and a fervent Catholic, alerted the police to the clinic's activities. John Blazi and Harold Berg, two police detectives, investigated the crime scene and confirmed there was, in fact, a birth control clinic operating in violation of the statute. Instead of New Haven state's attorney Ullman handling the case, this time, Julius Maretz, the circuit court prosecutor, took control.

"...we opened this clinic and after about ten days, the pressure was on...there was a campaign, just by one man, who picketed the clinic with pictures that were almost like what you see now in the anti-abortion picketing. He called everyone...," said Roraback in a later interview, referring to Morris.[3]

Instead of seizing all the clinic's medical records, Maretz was willing to negotiate with Griswold and agreed to settle for the names of two patients who were willing to come forward as having received contraceptives. Only one patient seen at the clinic agreed to cooperate—Joan Bates Forsberg, a thirty-three-year-old mother of three, who had visited the clinic and paid $2 for a supply of birth control pills as an alternative to going to New York to obtain contraceptives. She agreed to do whatever was necessary in order to help the clinic. Faced with the prospect of having all the records confiscated, Griswold and Buxton had to come up with another woman willing to cooperate. Buxton was able to find an alternative solution—he got in touch with Rosemary Stevens, whose husband was a member of the Yale Law School faculty. Stevens agreed to meet with Dr. Buxton at the clinic and admit to the police that she had met with the doctor and that she had received contraceptives from him. With the names of these two patients, the medical records of the clinic were saved.

Roraback was able to work out a deal with the prosecutor whereby the clinic would not be raided and the women who agreed to admit they had used the clinic's services would not be prosecuted. According to Roraback, she said to the prosecutor, "'Well if I give you the names of three of the women who have been to this clinic who would be willing to have their names used and cooperate with you on a prosecution, would you then not do the raid,' and he said, 'Yes.' So that's what we did."[4]

The women submitted statements to the police affirming that they had gone to the clinic, received birth control, and had returned home and used the contraceptives. With that, the police had their case and were ready to prosecute under the 1879 anti-contraception law.

The clinic had been successfully functional for 10 days, from November 1 to November 10, before being shut down. In that time, the clinic was open four times and had served approximately 75 women. The clinic had already been booked solid through December, with 15 appointments made per day the clinic was open, which was to be three times per week.

Roraback later remembered an interesting aspect of her involvement with the case during an interview. "When I was doing the Griswold case, I would frequently have, maybe once a month or something, calls from people who wanted to know how to get an abortion... I obviously knew the medical fraternity by that time. But the thing that really shocked me was one day a lawyer...called me and said he had a client who was...being held at the New Haven jail. She had gone into the Yale-New Haven Emergency Room with complications from one of these self-induced abortions and when she left—when she was being discharged from the hospital, she was arrested for having induced an abortion on herself. That was when I discovered that there was a rule at Yale-New Haven Hospital that if a woman came in, in that condition that they were to notify the police, and the police would come down and arrest them when they left...

"I remember I called up Lee Buxton and...told him what had happened and he was gasping. He couldn't believe it. He said, 'I'll call you back,' and I don't think it was more than fifteen minutes, he got back on the phone and said, 'There used to be such a rule. There is no more,' period. But that was the way things were treated at that time."[5]

Soon after the women made their statements, arrest warrants were issued for both Griswold and Buxton for violating the anticontraceptive statute. They were charged under Connecticut General Statutes Sections 53-32 and 54-196.

Section 53-32, Use of Drugs or Instruments to Prevent Contraception, read as follows: "Any person who uses any drug, medicinal article or instrument for the purpose of preventing contraception shall be fined not less than fifty dollars or imprisoned for not less than 60 days nor more than one year or be both fined and imprisoned."

Section 54-196, Accessories, read as follows: "Any person who assists, abets, counsels, causes, hires or commands another to commit any offense may be prosecuted and punished as if he were the principal offender."

Dr. Buxton and Griswold both pled not guilty to the charges, and though they were not held in jail, the activities of the clinic were seriously hampered. In order to avoid further problems, on the advice of Harper and the national Planned Parenthood, the clinic closed its doors for the time being. Over 200 women who had already booked appointments had to be told that the services were no longer available. In the letter sent out to cancel the appointments, a list of nearby drugstores where contraception could easily be found was listed, as well as the location and information for similar clinics in nearby states.

Buxton and Griswold's hearing was set for November 24, 1961, and they were to appear before Circuit Judge J. Robert Lacey. Again, Roraback filed a demurrer agreeing with the facts and circumstances as stated, but alleging that the law itself was unconstitutional. The demurrer argued that the statute was unconstitutional in that it "would deny him his rights to liberty and property without the due process of law, in violation of the Fourteenth Amendment." It also argued it was unconstitutional because it "would deny him his rights to freedom of speech and communication of ideas under the First and Fourteenth Amendments." Judge Lacey set a date for trial to begin and sent both sides off to prepare briefs for the trial, which would start December 8.

As with the previous litigation, the goal of this case was to get to the U.S. Supreme Court. There was no real expectation of triumphing in the lower courts, but the briefs still had to be prepared and oral arguments still had to be made each step of the way.

Using the Supreme Court's recent decision in *Poe v. Ullman*, specifically the dissenting opinions, as support for their contention that the law was unconstitutional, Roraback prepared the brief for Buxton and Griswold. The main thrust of her argument was, again, that their Constitutional rights were violated by this law; their freedom of expression was restricted, as was their right to life and liberty under the Fourteenth Amendment. At oral argument on December 8, Roraback urged the court to depart from the archaic nineteenth-century law that no longer had a rational bearing on society. The state's position was relatively simple—the law should be maintained because other courts continued to affirm it. Their three-page brief simply cited to the previous decisions of both Connecticut and federal courts that repeatedly upheld the law.

Just a few weeks after oral argument, on December 20, 1961, Lacey filed a written opinion in which he upheld the 1879 law and denied Roraback's demurrer. Because Connecticut courts had faced this exact issue repeatedly, coming to the same conclusion each time, Lacey felt it was his duty to affirm the law, and the decisions of the courts. Lacey noted that, "in the face of these decisions, this Court is confronted with the rule of stare decisis." Lacey also noted that the right to freedom of speech is "not an absolute right," as well as the fact that the state may "enact reasonable regulations in order to promote the general welfare as well as to promote and to advance public health and public morals." Lacey then scheduled a trial for January 2, 1962, in order to determine whether the law had actually been violated by Griswold and Buxton.

The trial of *State of Connecticut v. Griswold and Buxton* commenced the morning of January 2, 1962; approximately 100 people came to witness the trial, which lasted about six hours. Several witnesses were called for each side: the state called the police detectives who went to the clinic to confirm its existence; also called were three patients who had agreed to cooperate with the investigation. They testified they had gone to the clinic, received contraceptives, and used them. Little cross-examination was done by Roraback since the defense did not dispute what the witnesses said. After the patients were called, the state rested their case on the prima facie evidence that a clinic was in operation, that it distributed contraception, and that the patients, in fact, used the contraception.

The defense called Estelle Griswold as its first witness. Griswold had been waiting for her moment before the court for years; up until this point, she had taken a backseat to the litigation and the role of the attorneys. She took advantage of this opportunity to present a detailed and lengthy description of the clinic, the work they did, and her feelings on how contraception promoted family planning and the health of the mother. Also called to the stand was Dr. Buxton. The gist of his testimony focused on his medical expertise and experience in the field of obstetrics and gynecology, as well as the fact that throughout the country, doctors were free to do what he had done in Connecticut, namely give advice and prescribe contraception to married women. To reinforce Buxton's testimony regarding the health, safety, and moral implications of using birth control, two New Haven physicians who were unaffiliated with Planned Parenthood testified.

For the most part, the trial went smoothly; there were no protestors lining the streets outside; no death threats or bomb plots were uncovered. The only notable event was when James Morris, the citizen who initially reported the existence of the clinic to police, stood up in the middle of open court and began shouting. Refusing to comply with the judge's orders to remain quiet and seated, Morris was removed from the courtroom.

The day after the defense rested their case, on January 2, 1962, Judge Lacey made his final decision regarding whether Buxton and Griswold had, in fact, violated the statute. With the denial of Roraback's demurrer prior to the trial, it seemed rather obvious what his decision would be from the very beginning. He formally declared that both Buxton and Griswold were guilty of violating Connecticut General Statutes Sections 53-32 and 54-196. "It is therefore adjudged by the court that the accused is guilty in the manner and form as charged in said complaint." Both Buxton and Griswold were fined $100 for their actions.

A number of detailed findings regarding the case were issued by Judge Lacey on June 12, 1962, and Roraback soon appealed several of them. On September 13, 1962, Roraback filed an assignment of errors asserting that the circuit court erred in overruling the demurrers submitted for Griswold and Buxton, and because the court did not find that the statute was unconstitutional.

Oral arguments were heard before Judges Kosicki, Pruyn, and Dearington in the appellate court in New Haven on October 19, 1962. The court, recognizing they were dealing with important issues, noted in their opinion that:

> [t]he questions involved are deemed to be of great public importance and it is found that there are substantial questions of law which should be reviewed by the Supreme Court of Errors, namely:
> 1. Have the defendants been denied their rights to liberty and property without due process of law, in violation of the Fourteenth Amendment of the Constitution of the United States?
> 2. Have the defendants been denied their rights to freedom of speech and communication of ideas under the First and Fourteenth Amendments to the Constitution of the United States and Sections 5 and 6 of Article first of the Constitution of Connecticut?

Having recognized the importance of the issues, the court proceeded to affirm the trial court's decision on January 7, 1963, holding there was no error made at trial.

On January 31, Roraback filed a petition for certification by the Supreme Court of Errors to have the case reexamined by the state's highest court. Again, Roraback asked the court to find unconstitutional and repeal the antiquated nineteenth-century law. The petition asked that eight separate questions be certified and answered by the Supreme Court; for example, Roraback asked the court to decide whether the lower court erred

- in finding that offenses were committed in violation of the provisions of Section 53-32...when married women used contraceptives...
- in finding that the appellants assisted the commission of such offenses by supervising and participating in the operation of a medical center where these married women sought and obtained these contraceptives...
- in finding that the specific speech and conduct of these defendants constituted assisting, abetting, counseling, causing and commanding these married women to commit these offenses...
- in failing to find that the application of sections 53-32 and 54-196...violated their rights to freedom of speech and to life, liberty and property without due process of law...
- in failing to conclude that the defendant Dr. Buxton was required by the accepted standards of the medical profession to commit the actions which he did...

Roraback asserted that Buxton and Griswold could "not be charged as 'accessories' to the commission of an act which is itself not an 'offense,' and that there is no substantive offense charged or proven here, since the use by married women of drugs, medicinal articles and instruments to prevent contraception in their marital relations cannot be constitutionally held to come within the purview of permissible legislative action."

The petition was granted on February 19 of that year and oral arguments were prepared once again. While waiting for oral arguments, several notable events occurred. The 1963 bill that had been introduced to the legislature amending the law to create a physician's exception again failed to pass; it seemed as though a legislative amendment to the law was almost certainly impossible. Growing tired of the battle, however, was the Catholic Church; Connecticut representatives publicly came out and said they would no longer lobby in support of the laws that were on the books in Connecticut and Massachusetts. Also of note was Estelle Griswold's resignation from Planned Parenthood. Construction was underway at the newly purchased headquarters on Orange Street in New Haven. During the transition, the Griswolds were offered the chance to buy a carriage house on an adjacent piece of property to use as their primary residence. This had the effect of ruffling some feathers within the organization and it opened the door for criticism of Estelle's leadership and management of Planned Parenthood. Estelle, feeling hurt and unsupported, resigned, but other members of Planned Parenthood quickly talked her into withdrawing her resignation.

Oral argument before the Connecticut Supreme Court of Errors took place on November 12, 1963. Roraback had submitted an almost sixty-page brief in defense of her position. Julius Maretz, who had been the prosecuting attorney thus far, had been replaced by Joseph Clark. Arguments lasted only a little over two hours, and based on the line of questioning by newly appointed Chief Justice John King, it looked as though the court might rule in favor of Planned Parenthood. Much of the oral argument focused on the overbroad nature of the law.

Soon after oral arguments, Planned Parenthood made use of their new location on Orange Street and opened as an informational center. No doctors or nurses were on hand to give advice, exams, or prescriptions, but plenty of information was available and distributed. James Morris, the ever-present citizen who complained about the clinic in the first place,

Long an opponent of efforts to repeal Connecticut's birth control statute, James Morris of West Haven, Connecticut, pickets the new information center of Planned Parenthood League on Orange Street in New Haven, December 9, 1963. © *Bettmann/Corbis*.

continued his battle against contraception by picketing in front of the clinic with a large sign that read, "The Law is the Law or Is It? Morality is in danger!" Morris was there long enough to be photographed and the famous photo ran in a number of newspapers across the country.

On April 28, 1964, the Connecticut Supreme Court of Errors announced its decision. Based on a long line of previous decisions addressing the same statute, the court held that the law was constitutional. This was the logical and expected response by the court as it was unlikely they would have thrown out their previous decisions and dramatically changed direction. The unanimous opinion was written by Justice John Comley, and was relatively short. In rejecting the defendant's claims, the court adhered

> to the principle that courts may not interfere with the exercise by a state of the police power to conserve the public safety and welfare, including health and morals, if the law has a real and substantial relation to the accomplishment of those objects. The legislature is primarily the judge of the regulations required to that end, and its police statutes may be declared unconstitutional only when they are arbitrary or unreasonable attempts to exercise its authority in the public interest...Furthermore, as pointed out in *Buxton v. Ullman*, the General Assembly has not recognized that the interest of the general public calls for the repeal or modification of the statute as heretofore construed by us. It is our conclusion that the conviction of the defendants was not an invasion of their constitutional rights.

THE FINAL STOP

And so, the Connecticut courts had their final say regarding the issues of contraception and privacy. The last and final stop on this long and winding legal journey would be the U.S. Supreme Court. In going before the federal court, Fowler Harper, a more experienced appellate attorney, once again took the lead position, replacing Roraback. This time around though, Harper's health was precarious and so Roraback stayed ready. On July 22, 1964, Harper filed notice with the U.S. Supreme Court to let them know he was coming.

In his brief, Harper once again asserted that the statute was unconstitutional because it deprived the appellants, as well as their patients, of their liberty without due process, that it denied them their rights to freedom of speech and communication of ideas, and that on its face, it was unconstitutional as applied to married couples because it was an "unreasonable and unjustifiable invasion of their privacy contrary to the Fourth, Ninth and Fourteenth Amendments."

Harper continued, "[t]he statutes challenged regulate the practice of medicine in an arbitrary, unreasonable and unscientific manner which seriously restricts physicians in the practice of their profession and jeopardizes the lives and health of their patients."

Also included in Harper's briefs were the following arguments:

- use of contraceptives is beneficial to family planning;
- restriction to contraceptives increases the rate of illegal abortions and illegitimate births, which in turn leads to neglect and delinquency;
- making contraception available is in line with the national plan to fight poverty in that, "to fight poverty without birth control is to fight with one hand tied behind the back;"
- Buxton and Griswold's right to make a living is being unreasonably restricted by the state; and
- the rights of third parties will not be protected otherwise than through a criminal proceeding of this type.

In his conclusion, Harper noted that the "issues in these cases are of great importance to these appellants and their patients and of far-reaching importance to the medical profession. It is submitted that the First, Fourth, Ninth and Fourteenth Amendments to the Constitution forbid the State of Connecticut to enact laws which fly in the face of both common sense and science and which unreasonably and arbitrarily restrict physicians and clinic workers from giving their patients from receiving the best medical advice and care available."

Joseph Clark prepared the brief submitted on behalf of the state. The brief focused mainly on the fact that previous case law repeatedly held that this statute was properly maintained by the legislature for protection of the public health and morals. Clark also mentioned procedural issues with Harper's brief, including the assertion that Harper's constitutional claims were not brought in the correct fashion, and in fact, some of them could not be brought at all since they had not been brought up in previous stages of the litigation. Clark's hope that the court would dismiss the case for these procedural deficiencies did not last long.

On December 3, 1964, *Griswold v. Connecticut* survived the "Rule of Four" test with excellence as all nine justices voted to hear it. On December 7, the Court issued its official announcement noting jurisdiction and the case was officially placed on the Supreme Court's docket.

Unfortunately, Harper's health had taken a turn for the worse, and he was hospitalized on December 1, just days before the Court announced they would hear the case. Unable to argue from his hospital bed, Harper quickly found a colleague to assist Roraback with the rest of the proceedings. Thomas Emerson, a fellow Yale faculty member, accepted Harper's request and rapidly got himself up to speed. Just a few weeks later, on January 8, 1965, Harper died at the age of 67. Going forward with the case without Harper was a difficult task; he had truly acted as the backbone of the litigation thus far, and his death created a large void in the Planned Parenthood team.

The brief on behalf of Buxton and Griswold was submitted by Emerson on February 11, 1965, and began with a tribute to Harper, "[t]he authors of this brief wish to record their great and obvious debt to Professor Fowler V. Harper, who worked on this matter up to the time of his death on January 8, 1965." The American Civil Liberties Union, the Catholic Council on Civil Liberties, the Planned Parenthood Federation of America, as well as a group of 141 obstetricians and gynecologists throughout the country filed a number of amicus briefs in favor of reversal. The most surprising of the amicus was the Catholic Council. In their motion to file their brief, they stated that "the interest of the Catholic Council of Civil Liberties...is two-fold: CCCL's general concern as a civil liberties organization with the rights and freedoms of all; and more specifically, a belief that an argument presented from a Catholic perspective may truly be of aid to the Court in its adjudication of the sensitive issues raised by this case."

When oral arguments began on March 29, 1965, they brought quite the crowd with them. Members of the audience included Mrs. Robert F. Kennedy, wife of the New York senator, who had nine children, as well as Mrs. Edward Kennedy, wife of the Massachusetts senator, who had two children.

Emerson spoke on behalf of Buxton and Griswold and Clark spoke on behalf of the state. Their presentation was made to the nine Supreme Court justices—Earl Warren, Hugo Black, William Douglas, Tom Clark, John Harlan, William Brennan, Potter Stewart, Byron White, and Arthur Goldberg. Both attorneys were peppered with questions throughout their presentations. Emerson focused on hammering the arguments that there is a right to privacy implicit in the Constitution, as well as the fact that professional doctors should be free from the state's unnecessary intervention in the treatment of their patients regarding contraceptives. Clark argued that the statute was a valid exercise of the legislature's police power in that they were able to legislate to protect the health and morals of society as they saw fit.

Oral arguments only took two days, but it would take the Court more than two months to issue an opinion. On June 7, 1965 the Court issued a 7-2 decision in favor of Griswold and Buxton which repealed the statute; Potter Stewart and Hugo Black dissented from the plurality; Goldberg, Harlan, and White concurred in the Court's judgment. In all, six different opinions were written.

In the majority opinion, written by Justice Douglas, the Court noted that the case:

> concerns a relationship lying within the zone of privacy created by several fundamental constitutional guarantees. And it concerns a law which, in forbidding the *use* of contraceptives rather than regulating their manufacture or sale, seeks to achieve its goals by means having a maximum destructive impact upon that relationship. Such a law cannot stand in light of the familiar principle, so often applied by this Court, that a governmental purpose to control or prevent activities constitutionally subject to state regulation may not be achieved by means which sweep unnecessarily broadly and thereby invade the area of protected freedoms. Would we allow the police to search the sacred precincts of marital bedrooms for telltale signs of the use of contraceptives? The very idea is repulsive to the notions of privacy surrounding the marriage relationship.

The main thrust of Goldberg's concurring opinion was that he agreed that the statute was unconstitutional, but he did not agree with the assertion that "due process, as used in the Fourteenth Amendment incorporates all of the first eight Amendments." He did, however, agree that the right to privacy is a heretofore undocumented but fundamental right emanating from previous rights and implicit within the Constitution, and that the "Framers did not intend that the first eight amendments be construed to exhaust the basic and fundamental rights which the Constitution guaranteed to the people."

Harlan's concurrence noted that he agreed with the reversal, but not with the Court's justification. Harlan did not find it to be necessary that the law restricted a fundamental right as guaranteed by the Bill of Rights in order for it to be unconstitutional. Instead, in Harlan's view, "the proper constitutional inquiry in this case is whether this Connecticut statute infringes the Due Process Clause of the Fourteenth Amendment because the enactment violates basic values 'implicit in the concept of ordered liberty.'" As he had previously stated in his dissent in *Poe v. Ullman*, Harlan found that the statute did so violate the basic values of ordered liberty.

White's opinion spoke mostly about the fact that the statute was unconstitutional because the state did not have a compelling reason to keep it on the books. "I wholly fail to see how the ban on the use of contraceptives by married couples in any way reinforces the State's ban on illicit sexual relationships...I find nothing in this record justifying the sweeping scope of this statute, with its telling effect on the freedoms of married persons, and therefore conclude that it deprives such persons of liberty without due process of law."

Though the two dissenters both indicated they did not agree with the law, they both found it to be constitutional. Black stated that he found the law "every bit as offensive to me as it is to my Brethren of the majority and my Brothers Harlan, White and Goldberg." Even Stewart found it to be "an uncommonly silly law," noting that "the use of contraceptives in the relationship of marriage should be left to personal and private choice."

Black was unable to see past the fact that Griswold and Buxton "admittedly engaged with others in a planned course of conduct to help people violate the Connecticut law." Black also did not find the argument that a right to privacy was implicit in the constitution a convincing one. "The Court talks about a constitutional 'right of privacy' as though there is some constitutional provision or provisions forbidding any law ever to be passed which might abridge the 'privacy' of individuals. But there is not...I like my privacy as well as the next one, but I am nevertheless compelled to admit that government has a right to invade it unless prohibited by some constitutional provision."

Black also did not think it wise to overturn the statute, preferring to give the Connecticut legislature the benefit of the doubt. "Perhaps it is not too much to say that no legislative body ever does pass laws without believing that they will accomplish a sane, rational, wise and justifiable purpose." While Black recognized that the Court did in fact have a power to overturn unconstitutional laws, he found that "there is no provision of the Constitution which either expressly or impliedly vests power in this Court to sit as a supervisory agency over acts of duly constituted legislative bodies and set aside their laws because of the Court's belief that the legislative polices adopted are unreasonable, unwise, arbitrary, capricious or irrational."

Stewart saw the case, not as asking the justices to "say whether we think this law is unwise or even asinine. We are asked to hold that it violates the United States Constitution. And that I cannot do." Stewart, like Douglas, also could not fathom that a "right to privacy" existed in the Constitution. "The Court says it is the right of privacy 'created by several fundamental constitutional guarantees.' With all deference, I can find no

June 6, 1965, New Haven, Conn. Mrs. Estelle Griswold on left, medical advisor and executive director of Planned Parenthood Clinic in New Haven, and Mrs. Ernest Jahncke, president of Parenthood League of Conn., Inc., flash victory sign as the result of court's decision. © *Planned Parenthood of Connecticut.*

such general right of privacy in the Bill of Rights, in any other part of the Constitution, or in any case ever before decided by this Court." Stewart noted that "it is not the function of this Court to decide cases on the basis of community standards...It is the essence of judicial duty to subordinate our own personal views, our own ideas of what legislation is wise and what is not." Stewart saw the only constitutional way as taking the law off the books was for "the people of Connecticut [to] freely exercise their true Ninth and Tenth Amendment rights and persuade their elected representatives to repeal it."

Even though there were two strong dissents, with the plurality's decision in favor of Griswold and Buxton, the law, which had its beginnings in 1873, was officially repealed once and for all, almost 100 years later in 1965.

The Connecticut case, which had its roots in New Haven, affected the entire nation. For the first time, a law was struck down for violating the "right to privacy" which a plurality of the Court held existed implicitly within the Constitution. Never before had a citizen's privacy been held in such high regard. The era of government interference with the people's personal lives met the beginning of the end with *Griswold*. The case has been cited almost 10,000 times since 1965 by courts in every state in the nation, and every federal circuit. It has been talked about in over 6,300 articles in law reviews around the nation as well. *Griswold* changed the way American law treated privacy, and for that, it will always be remembered. In addition, *Griswold* became the foundation for later Court cases dealing with women's reproductive rights. In 1972, the U.S. Supreme Court ruled in *Eisenstadt v. Baird* that the right of privacy was extended to individuals. The case legalized birth control for unmarried women. In addition, in 1973 with *Roe v. Wade*, the Court recognized the right of women to choose abortion.

1. Connecticut Bar Foundation James W. Cooper Fellows Oral History of Connecticut Women in the Legal Profession Project, Catherine Roraback Interviews. September 14, 2004.
2. Connecticut Bar Foundation James W. Cooper Fellows Oral History of Connecticut Women in the Legal Profession Project, Catherine Roraback Interviews. May 4, 2004.
3. *Ibid*.
4. *Ibid*.
5. *Ibid*., September 14, 2004.

See Appendix D for the text of the U.S. Supreme Court decision in *Griswold v. Connecticut*.

5

The Circus Comes to New Haven
The Trial of the Black Panthers

In October of 1966, Bobby Seale and Huey Newton formed the Black Panther Party for Self Defense. The party's stated purpose was to promote and protect the civil rights of the African American citizens in California. Little did Seale know that the group he helped form would radically change the face of the nation, and cause him to be involved in some of the most heated legal proceedings the country had ever seen.

Bobby Seale was born Robert George Seale on October 22, 1936, in Dallas, Texas. He and his parents moved several times before ultimately settling in Oakland, California, during the 1940s. Bobby, as everyone called him, did not do well in school; feeling as though his skin color put him at a disadvantage, he left high school to join the U.S. Air Force. Three years after joining the Air Force, he was court-martialed and given a dishonorable discharge for disobedience. After leaving the Air Force, Seale returned to Oakland, working in factories and going to school for his high school diploma at night.

Huey Newton, born on February 17, 1942, in Monroe, Louisiana, was named after former Louisiana governor, Huey Pierce Long. He was the youngest of seven children, and he and his family relocated to Oakland during the 1940s. Newton was arrested for the first time at age 14 for gun possession and vandalism. He finished Oakland High School and went on to earn his Associate of Arts degree from Merritt College in Oakland. Though Newton did not earn a law degree, he studied law at Oakland City College and San Francisco Law School.

PANTHER BEGINNINGS

Seale and Newton met in the 1960s during the Cuban missile crisis; demonstrations and rallies were being held frequently in California and both men were students at Merritt College in Oakland at the time. They were both involved in numerous causes, and were passionate participants in the rallies. According to Seale's book *Seize the Time*, during one of the rallies, Newton was "holding down a crowd of about 250 people, and [Bobby] was one of the participants." Seale approached Newton to talk about civil rights laws, but according to Seale, Newton "shot him down." Several days after their initial encounter, Seale sought Newton out at the Merritt College Library in West Oakland and asked when Newton's group, the Afro-American Association, was meeting next. Newton provided an address and told him that they would be discussing the book, *Black Bourgeoisie* by E. Franklin Frazier at the next meeting.

The way Seale explains it, Newton was a natural and creative leader, and not afraid to step and think out of the box. The bond between the pair grew over the years, culminating in their ultimate partnership, the creation of the Black Panthers. Before the Black Panther Party was born, the two began the Soul Students Advisory Council (SSAC) at Merritt. The goal of the council was to create a group of students on campus that served the needs of black citizens, both at the school and in the community. Seale noted that they wanted to "serve the black community in a revolutionary fashion."

The pair's involvement in the SSAC did not last for long. They were wrongly arrested, seemingly only because their skin was black. They used money from the group's treasury to post bail and hired a lawyer. When controversy ensued over their use of the funds, they both resigned. According to Seale, they said, "We're going to the black community and we intend to organize in the black community and organize an organization to lead the black liberation struggle."

A few months after the break with the SSAC, in late September 1966, Newton said, "It's about time we get the organization off the ground, and do it now." This was the beginning of the Black Panther Party. "Huey and I began to write out a ten-point platform and program of the Black Panther party," Seale said. The point of creating a platform was so that people could relate to the organization and understand the party's concerns and goals. The program was divided into two main sections: "What we Want" and "What we Believe." Although the platform served as a basis for the organization, it also attracted potential members to the party.

The October 1966 version of the ten-point platform included the following:

- *We want freedom. We want power to determine the destiny of our Black Community.*

    We believe that black people will not be free until we are able to determine our destiny.

- *We want an immediate end to POLICE BRUTALITY and MURDER of black people.*

    We believe we can end police brutality in our black community by organizing black self-defense groups that are dedicated to defending our black community from racist police oppression and brutality. The Second Amendment to the Constitution of the United States gives a right to bear arms. We therefore believe that all black people should arm themselves for self-defense.

- *We want freedom for all black men held in federal, state, county and city prisons and jails.*

    We believe that all black people should be released from the many jails and prisons because they have not received a fair and impartial trial.

- *We want all black people when brought to trial to be tried in court by a jury of their peer group or people from their black communities, as defined by the Constitution of the United States.*

    We believe that the courts should follow the United States Constitution so that black people will receive fair trials. The 14th Amendment of the U.S. Constitution gives a man a right to be tried by his peer group. A peer is a person from a similar economic, social, religious, geographical, environmental, historical and racial background. To do this the court will be forced to select a jury from the black community from which the black defendant came. We have been, and are being tried by all-white juries that have no understanding of the "average reasoning man" of the black community.

- *We want land, bread, housing, education, clothing, justice and peace. And as our major political objective, a United Nations-supervised plebiscite to be held throughout the black colony in which only black colonial subjects will be allowed to participate for the purpose of determining the will of black people as to their national destiny.*

We hold these truths to be self evident, that all men are created equal; that they are endowed by their Creator with certain unalienable rights; that among these are life, liberty, and the pursuit of happiness. That, to secure these rights, governments are instituted among men, deriving their just powers from the consent of the governed; that, whenever any form of government becomes destructive of these ends, it is the right of the people to alter or to abolish it, and to institute a new government, laying its foundation on such principles, and organizing its powers in such form, as to them shall seem most likely to effect their safety and happiness. Prudence, indeed, will dictate that governments long established should not be changed for light and transient causes; and accordingly, all experience hath shown, that mankind are more disposed to suffer, while evils are sufferable, than to right themselves by abolishing the forms to which they are accustomed. But, when a long train of abuses and usurpations, pursuing invariably the same object, evinces a design to reduce them under absolute despotism, it is their right, it is their duty, to throw off such government, and to provide new guards for their future security.

After drafting the ten-point program, Newton decided the group needed a solid structure to build upon, and asked Seale whether he would prefer to be the chairman of the party or minister of defense; Seale told Newton to decide. Newton became minister of defense, and Seale became the chairman. According to Seale, they made over 1,000 copies of the ten-point program to distribute throughout the community. While passing out the platform at the North Oakland Neighborhood Anti-Poverty Center where Seale worked, someone inquired about the group's mascot and asked, "Why do you want to be a vicious animal like a panther?"

According to Seale, Newton explained that, "the nature of the panther is that he never attacks. But if anyone attacks him or backs him into a corner, the panther comes up to wipe that aggressor or that attacker out, absolutely, resolutely, wholly, thoroughly, and completely."

The first member of the Black Panther Party for Self Defense, besides Seale and Newton, was Bobby Hutton, often referred to as Little Bobby, because he was only 16 at the time. The three men opened an office for the party, which Seale said was important to Newton because the "establishment of an office meant that something was functional. The people in the black community could relate to it." The office, located on 56th and Grove Streets in Oakland, officially opened on January 1, 1967. The first meeting of the party was held one week later, and "the next thing we knew, we had about thirty, maybe forty members of the Party," Seale said.

A noteworthy aspect of the Panthers was their philosophy that black citizens should arm themselves with guns in order to patrol, and keep in check, the police force, which they commonly referred to as "pigs." Armed Panthers, with the aim of stopping police harassment, followed police patrols as the officers walked or drove through the ghettos of Oakland. Some people saw this use of guns as unnecessary and inappropriate; many were worried the Panthers were teaching children it was acceptable to use guns and were sending the wrong messages. The Panther's premise for carrying the guns was based on legal research conducted by Newton and Seale; Newton was taking classes at San Francisco Law School and made sure he knew the ins and outs of what he and his fellow citizens could and could not do, not only regarding the carrying of guns, but also concerning their Constitutional rights when stopped by police, how much information they had to give, and how far an officer could legally go when interrogating them. At that time, California law allowed citizens to carry concealed weapons.

The Panthers were also very cognizant about children; children were not allowed into the party offices because of the guns stored there. Newton began teaching black history classes for children and young adults at local community centers in order to promote education and involvement with the party. The party also promoted sobriety and did not allow members to be drunk while at the office; they were also active in producing anti-drug literature in the community. One of the Panther's main goals was to establish and develop community outreach programs. Some of the programs initiated by the party from 1966 to 1982 included consumer education classes; free food, furniture, shoes, dental, and optometry programs; community health classes; disabled persons services and transportation; employment referral services; police patrols; teen programs; and a Sickle Cell Anemia research program, among many others. Though some of their initial aims seemed to be public-spirited, many people in the community were put off and even frightened by some of the tactics displayed by the Panthers.

The party printed its first newspaper on April 25, 1967. The first *Black Panther, Black Community News Service*, as it was called, comprised two sheets of legal paper, printed on both sides. The impetus for starting the paper was the killing of party member Denzil Dowell by the police. The newspaper was used as a vehicle to publicize police brutality in the area as well as to promote Panther membership and Panther ideals. Party members Eldridge Cleaver and Huey Newton were instrumental in getting the paper off the ground; they soon met Emory Douglas, who quickly became involved in the party and the paper. His political cartoons drove home the Panther's ideology and his use of the pig to represent the police quickly became his trademark.

THE PANTHERS AND THE GOVERNMENT

Exacerbated with the Panther's widespread gun wielding, the California legislature quickly moved to change the law that authorized citizens to bear arms in public as long as the weapons were not concealed. Legislator Don Mulford introduced the bill that prohibited the carrying of firearms in public places and on public streets. The proposed legislation caused quite a stir, and the Panthers decided not to allow legislators to strike down this law, at least not without having their voices heard.

Newton and Seale organized a group of Panthers to go to the capital at Sacramento on May 2, 1967, in order to send a message to the legislature—and to all of America—that the Panthers were serious about their Constitutional rights and that they were not about to let anyone step on them. As Seale stated in his memoirs, "On 2 May 1967 we went across the bridge to Sacramento with a caravan of cars. There were 30 brothers and sisters—20 of the brothers were armed...A lot of people were looking. A lot of white people were shocked, just looking at us." The legislature was to conduct hearings on the proposed gun control legislation that day. The Panthers, whose "uniform" consisted of black berets, black leather jackets, black trousers, and blue shirts, walked up to the steps of the capital with their guns pointed in the air. The goal was to read to the Assembly "Executive Mandate Number One" as written by Newton:

> Excerpt Executive Mandate Number One
> Statement by the Minister of Defense
> Delivered May 2, 1967 at Sacramento, California, State Capitol Building
> The Black Panther Party for Self-Defense calls upon the American people in general and the black people in particular to

take careful note of the racist California Legislature which is now considering legislation aimed at keeping the black people disarmed and powerless at the very same time that racist police agencies throughout the country are intensifying the terror, brutality, murder, and repression of black people.

The Black Panther Party for Self-Defense believes that the time has come for black people to arm themselves against this terror before it is too late. The pending Mulford Act brings the hour of doom one step nearer. A people who have suffered so much for so long at the hands of a racist society, must draw the line somewhere. We believe that the black communities of America must rise up as one man to halt the progression of a trend that leads inevitably to their total destruction.

According to Seale, he read the mandate on the steps before the group decided to go in. When the Panthers were told that they could not enter the building with their guns, the decision was made to proceed forward. The group ended up on the floor of the senate where Seale again read the mandate. He read it again several times; the media eating it all up. They finally left and were heading home when car trouble forced them to stop at a nearby service station. It was there that police officers surrounded the group; according to Seale, they heard calls coming in over the police radio to "Arrest them all. On anything."

Twenty-six Panthers were arrested that day and taken to the jail in Sacramento. The tumultuous relationship between the Panthers and the government became even worse when the Mulford Act, as it had became known, was signed into law by then-Governor Ronald Reagan in 1967. Their day in Sacramento was far from a failure as it had the effect of raising awareness about the group to the national level and membership quickly expanded across the country. The Panthers continued to remain active over the next few years and regularly made headlines in the news, with the media portraying the Panthers as both heroes and thugs.

MURDER IN CONNECTICUT

On May 19, 1969, Panther Chairman Bobby Seale was scheduled to speak at Yale. He had traveled from California to Connecticut for the event, though it is unclear whether the speech took place or not. While in New Haven, Seale purportedly visited the Panther headquarters at 365 Orchard Street in New Haven.

The trouble brewing in New Haven made headlines on May 23, 1969, when news of Alex Rackley's murder surfaced. A *New York Times* article reported that Rackley's "mutilated body was tossed into the shallow Coginchaug River in Middlefield."

John Mroczka, a twenty-two-year-old Pratt & Whitney employee and Vietnam veteran, was taking a ride on his motorcycle on May 20, 1969, in Middlefield, a rural community that borders Middletown. An avid angler, he took a detour to his favorite spot to see if there were fish ready to be caught. Instead of finding a few trout, he found the remains of what would later be identified as Alex Rackley.

Rackley had been a member of the Black Panthers for about eight months, and some Panthers suspected that he had been acting as a police informer. Rackley was from Jacksonville, Florida, but had been residing in New York before traveling with other Panthers to Connecticut. He was the oldest of eight children. Some sources placed him at age 24 at the time of his death, others age 35. According to the book, *Murder in the Model City*, Rackley's birth certificate indicated he was only 19 when he died, just two weeks away from his twentieth birthday. While in New Haven, he was apparently tortured and eventually killed after being forced to stand what *The New York Times* called a "kangaroo trial." A kangaroo trial means a sham or a bogus legal proceeding in which a person is not allowed to defend oneself, only to take the abuse of the accusers.

Rackley's body was found at about 5:00 p.m. on May 21. His hands and feet were tied, and he had been shot twice, once in the chest and once in the head with a large-caliber pistol. There were also bruises on his body, burns from cigarettes and boiling water, ice-pick wounds, and rope marks around his wrists. The *Times* reported that the initial police reconstruction of the murder had Rackley being forcibly transported from New York to New Haven, and then held in the basement of the party's headquarters at 365 Orchard Street in New Haven against his will where his "trial" and torture took place. Police later believed that Rackley came to Connecticut of his own free will.

Only hours after Rackley's body was found, eight Black Panthers were arrested at party headquarters on Orchard Street at around 1:00 a.m. They were charged with murder, conspiracy to commit murder, kidnapping, conspiracy to commit kidnapping, and binding with criminal intent. Police raids on the headquarters, which lasted several days, also netted tape recordings of Rackley's last hours on earth. According to a *Times* interview with a police officer involved in the investigation, the tapes were about 40 minutes long and contained portions of Rackley's trial; the torture was reportedly referred to as "discipline." "Eighty percent of it is him trying to defend himself. It's very emotional stuff," the police officer said.

The eight party members arrested at this time included Ericka Huggins, 21; Warren Kimbro, 35; Margaret Hudgins, 21; Maud Francis, 17; Jeanne Wilson, 18; Rose Smith, 21; and George Edwards, 31, all of New Haven; and Francis Carter, 20, of Trumbull. Police held the group without bail at the New Haven State Jail. On May 28, the ninth party member was arrested in connection with Rackley's murder. Lorretta Luckes, 21, of Bridgeport was charged with the same offenses as the others. Lonnie McLucas, 23, a top Black Panther leader in Connecticut, was arrested in Salt Lake City on June 5; the police had been looking for him in North Carolina where his parents lived.

On June 24, 1969, after 15 minutes of deliberation, a grand jury in Middletown indicted Lonnie McLucas, Warren Kimbro, and George Sams Jr., who at the time was still at large, for first-degree murder. A grand jury in New Haven indicted all 11 Panthers on charges of kidnapping and nine of them on charges of aiding and abetting murder.

On June 5, Landon Williams, 25, and Rory Hithe, 18, were arrested in connection with the murder in Denver; they remained there for quite some time fighting extradition. Black Panther Chairman Bobby Seale, who police suspected of having ordered Rackley's murder, was arrested on August 19 in Berkley, California, making him the thirteenth of the 14 Panthers to be arrested in connection with the homicide. Seale was charged with kidnap, conspiracy to kidnap, murder, and conspiracy to murder. At the time of his arrest, Seale was still on probation for his involvement with the 1967 gun control demonstration at the legislature in Sacramento.

According to *The New York Times*, with Seale's arrest, "most of the top officers of the party, which had its national headquarters in Berkeley, were now in jail, out on bail, or living outside the country." The *Times* also noted that upon his being arrested, Seale's defense lawyer, Francis McTernan, quickly asserted that the Justice Department was "initiating a national campaign to harass the party." The *Times* also reported that McTernan asserted that not only was Seale's arrest "ridiculous," but that his $25,000 bond was "ridiculously high." According to the article, Attorney McTernan also said that Seale "knew absolutely nothing" about the New Haven charges, and predicted they would never be proved.

The last person to be arrested in connection with Rackley's murder was George Sams, Jr. Dressed as a minister, Sams had escaped to Canada. Police captured Sams on August 7, 1969, in Toronto.

THE PEOPLE BEHIND THE CHARGES

ERICKA HUGGINS

Ericka Huggins became politically active in 1963 after attending a protest march in Washington, D.C., where she had grown up. It was at that event that she decided she would become an active participant in working for social change in America. In an interview with the BBC, Huggins said that "I wanted to go [to the march], but my parents said no. I reminded my mother that she had always spoken of the need to step forward for our people and to make a difference. But she replied that she didn't mean for me to do it. I went anyway."

According to her interview, Huggins drove to California to join the Panthers. "I read about young people who were patrolling the police and encouraging people to say no to police brutality. This was the Black Panther Party and I wanted to be part of it," she said in the interview. In 1969, Huggins became involved with the party and served as a leader within the Los Angeles chapter. She held a leadership position in the party for 14 years, longer than any other female Panther. Her husband John, also a party member, was shot and killed in Oakland by members of a black nationalist group, a rival to the Black Panthers, just three weeks after their daughter was born. John Huggins had grown up in New Haven and when his body was brought to Connecticut for burial, Ericka Huggins journeyed to New Haven for the funeral and stayed, deciding to open a chapter of the party there. In 1970, *The New York Times* described Huggins as "a tall attractive woman with an Afro hairdo."

When Huggins was arrested and put in jail, she did not make friends with the prison guards or allow anyone to sway her; she maintained her innocence. She and the other arrested women were sent to the women's prison in Niantic where they were treated as convicted prisoners, instead of the pretrial detainees they actually were.

WARREN KIMBRO

In 1969, Warren Kimbro was working with an anti-poverty organization in New Haven. A group of Black Panthers recruited him to help launch a New Haven chapter of the party. Within a few months, the headquarters of the party was housed in Kimbro's home, Apartment B-13 at 365 Orchard Street.

From the time Kimbro was arrested until Bobby Seale was brought to Connecticut, Kimbro was jailed in the Montville prison where he befriended many of the guards. Once Seale arrived, the two men were separated—Seale was housed in Montville, while Kimbro was sent to a jail in Brooklyn, Connecticut, where George Sams, Jr. was also being held.

While at the prison in Brooklyn, Kimbro earned credits from Eastern Connecticut State University; professor and friend, Jim Tipton, along with two other colleagues, agreed to teach Kimbro college-level courses while he was in jail. He even wrote for the prison newspaper *The Tier* and served as a counselor to other inmates.

On January 16, 1970, Warren Kimbro pled guilty to second-degree murder and admitted to driving Rackley to Middlefield and killing him. Some Panthers asserted that Kimbro was forced to change his position and plead guilty by his brother, a police officer from Dade County, Florida. They pointed out that Warren Kimbro only changed his plea after his brother, William, whom he had not seen in two years, visited him in jail. William stayed in a hotel under an assumed name and the Office of the State's Attorney paid for his travel expenses. After her husband pled guilty, Kimbro's wife, Sylvia, withdrew the divorce proceeding that she had initiated.

Margaret Hudgins and Frances Carter

Frances Carter was one of the founding members of the New Haven chapter of the Black Panther Party and served as the chapter's secretary. Margaret, aka Peggy, Hudgins, was also an early member of the party. Hudgins and McLucas, as it was revealed at his trial, thought of each other as husband and wife, though they were not legally married.

Hudgins, 21 at the time of her arrest, pled guilty to aggravated assault after spending 467 days in jail without bail. Judge Harold Mulvey sentenced Hudgins to 18 months to five years in prison, but he suspended her sentence because she had served so much time already. Hudgins was one of five Panthers who challenged the state's right to deny them bail. Joining in the bail hearing were Ericka Huggins, Rose Marie Smith, George Edwards, and Frances Carter. After 11 days of testimony beginning on November 12, 1969, Judge Aaron Palmer denied the petition for bail for four of the five defendants. According to *The New York Times*, because Judge Palmer found that the "circumstances disclosed at the bail hearing indicate a fair likelihood that the defendants… [are] in danger of conviction," he was able to properly deny bail. He did find, however, that Frances Carter was not in danger of such a conviction, and ordered another hearing to determine the appropriate amount of bail.

When initially interrogated by police after Rackley's body was found, Carter admitted she had seen Rackley being held captive at Kimbro's apartment in New Haven. She was jailed for contempt of court after refusing to further testify against the other Panthers; she was denied bail.

The bail hearing was the first of its kind to be held in Connecticut. Because there was no state law to rely on in making his decision, Judge Palmer referred to recently decided cases from New Jersey that dealt with the same issue. The New Jersey cases required that the state go "beyond the legal requirement of probable cause, but not so far as proof beyond a reasonable doubt," in proving why bail should be denied.

Before the hearing, the women were imprisoned at the Niantic jail for women. There, Carter, who was pregnant, gave birth while shackled to her bed in the hospital where she was taken. Carter was granted bail in the amount of $2,500 on June 10, 1970.

Maud Francis and Jeanne Wilson

Maud Francis and Jeanne Wilson were the juveniles charged in connection with Rackley's murder. After police arrested both of them with the others on May 22, 1969, at 365 Orchard Street, they were taken into the custody of the juvenile court later that day. Because their cases were dealt with in juvenile court, their records were sealed. Francis and Wilson were released from incarceration in December of 1969.

Rose Marie Smith

Rose Smith was arrested with the other Panthers on May 22, 1969, at Panther headquarters. On June 23, she was indicted for aiding and abetting murder and kidnapping. On June 25, she was accused in a substitute information of conspiracy to murder, conspiracy to kidnap, and binding with intent to commit a crime. Two days later, she pled not guilty to all counts and charges. She was denied bail on December 29. After spending 467 days in jail without bail, Smith eventually changed her mind and pled guilty on one count of aggravated assault. Judge Mulvey sentenced her to 18 months to five years in prison, but he suspended her sentence because she had already served so much time in jail.

Loretta Luckes

New Haven police officers arrested Loretta Luckes on May 28, 1969, only a few weeks after she had joined the Black Panther Party. Luckes, who was pregnant at the time she was arrested, later gave birth in jail. On June 23, 1969, a New Haven superior court grand jury indicted Luckes for aiding and abetting murder and kidnapping. On June 25, 1969, she was accused in a substitute information of conspiracy to murder, conspiracy to kidnap, and binding with the intent to commit a crime. She pled guilty to all counts and charges that same day.

On December 1, 1969, a few hours after George Sams, Jr. pled guilty, Loretta Luckes changed her plea to guilty of conspiracy to kidnap. Luckes then testified against five other Panthers waiting in jail who were seeking to be released on bail. According to Luckes, all 14 people arrested in connection with the murder were at Panther headquarters on Orchard Street at some time during the four-day period that Rackley was there and being tortured. On September 10, 1970, almost a year after she pled guilty, Judge Mulvey sentenced her to a suspended sentence of 25 years. Luckes was the first of the Panthers to be sentenced. After spending 15 months in jail, she was released and placed on two years' probation.

George Sams, Jr.

George Sams, Jr., a native of Detroit, at one time held the rank of field marshal in the Black Panther Party. He is said to have spent most of his youth in New York institutions for "mental defectives," and even more time in jails. At one time, Seale expelled Sams from the party because of violence, but Stokely Carmichael, a friend of Sams and a person of power in the party, reinstated him.

On December 1, 1969, George Sams, Jr. pled guilty to second-degree murder in the slaying of Alex Rackley. Sams testified that Seale ordered him to kill Rackley. Sams' statement to police indicated that he had been ordered to help in the East Coast purging of disloyal Panthers, and that Seale personally ordered Rackley's death. Sams also admitted taking part in Rackley's torture, using boiling water to burn him. In addition, in his testimony Sams implicated Lonnie McLucas and Warren Kimbro as the other two Panthers directly involved in Rackley's murder.

Landon Williams and Rory Hithe

Both Landon Williams and Rory Hithe were high-ranking leaders in the national Black Panther Party. Arrested in Colorado on June 6, 1969, Williams and Hithe fought extradition to Connecticut for months. On December 14, 1969, they successfully delayed their extradition to Connecticut for an additional 35 days. George Sams, Jr. was flown to Colorado to identify and implicate Williams and Hithe in Rackley's murder. According to *The New York Times*, Sams identified them as "enforcers sent from California to purge East Coast chapters of the Panthers." In April 1971, Williams and Hithe chose to stop fighting the extradition orders and agreed to be voluntarily transported to Connecticut.

Bobby Seale

Police held Seale in California from August 19, 1969 until March 13, 1970, when he was flown to Connecticut to stand trial. On March 18, Seale appeared before Judge Harold Mulvey in New Haven superior court for a bail hearing. Seale stood with his attorney, Charles R. Garry from San Francisco, who was appearing with Connecticut attorney David N. Rosen. Garry could be considered the Panther's official lawyer as he had tried 38 Panther cases in the preceding three years. Judge Mulvey granted Seale a continuance in order for Seale's legal team to file preliminary motions. According to *The New York Times*, as Seale left the courtroom, whose spectator's gallery held several Panthers, he "raised a clenched fist and said: 'Right on, brothers!'" Reporters wrote that Seale's first appearance in court was "heavily-guarded." Seale showed up in an armored car and the courtroom was tightly secured as well.

Once Seale arrived in New Haven and his trial became imminent, both New Haven townspeople and the Panthers began to react. West Coast Panther leaders flew in and set up shop, beginning to plan demonstrations and rallies. Police guards were assigned twenty-four-hour duty at the superior court and new signs posted outside prohibited demonstrations, pickets, parades, or the like within 500 feet of the courthouse. David Hilliard, the most senior Panther leader not in jail, came to Connecticut to organize. According to *The New York Times*, after Seale's initial court appearance, ordinary people started to become active: "On Dixwell Avenue, a black man holds up a sign for motorists. Every so often he steps into the traffic. Like a bullfighter, he thrusts the piece of cardboard at the moving car. On it are four scribbled words: 'Free Bobby or else!'"

March 15, 1970: Bobby Seale is shown here strapped to an electric chair, indicating that he was facing the death penalty in the New Haven Black Panther trials. Seale credits this image with helping save his life. © *Emory Douglas, Image courtesy of Alden and Mary Kimbrough.*

Saturday, May 31, 1970 cover of the Black Panther newspaper. © *Emory Douglas, Image courtesy of the Center for the Study of Political Graphics.*

After Seale's first court appearance, Hilliard traveled to Storrs, Connecticut, and gave a speech to thousands of students at the University of Connecticut. Speeches to students in New Haven began to occur regularly, and soon student demonstrations spread beyond Connecticut; a group of 1,500 student demonstrators marched at Harvard to protest the Panther trials as well. The demonstrations at Harvard caused approximately $100,000 in damages due to broken windows and several cases of arson.

Almost exactly one month after Seale arrived in Connecticut, two more top Panthers were jailed. On April 14, David Hilliard and Emory Douglas wound up in jail after getting in a fight with sheriffs while at a court appearance for Seale. According to *The New York Times*, there was a dispute after Hilliard tried to receive a note from Seale, Douglas attempted to intervene, and both ended up arrested. They were charged with contempt and jailed for six months. The note Hilliard was attempting to deliver was sealed and impounded by Judge Mulvey. One week later, Hilliard and Douglas were released from prison after they apologized to Mulvey for their actions. Also apologizing to the court was Seale who, according to the *Times* said, "We understand the need for peace and decorum in the courtroom....We will maintain decorum in the courtroom." The note that Seale had given to Hilliard, which, according to Seale, was not "smuggled out" as had been reported, was actually an outline for a book he was working on. Mulvey ordered the note returned.

The day after the apologies, on April 22, George Sams, Jr. came to the witness stand for the first time to testify at a bail hearing for Seale. Seale's attorney Garry petitioned the court to have Sams examined by a psychiatrist, presenting a statement from a Detroit judge indicating that Sams had spent four years in a mental institution and that he was a "rather unstable individual." Mulvey agreed to the examination and appointed Dr. Robert Miller, then-director of the Fairfield Hills Hospital, to do the job.

The day after Sams testified, Seale's defense argued a motion to dismiss the indictments of the grand jury that were delivered in August 1969 charging Seale with kidnap and murder. Garry questioned seventy-three-year-old Sheriff John Slavin about the methodology for picking a grand jury, arguing the process was "haphazard, has no standards, and has all the elements of hand picked cronies." Twelve of the 20 members of the jury had been friends of Slavin including his barber, a former jail guard who had worked with the sheriff, and the son of a friend who wanted legal experience; one jury member was a lawyer picked from the corridor right before the proceedings began. Judge Mulvey had just dismissed a similar argument presented to him in regards to the grand jury that indicted the other

Panthers accused of murdering Rackley, indicating that he had been satisfied that the jury met both federal and state requirements.

Dr. Miller's psychiatric evaluation found Sams stable and able to give testimony in court. His report indicated that Sams was able to "report accurately, satisfactorily, and completely, events in which he was a participant, or to which he was a witness." Miller filed his report with the superior court on June 18, 1970.

THE MAY DAY RALLY

In the midst of all that was going on in court, the student body at Yale was making its own preparations. A rally was planned for the weekend of May 1 to protest government oppression of black citizens, and more specifically, Seale's impending murder trial. Many students were developing arrangements to provide food and shelter for the large crowds that were expected to show up. The students were not the only ones who decided to get involved. Kingman Brewster, then-President of Yale, became embroiled in the situation after making several comments at a faculty meeting. The meeting was called on April 23 to discuss the students' strike that had begun on April 21. Brewster's statement, which later became famous, included the following:

> I personally want to say that I am appalled and ashamed that things should have come to such a pass that I am skeptical of the ability of black revolutionaries to achieve a fair trial anywhere in the United States. In large part, the atmosphere has been created by police actions and prosecutions against the Panthers in many

Panther trial demonstration crowds New Haven green, May 1, 1970. © *Hartford Courant*.

The New Haven green rang with shouts of "Right On" and bristled with the clenched-fist symbol of the Panther Party at the rally on Saturday May 2, 1970. © *Hartford Courant*.

parts of the country. It is also one more inheritance from centuries of racial discrimination and oppression.

Brewster's comments and actions drew heated responses from the public at large, Yale alumni, the judiciary and even then-Vice President Spiro T. Agnew, who called for Brewster's resignation. As reported in *The New York Times* of April 29, 1970, Agnew called upon the Yale University alumni to demand "a more mature and responsible person" to head the college. Senior Presiding Judge Herbert MacDonald was quoted by the *Times* as saying Brewster and the students were the "ones who have created the atmosphere of which they now complain." MacDonald said that Brewster's remarks were an "awful letdown to the courts, the police, and the community in which Yale is located."

Between 12,000 and 15,000 people arrived in New Haven that weekend to participate in the rally and protest Seale's trial. The rally had been advertised as a peaceful protest, though the decision was made by the governor to request the help of federal troops; the attorney general sent in 4,000 troops. Students at Yale posted signs around the campus condemning the use of violence, as did many community groups. The signs read, "Violence is the tool of fascism," "Violence in the streets now means police retaliation in the black community later," and "Violence now will not help the New Haven Nine get out of jail."

Rock bands entertained the crowds and a number of people made speeches, including Panther leader David Hilliard. On Friday, May 1 at around 9:30 p.m., the peaceful mood of the day changed. Local police used canisters of tear gas to disperse a group of about 1,500 people who had begun throwing sulfur flares, rocks, and bottles. There were 11 arrests, although only a few minor injuries were reported. At approximately 11:50 p.m., an explosion occurred at Ingalls Hockey Rink on the Yale Campus about the same time as when a rock band that had been performing there was packing up to leave the rink. Two bombs that erupted in the basement under the stage caused the explosion. No one was seriously injured in the blast. Pleas from the Panther Party urging people off the streets were mostly heeded, and no further incidents occurred.

The rally continued peacefully on Saturday afternoon during which more than 7,000 people gathered on the New Haven green. Speakers at the Saturday rally included Area Captain of the Black Panther Party, Doug Miranda, and Bobby Seale's wife, Artie Seale. At an afternoon meeting in the courtyard of Branford College, Panthers urged the crowd to stay calm and refrain from using violence. "We are here to free the chairman, not to get maced," one Panther spokesperson told the crowd.

The police, though few in number, were equipped with full riot gear. At 2:00 p.m., an anonymous tip informed the National Guard that Molotov cocktails were being stored in a building near Canner and Livingstone Streets. Police officers found and confiscated three Coke bottles filled with gasoline and sealed with cloth wicks.

MOVING TOWARD TRIAL

The Monday after the rally, Judge Mulvey denied motions for immediate pretrial hearing on the suppression of evidence, as well as a preliminary motion to suppress an allegedly damaging statement made to the police by Lonnie McLucas. The motions concerned McLucas, Ericka Huggins, Margaret Hudgins, Rose Marie Smith, and George Edwards; Seale was not involved and not in court for the decision.

Soon after the defendants' motions were denied, the legal teams came up with new strategies to avoid trial. Theodore and Michael Koskoff, lawyers for McLucas, subpoenaed media representatives from 16 news outlets in an attempt to show that prejudicial media coverage made it impossible for their client to receive a fair trial. They filed a motion to dismiss McLucas' charges on the ground that an impartial jury could not be selected; in the alternative, they filed a similar motion for a six-month suspension of his trial. A separate trial for McLucas had been scheduled for June 9, 1970.

THE FIRST TRIAL: LONNIE MCLUCAS

McLucas' motions were unsuccessful and jury selection for his trial began on June 16. State's Attorney Arnold Markle assured the court that the state would not be seeking the death penalty for McLucas. The start of his trial was accompanied by a new set of courtroom rules; a ban on cameras and sound equipment was placed on the courthouse; the 500-feet perimeter remained in place for demonstrators outside the courthouse; and news interviews with the defendants or their lawyers were prohibited. United States Supreme Court Justices John Harlan and William Brennan both refused to hear challenges to the superior court's security rules.

While the lengthy hunt for an impartial jury continued, McLucas' defense used the time to file additional motions. They requested the court to have Huey Newton sent from prison in California in order to testify on behalf of McLucas. They also challenged Dr. Miller's psychiatric evaluation of George Sams, Jr., asserting it was inadequate and asked the court to allow them to choose another psychiatrist to examine him.

Signs banning demonstrations near the building were prominently displayed. April 22, 1970. © *Hartford Courant*.

Almost a month after jury selection began, and after 242 people were examined, including 12 blacks, a jury was selected for the McLucas trial. Twelve jurors and three alternates were chosen to hear the case; three of the regular jurors were black.

On July 13, the day before McLucas' trial was to begin, J. Edgar Hoover, then-director of the Federal Bureau of Investigation, released the Bureau's annual report. The report called the Black Panthers, "the most dangerous and violence-prone of all extremist groups." Koskoff moved for a mistrial, arguing that the report would have the effect of prejudicing the jury, but Judge Mulvey quickly denied the motion without comment.

McLucas' trial began as scheduled on Tuesday, July 14, 1970, more than a year after Rackley's body had been found. A central issue to be determined in this trial was to pinpoint who actually had given the orders for Rackley's death. On the first day, the jury was shown color slides of the victim's tortured body. They also heard testimony from Dr. Charles Chance, the medical examiner who initially examined Rackley—he estimated that Rackley had been alive when the second shot was fired into his head, the one allegedly shot by McLucas. On the second day, the jury heard testimony from Loretta Luckes who had previously pled guilty to a charge of conspiracy to kidnap. She told the jury that on the night Rackley was murdered, she saw Lonnie McLucas, Warren Kimbro, and George Sams take Rackley from headquarters with a wire hanger wrapped around his neck. Luckes also gave testimony describing the cruelty of George Sams, Jr., that many of the Panthers were afraid of him, and that he terrorized all those at the Panther headquarters.

On the third day, Frances Carter took the stand. She also testified about what happened at headquarters the day of the murder, and about Sams, Jr. In her testimony, she blamed Sams for the events surrounding Rackley's death and stated that he tried to dominate McLucas and had even disciplined McLucas that day for not participating in the torture of Rackley. Carter had been imprisoned for the previous five months on charges of contempt for refusing to testify about statements that she gave the police. On August 5, just a few weeks after she testified in the McLucas trial, her six-month sentence was reduced to five months and she was released from jail.

The string of witnesses continued for days. The jury heard from FBI agent Lynn Twede of Salt Lake City, who had interrogated McLucas on June 8, 1969, 18 days after the murder. Twede testified that McLucas admitted to firing a shot into Rackley to "make sure he was dead." Twede indicated that the reason given by McLucas for firing the shot was that he feared that "if he failed to do as ordered he would be shot by George

Sams." Koskoff attempted to have Twede's testimony suppressed because the interrogation of McLucas was done without his lawyer present even though Twede was aware that McLucas was represented by counsel. The motion was unsuccessful.

Warren Kimbro also took the stand and gave an account of the interrogation and torture of Rackley. His testimony did not incriminate Seale, an important point, since Seale was still being held without bail based solely on the testimony of George Sams, Jr., the only person who implicated him in Rackley's slaying. Kimbro also testified that he was unaware of a plan to kill Rackley until a gun was placed in his hand and he was ordered to shoot. Kimbro continued his testimony in saying that he only "assumed" that the order to execute Rackley came from the top, but that he never received such information firsthand. Kimbro also admitted to being frightened of Sams.

Several tape recordings of Rackley's torture were played to the jury, and then a transcript of the tapes was released to the news media. The jury could hear Ericka Huggins giving a description of how the beating of Rackley began and describing the "discipline" that Rackley received:

> HUGGINS: After the discipline, after the ten-point program was read there was more discipline and (Sams in the background: He said that he lied to us) he said that he lied to us, to the party and to Brother Landon about the fact that he could not read because he did read the ten point program. So then we began to realize how phony he was and that he was either an extreme fool or a pig so we began to ask questions with a little coercive force and the answers came after a few buckets of hot water. We found out that he is an informer. (Sams in the background: He's not an informer. He knows all the information.) Oh, he knows all the informers. He knows the informers in the chapter of the Black Panther Party in New York and that there's heavy infiltration there and a couple of names were given up. Shall I relate those names?
>
> SAMS: No
>
> HUGGINS: Okay. So that's basically what happened with Brother Alex and he's going to begin to tell us what, you know, what's really going on. You see. We have to know this.

Another tape of McLucas' confession was also played. In it, McLucas stated that Seale had been told about Rackley's detention at the headquarters and that his reaction to the information was passive, indicating that George (referring to Sams) would have to deal with it since he did not have time for such matters. During the recorded confession, McLucas also said that Sams told him that, "Whatever I say from now on is orders from national and they have to be carried out." This was the only authority McLucas claimed he was given to support the fact that the national Panther organization (*i.e.*, the party headquarters) was involved in ordering Rackley's killing.

While the trial progressed in the courtroom, supporters continued to rally outside, most of them white youths. There was no disruption to the court proceedings until July 28 when two such protesters were arrested for contempt. They threatened to blow up the courthouse after they were refused admission on the grounds that they were barefoot.

The days passed into weeks and the month of July came and went. The first witness to be called in August was George Sams, Jr., considered by many to be the state's star witness. His testimony, however, came only after hours of argument by Koskoff, who attempted to block the witness on the grounds that he was incompetent. The *Times* reported Judge Mulvey as saying, "I don't have the slightest hesitancy in saying this witness is competent to testify." His testimony began on August 6 and continued for three days; he was the last witness to be called by the state. The *Times* described Sams' testimony as "volatile" and "restless," with him "regularly rising out of his chair and stabbing his fingers into the air for emphasis."

Sams testified that he was authorized to "pop," or in other words, shoot, not only Rackley but also the two men who accompanied him the night he was murdered, McLucas and Kimbro, if they should exhibit any "nervous tendencies" after the job was done. He testified that such authorization came from Landon Williams. Sams also repeated the statement he gave to police earlier that the orders to kill Rackley came from upper-level party members, specifically Williams and Bobby Seale. Sams freely admitted that he was high on marijuana at the time Rackley was murdered and asserted that he did not order McLucas to fire the second shot into Rackley, but merely instructed him to see whether he was dead. While questioning the witness on cross-examination, Attorney Koskoff alluded to arguments that would be brought up by the defense, including the proposition that Sams planned Rackley's murder in order to effectuate a takeover of the party by Stokley Carmichael, who was then the "honorary" prime minister of the Black Panthers and a good friend of Sams.

Sams testified that he did not feel Rackley was an informer when he was killed, but that he was killed to straighten up the people in the New Haven chapter and to avenge the 21 Panthers that had been recently arrested in New York on unrelated charges.

Koskoff concluded his cross-examination of Sams and was able to establish several discrepancies between his testimony and the testimony of other witnesses. Sams denied doing things other witnesses had testified that he did. Sams testified in court that he smoked marijuana every day for four or five hours during the period before Rackley was killed and that he was high when he gave the order to shoot Rackley. In previous statements, Sams said he sometimes lost his memory when he was high, but during his testimony in court that day he insisted that he only lost it if he had smoked nine or 10 joints. He also originally said that after Rackley was murdered he traveled to Washington for a few hours on orders from Stokeley Carmichael. His testimony in court that day had him staying the night. Sams attributed the inconsistencies to "poor stenography" on the part of the police officers who took his statements when he was arrested the previous August and the fact that his memory had improved.

McLucas' defense began their case on August 12, 1970. According to the Times, their goal was to portray McLucas as a "passive bystander in the treatment of Rackley who never learned until the very last minute that he was to be killed. Thus it will be argued, he could not have been a conspirator." While the defense admitted to McLucas' participation in the events surrounding Rackley's death, they argued that the charges brought by the state—kidnapping resulting in death, conspiracy to kidnap, conspiracy to murder, and binding with the intent to commit a crime—were not applicable to McLucas.

Panther lawyer William Kunstler was the first witness to be called by the defense. The night before Kunstler took the stand, in a speech at Yale, he called for State's Attorney Markle to resign. The purpose of Kunstler's testimony was to refute Sams' assertions that a meeting between several Panther members occurred in Kunstler's New York offices immediately following Rackley's murder. Kunstler maintained that such a meeting never took place and that he had never met Sams before.

Linda Young and Robert Webb, two Panther members, followed Kunstler to the stand. Both testified about Sams' strained relations with the party as well as his various acts of assault. Judge Mulvey ruled that such evidence regarding Sams and his violent tendencies were "collateral issues," and thus prevented the jury from hearing the testimony. The defense next brought to the stand Dr. Robert Miller, the doctor who had concluded that Sams was competent to testify. He described Sams as having a personality type known as "psychopathic" and "sociopathic."

The next day the defense called New Haven Deputy Chief Inspector Nick Pastore to the stand. He had kept Seale under surveillance while the Panther leader was in New Haven, and those records had been subpoenaed by the defense in order to discredit testimony of his comings and goings by police. The records, however, proved to be the first evidence that corroborated Sams' testimony that Seale did, in fact, visit Panther headquarters before and after Rackley's death.

One of the next witnesses to come to the stand was Margaret Hudgins, another Panther member, who had been in detention for 14 months on charges in connection with Rackley's death. Hudgins testified about her interactions with McLucas on the night of the murder; she stated that McLucas said he was only going to "drop the brother off at the bus stop," and that he would be "right back." Upon his return, she testified that McLucas was "so upset that he laid down on the living room floor and just wouldn't talk to anyone." She told of McLucas putting his head in her lap and then starting to cry. She indicated that all McLucas would say that night was, "that crazy George is a mad man."

Other charged Panthers Erika Huggins and Rose Marie Smith were also brought to the stand on August 18, but both refused to testify on the grounds of possible self-incrimination.

On August 19, Lonnie McLucas took the stand to testify on his own behalf. He testified that he fired the shot, thinking that Rackley was already dead, doing so only because he did not want to end up "in the same position Rackley was in." McLucas testified of the fear that motivated him to follow Sams' orders, resisting Markle's insinuations that it was respect for Sams, a senior ranking party member, and not fear, that caused him to obey.

On August 21, Bobby Seale was the last to be led to the witness stand in the trial of Lonnie McLucas. Charles Garry, Seale's lawyer, urged him not to testify and informed him of his Fifth Amendment right not to take the stand, but Seale responded by saying, "I'd like to tell the truth." Seale denied knowing anything about Rackley before or after he went to the New Haven headquarters and denied knowing that Sams was in New Haven, or even active in the party. He stated, "I never ordered anyone killed. The party does not order anyone killed."

During final arguments, the attorneys were able to put their spin on the situation and speak to the jury for the last time. Markle argued that McLucas was a "dyed-in-the-wool" Black Panther who was ready to follow "any order that's given to him, without question and without fear." Theodore Koskoff described Rackley's murder a "motiveless" act of violence, completely orchestrated by Sams, whom he described as a "sadistic, viscous, brutal, psychopathic, mentally deranged criminal."

One of the jury's three black members, Mrs. Sennia Felton, failed to come to court on the last day of arguments; one of the alternates, all of whom were white, replaced her. The jury began deliberating at 12:10 p.m. on August 26, and continued until 5:00 p.m. that night. They told the court that they had not yet reached a decision. While the jury sat holed up in the courtroom, hundreds of supporters waited outside the courthouse for news. After the fifth day of deliberation, the jury sent a note to the court informing that they were at an impasse and could not reach a unanimous verdict. Judge Mulvey then asked the dissenting jurors to reconsider the view of the majority and sent them back to deliberate. At 5:00 p.m., they asked to retire for the night, still unable to agree on a verdict.

On August 31, the jury's sixth day of deliberation, the verdict was announced. The jury found Lonnie McLucas not guilty of kidnapping resulting in death, conspiracy to kidnap, and binding with intent to commit a crime. He was found guilty of conspiracy to murder, the least serious of the charges. The crime carried a maximum penalty of 15 years. His bail was set at $15,000. Outside the courthouse, Koskoff was quoted as saying, "I think they gave a black revolutionary a fair trial."

On September 17, McLucas was sentenced to 12 to 15 years. His bail was raised to $35,000 due to a new development in his case. It was revealed that he had been on probation for a previous conviction in North Carolina but had left the state without approval from his probation officer in September of 1969.

ONE TRIAL DOWN, SEVEN TO GO?

With McLucas' trial concluded, the state was left with seven Panthers to try. On September 22, 1970, George Edwards pled guilty to two counts of aggravated assault. Appearing before Judge Mulvey, Edwards admitted to being involved in Rackley's torture that took place at New Haven Panther headquarters. Edwards had been held in jail without bail since he was arrested on May 22, 1969. Edwards was given a suspended sentence after serving 513 days in jail and was released on probation on October 23, 1970.

Three days after Edwards pled guilty, two other Panthers awaiting trial pled guilty to aggravated assault as well. On September 25, Rose Marie Smith and Margaret Hudgins pled guilty to the reduced charges. On October 2, the two women were given suspended sentences and released on two years' probation. They had each spent 467 days in jail without bail.

With Edwards, Smith, and Hudgins pleading guilty by the end of September 1970, the state was left with the prospect of trying only four

Catherine Roraback, second from left, speaks with some of the Black Panther defendants and fellow attorney L. Scott Melville on the steps of New Haven Superior Court in October 1970. From left are Frances Carter, Roraback, Margaret Hudgins, Rose Marie Smith, and Melville. © *Hartford Courant.*

Panthers—Bobby Seale, Erika Huggins, and the two Panthers still fighting extradition in Colorado, Rory Hithe and Landon Williams. Any hope that these four Panthers would plead guilty disappeared on September 29 when Bobby Seale stated in superior court that, "[t]he charges against me are false." He pled not guilty to charges of first-degree murder and kidnapping resulting in death. Erika Huggins pled not guilty in April 1969 to the charges of aiding and abetting murder, kidnapping resulting in death, and binding with intent to commit a crime. Attorney Charles Garry, Seale's San Francisco lawyer, was not present when Seale submitted his plea. Seale told Judge Mulvey that he would "reluctantly" allow for David Rosen, a recent graduate of Yale Law School, to represent him during preliminary hearings, but insisted that Garry be present for further hearings. Catherine Roraback, a Connecticut lawyer already famous for her involvement in controversial cases, including *Griswold v. Connecticut*, represented Erika Huggins.

In a May 2004 interview, Roraback recounted her first experience in court with Ericka. "…When I went into the courtroom with Ericka Huggins, when she was first being arraigned in the Black Panther Case, she came in…having been brought in by the sheriffs and she looked around and said, 'Oh, my God!' and I said 'What's the matter?' I thought something had really happened and she said, 'It's all men.' I had been in practice at that point for…over twenty years and I'd forgotten. I'd forgotten that that was the fact of what trying a case in Connecticut was."[1]

Things got interesting on October 8, 1970, when Seale and Huggins filed suit claiming that their Constitutional right to be treated as innocent until proven guilty was being violated. They asserted that their confinement in jail without bail was "oppressive," and "far more onerous than necessary" to ensure their presence at trial. They filed suit against five parties, including the State Commissioner of Corrections, Ellis C. MacDougall; State's Attorney Arnold Markle; and Special Agent Charles Weeks, who was in charge of Connecticut FBI agents. Specifically, Seale and Huggins complained about the restrictions placed on Huggins' reading materials in jail (she was refused access to Seale's book *Seize the Time*, as well as works by Ho Chi Minh), denial of access to "reputable members of the press," censored mail, restrictions on visitation, harassment of visitors by prison officials, as well as restrictions on facial hair and jewelry. Most of these issues were resolved during a day-long conference attended by counsel for the parties and Commissioner MacDougall on December 24. The Council of Corrections ratified the agreement drawn up at the conference on February 8, 1971. Shortly after the ratification, Commissioner MacDougall resigned and was replaced by John Manson, who decided not to honor the agreement. The issue was again brought before the court, and on May 5, 1971, District Judge Robert Zampano announced that, except for Seale's claim that he was being held in administrative segregation, he and Huggins were not entitled to any of the relief that they had requested.

Meanwhile, before their trial began, attorneys for Seale and Huggins were filing a variety of motions, including one that challenged Connecticut's law on jury eligibility. They argued that by only choosing jurors from lists of registered voters, the chances that middle-class white citizens would be over-represented were great, a class of people "apt to have bigoted attitudes toward blacks." They called 36 witnesses to the stand to confirm the theory that a jury picked solely from registered voters would prejudice the defendants' ability to have a fair trial. On November 12, Judge Mulvey denied the challenge to the selection system. Counsel for Seale and Huggins argued a motion seeking to dismiss the charges against them on the grounds of prejudicial pretrial publicity. Mulvey denied that motion as well.

In a September 2004 interview, Catherine Roraback commented on working with Charles Garry. "Charlie Garry was an old-time male chauvinist. I mean, a good sense of humor. He was always cordial to women, but Charlie had grown up in a different era than I. Well, in different worlds...Charlie could never understand how I could represent Erica. I mean how I could create a defense for her because his idea of defending

February 6, 1971: Douglas' work repeatedly voiced the Black Panther Party's demand to free all political prisoners, including their own jailed party members. In this image, Douglas refers to the trial of Bobby Seale and Ericka Huggins in New Haven.
© *Emory Douglas, Image courtesy of Alden and Mary Kimbrough.*

a woman, which was very common in those days, was that you treated her as though she was a poor young thing. She was led astray by these, you know, terrible people that she didn't know what she was doing. You know, please be sorry for her and dismiss the charges, sort of thing. I mean, that was Charlie's concept of the defense for a woman, and I kept explaining to him that it just wouldn't take with a woman like Ericka. She was a very, very strong person and they had some evidence which was pretty horrendous too...."[2]

TRIAL NUMBER TWO BEGINS: A SEARCH FOR AN IMPARTIAL JURY

On November 12, Judge Mulvey announced that the trial of Seale and Huggins would begin the following Tuesday, November 17, 1970. Seale was charged with murder and kidnapping resulting in death and Huggins was charged with aiding and abetting murder, kidnapping resulting in death, and binding with intent to commit a crime. Mulvey ordered 500 prospective jurors to report to court; it was estimated that jury selection would take four to eight weeks.

The trial got off to a slow start with only two prospective jurors being questioned on the first day, neither of whom made the cut. The first juror, Charles Paradie of Wallingford, when questioned about his thoughts on the guilt or innocence of the defendants stated, there was "no question about the[ir] guilt or they wouldn't be here." Mulvey did not find this statement to be sufficient cause to dismiss the juror, thus forcing the defense to use their first challenge. The first two jurors were seated during the third day of *voir dire*—one white man and one black man.

After 12 days of jury selection, during which 218 potential jurors were questioned, only three remained on the jury. The fourth juror accepted by both sides had asked to be excused days after she was seated because an anonymous telephone call was made to her home and she "expressed anxiety about serving on a jury in a controversial murder case." At last, on March 11, a twelve-member jury with two alternates was finally seated, four months after jury selection began. The jury was composed of seven whites and five blacks; one alternate was white and one was black. The court had called 1,550 persons to report to the court, 1,035 of whom were actually questioned, breaking the country's record for largest venire pool.

TRIAL BEGINS

The case finally began on March 18, 1971. The first witness called by the state was Margaret Hudgins, the Panther who had also testified in the McLucas case. Interestingly, Hudgins was not a voluntary witness. As she was standing in line to enter the courthouse to watch the proceedings as a spectator, she was handed a subpoena to testify. Ignoring his opportunity to make an opening statement to the jury, State's Attorney Markle instead called Hudgins as the first witness. Hudgins' testimony was devoid of any mention of Bobby Seale, but she did report that Erika Huggins was in the room where Alex Rackley was being tortured the night of his murder. The questioning of Hudgins lasted several days.

The prosecution also called Warren Kimbro to testify; Kimbro had already pled guilty to second-degree murder and admitted to shooting Alex Rackley. Kimbro gave detailed accounts of Rackley's torture, including the beating of Rackley with sticks and burning him with boiling water. Kimbro testified that Huggins was present at the time Rackley was tortured, but not when he was scalded with boiling water. He did, however, testify that Huggins had not taken part in any of the torture that night.

Catherine Roraback and Charles Garry argued that the audio tape recording made of Rackley's torture should be suppressed due to the illegal nature of the search that had yielded the tape. Roraback argued that the search of Panther headquarters, which began on May 22, 1969, and went on for several days with no search warrant issued or requested, was illegal. Markle argued that even if the search was unreasonable overall, because it did not start out as unreasonable, the evidence seized should be admissible. Judge Mulvey ruled that since Seale was not arrested the day the search took place, he had no standing to argue that the evidence should be suppressed, leaving Roraback on her own with the argument. After Roraback and Markle filed briefs on the issue, Mulvey ruled that the evidence was admissible. He found the warrantless search to be justified because of the flight risk; had the police waited for a warrant, he reasoned, some of the Panthers could have escaped.

The trial hit its first snag in its second week when two jurors became unable to report to court; one was in bed with the flu, and the other in the intensive care unit at Yale-New Haven Hospital with injuries from a fall. Rather than use the jury's two alternates and run the risk of falling short of jurors and thus causing a mistrial, the decision was made to delay the trial for one week.

On April 5, the decision was made to delay the trial for another week in hope that at least one of the jurors would be well enough to return. The seriously injured juror, Dennis Adams, was told that surgery was necessary, making it unlikely that he would return, but Mulvey held out hope for the flu-stricken juror, Dorothy Goldson.

By April 13, trial began again. Kimbro resumed his testimony and was the first person since the trial started to refer to Bobby Seale in connection with Alex Rackley. He asserted that Seale was present when Landon Williams, a national Panther official, ordered Kimbro to listen to the torture tapes.

Kimbro had also testified at the earlier McLucas trial; during his questioning on the stand, he asserted that he had no idea that Rackley was to be killed, and that the order to kill came as a surprise. On April 14, that story changed. His new testimony indicated that he knew hours before Rackley was taken out of headquarters that he was to be killed. He testified that several Panthers, including Erika Huggins, had discussed the possibility earlier that day. Kimbro also indicated that Huggins had discussed whose car to use to transport Rackley, something he had not said in his earlier testimony at McLucas' trial. When Markle finished questioning Kimbro, Seale's attorney Charles Garry began his cross-examination, and the questioning continued for two-and-a-half days. Kimbro stuck to his new story throughout Garry's cross-examination. Attorney Roraback also questioned Kimbro, especially about why his story had changed concerning Ericka Huggins' suggestion about a car. The transcript of *State v. Seale and Huggins* shows that Roraback tried to shake down Kimbro's story:

> RORABACK: This is the first time you said it, is that correct, Mr. Kimbro, when you testified here in the last several days?
> KIMBRO: The first time I said it here, yes.
> RORABACK: And this is approximately two years after this alleged conversation took place?
> KIMBRO: Yes.
> RORABACK: And approximately fifteen months after the first statement you gave concerning—
> KIMBRO: Yes.
> RORABACK: And approximately nine months since you testified in the McLucas trial, is that right?
> KIMBRO: Yes.
> RORABACK: And you are claiming that your memory is better today, Mr. Kimbro, than it was seven or eight months after the incident?
> KIMBRO: Somewhat, yes.
> RORABACK: Who has refreshed it for you, Mr. Kimbro?

KIMBRO: Myself. Two years going over and over and over and over and over and over.

RORABACK: And adding and adding and adding and adding and adding?

After Kimbro's testimony ended, the state set about showing the jury evidence taken from the scene of the murder, including the rope, bullet shells, tape, and wire coat hanger that were found near Rackley's body. They were also able to exhibit five black and white photos of the murder scene, though they had wanted to show much more. The defense won on a motion to prevent additional photos and 13 color slides from being shown to the jury. Attorney Roraback, in arguing for the suppression of such evidence, stated that neither of the defendants had been charged with shooting the victim or witnessing the murder.

The state called Maude Francis as a witness on April 21. Francis was originally charged with the same offenses as Seale and Huggins, but her case was disposed of in juvenile court where the records are sealed, and she was released in December 1969. Francis placed Bobby Seale in the kitchen of Panther headquarters between the hours of 4:30 and 5:00 a.m. on the morning of May 20. She testified that during that time he tried to make a telephone call, but after being unable to get through, he left.

After Francis, and five weeks after the trial first began, the state began questioning their so-called "star" witness, George Sams, Jr. Sams again testified that the order to kill Rackley came directly from Seale, whom Sams quoted as saying, "A pig is a pig. Do away with him," allegedly referring to Rackley. Sams also implicated Erika Huggins in Rackley's torture more than any other witness before him. Sams claimed that she participated in beating Rackley and that she was the one to procure the first pot of boiling water used to burn him. According to *The New York Times*, Sams' testimony was so convoluted and unclear that several times the court reporter had to reread Sams' statements to the court.

On the second day of his testimony, during cross-examination by Seale's attorney, Sams engaged in what *The New York Times* called a "10-minute tirade" that left many people in the courtroom "stunned." "I'm not going to be no martyr for the party!" he shouted. "I have made up my mind I am going to expose the truth." Sams accused both Seale and Garry of telling lies and incriminating people to protect the image of the party. The state did not object to Sams' tirade, nor did Garry. It wasn't until Attorney Roraback objected that Sams was finally shut down. "It's about time somebody did, or we would be here all day," said Judge Mulvey. "It's all very interesting, but it's not pertinent to this case."

On April 28, after calling 11 witnesses over a six-week period, the prosecution rested their case against Seale and Huggins.

The defense began their case on May 6, 1971. The first witness called by the defense was Linda Young, a woman who had lived in the same house as Sams for several months before the Rackley murder. Charles Garry was able to use his questioning of Young to paint a picture of Sams for the jury; much of his medical history and background had been kept out of the trial, including his classification by psychiatrists as a "mental defective." Young was used as a vehicle to illustrate Sams' patterns of strange and violent behaviors. Young testified that he lied a lot, was "vicious and brutal," and that he beat her and tried to rape her. She also told the court that Sams had wanted to "get even" with Seale who had expelled Sams from the party for violence.

Garry next brought in five character witnesses to testify that Seale was an upstanding figure. The prosecution used this opportunity to question the witnesses about their knowledge of Seale's criminal record, outlining for the jury Seale's past run-ins with the law, which included a 1966 conviction for battery of a police officer, a 1966 conviction for assault with a dangerous weapon, and a 1968 conviction for possession of a firearm.

The jury also heard from Ericka Huggins herself who testified in her own defense. Her testimony began on May 11. During questioning by Roraback, Huggins' attorney, she was able to give a narrative description of what happened in the days preceding the murder and night Rackley was killed. She consistently spoke of her fear of Sams and indicated that he was the ringleader, that she was not involved in the beatings or torture, and that it was George Edwards, Warren Kimbro, and Lonnie McLucas who were the main players in the beatings.

Preparing Ericka to take the stand did not happen over night. During her September 2004 interview, Roraback said:

> I knew that when we were selecting the jury, I could not ask the questions of those jurors as to those words that Erica used on the tapes. If I said them, it would make it much too obvious. So for the two years before we actually got to having Erica on the witness stand, I would spend every morning looking in my mirror in the bathroom in New Haven there and practicing saying words that I had never used in my life before, but I finally got to the point where I could say with relative equanimity [expletive deleted] and a few others of that sort.[3]

In the same interview, Roraback recounted Attorney Markle's cross-examination of Huggins, specifically when he started asking her why she had not told anyone about what she knew in regards to Rackley's torture. "He said, 'You knew what was happening, why didn't you do something?' And she said, 'I tried,'...'Well, did you call the police...Why didn't you talk to Bobby Seale when he was there,' and she said, 'I tried,' and he said, 'What do you mean you tried'...'Mr. Markle, you have to understand, sometimes it's very hard for a woman to be heard by a man.'" Roraback said that Ericka's statement was one of the "most dramatic moments I've ever had in a case."[4]

On May 13, both attorneys for the defendants rested their case. Seale had not testified, though everyone was expecting him to. Garry had informed the court earlier in the trial that his client would, in fact, take the stand. Markle was forced to ask for a recess, indicating that his rebuttal witnesses were not prepared that day because he was expecting Seale to testify.

The next day, Markle petitioned the court to reopen his case; he wanted to introduce the transcript of Seale's testimony in the McLucas case. Judge Mulvey denied the motion without explanation or justification. As Markle began questioning one of his rebuttal witnesses, Sergeant Pasqual Carriero, who was with Nicholas Pastore on May 19, 1969, the night he claimed to have seen Seale enter party headquarters, Mulvey sus-

Ericka Huggins, free from jail for the first time in two years, joins her attorney Catherine Roraback in a grin on Tuesday, May 25, 1971, after murder and kidnap charges were dismissed against Huggins and Seale. ©*AP/WIDE WORLD PHOTOS, Photographer Dave Pickoff.*

Black Panther Bobby Seale is shown in this May 28, 1971 photo in New Haven. He was freed after serving 21 months is prison. ©*AP/WIDE WORLD PHOTOS.*

tained an objection by Garry, saying that Markle could have called this witness as part of his case-in-chief. "The rule is you don't put your case on piecemeal," he told Markle.

On May 18, arguments in the Seale-Huggins case concluded. The three attorneys gave their closing arguments to the jury. For six hours, they attempted to persuade the jury to believe their version of what happened and why the defendants acted in the manner they did.

On May 19, the jury, made up of seven whites and five blacks, began their deliberations. The end of the first day proved inconclusive—they had been unable to reach a verdict. On the sixth day of deliberations, the members of the jury announced that they had come to a decision. The note given by the jury to the judge read, "We are still deadlocked. We feel it is in vain to deliberate further." At 2:45 p.m. on May 25, Judge Mulvey declared a mistrial. The jurors were ordered by Mulvey to stay quiet about what went on behind the closed doors of the deliberation room. The lawyers were also instructed not to comment to the media on the situation. Both Garry and Markle indicated to the court that they would ask for a new trial.

After a conference attended by the attorneys in the case and Judge Mulvey on May 26, Mulvey announced that he was dropping the charges against both defendants, indicating that the "massive publicity" surrounding the trial would make it impossible to try them again fairly. Noting that she had been held for two years while she awaited trial without bail, Mulvey set Ericka Huggins free. Seale, on the other hand, was still awaiting trial in Chicago and so returned to jail until bail in that case was set. On May 28, bail was set for $25,000, and after 21 months in jail, Seale was released.

Seale's lawyer, Charles Garry, stands on his head in a yoga relaxation pose on the New Haven green as the jury deliberates on May 23, 1971. A boy looks like he's wondering what it's all about. ©*AP/WIDE WORLD PHOTOS.*

Soon after the trial ended and the charges were dropped, jurors and attorneys alike began to talk about what went on behind closed doors. It was reported that the initial vote taken by the jurors on their first day of deliberation was unanimously in favor of acquitting Seale on all charges. The results of the final vote taken was 10 jurors for acquittal of both defendants on all counts, one for conviction on all counts, and one for conviction of each defendant on one count.

State's Attorney Markle, who was released from the gag order on May 26, 1971, also spoke to reporters about his reaction to the outcome of the case. He stated:

> If this ruling is followed, it means someone who intends to commit a murder will commit a mass murder to attract the publicity. Then he'll get himself a lawyer to make all sorts of comments, none of which are proved and all of which are reported, then make sure every prospective juror knows something about the case, forces an uproar by whatever fringe followers he can find…and then having originally shot his parents, throw himself on the mercy of the court because he's an orphan.

Commenting on Attorney Garry, Markle said, "When he complains about massive media coverage and he stands on his head on the middle of the Green and he can't understand why there's so much publicity, I find it hard to take."

THE AFTERMATH

On June 23, 1971, less than one month after charges against Seale and Huggins were dropped, Warren Kimbro and George Sams were sentenced to life in prison by Judge Mulvey. Life terms were the mandatory sentence for charges of second-degree murder, the charge under which the two men had pled guilty. They would both be eligible for parole in less than 20 years and Markle indicated that he would appear before the parole board on their behalf.

Another month passed and on July 29, Superior Court Judge Aaron Palmer indicated that the publicity surrounding the Seale-Huggins trial would not prevent the selection of an impartial jury for the trial of Landon Williams and Rory Hithe, the last two defendants left to be tried in the Rackley case.

Several months later, on October 26, the last remaining defendants pled guilty to charges of conspiracy to murder. Williams and Hithe were given suspended sentences by Judge Otto LaMarchia on November 19.

With the last of the defendants sentenced, the New Haven trials of the Black Panthers came to an end nearly two-and-a-half years after the body of Alex Rackley was found in the Coginchaug River in Middlefield, Connecticut.

---

1. Connecticut Bar Foundation James W. Cooper Fellows Oral History of Connecticut Women in the Legal Profession Project, Catherine Roraback Interviews May 4, 2004.
2. Connecticut Bar Foundation James W. Cooper Fellows Oral History of Connecticut Women in the Legal Profession Project, Catherine Roraback Interviews September 14, 2004.
3. *Ibid.*
4. *Ibid.*

See Appendix E for the text of the *State of Connecticut v. Lonnie McLucas.*

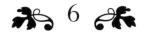

Desegregating Hartford Public Schools
Sheff v. O'Neill

In 1951, a group of 13 parents in Topeka, Kansas, sued the city's board of education. Their goal was to stop the forced racial segregation of the school district. In 1954, in *Brown v. Board of Education*, the U.S. Supreme Court unanimously decided that the "separate but equal" standard that had governed race relations in the United States was unconstitutional. "Separate educational facilities are inherently unequal," the Court stated. Chief Justice Earl Warren, writing for the unanimous court, noted that:

> Today, education is perhaps the most important function of state and local governments. Compulsory school attendance laws and the great expenditures for education both demonstrate our recognition of the importance of education to our democratic society. It is required in the performance of our most basic public responsibilities, even service in the armed forces. It is the very foundation of good citizenship. Today it is a principal instrument in awakening the child to cultural values, in preparing him for later professional training, and in helping him to adjust normally to his environment. In these days, it is doubtful that any child may reasonably be expected to succeed in life if he is denied the opportunity of an education. Such an opportunity, where the state has undertaken to provide it, is a right which must be made available to all on equal terms.

Though the Court's decision was firmly in place, the nature of the judicial system made it impossible for the verdict to be meaningfully implemented or enforced. It was years before school segregation was no longer the norm in the United States. Many schools chose to close their doors rather than desegregate. In 1957, Arkansas Governor Orval Faubus used the National Guard to block black students from enrolling in Little Rock High School. In 1963, Alabama Governor George Wallace personally closed the doors to two black students trying to enroll at the University of Alabama.

In 1964, Congress passed and President Lyndon B. Johnson signed the Civil Rights Act; Title VI of the Act prohibits segregation in schools that receive federal financial assistance. Innumerable cases on the subject of school segregation were filed at the state and federal level throughout the country, several of them making it to the U.S. Supreme Court. In *Green v. County School Board of New Kent County*, the Court mandated that school desegregation be dismantled, "root and branch," and mandated the school board to "fashion steps which promise realistically to convert promptly to a system without a 'white' school and a 'Negro' school, but just schools."

HARTFORD'S TROUBLES

After years of carrying out desegregation strategies, school integration in the United States reached an all-time high in 1988 with approximately 45 percent of black students attending schools with a white student majority. The numbers for the Hartford area, however, were not so promising. During the 1988–89 school year, the Hartford schools' racial makeup was over 91 percent minority; Bloomfield was 74 percent; and Windsor was 31 percent.

On April 26, 1989, the Connecticut Civil Liberties Union filed a lawsuit against the State of Connecticut. Seventeen children were chosen from the Hartford school system to represent the plaintiffs in the case—six white, six Puerto Rican, and five black children. Milo Sheff, a black student listed as the first plaintiff, was a fourth-grader at the Annie Fisher School in Hartford when the suit was filed.

According to Milo, the process he went through to become the named plaintiff was like being on TV's *American Idol*. "They had a whole bunch of kids that came in and they asked them questions about this and about that, about my school system and stuff I was going through at the time in my school and my background and so forth; it was like a trial," he said. As to why he thought he was the one ultimately chosen to represent the suit, Milo said, "[L]ots of the other kids couldn't articulate their thoughts the way I could; I was always around my mom and sister and uncles; my mom was an activist so I always knew what everything in life was, I wasn't naïve about anything."

When he first became involved with the lawsuit, Milo's impression of the law was heavily influenced by popular TV shows and media representations. "I thought it was going to be fast like *L.A. Law*, like a half hour show and I'm done; it was not anything like that."

The actual named plaintiffs in the case were Milo Sheff, represented by his mother Elizabeth Sheff; Wildaliz, Pedro, and Eva Bermudez, represented by their parents Pedro and Carmen Wilda Bermudez; Oskar and Waleska Melendez, represented by their parents Oscar and Wanda Melendez; Martin Hamilton, represented by his mother Virginia Pertillar; Darryl and Jewell Hughley, represented by their mother Rosetta Hughley; Neiima Best, represented by her mother Denise Best; Lisa Laboy, represented by her mother Adria Laboy; David William and Michael Joseph Harrington, represented by their parents Karen and Leo Harrington; Rachel and Joseph Leach, represented by their parents Eugene Leach and Kathleen Frederick; and Erica and Tasha Connolly, represented by their

Before an April 1989 news conference to announce the suit, Elizabeth Horton Sheff tries to calm her anxious son Milo, then 10, as John Brittain, the lead attorney, makes last minute notes. © *Hartford Courant.*

parents Carol Vinick and Tom Connolly. At the time that the lawsuit was brought, the ages of the children ranged from two years old to 18.

The named defendants in the lawsuit were William O'Neill, governor of Connecticut; State Board of Education; Abraham Glassman, A. Walter Esdaile, Warren J. Foley, Rita Hendel, John Mannix, Julia Rankin, members of the State Board of Education; Gerald Tirozzi, member of the State Board of Education and commissioner, Department of Education; Francisco Borges, treasurer, State of Connecticut; and J. Edward Caldwell, comptroller, State of Connecticut.

Six lawyers signed the complaint for the plaintiffs. They were John Brittain, University of Connecticut School of Law; Nancy Alisberg, Hispanic Advocacy Project Neighborhood Legal Services; Wesley Horton, Moller, Horton & Fineberg, P.C.; Wilfred Rodriguez, Hispanic Advocacy Project Neighborhood Legal Services; Martha Stone, Connecticut Civil Liberties Union Foundation; and Philip Tegeler, Connecticut Civil Liberties Union Foundation.

The complaint indicated that the case was brought "on behalf of school children in the Hartford school district, a great majority of whom—91 percent—are black or Hispanic, and nearly half of whom—47.6 percent—live in families that are poor." It was "also brought on behalf of children in suburban school districts that surround Hartford...to secure this basic constitutional right for plaintiffs and all Connecticut school children."

The goal of the lawsuit was to challenge Hartford's racially imbalanced school system. The concentration of white students in suburban schools and the black students in urban schools prompted the suit. The plaintiffs asserted that such an imbalance violated the Connecticut constitution's guarantee of equal educational opportunity. Interestingly, the suit did not allege that racist policies were the cause of such segregation; instead, they merely asserted that the situation itself was illegal and that it was the state's responsibility to do something about it.

The complaint read:

> [t]he State of Connecticut, by tolerating school districts sharply separated along racial, ethnic, and economic lines, has deprived the plaintiffs and other Hartford children of their rights to an equal educational opportunity, and to a minimally adequate education – rights to which they are entitled under the Connecticut Constitution and Connecticut statutes....These disparities in educational achievement between the Hartford and suburban school districts are the result of the educational and social poli-

cies pursued and/or accepted by the defendants, including the racial, ethnic, and socioeconomic isolation of the Hartford and suburban school districts.

The plaintiffs' complaint also asserted that integration would serve to enhance not only the plaintiff's educational experience, but also that of all students in Connecticut.

> Public school integration of children in the Hartford metropolitan region by race, ethnicity, and economic status would significantly improve the educational achievement of poor and minority children, without diminution of the education afforded their majority schoolmates. Indeed, white students would be provided thereby with the positive benefits of close associations during their formative years with blacks, Hispanics and poor children who will make up over 30 percent of Connecticut's population by the year 2000.

The case, brought in Connecticut Superior Court, specifically challenged the guarantees rooted in the Connecticut constitution, not the federal Constitution. In particular, Article Eighth, Section One of the Connecticut constitution provides that there will "always be free public elementary and secondary schools in the state." Section Four provides for a school fund, whose purpose is "to the support and encouragement of the public schools throughout the state, and for the equal benefit of all the people thereof." Article First, Section Twenty maintains that "[n]o person shall be denied the equal protection of the law nor be subjected to segregation or discrimination in the exercise or enjoyment of his civil or political rights because of religion, race, color, ancestry or national origin."

According to Attorney Wesley Horton, counsel for the plaintiffs, the fact that the Connecticut constitution did not specifically guarantee the right of a student to attend a non-segregated school was not fatal to their case. Their argument was that the education clause mandating free public education coupled with the equal protection clause created a fundamental right for all students to equal education.

Horton, in explaining their case to *The New York Times*, stated, "We are saying that there's something wrong in a state where one school system is all black and one is all white, and they're right next to each other. We say that is fundamentally wrong under the Connecticut Constitution and that the reason for it doesn't matter. The result is the same, and it's going to stop."

The complaint charged that:

> [f]or well over two decades, the State of Connecticut, though its defendant O'Neill, defendant State Board of Education, defendant Tirozzi, and their predecessors, have been aware of: (i) the separate and unequal pattern of public school districts in the State of Connecticut and the greater Hartford metropolitan region; (ii) the strong governmental forces that have created and maintained racially and economically isolated residential communities in the Hartford region; and (iii) the consequent need for substantial education changes, within and across school district lines, to end this pattern of isolation and inequality.

THE STATE ACKNOWLEDGES PROBLEMS

In January of 1988—the year before the suit was brought—then-Education Commissioner Gerald Tirozzi, a named defendant in the case, published a report entitled "A Report on Racial/Ethnic Equity and Desegregation in Connecticut's Public Schools." The report detailed and condemned the racial imbalance in Connecticut's schools. The report's findings and suggestions were frowned upon by those working to integrate, including the plaintiffs, because it provided no real mechanism for change.

According to the complaint, the Tirozzi report clearly informed the defendant board that "Many minority children are forced by factors related to economic development, housing, zoning and transportation to live in poor urban communities where resources are limited. They often have available to them fewer educational opportunities. Of equal significance is the fact that separation means that neither they nor their counterparts in the more affluent suburban school districts have the chance to learn to interact with each other, as they will inevitably have to do as adults living and working in a multi-cultural society. Such interaction is a most important element of quality education."

Some people thought that the report was inappropriate and that Tirozzi was stepping on a turf that was not his. For example, State Senator Philip Robertson called for Tirozzi's resignation, saying he was out-of-line for publishing such a report. "It is his responsibility to determine the direction of the State Department of Education, and this is a direction that is not his. The legislature is responsible for social change; the Department of Education is responsible for reading and writing and teaching youngsters arithmetic."

Tirozzi filed a follow-up report that was published in April 1989, shortly before the suit was filed. This report, "Quality and Integrated Education: Options for Connecticut," also did not receive a warm welcome, and served as an impetus for the filing of the case. The follow-up report was even weaker in its recommendations for integration; Tirozzi attributed his inability to formulate a more concrete set of recommendations to the state budget crisis.

This report indicated that "[r]acial and economic isolation have profound academic and affective consequences. Children who live in poverty—a burden which impacts disproportionately on minorities—are more likely to be educationally at risk of school failure and dropping out before graduation than children from less impoverished homes. Poverty is the most important correlate of low achievement. This belief was borne out by an analysis of the 1988 Connecticut Mastery Test data that focused on poverty....The analysis also revealed that the low achievement outcomes associated with poverty are intensified by geographic and racial concentrations."

In addition, the complaint stated that "[d]espite recognition of the 'alarming degree of isolation' of poor and minority schoolchildren in the City of Hartford and other urban school systems, Report at 3, and the gravely adverse impact this isolation has on the educational opportunities afforded to plaintiffs and other urban school children, the Report recom-

Attorney Wesley Horton at a UConn Law Alumni Banquet in 1989. *Courtesy of the University of Connecticut School of Law.*

Attorney and Professor John Brittain. Undated. *Courtesy of the University of Connecticut School of Law.*

mended, and the defendants have announced, that they intend to pursue an approach that would be 'voluntary and incremental.'"

According to the *Times*, the report called "upon school districts to take voluntary measures to promote integration, among them, creating more magnet schools and other regional educational programs. But should such voluntary methods fail, the report recommends that the Board of Education be given the power 'to impose a mandatory desegregation plan.'"

While some steps were being taken by the state, including the formation of several magnet schools, it was not enough for the plaintiffs. "Frankly, I'm delighted to see people taking action and not sitting back and waiting to see what the court does," Attorney Wesley Horton said, "but our case is going forward."

After the lawsuit was filed, *The New York Times* quoted Tirozzi as agreeing with the premise of the suit, but that he believed voluntary cooperation, and not legal action, was how the problems should be solved. Tirozzi's "voluntary cooperation" goal was the premise of his follow-up report. "I feel very strongly that continuing the voluntary approach is the way to go," he said. John Brittain, a lead lawyer for the plaintiffs and a then-professor at the University of Connecticut School of Law, was quoted by the *Times* as saying that relying on voluntary cooperation would "not produce any meaningful desegregation." He asserted that the purpose of the suit was to highlight and expose the problems in the school district in order for changes to occur. "We believe in mandatory voluntary cooperation," he said.

The complaint asserted that "separate educational systems for minority and non-minority students are inherently unequal. Because of the de facto racial and ethnic segregation between Hartford and the suburban districts, the defendants have failed to provide the plaintiffs with an equal opportunity to a free public education as required by Article First, §§1 and 20, and Article Eighth, §1, of the Connecticut Constitution, to the grave injury of the plaintiffs."

According to the complaint, the plaintiffs requested relief in the form of a declaratory judgment that would indicate:

- that public schools in the greater Hartford metropolitan region, which are segregated de facto by race and ethnicity, are inherently unequal...;
- that the public schools in the greater Hartford metropolitan region...do not provide plaintiffs with an equal educational opportunity, in violation of...the Connecticut Constitution;
- that the maintenance of public schools in the greater Hartford metropolitan region...deprives plaintiffs of an equal educational opportunity, and fails to provide plaintiffs with a minimally adequate education...and;
- that the failure of the defendants to provide plaintiffs with the equal educational opportunities to which they are entitled under Connecticut law...violates the Due Process Clause, Article First §8 and 10, of the Connecticut Constitution.

The plaintiffs also asked the court to issue a "temporary, preliminary and permanent injunction enjoining defendants, their agents, employees, and successors in office from failing to provide, and ordering them to provide "plaintiffs and those similarly situated with an integrated education;...with equal educational opportunities;...and with a minimally adequate educations."

NOT A NEW ISSUE

The complaint was not the first case of its kind. Previous decisions in Connecticut, New Jersey, and New York dealt with similar issues, but this was the first to ask for more than money to solve the problems. This case went beyond the need for more funds and insisted that substantial integration would be the only way to truly provide equal educational opportunities for the children of Connecticut.

In New Jersey, a similar case was brought in *Spencer v. Kugler*. In that case, a civil rights action was brought by black students alleging that their Fourteenth Amendment rights were violated by the school district's "failure to achieve racial balance among several districts in the state system of public schools." A major difference between *Spencer* and *Sheff* was that *Spencer's* arguments were based on the *federal* Constitution, while the *Sheff* argument was based on the *state* constitution.

The court in *Spencer* held that "school district lines based on municipal boundaries were reasonable so long as they were not designed or intended to foster segregation." The *Spencer* opinion concluded by stating that racial imbalances caused by housing patterns within the municipality-school districts were not "susceptible to federal judicial intervention....The New Jersey Legislature has by intent maintained a unitary system of public education, albeit that system has degenerated to extreme racial imbalance in some school districts; nevertheless the statutes in question as they are presently constituted are constitutional."

Even though *Spencer* was based on the federal Constitution, it was not a good precedent for the plaintiffs in the *Sheff* case.

WHY BRING THIS LAWSUIT?

In a 1990 interview with *The New York Times*, sixth-grader Milo Sheff spoke about his involvement in the lawsuit and why he wanted to be part of it. He said that it was important for the students to prevail because it would allow all people to have an equal education. When asked why he thought it was wrong for schools to be segregated, he said, "Because people don't get to know each other, and then they just judge each other according to the color of their skin...I also think schools should be mixed because I know I do not want my children racist, and I do not want to become a racist. The best way not to become a racist is to learn to talk to different people." He went on to say:

> If I had a magic wand, the schools would be mixed, the neighborhoods would be mixed. There'd be no zoning laws, no racism. You could live anywhere you wanted, and you wouldn't be denied loans or a job because of the color of your skin. If I had a magic wand I would make everything bad disappear.

Milo Sheff was more than just a face associated with the case—it became his life. "I used to get death threats, cameras following me around at school," he said. "I couldn't get into any trouble because the media would blow it out of proportion." It even affected how his teachers reacted to him in school. "Some teachers used to let me get away with murder; I would play my games all day long, and then with some teachers, I'd sneeze and they'd tell me to go to the vice principal's office for disrupting their class."

COMMUNITY REACTION TO THE SUIT

Some people, including students enrolled in Hartford schools, were skeptical that change would ever happen, even if the plaintiffs were successful. Tony Pitts, a junior at Weaver High in Hartford was quoted by *The New York Times* as saying, "Even if they win, you'll see so many private schools come out that it will all remain the same anyway." Other students voiced apprehension to being integrated with white suburban students, saying that such an environment might not be friendly.

In a *Hartford Courant*/Connecticut poll conducted by the University of Connecticut's Institute for Social Inquiry in January and February of 1993, state residents showed mixed emotions over the suit and its implications. In all, 500 adults from around the state were surveyed. The survey indicated that 42 percent said that integration made no difference for black students, and 46 percent said it made no difference for white students. Forty percent of those surveyed thought desegregation made education better for blacks while 21 percent thought it made education better for whites. According to the survey, 11 percent said desegregation made things worse for blacks, and 25 percent said it made things worse for whites. Less than half of those surveyed—43 percent—thought more should be done to integrate schools in their hometowns, while 47 percent said either less should be done or there should be no change.

TRYING TO BLOCK THE CASE

The defendants' first line of defense against the plaintiffs was to file a Motion to Strike the complaint. The defendants alleged that (1) the plaintiffs' claims were not justiciable; (2) unconstitutional state action had not been alleged; (3) the plaintiffs did not allege any causal connection between school district lines and educational performance; and (4) the existence of school districts that coincided with town boundaries did not violate state constitutional standards.

Judge Harry Hammer, who would oversee much of the *Sheff v. O'Neill* case, issued his Memorandum of Decision regarding the defendants' Motion to Strike on May 18, 1990. "The court finds that based upon the factual allegations of the complaint which the court must accept as true for the purposes of this motion, the plaintiffs have stated a justiciable claim because their pleadings present a 'substantial question or issue in dispute...which requires settlement between the parties.' Practice Book §390(b). The defendants' motion to strike the plaintiffs' complaint is denied."

On July 8, 1991, the defendants again attempted to block the case, this time by filing a Motion for Summary Judgment. The motion read, "[t]he defendants maintain that there is no dispute as to the material facts upon which this motion is predicated and that judgment should be entered as a matter of law in favor of the defendants and against the plaintiffs because the state has not engaged in conduct which violates the state constitution and because there is no remedy available to the plaintiffs."

Included with the motion were several affidavits reinforcing the state's argument, including one from Gerald Tirozzi. "To my knowledge, no child has ever been assigned or confined to a school district in Connecticut on the basis of his or her race, national origin, socio-economic status, or status as an 'at risk' student, *i.e.*, limited English proficient, single parent or family receiving AFDC. At the present time and as far back in history as I know, the State of Connecticut has always assigned children to particular school districts based exclusively on their city or town of residence." Also included with the motion was a "Bibliography of Definitions" of the words "discriminate," "discrimination," "segregate," and "segregation" to show that such actions had not taken place in Connecticut.

In responding to the defendants' Motion for Summary Judgment, the plaintiffs asserted that they did, in fact, make justiciable claims, and outlined them again for the court in their Opposition to Respondents' Motion for Summary Judgment filed on September 20, 1991. Their motion stated that:

- first, the defendants have permitted school districts to emerge in the Hartford area that are sharply segregated, de facto, on grounds of race and ethnic background;
- second, although the defendants recognize that racial and economic segregation has serious adverse educational effects, denying equal educational opportunity, they have permitted it to continue;
- third, the segregation that has arisen by race, by ethnicity and by economic status places Hartford school children at a severe educational disadvantage, denies them an education equal to that afforded to suburban school children, and fails to provide a majority with even a "minimally adequate" education;
- fourth, under Connecticut's education statutes, the defendants are obliged to correct these problems, and their failure to have done so violates the school children's rights.

Included with the Opposition Motion were several affidavits from people attesting to the fact that there were problems and that the state knew about them. One such affidavit was from John Allison, then-executive director of the Capital Region Education Council (CREC).

> I have reviewed the State's Memorandum in support of their Motion for Summary Judgment. In my professional opinion, I believe that the efforts they have laid out on pp. 17-43 of the Memorandum have had an insignificant effect on the racial, ethnic, and economic isolation within the Hartford Schools....
>
> There has been, to the best of my knowledge and belief, a lack of any coordinated effort by the State to effectively identify and fund educational sites for the purpose of achieving racial balance....The amount of funding the State has devoted to desegregation efforts has in fact substantially decreased over the past year. (Emphasis in original.)

Some of the efforts laid out in the defendants' memorandum that Allison alluded to included:

- the fact that Hartford's reimbursement rate for providing special education to disabled children was "consistently...approximately 20 percentage points higher" than for suburbs;
- the fact that the "state's contribution toward the total cost of educating the children in Hartford has consistently been more than twice the state's contribution toward the cost of educating children in the combined suburbs";
- that Hartford was the only school district in the area to receive grant money under the state's bilingual grant program;
- that Hartford "received approximately fifty percent more Professional Development Grant money per pupil than the combined suburbs each year the grants have been offered";
- that under the Education Enhancement Act Hartford received $6,000,000 over a three-year period beginning in 1986 to fund up to 240 new staff positions while suburban districts receiving no funds under the program;
- that Hartford received between three and four times as many dollars per pupil as the suburbs under the Summer School Incentive Grants program; and
- that the state provided between 1.45 and 1.86 times as many state matching dollars per pupil in Hartford than it did in the combined suburbs under the Child Nutrition State Matching Grant program.

Hernan LaFontaine, superintendent of schools for Hartford Public Schools from 1979 until June 1991, also submitted an affidavit. He stated that, "[t]he extreme concentration of children from poor and educationally disadvantaged backgrounds, and the extreme racial isolation of our school population, are serious detrimental influences on the quality of education in the Hartford Public Schools. The detrimental effects of racial isolation and high concentrations of poverty are exacerbated by educational resources that are both inadequate to the needs of our children, and inequitable as compared with resources available to students outside of the city."

On February 24, 1992, Judge Hammer denied the defendants' motion, noting his annoyance with their tactics in his decision. "The court is 'of the opinion that the issue was correctly decided' and the defendants' argument is repetitive. *Breen v. Phelps*, 186 Conn. 86, 99. 'Parties cannot be permitted to waste the time of the courts by the repetition in new pleadings of claims which have been set upon the record and overruled at an earlier stage of the proceedings.' *Hillyer v. Borough of Winstead*, 77 Conn. 304, 306....The defendants' motion for summary judgment is denied."

THE FIRST ROUND IN COURT BEGINS

By November 1991, the parties found themselves in court. The State of Connecticut, continuing in its efforts to block the case from proceeding, took the position that the complex legal issues raised by the case were far too extensive for a single judge to decide. Then-Assistant Attorney General John Whelan also argued that the state should not be held responsible for the voluntary residential patterns that caused schools to be predominantly black or white. He argued that there was no political or social mandate implemented by the state that was causing the segregation of the schools, and thus responsibility for any unintended segregation did not rest with the state. Attorney Horton responded that the issue was not how or why the segregation was occurring, but instead was the fact that such segregation was occurring at all.

In 1992, the parties were in the midst of preparing for trial. In defining their case in their Pre-Trial Memorandum, the plaintiffs asserted, "[f]orty years after the Supreme Court declared that '[s]eparate educational facilities are inherently unequal,' the schools in the Hartford are separate and unequal...The central issue presented by this case is whether these inequities can survive constitutional scrutiny." (Emphasis in original.)

The plaintiffs also described their case and informed the court that they would

> demonstrate the long term negative effects of racial and economic segregation. This is not simply a case of not enough resources being allocated to Hartford schools because of their particular needs. This is a case where young minds and hearts—both in Hartford and in the suburbs—are being deprived of opportunities to learn, to grow, to understand in a truly integrated environment. The various forms of segregation in the Hartford area schools insure that none of the students, regardless of race, ethnicity or economic status, will receive a truly adequate education.
>
> The time has now come for judicial intervention. The state has acknowledged its responsibility, but has demonstrated its in-

ability to act without a court order. This court should not hold another generation of children hostage to the state's good intentions.

Included with their pre-trial memorandum was a forty-three-page list of exhibits the plaintiffs planned to introduce at trial, quickly alerting the court that this case would be neither simple nor quick.

The defendants also filed a pre-trial memorandum on November 16, 1992, in which they asserted that "[t]here is no constitutional wrong upon which the court can find the defendants liable." In describing what evidence the court would hear throughout the trial, the defendants maintained that "[t]he plaintiff will introduce no evidence of unconstitutional governmental acts. Rather, the evidence will show that the state has identified certain problems and concerns relating to our schools and has taken steps to address those problems and concerns."

The defendants characterized what the plaintiffs were asking the court to do as impossible, unprecedented, and inappropriate:

> They [the plaintiffs] are asking the court to impinge on the designated functions of other branches of state government by ordering them to take measures to remedy complex social and ed-

December 16, 1992. Then-Hartford Mayor Carrie Saxon Perry, left, Milo Sheff and his mother, Elizabeth Horton Sheff, attending a pre-trial prayer session the day opening arguments started in the case. The bear was a gift intended to provide comfort as the case proceeded. © *Hartford Courant*.

ucational problems....The court has never before injected itself into the process of addressing social and educational problems in this way. The court has always insisted that unconstitutional government action be proven before stepping in, and, even then, the court has only stepped in to the extent necessary to rectify the unconstitutional government action.

The court should reject the plaintiffs' invitation to depart from its traditional role as a body which corrects legal wrongs. The court should not turn itself into a body which determines educational policies and practices for the state.

Accompanying the pre-trial memorandum was a twenty-seven-page list of exhibits the defendants planned to introduce at trial. Nine revisions to the list later, it was eventually expanded to 33 pages.

On December 16, 1992, the trial began. *The New York Times*, in describing the impact this case could have, said, "[t]he Sheff case holds the potential of redefining the central element in many Connecticut communities, the local school district, an element of great pride in wealthy suburbs and of frustration in poor cities and towns."

Attorneys Wesley Horton and John Brittain made the opening arguments for the plaintiffs. Horton began by saying, "[y]our Honor, this is a historic day. This is a start of a trial to determine whether 25,000 children attending the Hartford Public Schools will ever have an equal educational opportunity." He asserted that "unless this Court takes action, another generation of Hartford Public Schools will be condemned to racial and economic isolation in a system with inadequate resources, and these 25,000 children will not be able to achieve up to their potential. In short, your Honor, what this case is about is no less than saving 25,000 children."

John Brittain used Langston Hughes' poem, "A Dream Deferred," to open his speech. "Judge Hammer, this is a case of a dream deferred. What happens to a dream deferred? 'Does it dry up like a raisin in the sun?'....Nineteen children, many of them here, from eleven families of African Americans, Puerto Ricans, and whites in Hartford and West Hartford, filed this lawsuit three and a half years ago, because the school district boundary lines have created a minority enclave of disadvantage in virtually every measurable category of education."

John Whelan made opening arguments for the defendants, acknowledging that the situation in Hartford was not good:

> The defendants share the plaintiffs' concerns. The defendants care very deeply about the children of this state, about the qual-

ity of education that's being provided to the children in this state, and about promoting integration, not just in our schools, but throughout our society....But the question in this case is not that issue. The question in this case is, has the Constitution been violated? Stated differently, the question is whether the Court should replace parents, teachers, local boards of education, the State Board of Education, and the Legislature, in being an architect of the social and educational policies that need to be developed to address these problems.

The initial issue before Judge Hammer in superior court in West Hartford was the claim brought by the plaintiffs that children in Connecticut were constitutionally guaranteed a free, equal, and adequate education. On the first day, they started presenting their case by calling two witnesses, one of which was David Carter, then-president of Eastern Connecticut State University. Carter was asked to provide the court with a definition of "equal educational opportunity." "It's when a student has an opportunity to achieve in his or her potential to the maximum," Carter said.

The defendants' position that the state was not responsible for demographic patterns and a lack of diversity in Hartford's public schools was muddied in the midst of the trial by then-Governor Lowell Weicker's State of the State Address delivered on January 6, 1993. In his address, Weiker urged the legislature and local school leaders to voluntarily integrate Connecticut's schools. He proposed having equal racial mixes in urban and suburban schools by the 1999–2000 school year. "A court-run school system is not for Connecticut—its children or its adults," he said. Acknowledging a court-mandated solution was a possibility, he said, "[i]f we fail to act, the courts, sooner or later, will do that which by election was entrusted to us." He also stated that Hartford's school system, as it existed then, was harmful to Connecticut's children and that the state had a duty to make it right. "The racial and economic isolation in Connecticut's school system is indisputable. Whether this segregation came about through the chance of historical boundaries or economic forces beyond the control of the state or whether it came about through private decisions or in spite of the best educational efforts of the state. What matters is that it is here and must be dealt with."

Reaction to Weicker's address was mixed. John Brittain, attorney for the plaintiffs, believed that the speech undercut the state's position, and was quoted by *The New York Times* as saying, "I don't know why I wouldn't call the Governor tomorrow as a witness." On the other side of the coin, State Representative Paul Knierim, a Republican from Simsbury and ranking member of the Education Committee, said, "I don't think it should be our objective to try to make all school districts have the same statistical racial or ethnic makeup regardless of settlement patterns. I'm fearful that that's the governor's thrust with this."

Then-House Majority Leader Edward Krawiecki went so far as to say that the governor was trying to "skew" the *Sheff* case with his speech. "What he was trying to do is put another piece of evidence outside the courtroom, before the judges and all the attorneys that are arguing this case,—that, look, the legislature and the executive branch are prepared to roll up their sleeves and go to work."

The same day as Weicker's address, on January 6, 1993, Elizabeth Sheff took the stand as a witness. She testified that during his first seven years of school, her son, Milo, did not have one white classmate. She commented on how such lack of diversity would not serve to develop well-balanced children. "I was able to learn and grow with people of different perspectives," she said, "and it afforded me the opportunity to be able to look at people as people. I hold no shadows in my heart based on the color of people's skin or the angle of their eyes or their material possessions. I've been able to look at people as God would have us look at them, as people. My son is not being afforded that opportunity, and I think that that is not good."

On January 12, almost a month after the trial began, Milo Sheff took the stand as a witness, the first student to do so in the case. Sheff told the court that in his eight years of public education in the Hartford School District, he had had one white classmate. Sheff also described his first experience at summer camp, where he was the only black camper. "It was hard to relate because I didn't know what to talk about. I dressed different, I talked different, we didn't have the same interests. It was really hard at first," he said. When asked whether it made a difference to him that he had only one white classmate over his past eight years of school, Milo replied that "[i]t makes a lot of difference in the terms that we need to put more of everybody in the class. It's really hard to know about somebody if you haven't talked to them. So we need to put everybody in the class, a mixture of people in the class." When asked if he would like the chance to go to school with a mixture of white and black students, Milo said, "Yea, that would be good for them. And good for everybody. It's good for the whole, so everybody could learn about each other, so when they get to the workforce you won't be confused and how I was in the first week I was there at camp."

Assistant Attorney General Whelan for the defense did not exercise his option to cross-examine Milo.

After calling 41 witnesses, the plaintiffs rested their case on January 28, 1993. The plaintiffs were obviously more than pleased with their progress. The *Courant* quoted John Brittain as saying, "I believe [the testimony] exceeded what we expected. We didn't expect the disparity to appear so stark. People have come up to us and said, 'We didn't know it was like that.'"

On February 2, the state began the presentation of their case, maintaining the argument that the state was not responsible for the segregation that was naturally occurring in the state. They also argued that the solution to such a problem was too big a task for one judge, and that the proper means of engineering a solution was to leave it in the hands of the legislature. Supporting the notion that the legislature would be the best branch to handle the problem was the fact that five days before the state started its case—on January 28—the legislature proposed an integration timetable for Connecticut communities. The goal was for regional education councils to submit integration plans by 1994 and begin implementing them the next year.

Whelan told the court that one of the state's primary aims in the case was to "present the court with some of the positive things that are going on, both in terms of demographics and in terms of positive efforts by the state to address both the issues of diversity and the needs of disadvantaged children."

The state's witnesses painted a somewhat rosier picture of Hartford public schools. Lloyd Calvert, former school superintendent in West Hartford, Trumbull, and Windsor was serving as a consultant for the state. Calvert testified that "[t]here's a shifting. The share [of minorities] in Hartford is becoming smaller, whereas the share in the 21 districts [surrounding Hartford] is becoming larger." Robert Nearine, special assistant for evaluation, research, and testing for the Hartford Public Schools, testified that Hartford school children's test scores were "below average, but not substantially below average."

In all, the state called 13 witnesses to the stand and rested its case on February 26, 1993.

POST-TRIAL DOCUMENTS AND DELIBERATIONS

After two months of testimony, the trial ended on February 26, 1993, though closing arguments by the attorneys would not take place until November 30, 1994. The next step was for each side to prepare and submit post-trial memorandums outlining their arguments as well as what they wanted Judge Hammer to do. Oral summaries of the briefs before the court would be scheduled as well. It would be more than two years before Judge Hammer made his decision.

"What is at stake in this case is the nature of the fundamental right that the Connecticut Constitution protects in ensuring all children an education," the plaintiffs argued in their Post-Trial Memorandum. "It is axiomatic that poor urban children deserve the same educational opportunities as middle class suburban children. Each child is precious, and each is an important resource for our future."

The memorandum reviewed the case the plaintiffs put on for the court, highlighting the fact that poverty was a major cause of the disparity between urban and suburban education. They also argued that in the Hartford schools, resources were deficient in every area, including school supplies, technology hardware and training, teachers, curriculum, guidance counselors, library materials, even a lack of chairs and classroom space. "The Hartford schools lack the staff necessary to provide the students in the district with an adequate education. At trial, Hartford educators described a school district that cannot afford to employ an adequate number of staff in critical areas. For example, Assistant Superintendent John P. Shea testified that schools' 'very valid' requests for additional teachers and other staff are routinely rejected because of a lack of resources."

The memorandum also attacked what the plaintiffs referred to as the state's "History of Inaction," going back to 1965 and outlining every report that was commissioned and every recommendation that was made for Hartford, but never followed. "Looking back over the thirty-year history of Connecticut's experience with racial and economic isolation in the Hartford schools, it is incontrovertible that the defendants were fully aware of increasing levels of racial isolation in the Hartford area; that the recognized the harms of segregation and the link between quality education and integrated education; that defendants were aware of techniques available to achieve desegregation; and that they received recommendations that could have significantly ameliorated the problem. Yet, during this entire period, virtually nothing significant has been done."

In concluding, the plaintiffs urged the court not to be "deterred by promises of future voluntary actions by the defendants. The state has filled many documents with many visions and promises of quality and integrated education in the past, but nothing has been done....Decades of delay and neglect by state authorities have deprived the plaintiff children of their fundamental right to an equal educational opportunity. The continued concentration of the poorest students in the most racially isolated school district with the worst academic performance in the state creates a compelling and urgent need for this court to act."

The defendants' post-trial brief similarly highlighted the same points they had been asserting since the complaint was filed, namely that the "plaintiffs have not established that the defendants have violated the equal protection, due process and education provisions of the Constitution...[they] have not proven that the constitutional obligation to provide free elementary and secondary schools imposes a specific obligation on the state to meet certain levels of racial and economic integration and educational achievement."

The defendants also argued that the state was handling the situation in the best and most efficient way possible, through the general assembly. The defendants in their brief stated, "Consistent with the constitution, the general assembly has taken appropriate action to address racial, ethnic and socioeconomic isolation and to address the underachievement of children living in poverty in our cities."

The brief also commented on the issue of the suit's broad scope, and their opinion that the problems addressed by the suit were too wide-ranging and complex to be fixed by the judicial branch. "The problem of racial, ethnic and socioeconomic isolation and poor educational performance in Hartford and other urban areas are complex social conditions that cannot be resolved in the limited context of a case such as this, but must be addressed by a broad spectrum of initiatives which can only be directed by the general assembly."

In reviewing the evidence presented at trial, the defendants asserted that

> [t]he only conclusion that can be drawn from the evidence is that there is no reasonable basis upon which to find that the defendants have violated the constitution and that the court should not usurp what is properly the role of the General Assembly... The plaintiffs' failure to offer any substantial evidence of a constitutionally-required course of conduct which the defendants did not follow, is reason enough for the court to find that the constitution has not been violated.

The defendants do not claim that the job which state policymakers have set for themselves has been fully accomplished. State policymakers continue to look for new ways to advance the rational state policy of promoting greater diversity in our schools. But neither the inability to fully meet our goals nor the constant consideration of new and different approaches to these problems are reason for the court to find that the constitution has been violated.

In concluding, the defendants asked the court to "recognize the plaintiffs' case for what it is—a request by a small group of individuals for a writ of mandamus that would dramatically intrude upon the broad discretion which must be exercised by the General Assembly, the State Board of Education, the Commission of Education, twenty-two cities, towns and school districts in the Hartford area, and the citizens of this state through their elected representatives. No court has the authority to grant the kind of relief the plaintiffs are seeking under the facts of this case."

Closing arguments were heard on November 30, 1994, nearly two years after the trial began. Attorneys Horton and Brittain again spoke for the plaintiffs, while Attorney General Richard Blumenthal and Assistant Attorney General Bernard McGovern spoke on behalf of the defendants. John Whelan, who had been arguing for the defendants thus far, had died suddenly on April 28, 1994.

"The school children in this case have been deeply disappointed over the slow case of equal educational opportunities, as our long thirty-year chart shows," said Brittain. "At the current pace, it could be the year two thousand and fifty before integration reaches the Hartford region... Many believe that the *Sheff versus O'Neill* case is to Connecticut what *Brown versus Board of Education* was to the South and later to the nation."

Horton told Judge Hammer that if he "[agreed] that the students in Hartford are not receiving equal educational opportunity, then...the combination of Article Eight, Section One, plus the equal protection clause...wins our case..."

"Your honor, we're not here because of some vague moral principles or such like, we're here because of the law," he said. "We're here because we say the law requires that all students receive an equal educational opportunity, and they're not receiving it. Your Honor, the plaintiffs have proved their case and they're entitled to judgment."

Attorneys Blumenthal and McGovern responded to the plaintiffs arguments by continuing to assert that the plaintiffs had failed to prove the state did anything wrong. "...[I]f I were here for no other reason, it would be to dispute the claim that Mr. Brittain made in the course of his argument that the State's position is that nothing should be done about the problems that they are asking this court to address," Blumenthal said. "I would most vigorously dispute that contention. In fact, the State's position is, the governor's position is, my position is that more can and should and must be done about the problem. They must be done as a moral imperative, as a social imperative, but the key question for this Court is whether there's been a violation of constitutional law."

McGovern closed by saying "[w]e believe that there has been no violation of law, no violation of any of the specific provisions of law that have been advanced by the plaintiffs here...certainly, there's no constitutional entitlement to any special programs or any special resources, other than a general equal educational expenditure."

WAITING TO HEAR FROM HAMMER

While the parties were waiting for a decision, the legislature began seriously dealing with the issue of segregation. On June 28, 1993, the governor signed into law Public Act 93-263, "An Act Improving Educational Quality and Diversity." The new law set forth a specific timetable giving local and regional boards of education until April 1, 1994 to "assess the needs of the school district and the communities served by the school district...On or before September 15, 1994, each region shall develop...and submit a regional plan to the commissioner [of education] for review." The Act defined such a plan as "a voluntary cooperative interdistrict or regional plan to (i) improve the quality of school performance and student outcomes through initiatives which may include, but are not limited to, magnet schools and programs, interdistrict schools and programs, regional vocational-technical schools, regional vocational-agricultural programs, interdistrict student attendance including school choice, charter schools, early childhood education and parent education, summer school, extracurricular activities, and student community service, paired schools, teacher and administrator exchange and interactive telecommunications; (ii) reduce barriers to opportunity including, but not limited to, poverty, unemployment and the lack of housing and transportation; (iii) enhance student diversity and awareness of diversity or (iv) address the programmatic needs of limited English proficient students with quality limited English proficient and bilingual programs." The Act also mandated that "[e]ach such plan shall provide equal opportunity for all students, including such additional services as may be necessary to ensure meaningful participation in a program."

Financing for such programs were vaguely addressed in the Act, putting the power of approving requested funds in the hands of the education commissioner; no funds for implementing such programs were guaranteed by the new law. It also indicated that school districts which "failed to participate in good faith" in the planning could be denied funds regularly paid to it by the state treasury.

A DISAPPOINTING DECISION

Judge Hammer's opinion was released on April 12, 1995, almost six years to the day after the complaint was first filed. After examining all the evidence and issues of law, Hammer decided not to make a decision as to whether the children's constitutional rights had been violated—finding that maintaining racially balanced schools was not a duty of the state—and entered judgment in favor of the defendants.

In his decision, Hammer noted that the plaintiffs did not "[establish] any of what Justice Douglas described as the 'more subtle' types of state action that are ordinarily presumed in 'de facto segregation' cases, including more specifically the factors of residential segregation, as well as attendance zone boundaries, which are exclusively the statutory duty of local boards of education under § 10-220 of the General Statutes. The court also finds in accordance with the holding of *Spencer v. Kugler*, that '[r]acially balanced municipalities are beyond the pale of either judicial or legislative intervention.' The court therefore finds that the plaintiffs have

April 12, 1995. Milo Sheff, center, talks during a press conference about the verdict on the *Sheff v. O'Neill* case. Surrounding Sheff are, clockwise from lower left, law professor John Brittain, CCLU lawyer Phil Tegeler, co-plaintiffs in the case Carol Vinick and her daughter Tasha Connoly, 9, Milo's mother Elizabeth Horton Sheff, and CCLU Legal Director Martha Stone. © *Hartford Courant*.

failed to prove that 'state action is a direct and sufficient cause of the conditions' which are the subject matter of the plaintiffs' complaint as alleged in the defendants' sixth special defense, and that accordingly the constitutional claims asserted by the plaintiffs need not be addressed."

Then-Governor John Rowland's reaction to the decision was to break out the bubbly. Upon hearing of Hammer's decision, Rowland presented Attorney General Richard Blumenthal with a bottle of champagne during a press conference regarding the outcome of the case. Blumenthal, who according to the *Hartford Courant* does not drink, said, "I was as surprised as anyone by the champagne. I had no idea it was coming and would have advised against it...I have never celebrated any victory in court with champagne, but least of all this one." Outcry against Rowland's actions came swiftly. Elizabeth Horton Sheff was quoted by the *Courant* as saying that it was in "poor taste for the governor to be toasting the fact that Judge Hammer decided not to decide whether our children have constitutional rights." State Senator Toni Harp commented, "I would hope that the governor, in reviewing his toast, understands that he's toasting to the lack of mobility for children of color."

Rowland apologized to black community leaders on April 20, 1995, explaining that he "didn't really understand the implication that some people would read into it....The attorney general's office had worked for almost six years on this case representing the state. We were applauding that hard work, not the result and not the outcome."

"The only real victory and celebration will be when we achieve the goal of giving our schoolchildren the best quality and diversity of education that's possible," Blumenthal said, "and we all ought to be working [toward] that goal together and put the champagne on ice until we achieve it."

Martha Stone, attorney for the plaintiffs, in reaction to Hammer's decision was quoted by the *Courant* as saying, "We're not about to give up the fight. We do feel we proved there is unequal educational opportunity for these 26,000 [Hartford] children."

"We will continue here," said Elizabeth Horton Sheff. "We are disappointed. Truly, truly I feel we have proved over and over again in court the unequal educational opportunities of children in the city of Hartford. I am truly disappointed but undaunted, because the first rule of struggle is perseverance."

Eugene Leach, parent of Rachel and Joseph Leach who were named plaintiffs in the case was quoted by the *Courant* as calling Hammer's decision an "evasion of responsibility...We haven't got the satisfaction that we sought. This makes it crystal clear that we must appeal the decision. There can't be any doubt about this," he said.

Hammer's reliance on federal precedent, especially his excessive quotation of Supreme Court Justice William Douglas, left many puzzled. William Taylor, a desegregation attorney from Washington, D.C., was quoted by the *Courant* as saying that Hammer's reliance on Douglas was "puzzling," and even "inappropriate." George Mason University sociologist David Armor also weighed in on the issue. "The federal law doesn't apply here. That's why they brought the case in the state court. I don't personally understand."

John Brittain, attorney for the plaintiffs, was also not pleased with the federal interpretation of the case that was brought specifically in state court. "We mentioned under the Connecticut Constitution that there was no such requirement [of intentional discrimination]," he said. "Harry Hammer swept the case under the rug."

Defendant Education Commission Gerald Tirozzi also did not necessarily agree with the opinion. "In winning, everyone in the state is losing...Someone is at fault and someone has to find a solution to the problems," he said.

Before the plaintiffs' attorneys even finished reading Hammer's seventy-page decision, they pledged they would appeal the case to the Connecticut Supreme Court. Just six days after the decision was issued, protests about the results began in Hartford. Nearly 200 students walked out of their classes at Hartford and Weaver Highs on April 18, 1995. Because they were led by community leaders, the students were not sanctioned for leaving classes. Prayers and hymns were recited at the State Capitol that morning and followed by an evening rally at St. Monica's Church in Hartford.

Then-Hartford Mayor Michael Peters participated in the day's events and told the *Courant* that he planned to file an amicus, or friend of the court, brief on behalf of the plaintiffs in their appeal of the case. "I am going to ask the city of Hartford to be a part of this lawsuit," he said. A few weeks later on May 5, John DeStefano, then-mayor of New Haven, said he would also seek the support of the city council to file an amicus brief on behalf of the plaintiffs.

On August 8, 1995, the cities of Hartford and New Haven, and the Bridgeport Board of Education were authorized to appear and file a brief as amici curiae. Their briefs were limited to 20 pages in length.

The *Courant* commissioned another poll by the Institute for Social Inquiry at the University of Connecticut regarding the results of Hammer's decision. The poll interviewed 418 white and 69 nonwhite people from April 18 to April 25. According to the poll, 58 percent of residents interviewed "strongly" or "somewhat" favored Hammer's ruling against the plaintiffs, 63 percent of nonwhites polled opposed Hammer's decision, and 64 percent of whites supported it.

APPEALING THE DECISION

On April 27, 1995, less than two weeks after the decision was issued, and exactly six years and one day after the initial complaint was filed, the plaintiffs submitted their appeal. In their Preliminary Statement of the Issues, the plaintiffs informed the court they would be raising the following issues:

1. Did the court err in refusing to follow the construction of Article First, §§1 and 20 and Article Eighth, §1 of the Connecticut Constitution established in *Horton v. Meskill*, which held that the state is required to assure to all of Connecticut's public school students an equal educational opportunity?
2. Did the court err in failing to recognize as "state action" the state's extensive involvement in public education in denying plaintiffs' claims of racial and ethnic segregation, unequal educational opportunity and lack of a minimally adequate education?
3. Did the court err in failing to recognize that the state constitution gives rise to an affirmative duty on the state to address racial and ethnic segregation, unequal educational opportunity and lack of a minimally adequate education and that the state failed to act to remedy these constitutional and statutory deficiencies?
4. Did the admitted and undisputed evidence require the court as a matter of law to find that the students in the Hartford public schools are not receiving an equal educational opportunity?

On May 1, 1995, word came from the Connecticut Supreme Court that the justices had agreed to hear the case. The court called a meeting with the attorneys on May 11 to discuss how the case would proceed. They asked Judge Hammer for a more concise ruling of fact on several of the key issues in the case. According to Boston University Professor Christine Rossell who served as a witness for the defendants, the court's request of Hammer was "a diplomatic way of saying they don't like

Hammer's decision...or they don't like the form of it. Essentially what they want is [for] Judge Hammer to write a new opinion."

The court also directed the parties to come up with an outline of what facts they agreed and disagreed on by May 25. They asked Hammer to have his revised findings in by June 15. Much of the court's orders stemmed from a motion to expedite the appeal filed by the plaintiffs on May 10, 1995. The plaintiffs proposed that the parties prepare a joint stipulation of facts and provided the deadlines ultimately adopted by the court. They also asked that Hammer "promptly review the stipulation."

The defendants filed their preliminary Statement of the Issues on May 10 as well. They informed the court of the issues they thought had to be decided in the appeal, namely, "whether the court correctly held that the defendants have taken no action...which has caused the present racial and ethnic student composition of the Hartford public schools, and therefore, have not deprived the plaintiff students of equal protection nor caused them to be segregated or discriminated against on the basis of their races or national origins nor denied them due process...?" The defendants also presented the court with three alternate grounds upon which it could affirm Hammer's judgment:

1. Whether Art. I, §§1, 8, 10, and 20 and Art. VIII, §1, either separately or collectively, require no specific level of racial, ethnic or socioeconomic integration in the state's public elementary and secondary schools nor a specified level of educational achievement by students in those schools?
2. Whether, in the absence of any state action causing the plaintiffs' school assignments or their educational programs to be based upon their races or national origins and when the General Assembly has enacted and kept in force legislation which assures for the plaintiffs substantially equal educational expenditures in relation to all other public elementary and secondary public school students in the state, the plaintiffs have not been statutorily denied "equal educational opportunity..."
3. Whether the plaintiffs' claim that they are denied a "minimum adequate education" or any particular educational program...is nonjusticiable?

Due to the enormous volume of paperwork to go through, Hammer quickly asked for help in rewriting his findings. Parties on both sides worked to reduce the number of issues that were in dispute to make

Hammer's job less consuming. The *Courant* quoted John Brittain as saying, "I don't think anyone would begrudge him if he needs extra time, because it's an enormous amount of work." Two days before the June 15 deadline, the Connecticut Supreme Court agreed to extend the date of completion to June 27.

Hammer submitted his twenty-eight-page findings to the court on June 27. His findings covered the following areas:

- the historical background of the case, the "State's involvement in the racial, ethnic and socioeconomic isolation of the Hartford school system and the state's response to those conditions and to the educational underachievement of the children who attend the Hartford public schools";
- whether the Hartford school system provided the "plaintiffs with a minimally adequate education under the equal protection and education clauses of the state constitution;
- whether the Hartford school system provided "equal educational opportunities to the plaintiffs under the equal protection and education clauses of the state constitution," as well as the nature and scope of the remedy.

According to the *Courant*, Hammer "concurred with the state's argument that schools are not equipped to deal with serious social problems such as poverty, hunger, drug abuse and parental neglect," and more significantly found that "the state had no role in causing racial segregation and that court-ordered desegregation plans do not work well."

In responding to Hammer's new findings, John Brittain was quoted as saying, "It's a very sad day. The judge blamed the poor children for their lack of equal educational opportunity and essentially adopted the premise...that there is nothing that can be done."

Oral arguments began and ended on September 28, 1995. The first question was posed by Justice David Borden only minutes after Attorney Wesley Horton began his argument. "I don't think anybody disagrees that [racial] diversity is good for society and the educational process," Borden said. "The question is, is that required by the constitution?" For over two hours both sides were asked pointed questions designed to get at the issues that would decide the case, specifically whether Connecticut's constitution required the state to provide an equal educational opportunity. Horton represented the plaintiffs while Attorney General Richard Blumenthal spoke for the state.

More than nine months after the court heard oral arguments, the decision was handed down on July 9, 1996. Justice Peters, writing for a sharply divided court stated:

> The public elementary and high school students in Hartford suffer daily from the devastating effects that racial and ethnic isolation, as well as poverty, have had on their education. Federal constitutional law provides no remedy for their plight. The principal issue in this appeal is whether, under the unique provisions of our state constitution, the state, which already plays an active role in managing public schools, must take further measures to relieve the severe handicaps that burden these children's education. The issue is as controversial as the stakes are high. We hold today that the needy schoolchildren of Hartford have waited long enough. The constitutional imperatives contained in article eighth, § 1, and article first, §§ 1 and 20, of our state constitution entitle the plaintiffs to relief. At the same time, the constitutional imperative of separation of powers persuades us to afford the legislature, with the assistance of the executive branch, the opportunity, in the first instance, to fashion the remedy that will most appropriately respond to the constitutional violations that we have identified. The judgment of the trial court must, accordingly, be reversed.

Retired Chief Justice Ellen Ash Peters of the Connecticut Supreme Court, author of the ruling in *Sheff v. O'Neill*, speaks during a symposium at the University of Connecticut School of Law on November 9, 2006, marking the 10th anniversary of *Sheff*. To her right is Attorney Wesley Horton. *UConn Advance, Photo by Spencer Sloan.*

The court ruled in favor of the plaintiffs, acknowledging the fact that public school segregation, even though unintentional, violated Connecticut's constitution. What the court did not do, however, was provide specific remedies to correct the segregation. Instead, the court directed "the legislature and the executive branch to put the search for appropriate remedial measures at the top of their respective agendas." Though the court imposed no definite deadlines for the Connecticut governor and legislature to come up with a solution, the court did note that, "[i]n staying our hand, we do not wish to be misunderstood about the urgency of finding an appropriate remedy for the plight of Hartford's public schoolchildren. Every passing day denies these children their constitutional right to a substantially equal educational opportunity. Every passing day shortchanges these children in their ability to learn to contribute to their own well-being and to that of this state and nation."

The plaintiffs had finally prevailed in court. Whether the favorable court decision would translate into meaningful change for Hartford's schoolchildren, however, was another matter altogether.

Reaction to the ruling was both very positive and very negative, with some criticism coming directly from the court itself. Justice Borden, who wrote separately to note his dissenting opinion, said that the majority's decision was "long on rhetoric and short on reasoning." Borden's dissent asserted that "the majority has used this court's power to interpret the constitution in order to mandate a vast and unprecedented social experiment, using the state's schools and schoolchildren as test data, and thereby to construct what the majority perceives to be the necessary bridge over the racial divide."

Governor Rowland was quoted by the *Courant* as saying, "We don't like the decision, but we're working with it." Attorney General Blumenthal said, "We disagree profoundly with the result."

LEGISLATIVE REACTION

One of the first steps the state took in complying with the court's mandate was to form a twenty-two-member Education Improvement Panel to advise the legislature. The contentious issue surrounding this panel was its makeup. Senate Minority Leader William DiBella of Hartford was in charge of naming members to the panel, and with just two slots left to fill, only one of the 20 members of the board lived in Hartford; 14 members were white with four black and two Hispanic.

The group's initial meeting was on August 25, 1996; the deadline for their findings and recommendations, as imposed by Governor Rowland, was January 22, 1997. According to the *Courant*, some of the options the panel would be looking at included expanding charter schools, increasing school choice programs whereby parents could enroll their children in districts outside their town, expand Project Concern whereby Hartford students could attend schools in nearby districts, provide regional magnet schools with more support, create elite schools for Hartford students, provide financial incentives to districts that build schools that are racially integrated, earmark state aid for fundamental supplies like textbooks and computers in Hartford, change zoning laws, and redraw school district boundaries.

By January 22, the panel had come up with 15 recommendations for the legislature. The three major proposals were school choice expansion, expansion of preschool programs, and the construction of racially integrated schools. The panel also recommended hiring more minority teachers, expanding adult education programs, creating and imposing sanctions on "failing" schools to promote accountability, expanding and improving bilingual education programs, encouraging parent involvement, and imposing measures to reduce poverty.

The legislature's response to the recommendation came in the form of several bills including "An Act Enhancing Educational Choices and Opportunities," "An Act Ensuring Affordable Housing for Residents of the State in Response to the Decision in *Sheff v. O'Neill*," "An Act Extending the Time for the Department of Education to Review the Racial Imbalance Statutes and Regulations," "An Act Concerning Withdrawal of Towns from Regional School Districts and Dissolution of Regional School Districts," "An Act Concerning the Hartford Public Schools and School District Accountability," and "An Act Concerning Revisions to the Education Statutes."

On April 18, 1997, "An Act Concerning the Hartford Public Schools" was signed into law. "It is hereby found and declared that the Hartford school district is in a state of crisis and that the continued existence of this crisis is detrimental to the children of the city and in conflict with the educational interests of the state and the resolution of the crisis is a matter of paramount public interest...." The Act disbanded the Hartford Board of Education and created in its place a Board of Trustees that would be responsible for getting Hartford schools back on its feet.

On June 26, 1997, "An Act Enhancing Educational Choices and Opportunities" was passed into law. "In order to reduce racial, ethnic and economic isolation, each school district shall provide educational opportunities for its students to interact with students and teachers from other racial, ethnic, and economic backgrounds and may provide such opportunities with students from other communities."

By March 1998, the plaintiffs felt that not enough was being done and that the situation in the Hartford public schools remained largely the same as before the supreme court had issued its decision. They sought judicial relief and, according to the *Courant*, asked the judge to order "the design and implementation of a comprehensive remedial plan for the schools and districts...no later than the 1998-99 school year." A hearing on the issue was ordered and the state was obligated to prove to the court that they were in fact taking steps to reduce the racial segregation present in Hartford schools. A trial date was scheduled and rescheduled; the parties finally returned to court on September 8, 1998. The case was heard before Judge Julia L. Aurigemma at Middlesex Superior Court in Middletown, which had a special docket for complex litigation cases.

William M. Gordon, a school desegregation specialist, testified for the plaintiffs about the state's legislative response to the supreme court's ruling. "There are a lot of good things in it, but it is not a desegregation plan," he said. Gordon also noted that the legislation did not "define desegregation. It doesn't have any timelines. It doesn't have any particular goals." For three days, the plaintiffs presented evidence and witnesses to show the state was not taking meaningful steps to desegregate Hartford schools.

On September 11, the state defended the actions it had taken thus far, and urged the court to give them more time, asserting that a solution to the problem would not and could not happen overnight. The hearing continued until September 22; oral arguments were heard on December 7. Each side submitted briefs to the court before final arguments. The state argued that the legislative response was not intended to be a "quick fix to produce impressive numbers, which would be destined to disintegrate in a few years from a lack of public support and a dearth of real educational improvement. Rather, it is a strategy for long-term educational reform to attain the twin goals of diversity and quality." The plaintiffs argued that the programs offered by the state, "however desirable they may be educationally, are wholly irrelevant to the question of reduction of racial isolation."

Issuing her opinion a year after relief was sought, on March 3, 1999, Judge Aurigemma found that "[t]he plaintiffs have sought court intervention before the state has had an opportunity to take even a 'second step' in the remedial process. The state has acted expeditiously and in good faith to respond to the decision of the Supreme Court in this case...The legislative and executive branches should have a realistic opportunity to implement their remedial programs before further court intervention." The court declined to grant the plaintiffs request for relief and found that "the state has complied with the decision of the Supreme Court."

In a press release praising the decision, Attorney General Blumenthal said that the state was "pleased that the Court has recognized that our Legislature is acting positively in good faith to improve the quality and diversity of education for all students in Connecticut, in compliance with the State Supreme Court's ruling in *Sheff v. O'Neill*." He also acknowledged that the problems facing Hartford had not yet been solved. "Much progress has been achieved. Much more remains to be accomplished, and must be accomplished, under the ongoing initiatives and programs devised by legislative and executive officials who have made the diversity and quality of education central goals and priorities now and in the immediate future."

The plaintiffs agreed not to appeal the ruling. "We've decided our best course of action is to wait and see how the legislature performs this session and what progress is made in the upcoming school year," said Philip D. Tegeler, legal director of the Connecticut Civil Liberties Foundation and a *Sheff* lawyer, as quoted in the *Hartford Courant*.

The plaintiffs returned to court in December 2000. "We've waited through two legislative sessions," Wesley Horton said. "There's more of a problem today than there was two years ago." Finding the results of the state's action to be unacceptable, the plaintiffs filed a motion to ask for another declaratory judgment that the action was inadequate.

"We find ourselves in 2001, five years after the decision ... [and] we have not seen any reduction of racial and ethnic isolation in Hartford," said Dennis Parker, a member of the *Sheff* legal team and lawyer with the NAACP Legal Defense Fund, as quoted in the *Hartford Courant*. "The steps taken do not come close to what is required."

This time, instead of merely filing a motion for a declaratory judgment, the plaintiffs submitted a comprehensive plan they designed to desegregate Hartford schools. The four-year plan was created by Leonard Stevens, a desegregation consultant who had designed similar plans across the country. According to the *Courant*, the plan called for "[f]ull state funding of regional magnet schools...[a]dditional money to help Hartford convert several of its public schools to magnets designed to enroll city and suburban children...[and] [a] provision allowing parents, not school districts, to determine who gets into magnet schools or the urban-suburban choice program."

The funding aspect of the plan involved state aid dollars literally traveling with the children. According to the *Courant*, "[u]nder the plan, mostly white suburban districts would lose part of their state aid as they send students to magnet schools but would gain money by accepting black and Hispanic students from Hartford under a voluntary urban-suburban transfer program."

The state argued that such a plan, potentially costing hundreds of millions of taxpayer dollars, would do more harm than good, and that a judicially imposed plan was not going to solve the problem.

The trial was again heard by Judge Aurigemma, this time in New Britain. The hearings, during which both sides presented evidence and testimony regarding Hartford's progress, or lack thereof, lasted more than three weeks in April and May of 2002. At the conclusion of the testimony, Aurigemma asked both sides to submit proposals as to how she should rule and what should happen next.

In the time between the end of the hearings and before oral arguments, attorneys for both sides came together with hopes of negotiating a settlement instead of leaving the decision in the hands of the court. The *Courant* quoted Aurigemma commenting on the negotiation efforts. "If the plaintiffs and the state can find a way to live with a resolution, that would be excellent," she said. "It would be a good thing for everyone." Negotiations lasted several months though neither side publicly stated what was being discussed or whether progress was being made.

On January 22, 2003, it was revealed that the negotiations were successful and the parties had come to an agreement. The *Courant* reported that the secretive negotiations took place in various locations including the "posh" Hartford Club as well as Horton's office, and the major draws were bowls of candy and blueberry muffins supplied by Horton's wife Chloe.

An eleven-page settlement and stipulation was submitted to the General Assembly for ratification. The agreement consisted of a "timetable for planned, reasonable progress in reducing student isolation in the Hartford public schools until June 30, 2007." Both parties recognized that "efforts will need to continue beyond 2007 to further reduce isolation in the Hartford Public Schools."

The stipulation asserted that, "by the end of the term of this Stipulation, at least 30 percent of minority students residing in Hartford will have an educational experience with reduced isolation...." The agreement also noted consequences for failure to meet the goals. "[D]efendants' inability to make significant progress towards this goal may be considered by the Court, as one factor, in determining what future plans or orders may be necessary to achieve future compliance."

The stipulation called for the creation of two new magnet schools a year, for a total of eight new schools by 2007, that would service 600 students each. It also mandated for the Open Choice program to expand to 1,000 students in the first year, 1,200 in the second, 1,400 in the third, and 1,600 in the fourth. Expansion of interdistrict cooperative programs was also required. The costs of implementation were estimated at $4.5

million for the first year, and went up to $18.09 million in the fourth year; in all, the state would be required to allocate more than $45 million over the four year period.

Regular monitoring of the plan's progress was provided for, and the parties agreed to meet at least twice a year to discuss the implementation of the plan. The plaintiffs' ability to return to court was also limited by the stipulation—the parties were directed to resolve issues on their own before going to court. If an issue remained unresolved, the plaintiffs could return to court only to ask for a judicial determination of whether a material breach of the stipulation occurred. On February 25, the settlement was approved by the Connecticut legislature.

Just eight months after the settlement was approved and went into effect, the plaintiffs made it clear they still felt the state was not working fast enough. Philip D. Tegeler, legal director of the Connecticut Civil Liberties Union, who had been with the *Sheff* case since the original filing in 1989, was quoted by the *Courant* on October 18, 2003, as saying, "We appear to be far behind in terms of compliance with the agreement in the first year." The Open Choice program had expanded by only 500 students instead of the 1,000 the settlement mandated and problems with funding held up magnet school creation.

By the beginning of August 2004, then-State Education Commissioner Betty Sternberg admitted that it was unlikely the state would meet all the terms of the 2003 settlement. It was not until 10 months after Tegeler spoke out about the problems that the plaintiffs found themselves back in court. They again petitioned to have the state held accountable, this time in the form of a determination that the state had materially breached the agreement. The motion indicated that the settlement timetable called for 2,400 Hartford children to enroll by 2004 in two new magnet schools that opened in 2003 and three others that were scheduled to open in 2004, but that they estimated that fewer than 900 students would actually enroll. At the time the motion was filed, the racial makeup of Hartford schools was 95 percent black and Latino.

Sternberg was quoted by the *Courant* as saying, "We're doing everything in our capacity to meet the requirements. From an educational point of view, we think we're moving in the right direction. The legal issue will have to be decided in court." Elizabeth Horton Sheff was quoted as saying, "They've fallen short of the entire agreement...The state has not, as agreed, given enough money to even get [the new magnet schools] going."

Perhaps prompted by the filing of the motion, the state promised to provide Hartford with funds to get the magnet schools up and running. The state promised $810,000 to cover start-up costs for the new magnet schools and agreed to sell Hartford 14.4 acres of property to build a magnet school for $1 instead of the $230,000 as originally negotiated.

Judge Susan Peck heard arguments on the motion at superior court in New Britain on June 20, 2005, but deferred making a decision right away, though she did indicate she was more inclined to find for the state. "Based on what I have before me, I can't find that the state is in breach of this agreement," she said. "I don't know how I could find [the state] in material breach based on this language unless they didn't have a game plan or they didn't open the schools or they failed to operate two new magnet schools each year. How do you open two schools and expect that on day one they will be filled to capacity or even to substantial capacity? They're untested. They're untried."

By the third year of the agreement, Hartford schools were far behind in terms of compliance with the settlement requirements. Hartford schools had achieved slightly less than half the target student body numbers in the magnet schools, and the students who were attending magnet schools were mostly non-white. By January 2006, the plaintiffs were talking with state officials to determine what the next phase of the plan would look like. In June 2006, 22 magnet schools existed in Hartford, though not all of them were open. According to the *Courant*, of the nine schools that were opened after the 2003 settlement, white students made up only 4 percent to 19 percent of total students; these numbers fell far below the 30 percent requirement imposed by the settlement.

In May 2007, the parties formulated a tentative agreement to extend and revise the existing agreement which was set to expire in June 2007. The new agreement called for more money—approximately $112 million—over five years to promote magnet and charter schools in order to foster integration. This agreement, however, acknowledged the fact that magnet schools in Hartford had not been as successful as hoped. The new plan called for the creation of magnet schools in suburban towns, not Hartford. The new agreement would have to be approved first by the legislature and then by the courts in order to go into effect. Tired of waiting for the legislature's approval, the plaintiffs filed a motion in court on July 5, 2007, in order to require the state to take immediate action to desegregate. "Time is wasting, and kids are not being properly educated," the *Courant* quoted Elizabeth Wesley Horton.

While the motion in court was pending, the legislature declined to approve the new agreement at a special session called in July. The legislature had received the proposal two days before the regular session ended. The refusal was influenced by Hartford Mayor Eddie Perez who had been vocal about his disapproval of the agreement. The *Courant* reported that Perez felt "the agreement could lead to excessive construction and busing costs that his city cannot afford. He noted the city still has not been reimbursed for more than $3.2 million in construction costs at one magnet school."

"If the city of Hartford doesn't think it's good, we have to take that into account," said then-Senate Majority Leader Martin Looney, a New Haven Democrat, as reported in the *Courant*. "It's their city, their schools."

The parties appeared in court for a hearing on the motion beginning on November 6, 2007. The plaintiffs asked for stricter guidelines for desegregation efforts. They also asked to double the number of Hartford students attending suburban schools and to create more Hartford magnet schools. Witnesses for the plaintiffs spoke of the state's inconsistent enforcement of the settlement requirements, especially the fact that it left much of the enforcement to the city of Hartford, who was not a party to the case, and thus not responsible for carrying out the mandate of the court.

Casey Cobb, (left) associate professor of educational leadership at the University of Connecticut, speaks with John Brittain (right) during the Public School Choice in a Post-Desegregation World conference at UConn's Center for Education Policy Analysis in November 2007. *UConn Advance, Photo by Frank Dahlmeyer.*

According to the *Courant*, State Education Commissioner Mark McQuillan testified that he would like the court to expand his "legal authority to force suburban districts to accept students of color from Hartford." The state argued that one of the main problems they faced was not being able to force suburban school districts to open up seats to Hartford children under the Open Choice program.

Closing arguments were held on January 3, 2008. According to the *Courant*, the plaintiffs asked the court "to issue a detailed order spelling out exactly what the state should do to integrate city students with their suburban counterparts. A lawyer for the city urged the court to appoint a monitor to oversee the task. An attorney for the state of Connecticut argued that no order, nor monitor was necessary or desirable. The state education commissioner can bring about the desegregation goals without judicial intervention."

Even though Judge Berger had 120 days to issue a ruling, just a few weeks later on January 24, he announced his decision to halt the judicial action. He informed the parties that he would refrain from ruling on the case until the legislature officially decided on the proposal submitted to them, which had not yet been officially ratified or withdrawn. The legislature had until February 25, 2008, to approve or deny the settlement; if they did not do so within that time frame, the settlement would automatically be approved.

State Senator Don Williams introduced a resolution to approve the settlement. On February 14, 2008, the resolution was referred to the Joint Committee on Education. Representative James Amman introduced an identical resolution in the House, which was referred to the Joint Committee on Education on February 11. No resolutions seeking to deny the resolution had been introduced at the time of printing and neither the Senate nor the House had voted on the resolutions. It is unclear whether the new settlement will be approved, or if once again, the plaintiffs will return to court. The February 25 deadline came and went with no decision made by the legislature; the settlement did not automatically go into effect, however, as an extension of time had been granted. The legislature was granted until March 6 to accept or deny the agreement. On March 4, 2008, the agreement was withdrawn from the General Assembly. The *Courant* cited "legislators with knowledge of the talks," as saying that the two sides were in the process of negotiating broader changes than originally proposed in the withdrawn agreement. Attorney General Blumenthal was quoted as saying they hoped to submit a new plan by the end of March 2008.

Milo Sheff said he was not surprised that the state has been unable to solve the problems in Hartford public schools. "We live in Connecticut. How long have you been driving down the same street with the same potholes," he said. "Do you really think they are going to be able to fix an entire school system?...It's not the system that's failing it's the people that are failing the system. We need to elect people who speak for us not to us."

One thing is clear, the problems Hartford has been facing for decades are far from solved. It seems likely that the plaintiffs will refuse to stop trying to integrate the schools, and with any luck they will continue to receive cooperation from the state, which has thus far made a valiant effort to overcome Hartford's segregation. Segregated schools present a multitude of problems, none of which can be fixed overnight, or even in the span of a few years.

APPENDIX A

Connecticut Justice and Mercy

By Ruth MacKenzie*

At the May 1693 session of the Connecticut General Court, the long-established common-law procedure governing jurors empanelled for a criminal trial was put into written law.[1] On the surface, this action might appear to reflect a continuance of previous interest in codifying the inherited English common law. Actually it was more a case of openly locking the barn door after first removing a horse by stealth: the Court was writing "Finis" to a chapter of chicanery in which Governor Treat, William Pitkin, Samuel Wyllys, and others of lesser stature had all been involved.

The chicanery, however, had not been lightly or meanly motivated; it had been the last desperate resort of honorable men. When all else failed and a final choice had to be made, they had placed the newly regained, but still precarious, stability of their colony, as well as justice for an individual, above the demands of Puritan conscience. Had they not done so, history might well have placed Connecticut in the dubious niche now reserved for Salem and Massachusetts alone.

The troubles whose solution posed so great a moral problem originated in the spring of 1692. At that time the people of eastern Massachusetts, goaded on by fanatical religious and civil leaders, were indulging in their orgy of legal homicide. But public hysteria was not confined to the Salem area; the good people in the Fairfield County section of Connecticut suddenly realized that they, too, were harboring the Devil's own. Fortunately, from their point of view, this assault by the forces of evil was a contingency for which they were well prepared. In 1642, the General Court had established as the second of the twelve "Capitall Lawes" of the colony:

Yf any man or woman be a witch (that is) hath or consulteth wth a familiar spirit, they shall be put to death. Ex: 22.18 Lev: 20.27 Deu: 18.10, 11.[2]

The same capital laws had also been included verbatim in the Code of Laws drawn up by Roger Ludlow and established by the Court in 1650. Thus armed with legal weapons the hunt was on, and the hunters raced in for the kill.

Fortunately for Connecticut's historical image, its leaders were men marked more by skepticism than by fanaticism: the more enlightened ministers, while not denying the verity of witchcraft, gave little credence to the claims from Fairfield; the secular officials, whatever their own beliefs, were more afraid of the flammatory worldly situation around them than of Satan himself. Conditions were unstable enough without this new element. The government of the colony was just settling down again after years of upheaval. Charter rights had been lost and recently regained, and the wounds from the political infighting were still raw. As new centers of population developed in outlying sections of older towns, local struggles for self-determination broke out; the General Court, in ruling upon claims and counterclaims, was often incurring more ill-will than gratitude from both sides. In addition, the intermittent war against the French and the Indians had turned hot again, and the tax burden was increasingly heavy. The people of the colony were confused, on edge, and looking for scapegoats. Connecticut was too much of a tinder box to allow play with any matches.

A special session of the colony's legislative body was called on June 22, 1692, to take cognizance of the charges of witchcraft that had been filed in Fairfield County. The crime charged being a capital offense, it came under the jurisdiction of the highest court, the Court of Assistants. The records of this special June session of the General Court state:

Whereas there are at present in the county of Fayrefeild several persons in durance upon capitall crimes, which are not soe capeable to be brought to a tryall at the usual Court of Assistants, by reason of the multiplicity of witnesses that may be concerned in the case, &c this Court doe grant to the Governor, Deputy Governor and Assistants to a number of at least seven a commission of oyer and terminer to keep a special court in Fayrefeild the second Wednesday in December next, to hear and determine all such capitall cases and complaints as shall be brought before the sayd court.[3]

Accordingly, it was a distinguished party of gentlemen who rode down the King's Highway to Fairfield in September. Besides Governor Robert Treat and Deputy Governor William Jones, there were four Assistants including William Pitkin who had by that time established his reputation as one of the foremost lawyers in all New England. Waiting for them at the end of their journey were the two Assistants from Fairfield: Major Nathan Gold, Fairfield's most prominent citizen, and Colonel John Burr of the family that later produced Aaron Burr.

The troubles that the officials had come to resolve had originated, not in Fairfield itself, but in the neighboring village of Standford (Stamford). Here, in the home of Daniel Wescot, lived a seventeen-year-old French bound girl named Catherine Branch. From depositions taken at the time, it is obvious that this Catherine, or Kate, was subject to some kind of seizures, probably epileptic in nature. The girl was perhaps ridden by the fear of losing her comfortable niche in a home if the true nature of her affliction became known, but the attacks couldn't be hidden. In the beginning she attempted to explain them away by the simple cry of, "Bewitched!",[4] but that did not long suffice; it was common knowledge that witches were not in the habit of wreaking their evil in anonymity for long. So, yielding to public pressure, Kate began to describe, and, later, to name her tormentors. Once launched in the role of star performer in a drama that held the rapt attention of all the village, the temptation to improve upon her own histrionics became irresistible, and she showed shrewd and calculated cunning in her choice of victims.

Daniel Wescot was completely taken in by Kate's performance, but his wife was not so gullible at first. In the testimony of one witness in the case:

The testimony of Lidia Penoir saith that she heard her Aunt Abigail Wescot say that her servant Catherine Branch was such a lying girl that not anybody could believe one word...she said...and that...she did not believe that Mercy nor Goody Miller, nor Hannah nor any of these women...was any more witches than she was and that her husband would believe Catherine before he would believe Mr. Bishop or Lieutenant Bell or herself.[5]

Kate took care of the suspicions of her mistress by adding a new name, that of Elizabeth Clausen, to the witches' roll.[6] A full-scale feud, typical of a small town, had long been enjoyed by Abigail Wescot and Goody Clausen; each was only too ready to believe the worst of the other.

The "Hannah" of Lidia's testimony was Hannah Harvey, daughter of Josiah Harvey of Fairfield, and, more importantly, granddaughter of a Mrs. Thomas Staples who had been under suspicion years before of the same evil-doing. Only prompt and bold action by her husband had prevented the suspicions from growing into formal charges. His threat to hit back where it would hurt a Yankee most—in the pocketbook—was recognized as no idle one, and the tongues abruptly hushed.[7] Now, Kate revived the old gossip against the elderly and widowed Mrs. Staples, tossing in, for good measure, Hannah and her mother and the not so veiled allusion:

...& Kate sayd what Creature is that with a great head & wings & noe boddy: & All black: sayeing hanah is that your father: I believe it is for you are a wich: & sd Kate sayd hanah is yor fathers name....[8]

It is likely that Josiah Harvey, tax collector and quondam schoolmaster in Fairfield, had more than one enemy in the town. Education in Connecticut at that time was compulsory but neither free nor universally popular. Mr. Harvey had had frequent difficulties in collecting fees from reluctant parents. Hannah's twin crimes may have been that she, too, was seventeen but the pampered daughter in a well-to-do family.

But the chief defendant in the September trial was a complete outsider in the beginning.

Mercy Disbrow lived in the Compo district (now the town of Westport) of Fairfield. By her own testimony,[9] and there is no reason to disbelieve it, she had never even heard of Kate until the girl made accusations against her. The probable explanation for her involvement lay in the fact that some eight or nine years previously Mr. Wescot had quarreled with Mercy. The deep bitterness engendered had not lessened with time, so Kate could safely revel in being the helpless target of Mercy's wrath towards her master:

...She cryd out in her fit mercy why do you meddle with me I never did you any wronge, whats yt to me if my master did. being composed her master asked her what causd her to talke at that rate & wt ye woman sd to her. She made answer ye woman toulde her yt he had wronged her in giving Evidence against her. after this being in her fit again, discoursing as before; why do you meddle with me wts yt to me if my master did, I have toulde him of it, and he sd nothing, I believe you Ly....[10]

By such a thin thread was Mercy Disbrow enmeshed in the events that followed.

Although the bound girl had thus lit the fuse, her role was soon played out; before September she was thoroughly discredited as a witness, but the damage was done. Others rushed through the breach she had blasted, and Mercy was the chief target.

This unfortunate woman had been an Ishmael since her childhood in New Haven. She was the daughter of a man who was publicly whipped as a petty thief. Nor had Fairfield's welcome been warm when its old and beloved minister later married Mercy's widowed mother and brought her little family home with him. Now in middle age, Mercy, even in appearance, flaunted her contempt for the opinion of others. Mr. Wescot had no difficulty in recognizing his old enemy from Kate's description:

...her master askd her what kinde of woman she was that Last appeared to her she sd she was a black woman, thick Lips, & of a middle stature, he Likewise askd her of what age she was, she answered neither olde nor younge, & yt she had on an olde Large Samar,...a dirty shift & a dirty Cap....[11]

All through the summer of 1692, while Mercy stagnated in jail awaiting trial, neighbors busily rummaged through trunks of memory for further evidence of her evil deeds. Choice items weren't hard to come by—mishaps are common in a pioneer community, and Mercy's tongue had slashed like summer lightning—so it wasn't hard to link damning sequences and rush new testimony to the Stamford Commissioner.

A different man might have dampened some of the enthusiasm, but Commissioner Selleck was completely taken in by Kate's performance and was zealous in fulfilling his obligations both to God and the Crown. He was deeply disturbed when, late in June, he had to inform Major Gold, the Fairfield Assistant, that one of the accused could not be brought to trial:

...mr pell & Justice theale would not doe anny thing toward Examining Goody miller when they mett at bedford...at first he [Mr. Pell] sayd he would doe it: but advising with her brothers: would not doe it: but sayd he would advise with Athurny genrall mr graham: but abram Ambler tould Danll wescot: he knew what would become of her if she was sent doune to us here:...Sr. I have here Inclosed...which sys that: the authorny Genrall was not willing to incoridge: the proceedings against: goody miller: but I am of the minde that if the authiurity here would send to the gouvner of new Yeork...I will Improue my Interest for Coll heathcott: whoe hath the greatest Interest In this present gouernor of any man in new yeorke: for tis great pitty shee can not be hadd....[12]

Mr. Selleck's hope of cooperation from the New York authorities proved to be futile. Their attitude was one of ridicule towards what they felt was a madness sweeping New England.

The letter to Mr. Gold must have been a difficult one to write. In addition to word of Goody Miller's unavailability, Commissioner Selleck also had to break the news of the charges against the Harvey family—and Josiah Harvey was Nathan Gold's stepson.

Of all those accused by Kate, only five were finally ordered to appear before the Court of Assistants: Mercy Disbrow, Elizabeth Clausen, and the three women in Josiah Harvey's family. Mercy and Elizabeth, being considered the most dangerous, and since witches could do no harm while incarcerated, were taken to the jail in Fairfield to await trial.

On September 14th the trial began. The first order of business was the appointment of attorneys for the Crown, and it might, or might not, have been significant in the light of what happened later that one was a step-nephew of Mercy Disbrow. (It should be noted that it was not possible for the courts in those days to even strive towards a degree of objectivity we deem vital for a fair trial. Every community was close-knit by propinquity, blood relationship, and marriage ties.)

A bill against Mercy was committed to the Grand Jury which promptly returned a Billa Vera:

Mercy disborough wife of Thomas Disbrough of compo in fayrefeed thou art here indicted by the Name of Mercy disborough that not hauing the fear of God before thine eyes thou hast had familiarety wth satan the Grand enemie of God & man & that by his instigation & help thou hast in a preternatural way afflicted & don Harm to the body's & estates of sundry of their Maties subject or to some of them contrary to the peace of ye souereign Lord the King & queen their crowne & dignity & That on the 25 of April in the 4th year of their Maties reigne & at sundry other times, for which by the Law of God & the Lawes of this colony thou desarvest to dye.[13]

The Grand Jury returned a similar Billa Vera against Elizabeth Clausen, and both women pleaded not guilty. Since there is no record of any attorneys for the defense, it was probably assumed that the Devil was advocate enough if guilty, and none needed if innocent.

There was little evidence on hand against Mrs. Staples, her daughter, and her granddaughter except for that of the now discredited Kate, so the Grand Jury presented them only as being under suspicion for the crime of witchcraft. Three times on each of the next two days the Court made proclamation for all who would to step forward and testify against them.

Perhaps the stern figure of Nathan Gold sitting there on the judges' bench was a dampening influence. Only two stepped forward to testify. The Court then proclaimed:

...nothing of consequence appearing agnst them they the afoarsayd persons were quitted by proclamation & all persons were comanded to forbear speakeing evil of the foresayd persons for the future upon payn of displeasure....[14]

But the case against the other two women was quite a different matter. One by one the crowd of witnesses came forward to swear before the Secretary of the colony to the depositions made earlier. On and on droned the procedure until they all had been heard and the case given to the jury. But, after long deliberations, the jury reported that they couldn't agree upon a verdict in either case.

Faced with this impasse, the judges deemed it best to get further instructions from the General Court which was due to meet in Hartford in October. Accordingly the prisoners were remanded to jail, and the jurors instructed to hold themselves in readiness for a resumption of deliberations.[15]

The month that followed was a busy one. A meeting of the most prominent ministers was called in Hartford, and the evidence offered at the trial turned over to them for evaluation. In their written opinion, dated October 17th, the ministers made four points: the water test (given to, and failed by, both women) was unlawful, sinful, and therefore not evidence; only an able doctor could judge whether the excrescences found upon the prisoners' bodies were unnatural or not (the local court had appointed housewives to make the search); as for Kate's evidence, it was open to suspicion of counterfeiting, and there was reason to believe that she suffered from some condition that had afflicted her mother; all the accidents and such like attributed to the women were very slender and uncertain grounds upon which to base a charge of witchcraft.[16] So spoke the ministers. But unfortunately there was no strong voice returning to a Fairfield County pulpit to emphasize their message. Fairfield's pastor of many years had died in March, and his young successor was in the process of settling into his new parsonage at the time of the meeting; the message itself was completely contrary to the stand taken by the ministers in the villages of Stamford and Norwalk from the beginning of the troubles. Mr. Bishop, in Stamford, had indeed fought hard and openly to deliver Kate from the evil forces bedeviling her in the spring.[17]

The opinion itself was written and signed at the conclusion of the Hartford meeting by two of the ministers present, Joseph Eliot of Guilford and Timothy Woodbridge of Hartford. Those two men point to the man who was to play an important role in all that followed—their mutual father-in-law, Samuel Wyllys of Hartford.

Samuel Wyllys had, along with Nathan Gold and others, been one of the original grantees of the Connecticut Charter, and his voice in the affairs of the colony had always been powerful. Connecticut's famous Charter Oak graced his lawn. Whatever the reason—age, health, or other commitments—that kept him from being one of the Assistants at the trial, it was definitely not lack of interest. His interest in alleged cases of witchcraft had dated back at least thirty years. In 1662 when there had been another epidemic of the same fever, he had been a judge at the trial of three persons who were condemned and hanged.[18] His attitude at that time is not known: he may have been outraged at the verdict; or, like Judge Sewell of Boston, realized later that he had been in error.

What went on in private conferences in Hartford, and what share Samuel Wyllys had in the planning that was done, we can only surmise from later events. The only recorded action was that of the General Court:

The Govr hauing giuen an accot how far they have proceeded against Eliz. Clawson and Mercy Disborough by reason that the jury could not agree to make a verdict, this Court (?) the Governor to appoynt time for the sayd Court to meet againe as soone as may be. and that the jury be called together and that they make a verdict upon the case and the Court to put a finall issue thereto.[19]

So back to Fairfield rode Governor Treat and his party. Two of the original judges, William Pitkin and Andrew Leete, did not return, but another Assistant came in replacement to fill the required quota.[20] Did Mr. Pitkin, aware of, or a party to, the planning that must have been done feel that his presence there was an unnecessary risk to his professional reputation? Or had it been decided that the weight of that reputation should be held in reserve?

Whatever the answers to these questions, this stands out: the strategy of a last resort maneuver had been worked out and the first step set in motion in case the ministers' appeal to reason proved to have fallen upon unheeding ears; the attorneys for the Crown, as well as all the judges, were well briefed in the course that was laid out. No witch would dangle from the scaffold in Connecticut this time.

The Court of Oyer and Terminer was reconvened on October 28th, and the jury called upon to consider again the indictment against Mercy. This time they had no difficulty in reaching a quick verdict—guilty as charged. Sent out to reconsider their decision, they promptly returned and said they saw no reason to change it. So the Court, without further effort to influence the unwanted verdict, went through the motions of approving it, and Governor Treat passed the obligatory sentence of death.[21]

Then Elizabeth Clausen's case was taken up. During the recess, friends had been active, and new, favorable depositions made. The jury found her not guilty, and the Court ordered her freed.[22]

The trial was over. Twelve men, good and true to their faith, hand handed a blow to the Devil—and, incidentally, asserted their independence of the Golds, the Burrs, and the powers from Hartford. Fairfield was satisfied.

But while the trial was over, the case was not ended. A petition was immediately presented to the General Court calling attention *now* to the fact that the second half of the trial had been completely illegal![23]

One of the original jurors, Thomas Knowles of Stratford, had been unavailable and reportedly out of the colony on October 28th[24] despite the firm injunction of the Court when the trial was recessed. When the reconvening of the trial found him missing, his name was simply crossed out of the original list of jurors,[25] Joseph Rowland, son of the innkeeper, selected to fill his place, and the trial resumed until the verdict was reached and sentence passed. The Governor, the Secretary, the Assistants, the two attorneys for the Crown—not one of those gentlemen raised a word in protest either at the substitution or after the unwanted verdict was handed up.

And who was the strangely missing Mr. Knowles? He was no isolated countryman whose horizon was bounded by his own stone walls; he was a former deputy to the General Court. The fact that the jury found it impossible to reach a verdict while he was on it but reached quick agreement when Mr. Rowland took his place argues that he had been either the solitary holdout or the only strong voice for acquittal.

Upon receiving the petition, the General Court in Hartford promptly appointed Samuel Wyllys, William Pitkin, and Nathaniel Stanley as a committee empowered to review the trial and *take such action as they saw fit*.

The committee reported back to the next session of the General Court in May, 1693:

...Reasons for Repreiueing Mrs Mercy Disbrough from being put to death until this Court had Cognizance of her case:

First because wee that Repreiued her had power by the Law so to do: Secondly Because we had and haue sattisfying Reasons that the Sentence of Death passed against her ought not to be execcuted which Reasons we giue to this Court to be Judged of.

1st The Jury that brought her in Guilty (which uerdict was the Ground of her Condemnation) was not the same Jury who were first charged with this Prisoners deliuerance and who had it in charg many weeks Mr Knowles was on the Jury first sworn to try this woman and he was at or about york when the Court sate the second time and when the uerdict was giuen the Jury was altered and Another man sworn

It is so inuiolable a practice in Law that the Indiuidal Jurors and Jury that is Charged with the deliuerance of a prisoner in a Capital Case and on whom the Prisoner puts him or her self to be tryed must try it and they only that al the presidents in Old England and New Confirm it and not euer heard of til this time to be inouated. And not only president but the Nature of the thing inforces it for to these Jurors the Law gaue power uested it in them they had it in right of Law, and it is incompatible and impossible that it should be uested in these and in others too for then two Juries may haue the same power in the same Case one man altered the Jury is altered.

Tis the Birthright of the Kings subjects so and no otherwise to be tryed and they must not be despoyled of it.

due form of Law is that alone wherein the ualidity of uerdicts and Judgments in such Cases stands and if a real and Apparent Murtherer be Condemned and Excetued out of Due form of Law it is Inditable against them that do it for in such a Case the Law is superseded by Arbitrary doings.

What the Court accepts and the prisoner accepts differing from the Law is Nothing what the Law admitts is al in the Case.

If one Juror may be changed two, ten, the whole may be so. and solemn oaths made uain

wee durst not but dissent from and declare against such alterations by our Repreiueing therfore the said Prisoner when we were informed of this Buisiness about her Jury, and we pray this honored Court to take heed what they do in it now it is roled to thair dore and that at least they be wel sattisfied from able Lawyers that such a Chang is in Law alowable ere this prisoner be excecuted least they bring themselues into inextricable troubles and the whole Country Blood is a great thing and we cannot but open our mouths for the dumb in the Cause of one appointed to die by such a verdict.

The Committee's report went on to doubt the validity of the evidence, and concluded:

...and the miserable toyl they are in in the Bay for Adhereing to these last mentioned Litigious things is warning enof, those that wil make witchcraft of such things wil make hanging work apace and we are informed of no other but such as these brought against this woman....

There was a final postscript:

The Court may please to Consider also how farr these proceedings do put a difficulty on any further tryal of this woman.[26]

So did the good fathers put an end to the hysteria besetting their colony. Emotions could not hold one high pitch indefinitely: denied a sacrifice to goad them on, and probably influenced by a return to season in Massachusetts, they simmered down.

Mercy returned to her home and her family. A different, and equally unjust, attack was mounted against her later[27] but it came to nothing. She lived out her years safe from, if not at peace with, her neighbors.

Stability had been restored and Mercy set free, but the work of the lawmakers was not over. Others with more peccable motives might also try tampering with the integrity of jury trials now that a precedent had been set. So that May 1693 session of the General Court took further action after receiving its committee's report. They wrote into their records this new statute:

For the beter regulating of proceedings in our courts of judicature and to prevent the frustration and unnecessary delay of justice to the needless increase of charge and expense to the country. especially in the tryall of capitall and criminal cases, this Court doe order for the future that all jurie or juries when impaneld and sworn in court and hauing heard the pleas and euidences for and against any person or persons indicted or complayned of, shall imediatly withdraw themselues into some convenient roome or place by the court appoynted them and their abide untill they are agreed of a uerdict or uerdicts, unless in case of some difficulty ariseing among them about the matter giuen them in charge they desire farther light or information from the court, and then *and then* to return and abide as before, and the court are to appoynt som officer to themselues belonging to see this order accordingly attended.

It is allso ordered that all jury men that are warned and returned to seru on the jury and shall neglect to attend shall be fined the sume of twenty shillings to the treasury of the county, except he can render a sufficient reason for his non attendance.[28]

As the years went by, the tale of Mercy Disbrow was forgotten. So, too, was any memory of Connecticut witches. In 1820 Hartford's controversial editor, William Stone, in sorting out the voluminous Wyllys family papers, came across an old bundle marked "Trials for witchcraft." Soon after, he wrote in the "New York Commercial Advertiser":

It has generally been denied that any trials of this nature ever occurred in Connecticut. No mention is made of any such trials in any book that has fallen under my observation: indeed it is the prevailing opinion, that none ever did take place....[29]

Even after his death, Samuel Wyllys had served well the colony he helped to found. The stain that would have blemished its name in history lay buried until time granted a more tolerant perspective.

Notes

This article was first published in the *Connecticut Bar Journal*, Volume XXXIX, Number 4, December 1965, pp. 558–573.

---

* In the letter accompanying the manuscript the author makes the following observations:

"The contents of the article are based upon research in depth, and all statements, unless clearly indicated by the wording that they are surmises or "educated guesses," can be documented, usually by primary source material. In the footnotes I have given some of the many sources in which facts bearing upon this case can be found. Some of the other sources that proved helpful, especially for background information, were: Fairfield Town Records; Fairfield Probate Records; *1 Ancient Record Series* (New Haven Historical Society); *1* Schenck, *History of Fairfield* (1889); Taylor, *The Witchcraft Delusion in Colonial Connecticut* (1908); Savage, *Genealogy of the Early New England Settlers* (1860); the New Haven Colony Records; the other original trial documents, preserved by Samuel Wyllys, which are now in the libraries mentioned in the article.

"Unfortunately there is one key document which I have been unable to trace. It is the memorial presented to the General Court after the conclusion of the trial. It was apparently among the papers found by Mr. Stone in 1820 but has since either been destroyed or mislaid, as no one seems to know its whereabouts. Knowing who signed it and what was stated in it might fill in a little more of the picture."

[1] *4 Public Records of the Colony of Connecticut* 98, 99 (Case, Lockwood & Brainard ed. 1868).

[2] *1 Public Records of the Colony of Connecticut* 77 (Brown and Parsons ed. 1850).

[3] *4 Public Records of the Colony of Connecticut* 76 (1868). *See Also* footnote on page calling attention to the original recorder's error in giving December instead of September as the date of the trial.

[4] *4 Oyer and Terminer Court Records of Trials for Witchcraft in Connecticut* (Wyllys Papers), in Annmary Brown Memorial, Brown University Library, Providence, Rhode Island and here identified by their notation. W-19.

[5] *Samuel Wyllys Collection* # 32 (State Library, Hartford).

[6] *Oyer and Terminer Court Records of Trials for Witchcraft in Connecticut* W-19.

[7] *1 Jacobus, History and Genealogy of the Families of Old Fairfield* (Part iv) 391 (1932).

[8] Oyer and Terminer Court Records of Trials for Witchcraft in Connecticut W-21.

[9] *Ibid* W-19.

[10] *Ibid* W-19.

[11] *Ibid* W-19.

[12] *Ibid* W-22.

[13] *Ibid* W-39.

[14] *Ibid* W-39.

[15] *Ibid* W-39.

[16] *Ibid* W-30.

[17] *Ibid* W-21, W-22.

[18] Love, *Colonial History of Hartford* 285n (1914).

[19] *4 Public Records of the Colony of Connecticut* 79 (1868).

[20] *Oyer and Terminer Court Records of Trials for Witchcraft in Connecticut* W-39.

[21] *Ibid* W-39.

[22] *Ibid* W-39.

[23] Hartford Times and Weekly Advertiser, August 8, 1820.

[24] *Oyer and Terminer Court Records of Trials for Witchcraft in Connecticut* W-36.

[25] *Samuel Wyllys Collection*, Supplement #5.

[26] *Oyer and Terminer Court Records of Trials for Witchcraft in Connecticut* W-36.

[27] Letter dated June 3, 1696, from Rev. Gershom to Joseph Bulkeley of Wethersfield to Joseph Bulkely of Fairfield. (Letter now in possession of the Connecticut Historical Society.)

[28] *4 Public Records of the Colony of Connecticut* 98, 99 (1868). These provisions are the forerunner of the present Conn. Gen. Stat. (Rev. 1958) §§ 51-246 and 51-237.

[29] *Hartford Times* and *Weekly Advertiser*, August 8, 1820.

APPENDIX B

Prudence Crandall: "Letter to the Windham County Adviser"

(MAY 7, 1833). FIRST PUBLISHED IN FRUITS OF COLONIZATION, 1833.

LETTER FROM PRUDENCE CRANDALL

Canterbury, May 7, 1833

Mr. Holbrook: Whatever reluctance I may feel to appear before the public, circumstance require that I should do so. After all that has been said in various newspapers about me and my school and my friends it seems that I owe it to them and to myself to make a simple statement that you and others may know the object of my present school and also what first induced me to establish it; and to exonerate my friends and myself from several unreasonable censures and misrepresentations that are in circulation.

A colored girl of respectability—a professor of religion—and daughter of honorable parents called on me sometime during the month of September last and said in a very earnest manner "Miss Crandall, I want to get a little more learning, if possible enough to teach colored children and if you will admit me to your school, I shall forever be under greatest obligation to you. If you think it will be the means of injuring you, I will not insist on the favor."

I did not answer her immediately, as I thought if I gave her permission some of my scholars might be disturbed. In further conversation with her however I found she had great anxiety to improve in learning.

Her repeated solicitations were more than my feelings could resist and I told her if I was injured on her account I would bear it—she might enter as one of my pupils. The girl had not long been under my instruction before I was informed by several persons that she must be removed or my school would be greatly injured.

This was unpleasant news for me to hear but I continued her in my school. Previous to any excitement concerning her there fell in my way several publications that contained many facts relative to the people of color of which I was entirely ignorant. My feelings began to awaken. I saw that the prejudice of whites against color was deep and inveterate. In my humble opinion it was the strongest if not the only chain that bound those heavy burdens on the wretched slaves, which we ourselves are not willing to touch with one of our fingers. I felt in my heart to adopt the language of the Sacred Preacher when He said—"So I turned to consider all the oppressions that are done under the sun and behold the tears of such as were oppressed, and they had no comforter; and on the side of their oppressors there was power but they had no comforter. Therefore, I praised the dead that are already dead more than the living which are yet alive."

I said in my heart, here are my convictions. What shall I do? Shall I be inactive and permit prejudice, the mother of abominations, to remain undisturbed? Or shall I venture to enlist in the ranks of those who with the Sword of Truth dare hold combat with prevailing iniquity? I contemplated for a while the manner in which I might best serve the people of color. As wealth was not mine, I saw no other means of benefiting them, than by imparting to those of my own sex that were anxious to learn, all the instruction I might be able to give; however small the amount. This I deem my duty, how to perform it, I knew not. With the friends of the people of color, called "Abolitionists" I was entirely unacquainted save by reputation.

Having for some time wished to visit New York or some other places of schools and also to purchase for the benefit of my scholars, school apparatus, I come to the conclusion that I would perform my long contemplated journey and visit the schools in Boston while at the same time the most prominent object of my tour was to visit William L. Garrison—to obtain his opinion respecting the propriety of establishing a school for colored females—and the prospect of success should I attempt it. Being an entire stranger in Boston previous to my journey, I took the liberty to inquire of several of my neighbors if they had any friends in Boston to whom they would be willing to give me a line of introduction. Rev. Mr. Kneeland and Rev. Mr. Platt were the only persons I found who had any acquaintance in the place. These gentlemen very kindly gave me letters to distinguished clergymen in that city. Neither to these gentlemen, my scholars, nor my neighbors, did I make known all my business. And I felt perfectly justified in telling them I was going to visit schools, which I did; and to purchase the before-mentioned apparatus, which was at that time my determination; and the want of money was the only reason why I did not purchase.

Now because I did not see fit to expose my business before I knew whether I could obtain a sufficient number of colored pupils to sustain my school and also did not purchase the apparatus (which was too costly), I am charged that too in a public manner of falsehood or at least willful prevarication. False and scandalous reports about me and my friends are in constant circulation, some of which are dispersed by the papers far and near. In the piece signed "A friend of the Colonization Cause" that first appeared in the Norwich Republican, which you have copied into your paper, the author upon his own authority ahs declared that there are a few men in Boston and Providence who have laid the foundation of this school which is entirely false as I was wholly self moved in the plan, though I gratefully acknowledge their kind approbation. Furthermore, he asks, "and what do they intend to do with this institution?" After making several ungenerous and detestable replies the sentence is closed with this remark— "In a word they hope to force the races (black and white) to amalgamate." This is utterly false—the object, the sole object, at this school is to instruct the ignorant and fit and prepare teachers for the people of color that they may be elevated and their intellectual and moral wants supplied.

You are apprised that the Rev. S. J. May is the warm friend and advocate of my school. He had plead my cause manfully, and I trust he will reap a just reward.

The truth of his remonstrance with A. T. Judson Esq., and others, I presume no one will attempt to deny in any material point. After what he has published, it is unnecessary to enlarge, but simply to give this, my public declaration, in favor of the correctness of all the statements he has made, respecting myself and my school, many of which he made upon my authority.

Respectfully yours, Prudence Crandall

Connecticut General Assembly, "An act in addition to an Act entitled 'An Act for the admission and settlement of Inhabitants of Towns.'" (May 24, 1833).

WHEREAS, attempts have been made to establish literary institutions in this State for the instruction of colored persons belonging to other states and countries, which would tend to the great increase of the colored population of the State, and thereby to the inury of the people: Therefore,

Sec. 1. Be it enacted by the Senate and House of Representatives, in General Assembly convened, That no person shall set up or establish in this State, any school, academy, or literary institution, for the instruction or education of colored persons who are not inhabitants of this State, nor instruct or teach in any school, academy, or literary institution whatsoever in this State, or harbor, or board, for the purpose of attending or being taught or instructed in any such school, academy or literary institution, any colored person who is not an inhabitant of any town in this state, without the consent in writing, first obtained of a majority of the civil authority, and also of the select men of the town in which such school, academy, or literary institution is situated; and each and every person who shall knowingly do any act forbidden as aforesaid, or shall be aiding or assisting therein; shall, for the first offence shall forfeit and pay to the treasurer of the state, a fine of one hundred dollars, and for the second offence shall forfeit and pay a fine of two hundred dollars; and so double for every offence of which he or she shall be convicted. And all informing officers are required to make due presentment of all breaches of this act. Provided, That nothing in this act shall extend to any district school established in any school society, under the laws of this state, or to any incorporated academy or incorporated school for instruction in this state.

Sec. 2. Be it further enacted, That any colored person, not an inhabitant of this state, who shall reside in any town therein for the purpose of being instructed as aforesaid, may be removed in the manner prescribed in the sixth and seventh sections of the act to which this is in addition.

Sec. 3. Be it further enacted, That any person, not an inhabitant of this state, who shall reside in any town therein, for the purpose of being instructed as aforesaid, shall be an admissible witness in all prosecutions under the first section of this act, and may be compelled to give testimony therein, notwithstanding any thing contained in this act, or the act last aforesaid.

Sec. 4. Be it further enacted, That so much of the seventh section of the act to which this is an addition, as may provide for the infliction of corporeal punishment, be, and at the same is hereby repealed.

SAMUEL INGHAM, Speaker of the House of Representatives.
EBENEZER STODDARD, President of the Senate.
Approved, May 24, 1833.

APPENDIX C

LEXSEE 40 U.S. 518

THE UNITED STATES, APPELLANTS, V. THE LIBELLANTS AND CLAIMANTS OF THE SCHOONER AMISTAD, HER TACKLE, APPAREL, AND FURNITURE, TOGETHER WITH HER CARGO, AND THE AFRICANS MENTIONED AND DESCRIBED IN THE SEVERAL LIBELS AND CLAIMS, APPELLEES.

SUPREME COURT OF THE UNITED STATES

40 U.S. 518; 10 L. Ed. 826; 1841 U.S. LEXIS 279

March 9, 1841, Decided

PRIOR HISTORY: [***1] ON appeal from the Circuit Court of the United States for the District of Connecticut.

On the 23d day of January, 1840, Thomas R. Gedney, and Richard W. Meade, officers of the United States surveying brig Washington, on behalf of themselves and the officers and crew of the brig Washington, and of others interested and entitled, filed a libel in the District Court of the United States, for the District of Connecticut, stating that off Culloden Point, near Montauck Point, they took possession of a vessel which proved to be a Spanish schooner called the Amistad, of Havana, in the island of Cuba, of about 120 tons burden; and the said libellants found said schooner was manned by forty-five negroes, some of whom had landed near the said point for water; and there were also on board, two Spanish gentlemen, who represented themselves to be, and, as the libellants verily believe were part owners of the cargo, and of the negroes on board, who were slaves, belonging to said Spanish gentlemen; that the schooner Amistad sailed on the 28th day of June, A.D. 1839 from the port of Havana, bound to a port in the province of Principe, both in the island of Cuba, under the command of Raymon Ferrer [***2] as master thereof: that the schooner had on board and was laden with a large and valuable cargo, and provisions, to the amount, in all, of forty thousand dollars, and also money to the sum and amount of about two hundred and fifty dollars; and also fifty-four slaves, to wit, fifty-one male slaves, and three young female slaves, who were worth twenty-five thousand dollars; and while on the voyage from Havana to Principe, the slaves rose upon the captain and crew of the schooner, and killed and murdered the captain and one of the crew, and two more of the crew escaped and got away from the schooner; that the two Spaniards on board, to wit, Pedro Montez, and Jose Ruiz, remained alive on board the schooner after the murder of the captain, and after the negroes had taken possession of the vessel and cargo; that their lives were spared to assist in the sailing of the vessel; and it was directed by the negroes, that the schooner should be navigated for the coast of Africa; and Pedro Montez, and Jose Ruiz did, accordingly, steer as thus directed and compelled by the negroes, at the peril of their lives, in the daytime, and in the night altered their course and steered for the American shore; [***3] but after two months on the ocean, they succeeded in coming round Montauck Point, then they were discovered in coming by the libellants, and the two Spanish gentlemen begged for and claimed the aid and protection of the libellants. That the schooner was accordingly taken possession of, and recaptured from the hands and possession of the negroes who had taken the same; that the schooner was brought into the port of New London, where she now is; and the schooner would with great difficulty, exposure, and danger have been taken by the libellants, but for the surprise upon the blacks who had possession thereof, a part of whom were on shore; and but for the aid and assistance and services of the libellants, the vessel and cargo would have been wholly lost to the respective owners thereof. That the cargo belongs to divers Spanish merchants and others, resident in the island of Cuba, and to Pedro Montez and Jose Ruiz, the latter owning most of the slaves.

The libellants stated, that having saved the schooner Amistad and cargo, and the slaves, with considerable danger, they prayed that process should be issued against the same, and that the usual proceedings might be had by the Court, by [***4] which a reasonable salvage should be decreed out of the property so saved.

Afterwards, Henry Green and Pelatiah Fordham, and others, filed a petition and answer to the libel, claiming salvage out of the property proceeded against by Thomas R. Gedney and others, and stating that before the Amistad was seen or boarded by the officers and crew of the Washington, they had secured a portion of the negroes who had come on shore, and had thus aided on saving the vessel and cargo.

On the 29th of August, 1839, Jose Ruiz and Pedro Montez, of Cuba, filed claims to all the negroes on board of the Amistad, except Antonio, as their slaves. A part of the merchandise on board the vessel was also claimed by them. They alleged that the negroes had risen on the captain of the schooner, and had murdered him; and that afterwards they, Ruiz and Montez, had brought her into the United States. They claimed that the negroes and merchandise ought to be restored to them, under the treaty with Spain; and denied salvage to Lieutenant Gedney, and to all other persons claiming salvage.

Afterwards, Ruiz and Montez each filed in the District Court, a separate libel, stating more at large the circumstances of [***5] the voyage of the Amistad, the murder of the captain by the negroes, and that the negroes afterwards compelled them to steer the vessel towards Africa, but that they contrived to bring her to the coast of the United States, where she was captured by the United States brig Washington. Ruiz, in his libel, stated the negroes belonging to him to have been forty-nine in number, "named and known at Havana, as follows: Antonio, Simon, Jose Pedro, Martin, Manuel, Andreo, Edwards, Celedonia, Burtolono, Ramia, Augustin, Evaristo, Casamero, Merchoi, Gabriel, Santorion, Escolastico, Rascual, Estanislao, Desidero, Nicholas, Estevan, Tomas, Cosme, Luis, Bartolo, Julian, Federico, Salustiano, Ladislao, Celestino, Epifanio, Eduardo, Benancico, Felepe, Francisco, Hipoleto, Berreto, Isidoro, Vecente, Deconisco, Apolonio, Esequies, Leon, Julio, Hipoleto, and Zenon; of whom several have died." Their present names, Ruiz stated, he had been informed, were, "Cinque, Burnah 1st, Carpree, Dammah, Fourrie 1st, Shumah, Conomah, Choolay, Burnah 2d, Baah, Cabbah, Poomah, Kimbo, Peea, Bang-ye-ah, Saah, Carlee, Parale, Morrah, Yahome, Narquor, Quarto, Sesse, Con. Fourrie 2d, Kennah, Lammane, Fajanah, Faah, Yahboy, [***6] Faquannah, Berrie, Fawnu, Chockammaw, and Gabbow."

The libel of Pedro Montez stated that the names of three negroes on board the Amistad, belonging to him, were Francisco, Juan, and Josepha; the Spanish name of the fourth was not mentioned; and the four were not called Teme, Mahgra, Kene, and Carria.

All these were stated to be slaves, and the property of the claimants, purchased by them at Havana; where slavery is tolerated and allowed by law; and they and the merchandise on board the vessel, the claimants alleged, by the laws and usages of nations, and of the United States of America, and according to the treaties between Spain and the United States, ought to be restored to the claimants without diminution, and entire.

The vessel, negroes, and merchandise were taken into his possession, by the Marshal of the district of Connecticut, under process issued by order of the Court.

On the 19th of September, 1837, William S. Holabird, Esq., attorney of the United States, for the district, filed a suggestion in the District Court, stating that, since the libel aforesaid, of Thomas R. Gedney, Esq., was filed in this Court, viz. within the present month of September, in the year of our [***7] Lord 1839, the duly accredited minister to the United

States, of her Catholic Majesty, the Queen of Spain, had officially presented to the proper department of the United States government, a claim, which is now pending, upon the United States, setting forth that "the vessel aforesaid, called the Amistad, and her cargo aforesaid, together with certain slaves on board the said vessel, all being the same as described in the libel aforesaid, are the property of Spanish subjects, and that the said vessel, cargo, and slaves, while so being the property of the said Spanish subjects, arrived within the jurisdictional limits of the United States, and were taken possession of by the said public armed brig of the United States, under such circumstances as make it the duty of the United States to cause the same vessel, cargo, and slaves, being the property of said Spanish subjects, to be restored to the true proprietors and owners of the same without further hindrance or detention, as required by the treaty now subsisting between the United States and Spain." The attorney of the United States, in behalf of the United States, prayed the Court, on its being made legally to appear that the claim [***8] of the Spanish minister is well founded, and is conformable to the treaty, that the Court make such order for the disposal of the said vessel, cargo, and slaves as may best enable the United States in all respects to comply with their treaty stipulations, and preserve the public faith inviolate. But if it should be made to appear that the persons described as slaves, are negroes and persons of colour, who have been transported from Africa, in violation of the laws of the United States, and brought within the United States, contrary to the same laws, the attorney, in behalf of the United States, claimed that, in such case, the Court will make such further order in the premises as may enable the United States, if deemed expedient, to remove such persons to the coast of Africa to be delivered there to such agent or agents as may be authorized to receive and provide for them, pursuant to the laws of the United States, in such case provided, or to make such other order as to the Court may seem fit, right, and proper in the premises.

"On the same day, September 19, 1839, the negroes, by their counsel, filed an answer to the libel of Lieutenant Gedney and others, claiming salvage, and to [***9] the claim of Ruiz and Montez, claiming them as slaves, as also to the intervention of the United States, on the application of the minister of Spain; in which they say, that they are natives of Africa, and were born free, and ever since have been and still of right are and ought to be free and not slaves; that they were never domiciled in the island of Cuba, or in the dominions of the Queen of Spain, or subject to the laws thereof. That on or about the 15th day of April, 1839, they were, in the land of their nativity, unlawfully kidnapped, and forcibly, and wrongfully, by certain persons to them unknown, who were there unlawfully and piratically engaged in the slave trade between the coast of Africa and the island of Cuba, contrary to the will of these respondents, unlawfully, and under circumstances of great cruelty, transported to the island of Cuba for the unlawful purpose of being sold as slaves, and were there illegally landed for that purpose. That Jose Ruiz, one of the libellants, well knowing all the premises, and confederating with the persons by whom the respondents were unlawfully taken and holden as slaves, and intending to deprive the respondents severally of their liberty, [***10] made a pretended purchase of the respondents, except the said Carria, Teme, Kene, and Mahgra; and that Pedro Montez, also well knowing all the premises, and confederating with the said persons for the purpose aforesaid, made a pretended purchase of the said Carria, Teme, Kene, and Mahgra; that the pretended purchases were made from persons who had no right whatever to the respondents or any of them, and that the same were null and void, and conferred no right or title on Ruiz or Montez, or right of control over the respondents or either of them. That on or about the 28th day of June, 1839, Ruiz and Montez, confederating with each other, and with one Ramon Ferrer, now deceased, captain of the schooner Amistad, and others of the crew thereof, caused respondents severally, without law or right, under color of certain false and fraudulent papers by them procured and fraudulently used for that purpose, to be placed by force on board the schooner to be transported with said Ruiz and Montez to some place unknown to the respondents, and there enslaved for life. That the respondents, being treated on board said vessel by said Ruiz and Montez and their confederates with great cruelty and oppression, [***11] and being of right free as aforesaid, were incited by the love of liberty natural to all men, and by the desire of returning to their families and kindred, to take possession of said vessel while navigating the high seas, as they had a right to do, with the intent to return therein to their native country, or to seek an asylum in some free state, where slavery did not exist, in order that they might enjoy their liberty under the protection of its government; that the schooner, about the 26th of August, 1839, arrived in the possession of the respondents, at Culloden Point near Montauk, and was there anchored near the shore of Long Island, within hailing distance thereof, and within the waters and territory of the state of New York; that the respondents, Cinque, Carlee, Dammah, Baah, Monat, Nahgüis, Quato, Con, Fajanah, Berrie, Gabbo, Fouleaa, Kimbo, Faquannah, Cononia, otherwise called Ndzarbla, Yaboi, Burnah 1st, Shuma, Fawne, Peale, Ba, and Sheele, while said schooner lay at anchor as aforesaid, went on shore within the state of New York to procure provisions and other necessaries, and while there, in a state where slavery is unlawful and does not exist, under the protection of the [***12] government and laws of said state by which they were all free, whether on board of said schooner, or on shore, the respondents were severally seized, and well those who were on shore as aforesaid, as those who were on board of and in possession of said schooner, by Lieutenant Gedney, his officers, and crew of the United States brig Washington, without any lawful warrant or authority whatever, at the instance of Ruiz and Montez, with the intent to keep and secure them as slaves to Ruiz and Montez, respectively, and to obtain an award of salvage therefor, from this honourable Court, as for a meritorious act. That for that purpose, the respondents were, by Lieutenant Gedney, his officers and crew, brought to the port of New London; and while there, and afterwards, under the subsequent proceedings in this honourable Court taken into the custody of the marshal of said district of Connecticut, and confined and held in the jails in the cities of New Haven and Hartford, respectively, as aforesaid. Wherefore, the respondents pray that they may be set free, as they of right are and ought to be, and that they be released from the custody of the marshal, under the process of this honourable [***13] Court, under which, or under colour of which they are holden as aforesaid.

Jose Antonio Tellincas, and Aspe and Laca, subjects of Spain, and merchants of Cuba, presented claims for certain merchandise which was on board the Amistad when taken possession of by Lieutenant Gedney; denying all claims to salvage, and asking that the property should be restored to them.

On the 23d day of January the District Judge made a decree, having taken into his consideration all the libels, claims, and the suggestion of the District Attorney of the United States, and the claim preferred by him that the negroes should be delivered to the Spanish authorities, the negroes to be sent by them to Cuba, or that the negroes should be placed under the authority of the President of the United States, to be transported to Africa.

The decree rejected the claim of Green and others to salvage with costs. The claim of Lieutenant Gedney and others to salvage on the alleged slaves was dismissed. The libels and claims of Ruiz and Montez being included under the claim of the minister of Spain, were ordered to be dismissed, with costs taxed against Ruiz and Montez respectively.

"That that part of the claim of the [***14] minister of Spain which demands the surrender of Cinques and others, who are specifically named in the answer filed as aforesaid, be dismissed, without cost."

That the claim of the vice counsul of Spain, demanding the surrender to the Spanish government of Antonio, a slave owned by the heirs of Captain Ferrer, should be sustained; and ordered that Antonio should be delivered to the government of Spain, or its agent, without costs.

The claims of Tellincas and Aspe and Laca, for the restoration of the goods specified by them, being part of the cargo of the Amistad, was sustained, and that the same goods be restored to them, deducting one-third of the gross appraised value of them, which was allowed as salvage to the officers and crew of the Washington. A like salvage of one-third of the gross value of the Amistad, and the other merchandise on board of her, was also adjudged to the salvors. The costs were to be deducted from the other two-thirds.

"And, whereas the duly accredited minister of Spain, resident in the United States, hath, in behalf of the government of Spain, for the owners of said schooner, and the residue of said goods, claimed that the same be restored to that government [***15] for the said owners, they being Spanish subjects, under the provisions of the treaty subsisting between the United States and Spain: And, whereas it hath been made to appear to this Court, that the said schooner is lawfully owned by the subjects of Spain, as also the residue of said goods not specifically claimed: And, whereas the aforesaid Don Pedro Montez, and Jose Ruiz, have in person ceased to prosecute their claim as specified in their respective libels, and their said claims fall within the demand and claim of the Spanish minister, made as aforesaid: And, whereas the seizure of the said schooner and goods by the said Thomas R. Gedney and others, was made on the high seas, in a perilous condition, and they were first brought into the port of New London, within the District of Connecticut, and libelled for salvage,"

[The decree then proceeds to adjudge to Lieutenant Gedney and others, as salvage, one-third of the gross proceeds of the vessel and cargo, according to an appraisement which had been made thereof; and, if not paid, directed the property to be sold, and that proportion of the gross proceeds of the sale to be paid over to the captors, the residue, after payment of all [***16] costs, to be paid to the respective owners of the same.]

Upon the answers of the negroes, and the representations of the District Attorney of the United States, and of Montez and Ruiz, the decree proceeds:

"This Court having fully heard the parties appearing with their proofs, do find that the respondents, severally answering as aforesaid, are each of them natives of Africa, and were born free, and ever since have been, and still of right are free, and not slaves, as is in said several libels claims or representations alleged or surmised; that they were never domiciled in the Island of Cuba, or the dominions of the Queen of Spain, or subject to the laws thereof; that they were severally kidnapped in their native country, and were, in violation of their own rights, and of the laws of Spain, prohibiting the African slave trade, imported into the island of

Cuba, about the 12th June, 1839, and were there unlawfully held and transferred to the said Ruiz and Montez, respectively; that said respondents were within fifteen days after their arrival at Havana, aforesaid, by said Ruiz and Montez, put on board said schooner Amistad to be transported to some port in said island of Cuba, and [***17] there unlawfully held as slaves; that the respondents or some of them, influenced by the desire of recovering their liberty, and of returning to their families and kindred in their native country, took possession of said schooner Amistad, killed the captain and cook, and severely wounded said Montez, while on her voyage from Havana, as aforesaid, and that the respondents arrived in possession of said schooner at Culloden Point near Montauck, and there anchored said schooner on the high seas, at the distance of half a mile from the shore of Long Island, and were there, while a part of the respondents were, as is alleged in their said answer, on shore in quest of water and other necessaries, and about to sail in said schooner for the coast of Africa, seized by said Lieutenant Gedney, and his officers and crew, and brought into the port of New London, in this district. And this Court doth further find, that it hath ever been the intention of the said Montez and Ruiz, since the said Africans were put on board the said schooner, to hold the said Africans as slaves; that at the time when the said Cinque and others, here making answer, were imported from Africa into the dominions of Spain, [***18] there was a law of Spain prohibiting such importations, declaring the persons so imported to be free; that said law was in force when the claimants took the possession of the said Africans and put them on board said schooner, and the same has ever since been in force."

The decree of the District Court recites the decree of the government of Spain of December, 1817, prohibiting the slave trade, and declaring all negroes brought into the dominions of Spain by slave traders to be free; and enjoining the execution of the decree on all the officers of Spain in the dominions of Spain.

The decree of the District Court proceeds:

And this Court doth further find, that when the said Africans were shipped on board the said schooner, by the said Montez and Ruiz, the same were shipped under the passports signed by the Governor General of the Island of Cuba, in the following words, viz.:

Description.
Size.
Age.
Colour.
Hair.
Forehead.

Eyebrows.
Eyes.
Nose.
Nouth.
Beard.
Peculiar signs.
Havana, June 22d, 1839.

I grant permission to carry three black ladinoes, named Juana, Francisca, and Josefa, property of Dr. Pedro Montez, to Puerto Principe, by sea. They must present themselves [***19] to the respective territorial judge with this permit.

Duty, 2 reasls. ESPLETA.

(Endorsed) Commander of Matria.

Let pass in the schooner Amistad, to Guana ja, Ferrer, master. Havana, June 27th, 1839

MART & Co.
Description.
Size.
Age.
Colour.
Hair.
Forehead.
Eyebrows.
Eyes.
Nose.
Mouth.
Beard.
Peculiar signs.
Havana, June 26th, 1839.

I grant permission to carry forty-nine black ladinos, named Antonio, Simon, Lucas, Jose, Pedro, Martin, Manuel, Andrios, Edwardo, Celedernnio, Bartolo, Raman, Augustin, Evaristo, Casimero, Meratio, Gabriel, Santome, Ecclesiastico, pasenal, Stanislao, Desiderio, Nicolas, Estevan, Tomas, Cosme, Luis, Bartolo, Julian, Federico, Saturdino, Ladislas, Celestino, Epifano, Fronerie, Venaniro, Feligre, Francisco, Hypolito, Benito, Isdoro, Vicente, Dioniceo, Apolino, Esequiel, Leon, Julio, Hipolito, y Raman, property of Dr. Jose Ruiz, to Puerto Principe, by sea. They must present themselves with this permit to the respective territorial judge.

ESPLETA.

Duty, 2 reals.

(Endorsed) Commander of Matria.
Let pass in the schooner Amistad, to Guanaja, Ferrer, master.
Havana, June 27th, 1839.
MART & Co."

"Which said passorts do not truly describe [***20] the said persons shipped under the same. Whereupon, the said claim of the minister of Spain, as set forth in the two libels filed in the name of the United States by the said District Attorney, for and in behalf of the government of Spain and her subjects, so far as the same relate to the said Africas named in said claim, be dismissed."

"And upon the libel filed by said District Attorney in behalf of the United States, claiming the said Africans libelled as aforesaid, and now in the custody of the Marshal of the district of Connecticut, under and by virtue of process issued from this Court, that they may be delivered to the President of the United States to be transported to Africa. It is decreed that the said Africans now in the custody of said Marshal, and libelled and claimed as aforesaid, (excepting Antonio Ferrer, be delivered to the President of the United States by the Marshal of the district of Connecticut, to be by him transported to Africa, in pursuance of the law of Congress, passed March 3d, 1819, entitled 'An act in addition to the acts prohibiting the slave trade.'"

After the decree was pronounced, the United States, "claiming in pursuance of a demand made upon them [***21] by the duly accredited minister of her Catholic Majesty, the Queen of Spain, to the United States, moved an appeal from the whole and every part of the said decree, except part of the same in relation to the slave Antonio, to the Circuit Court" of Connecticut.

Antonio Tellincas, and Aspe and Laca, claimants, &c., also appealed from the decree to the Circuit Court, except for so much of the decree as sustains their claims to the goods, &c.

The Africans, by their African names, moved in the Circuit Court, in April, 1840, that so much of the appeal of the District Attorney of the United States, from so much of the decree of the District Court as related to them severally, may be dismissed; "because, they say that the United States do not claim, nor have they ever claimed any interest in the appellees, respectively, or either of them, and have no right, either by the law of nations, or by the Constitution or laws of the United States to appear in the Courts of the United States, to institute or prosecute claims to property, in behalf of the subjects of the Queen of Spain, under the circumstances appearing on the record in this case; much less to enforce the claims of the subject of a [***22] foreign government, to the persons of the said appellees, respectively, as the slaves of the said foreign subjects, under the circumstances aforesaid."

The Circuit Court refused the motion.

The Circuit Court affirmed the decree of the District Court, pro forma, except so far as respects the claims of Tellincas, and Aspe and Laca.

After this decree of the Circuit Court, the United States, claiming in pursuance of a demand made upon them by the duly accredited minister of her Catholic Majesty, the Queen of Spain to the United states, moved an appeal from the whole and every part of the decree of the Court, affirming the decree of the District Court to the Supreme Court of the United States, to be holden at the city of Washington, on the second Monday of January, A.D. eighteen hundred and forty-one; and it was allowed.

The Court as far as respects the decree of the District Court allowing salvage on the goods on board the Amistad, continued the case to await the decision of the Supreme Court, on that part of the decree appealed from.

The Circuit Court in the decree, proceed to say, that "they had inspected certain depositions and papers remaining as of record in said Circuit Court, [***23] and to be used as evidence, before the Supreme Court of the United States, on the trial of said appeal.

Among the depositions, were the following.

"I, Richard Robert Madden, a British subject, having resided for the last three years and upwards, at Havana, where I have held official situations under the British government, depose and say, that I have held the office of superintendent of liberated Africans during that term, and still hold it; and have held for the term of one year, the office there, of British commissioners, in the Mixed Court of Justice. The duties of my office and of my avocation, have led me to become well acquainted with Africans recently imported from Africa. I have seen and had in my charge many hundreds of them. I have seen and had Africans in the custody of the marshal of the district of Connecticut, except the small children. I have examined them and observed their language, appearance, and manners; and I have no doubt of their having been, very recently, brought from Africa. To one of them, I spoke, and repeated a Mohammedan form of prayer in the Arabic language; the man immediately recognised the language, and repeated a few words of it after me, and [***24] appeared to understand it, particularly the words 'Allah akbar,' or God is great. The man who was beside this negro, I also addressed in Arabic, saying—'salaam ailkoem,' or peace be to you; he immediately, in the customary oriental salutations, replied—'aleckoum salaam,' or peace be on you. From my knowledge of oriental habits, and of the appearance of the newly imported slaves in

Cuba, I have no doubt of those negroes of the Amistad being bona fide Bozal negroes, quite newly imported from Africa. I have a full knowledge of the subject of slavery—slave trade in Cuba; and I know that no law exists, or has existed since the year 1820, that sanctions the introduction of negroes into the island of Cuba, from Africa for the purpose of making slaves, or being held in slavery; and, that all such Bozal negroes, as those recently imported are called, are legally free; and no law, common or statute, exists there, by which they can be held in slavery. Such Africans, long settled in Cuba, and acclimated, are called ladinos, and must have been introduced before 1820, and are so called in contradistinction to the term creole, which is applied to the negroes born in the island. I have [***25] seen, and now have before me, a document, dated 26th June, 1839, purporting to be signed by Ezpeleta, who is captain general of the island, to identify which, I have put my name to the lefthand corner of the document, in presence of the counsel of the Africans; this document, or "trasspasso," purporting to be a permit granted to Don I. Ruiz, to export from Havana to Porto Principe, forty-nine negroes, designated by Spanish names, and called therein ladinos, a term totally inapplicable to newly imported Africans. I have seen, and now have before me, another document, dated 22d June, 1839, and signed in the same manner, granted to Don Pedro Montez, for the removal of three negro children from Havana to Porto Principe, also designated by Spanish names, and likewise called 'ladions,' and wholly inapplicable to young African children, who could not have been acclimated, and long settled in the island; which document, I have identified in the same manner as the former. To have obtained these documents from the governor, for bona fide Bozal negroes, and have described them in the application for it, as ladinos, was evidently a fraud, but nothing more than such an application and the payment [***26] of the necessary fees would be required to procure it, as there is never any inquiry or inspection of the negroes on the part of the governor or his officers, nor is there any oath required from the applicant. I further state, that the above documents are manifestly inapplicable to the Africans of the Amisted, I have been here and in New Haven; but such documents are commonly obtained by similar applications at the Havana, and by these means, the negroes recently and illegally introduced, are thus removed to the different ports of the island, and the danger obviated of their falling in with English cruisers, and then they are illegally carried into slavery. One of the largest dealers and importers of the island of Cuba, in African slaves, is the notorious house of Martiner & Co., of Havana; and for years past, as at present, they have been deeply engaged in this traffic; and the Bozal Africans, imported by these and all other slave traders, when brought to the Havana, are immediately taken to the barracoons, or slave marts; five of which are situated in the immediate vicinity of the governor's county house, about one mile and a half from the walls of Havana; and from these barracoons, [***27] they are taken and removed to the different parts of the island when sold; and having examined the endorsements on the back of the transspasso, or permits for the removal of the said negroes of the Amistad, the signature to that endorsement appears to be that of Martiner & Co.; and the document purports to be a permit of pass for the removal of the said negroes. The handwriting of Martiner & Co., I am not acquainted with. These barracoons, outside the city walls, are fitted up exclusively for the reception and sale of Bozal negroes; one of these barracoons or slave marts, called la miserecordia, or 'mercy,' kept by a man, named 'Riera,' I visited the 24th September last, in company with a person well acquainted with this establishment; and the factor or major domo of the master, in the absence of the latter, said to me, that the negroes of the Amistad had been purchased there; that he knew them well; that they had been bought by a man from Porto Principe, and had been embarked for that place; and speaking of the said negroes, he said, 'che, castima,' or what pity it is, which rather surprised me; the man further explained himself, and said, his regret was for the loss of so many [***28] valuable Bozals, in the event of their being executed in the United States.

"One of the houses most openly engaged, and notoriously implicated in the slave trade transactions, it that of Martiner & Co.; and their practice is to remove their newly arrived negroes from the slave ships to these barracoons, where they commonly remain two or three weeks before sold, as these negroes of the Amistad, illegally introduced by Martiner & Co., were in the present instance, as is generally reported and believed in the Havana. Of the Africans which I have seen and examined, from the necessity which my office imposes on me at the Havana of assisting at the registry of the newly imported Bozals, emancipated by the Mixed Court, I can speak with tolerable certainty of the ages of these people, with the exception of the children, whom I have not seen. Sa, about 17; Ba, 21; Luckawa, 19; Tussi, 30; Beli, 18; Shuma, 26; Nama, 20; Tenquis, 21; the others, I had not time to take a note of their ages.

"With respect to the Mixed Commission, its jurisdiction extends only to cases of captured negroes brought in by British or Spanish cruisers; and notwithstanding the illegalities of the traffic in slaves, [***29] from twenty to twenty-five thousand slaves have been introduced into the island during the last three years; and such is the state of society, and of the administration of the laws there, that hopeless slavery is the inevitable result of their removal into the interior."

On his cross-examination the witness stated, that he was not acquainted with the dialects of the African tribes, but was slightly acquainted with the Arabic language. Lawful slaves of the island are not offered for sale generally, or often placed in the barracoons, or man marts. The practice in Havana is to use the barracoons "for Bozal negroes only." Barracoons are used for negroes recently imported, and for their reception and sale. The native language of the Africans is not often continued for a long time on certain plantations. "It has been to me a matter of astonishment at the shortness of time in which the language of the negroes is disused, and the Spanish language adopted and acquired. I speak this, from a very intimate knowledge of the condition of the negroes in Cuba, from frequent visits to plantations, and journeys in the interior; and, on this subject, I think I can say my knowledge is as full as [***30] any person's can be.

"There are five or six barracoons within pistol shot of the country residence of the Captain General of Cuba. On every other part of the coast where the slave trade is carried on, a barracoon or barracoons must likewise exist. They are a part of the things necessary to the slave trade, and are for its use only; for instance, near Matanzas there is a building or shed of this kind and used for this purpose.

"Any negroes landed in the island since 1820, and carried into slavery, have been illegally introduced; and the transfer of them under false names, such as calling Bozal, Ladinos, is, necessarily, a fraud. Unfortunately, there is no interference on the part of the local authorities; they connive at it, and collude with the slave traders; the governor, alone, at the Havana, receiving a bounty or impost on each negro thus illegally introduced, of ten dollars a head. As to the Mixed Commission, once the negroes clandestinely introduced are landed they no longer have cognisance of the violation of the treaty; the governor has cognisance of this and every other bearing of the Spanish law on Spanish soil. This head-money has not the sanction of any Spanish law [***31] for its imposition; and the proof of this is, it is called a voluntary contribution."

Also a statement, given by the District Attorney, W. S. Holabird, Esq., of what was made to him by A. G. Vega, Esq., Spanish Consul, January 10th, 1840: "That he is a Spanish subject; that he resided in the island of Cuba several years; that he knows the laws of that island on the subject of slavery; that there was no law that was considered in force in the island of Cuba, that prohibited the bringing in African slaves; that the Court of Mixed Commissioners had no jurisdiction except in cases of capture on the sea; that newly imported African negroes were constantly brought to the island, and, after landing, were bona fide transferred from one owner to another, without any interference by the local authorities or the Mixed Commission, and were held by the owners, and recognised as lawful property; that slavery was recognised in Cuba by all the laws that were considered in force there; that the native language of the slaves was kept up on some plantations for years. That the barracoons are public markets, where all descriptions of slaves and sold and bought; that the papers of the Amistad are genuine, [***32] and are in the usual form; that it was not necessary to practise any fraud to obtain such papers from the proper officers of the government; that none of the papers of the Amistad are signed by Martiner, spoken of by R. R. Madden in his deposition; that he (Martiner) did not hold the office from whence that paper issued."

Also a deposition of James Ray, a mariner on board of the Washington, stating the circumstances of the taking possession of the Amistad, and the Africans, which supported the allegations in the several libels, in all essential circumstances.

The documents exhibited as the passports of the Spanish authorities at Havana, and other papers relating to the Amistad, and her clearance from Havana, were also annexed to the decree of the Circuit Court, in the original Spanish. Translations of all of these, which were deemed of importance in the cause, are given in the decree of the District Court.

Sullivan Haley stated in his deposition, that he heard Ruiz say, that "none of the negroes could speak Spanish; they are just from Africa."

James Covey, a coloured man, deposed that "he was born at Berong-Mendi country; left there seven and a half years ago; was a slave, and [***33] carried to Lumboko. All these Africans were from Africa. Never saw them until now. I could talk with them. They appeared glad because they could speak the same language. I could understand all but two or three. They say they from Lumboke; three moons. They all have Mendi names, and their names all mean something; Carle, means bone; Kimbo, means cricket. They speak of rivers which I know; said they sailed from Lumboko; two or three speak different language from the others; the Timone language. Say-ang-wa rivers spoken of; these run through the Vi country. I learned to speak English at Sierre Leone. Was put on board a man-of-war one year and a half. They all agree as to where they sailed from. I have no doubt they are Africans. I have been in this country six months; came in a British man-of-war; have been in this town (New Haven) four months with Mr. Bishop; he calls on me for no money, and do not know who pays my board. I was stolen by a black man who stole ten of us. One man carried us two months' walk. Have conversed with Sinqua; Barton has been in my town, Gorang. I was sailing for Havana when the British man-of-war captured us."

The testimony of Cinque and the [***34] negroes of the Amistad, supported the statements in their answers.

The respondents also gave in evidence the "Treaty between Great Britain and Spain, for the abolition of the slave trade, signed at Madrid, 23d September, 1817."

LAWYERS' EDITION HEADNOTES:

Admiralty—salvage—capture by United States brig of Spanish vessel in possession of negroes who had been kidnapped but had revolted—construction of laws and treaties regarding slave trade—regarding pirates and robbers—ship's papers, effect of fraud—evidence.—

Headnote:

The Spanish schooner Amistad, on the 27th day of June, 1839, cleared out from Havana, in Cuba, for Puerto Principe, in the same island, having on board Captain Ferrer, and Ruiz and Montez, Spanish subjects. Captain Ferrer had on board Antonio, a slave; Ruiz had forty-nine negroes; Montez had four negroes, which were claimed by them as slaves, and stated to be their property, in passports or documents signed by the Governor-General of Cuba. In fact, these African negroes, had been, a very short time before they were put on the Amistad, brought into Cuba, by Spanish slave traders, in direct contravention of the treaties between Spain and Great Britain, and in violation of the laws of Spain. On the voyage of the Amistad, the negroes rose, killed the captain, and took possession of the vessel. They spared the lives of Ruiz and Montez, on condition that they would aid in steering the Amistad for the coast of Africa, or to some place where negro slavery was not permitted by the laws of the country. Ruiz and Montez deceived the negroes, who were totally ignorant of navigation, and steered the Amistad for the United States; and she arrived off Long Island, in the State of New York, on the 26th of August, and anchored within half a mile of the shore. Some of the negroes went on shore to procure supplies of water and provisions, and the vessel was then discovered by the United States brig Washington. Lieutenant Gedney, commanding the Washington, assisted by his officers and crew, took possession of the Amistad, and of the negroes on shore and in the vessel, brought them into the District of Connecticut, and there libeled the vessel, the cargo, and the negroes for salvage. Libels for salvage were also presented in the District Court of the United States, for the District of Connecticut, by persons who had aided, as they alleged, in capturing the negroes on shore on Long Island, and contributed to the vessel, cargo, and negroes being taken into possession by the Brig Washington. Ruiz and Montez filed claims to the negroes as their slaves, and prayed that they, and parts of the cargo of the Amistad, might be delivered to them, or to the representatives of the crown of Spain. The attorney of the district of Connecticut filed an information stating that the Minister of Spain had claimed of the government of the United States that the vessel, cargo, and slaves should be restored, under the provisions of the treaty between the United States and Spain, the same having arrived within the limits and jurisdiction of the United States, and had been taken possession of by a public armed vessel of the United States, under such circumstances as made it the duty of the United States to cause them to be restored to the true owners thereof. The information asked that the court would make such order as would enable the United States to comply with the treaty: or, if it should appear that the negroes had been brought from Africa, in violation of the laws of the United States, that the court would make an order for the removal of the negroes to Africa, according to the laws of the United States. A claim for Antonio was filed by the Spanish consul, on behalf of the representatives of Captain Ferrer, and claims are also filed by merchants of Cuba for parts of the cargo of the vessel, denying salvage, and asserting their right to have the same delivered to them under the treaty. The negroes, Antonio excepted, filed an answer denying that they were slaves, or the property of Ruiz, or Montez; and denying the right of the court under the Constitution and laws of the United States to exercise any jurisdiction over their persons. They asserted that they were native free-born Africans, and ought of right to be free; that they had been, in April, 1839, kidnapped in Africa, and had been carried in a vessel engaged in the slave trade from the coast of Africa to Cuba, for the purpose of being sold; and that Ruiz and Montez, knowing these facts, had purchased them, put them on board the Amistad, intending to carry them to be held as slaves for life, to another part of Cuba, and that, on the voyage, they rose on the master took possession of the vessel and were intending to proceed to Africa or to some free State, when they were taken possession of by the United States armed vessel, the Washington. After evidence had been given by the parties, and all the documents of the vessel and cargo, with the alleged passports, and the clearance from Havana had been produced the District Court made a decree, by which all claims to salvage of the negroes were rejected, and salvage amounting to one third of the vessel and cargo was allowed to Lieutenant Gedney, and the officers and crew of the Washington. The claim of the representatives of Captain Ferrer, to Antonio, was allowed; the claims of Ruiz and Montez being included in the claim of the Spanish minister, and of the minister of Spain, to the negroes as slaves, or to have them delivered to the Spanish minister, under the treaty, to be sent to Cuba, were rejected; and the court decreed that the negroes should be delivered to the President of the United States, to be sent to Africa, pursuant to the Act of Congress of 3d March, 1819. From this decree the District Attorney of the United States appealed to the Circuit Court, except so far as the same related to Antonio. The owners of the cargo of the Amistad also appealed from that part of the decree which allowed salvage on their goods. Ruiz or Montez did not appeal, nor did the representatives of the owner of the Amistad. The Circuit Court of Connecticut, by a proforma decree, affirmed the decree of the District Court reserving the question of salvage on the merchandise on board the Amistad. The United States appealed from this decree. The decree of the Circuit Court was affirmed; saving that part of the same which directed the negroes to be delivered to the President of the United States, to be sent to Africa; which was reversed, and the negroes were declared to be free.

The sixth article of the Treaty with Spain, of 1795, continued in full force, in this particular, by the treaty ratified in 1821, seems to have had principally in view, cases where the property of the subjects of either State had been taken possession of within the territorial jurisdiction of the other during war. The eighth article provides for cases where the shipping of the inhabitants of either State are forced, through stress of weather, pursuit of pirates, or enemies, or any other urgent necessity, to seek shelter in the ports of the other. There may well be some doubts entertained whether the case of The Amistad, in its actual circumstances, falls within the purview of this article.

The ninth article of the treaty provides, that all ships and merchandise, which shall be rescued out of the hands of any pirates and robbers, on the high seas, which shall be brought into some port of either State, shall be delivered to the officers of the port in order to be taken care of, and "restored entire to the proprietary, as soon as due and sufficient proof shall be made concerning the property thereof." To bring the case of the Amistad within this article, it is essential to establish: First, that the negroes, under all the circumstances, fall within the description of merchandise, in the sense of the treaty. Second. That there has been a rescue of them on the high seas, out of the hands of pirates and robbers. Third. That Ruiz and Montez are the true proprietors of the negroes, and have established their rights by competent proofs. If those negroes were, at the time, lawfully held as slaves under the laws of Spain, and recognized by those laws as property capable of being bought and sold, no reason is seen why this may not be deemed, within the intent of the treaty, to be included under the denomination of merchandise, and ought, as such, to be restored to the claimants; for upon that point the laws of Spain would seem to furnish the proper rule of interpretation. But, admitting that to be the construction of the treaty, it is clear in the opinion of the court that neither of the other essential facts and requisites has been established by proof, and the onus probandi of both lies upon the claimants, to give rise to the casus foederis.

The negroes were never the lawful slaves of Ruiz, or Montez, or of any other Spanish subject. They are natives of Africa; and were kidnapped there, and were unlawfully transported to Cuba, in violation of the laws and treaties of Spain, and of the most solemn edicts and declarations of the government.

By the laws, treaties, and edicts of Spain, the African slave trade is utterly abolished; the dealing in that trade is deemed a heinous crime; and the negroes thereby introduced into the dominion of Spain are declared to be free.

There is no pretense to say the negroes of the Amistad are "pirates" and "robbers;" as they were kidnapped Africans, who, by the laws of Spain itself were entitled to their freedom.

Although public documents of the government accompanying property found on board of the private ships of a foreign nation are to be deemed prima facie evidence of the facts which they state, yet they are always open to be impugned for fraud; and whether that fraud be in the original obtaining of those documents, or in the subsequent fraudulent and illegal use of them, where once it is satisfactorily established, it overthrows all their sanctity, and destroys them as proof.

Fraud will vitiate any, even the most solemn transactions; and any asserted title founded upon it is utterly void.

The language of the Treaty with Spain of 1795 requires the proprietor "to make due and sufficient proof" of his property; and that proof cannot be deemed either due or sufficient, which is stained with fraud.

Nothing is more clear in the laws of nations, as an established rule to regulate their rights and duties and intercourse, than the doctrine that the ship's papers are prima facie evidence of what they state; and that if they are shown to be fraudulent, they are not to be held proof of any valid title whatever. This rule is applied in prize cases; and is just as applicable to the transactions of civil intercourse between nations in times of peace.

In the solemn treaties between nations it never can be presumed that either State intends to provide the mans of perpetrating or protecting frauds; but all the provisions are to be construed as intended to be applied to bona fide transactions.

The seventeenth article of the treaty with Spain which provides for certain passports and certificates as evidence of property on board of the ships of both States, is, in its terms, applicable only to cases where either of the parties is engaged in war. This article required a certain form of passport to be agreed upon by the parties and annexed to the treaty. It never was annexed; and, therefore, in the case of The Amiable Isabella, 6 Wheaton, 1, it is held inoperative.

Supposing the African negroes on board the Amistad not to be slaves, but kidnapped, and free negroes, the treaty with Spain cannot be obligatory upon them; and the United States are bound to respect their rights, as much as those of Spanish subjects. The conflict of rights between the parties, under such circumstances, becomes positive and inevitable, and must be decided upon the invariable principles of justice and international law.

The treaty with Spain never could have been intended to take away the equal rights of all foreigners who should assert their claims to equal justice before the courts of the United States; or to deprive such foreigners of the protection given to them by other treaties, or by the general laws of nations.

There is no ground to assert that the case of the negroes who were on board of the Amistad comes within the provisions of the Act of Congress of 1799, or of any other of the prohibitory slave trade acts. These negroes were never taken from Africa, or brought to the United States in contravention of these acts. When the Amistad arrived she was in possession of the negroes, asserting their freedom; and in no sense could possibly intend to import themselves into the United States as slaves, or for sale as slaves.

The carrying of the Amistad and her cargo into Connecticut by Lieutenant Gedney, and the officers and crew of the Washington, was a highly meritorious and useful service to the proprietors of the ship and cargo, and such, as by the general principles of the maritime law, is always deemed a just foundation for salvage. The rate allowed by the court (one third) does not seem beyond the exercise of a sound discretion, under the very peculiar and embarrassing circumstances of the case.

SYLLABUS

The Spanish schooner Amisted, on the 27th day of June, 1839, cleared out from Havana, in Cuba, for Puerto Principe, in the same island, having on board, Captain Ferrer, and Ruiz and Montez, Spanish subjects. Captain Ferrer had on board Antonio, a slave; Ruiz had forty-nine negroes; Montez had four negroes, which were claimed by them as slaves, and stated to be their property, in passports or documents, signed by the Governor General of Cuba. In fact, these African negroes had been, a very short time before they were put on board the Amistad, brought into Cuba, by Spanish slave traders, in direct contravention of the treaties between Spain and Great Britain, and in violation of the laws of Spain. On the voyage of the Amistad, the negroes rose, killed the captain, and took possession of the vessel. They spared the lives of Ruiz and Montez, on condition that they would aid in steering the Amistad for the coast of Africa, or to some place where negro [***35] slavery was not permitted by the laws of the country. Ruiz and Montez deceived the negroes, who were totally ignorant of navigation, and steered the Amistad for the United States; and she arrived off Long Island, in the state of New York, on the 26th of August, and anchored within half a mile of the shore. Some of the negroes went to shore to procure supplies of water and provisions, and the vessel was then discovered by the United States brig Washington. Lieutenant Gedney, commanding the Washington assisted by his officers and crew, took possession of the Amistad, and of the negroes on shore and in the vessel, brought them into the District of Connecticut, and there libelled the vessel, the cargo, and the negroes for salvage. Libels for salvage were also presented in the District Court of the United States, for the District of Connecticut, by persons who had aided, as they alleged, in capturing the negroes on shore on Long Island, and contributed to the vessel, cargo, and negroes being taken into possession by the brig Washington. Ruiz and Montez filed claims to the negroes as their slaves, and prayed that they, and parts of the cargo of the Amistad, might be delivered to them, [***36] or to the representatives of the crown of Spain. The attorney of the District of Connecticut filed an information stating that the Minister of Spain had claimed of the government of the United States that the vessel, cargo, and slaves should be restored, under the provisions of the treaty between the United States and Spain, the same having arrived within the limits and jurisdiction of the United States, under such circumstances as made it the duty of the vessel of the United States, under such circumstances as made it the duty of the United States to cause them to be restored to the true owners thereof. The information asked that the Court would make such order as would enable the United States to comply with the treaty; or, if it should appear that the negroes had been brought from Africa, in violation of the laws of the United States, that the Court would make an order for the removal of the negroes to Africa, according to the laws of the United States. A claim for Antonio was filed by the Spanish consul, on behalf of the representatives of Captain Ferrer, and claims are also filed by merchants of Cuba for parts of the cargo of the vessel, denying salvage, and asserting their right [***37] to have the same delivered to them under the treaty. The negores, Antonio excepted, filed an answer denying that they were slaves, or the property of Ruiz, or Montez; and denying the right of the Court under the Constitution and laws of the United States to exercise any jurisdiction over their persons. They asserted that they were native free-born Africans, and ought of right to be free; that they had been, in April 1839, kidnapped in Africa, and had been carried in a vessel engaged in the slave trade from the coast of Africa to Cuba, for the purpose of being sold; and that Ruiz and Montez, knowing these facts, had purchased them, put them on board the Amistad, intending to carry them to be held as slaves for life, to another part of Cuba, and that, on the voyage, they rose on the master, took possession of the vessel, and were intending to proceed to Africa, or to some free state, when they were taken possession of by the United States armed vessel, the Washington. After evidence had been given by the parties, and all the documents of the vessel and cargo, with the alleged passports, and the clearance from Havana had been produced the District Court made a decree, by which all [***38] claims to salvage of the negroes were rejected, and salvage amounting to one-third of the vessel and cargo, was allowed to Lieutenant Gedney, and the officers and crew of the Washington. The claim of the representatives of Captain Ferrer, to Antonio, was allowed: the claims of Ruiz and Montez being included in the claim of the Spanish minister, and of the minister of Spain, to the negroes as slaves, or to have them delivered to the Spanish minister, under the treaty, to be sent to Cuba, were rejected: and the Court decreed that the negroes should be delivered to the President of the United States, to be sent to Africa, pursuant to the act of Congress of 3d March, 1819. From this decree the District Attorney of the United States appealed to the Circuit Court, except so far as the same related to Antonio. The owners of the cargo of the Amistad also appealed from that part of the decree which allowed salvage on their goods. Ruiz or Montez did not appeal, nor did the representatives of the owner of the Amistad. The Circuit Court of Connecticut, by a pro forma decree, affirmed the decree of the District Court, reserving the question of salvage on the merchandise on board the Amistad. [***39] The United States appealed from this decree. The decree of the Circuit Court was affirmed; saving that part of the same, which directed the negroes to be delivered to the President of the United States, to be sent to Africa; which was reversed, and the negroes were declared to be free.

The sixth article of the treaty with Spain, of 1795, continued in full force, in this particular, by the treaty ratified in 1821, seems to have had principally in view, cases where the property of the subjects of either state, had been taken possession of within the territorial jurisdiction of the other, during war. The eighth article provides for cases where the shipping of the inhabitants of either state are forced, through stress of weather, pursuit of pirates, or enemies, or any other urgent necessity, to seek shelter in the ports of the other. There may well be some doubts entertained whether the case of the Amistad, in its actual circumstances, falls within the purview of this article.

The ninth article of the treaty provides, that all ships and merchandise, which shall be rescued out of the hands of any pirates and robbers, on the high seas, which shall be brought into some port of either [***40] state, shall be delivered to the officers of the port in order to be taken care of, and "restored entire to the proprietary, as soon as due and sufficient proof shall be made concerning the property thereof." To bring the case of the Amistad within this article, it is essential to establish: First, that the negroes, under all the circumstances, fall within the description of merchandise, in the sense of the treaty. Secondly, That there has been a rescue of them on the high seas, out of the hands of pirates and robbers. Thirdly, That Ruiz and Montez are the true proprietors of the negroes, and have established their title by competent proofs. If those negroes were, at the time, lawfully held as slaves under the laws of Spain, and recognised by those laws as property capable of being bought and sold, no reason is seen why this may not be deemed, within the intent of the treaty, to be included under the denomination of merchandise, and ought, as such, to be restored to the claimants; for upon that point the laws of Spain would seem to furnish the proper rule of interpretation. But, admitting that to be the construction of the treaty, it is clear in the opinion of the Court, that neither [***41] of the other essential facts and requisites has been established by proof and the onus probandi of both lies upon the claimants, to give rise to the casus foederis.

The negroes were never the lawful slaves of Ruiz, or Montez, or of any other Spanish subject. They are natives of Africa; and were kidnapped there, and were unlawfully transported to Cuba, in violation of the laws and treaties of Spain, and of the most solemn edicts and declarations of that government.

By the laws, treaties, and edicts of Spain, the African slave trade is utterly abolished; the dealing in that trade is deemed a heinous crime; and the negroes thereby introduced into the dominions of Spain, are declared to be free.

There is no pretence to say the negroes of the Amisted are "pirates" and "robbers;" as they were kidnapped Africans, who, by the laws of Spain itself were entitled to their freedom.

Although public documents of the government accompanying property found on board of the private ships of a foreign nation, are to be deemed prima facie evidence of the facts which they state, yet they are always open to be impugned for fraud; and whether that fraud be in the original obtaining of those documents, [***42] or in the subsequent fraudulent and illegal use of them, where once it is satisfactorily established, it over-throws all their sanctity, and destroys them as proof.

Fraud will vitiate any, even the most solemn transactions; and any asserted title founded upon it, is utterly void.

The language of the treaty with Spain of 1795, requires the proprietor "to make due and sufficient proof" of his property; and that proof cannot be deemed either due or sufficient, which is stained with fraud.

Nothing is more clear in the laws of nations as an established rule to regulate their rights and duties, and intercourse, than the doctrine that the ship's papers are prima facie evidence of what they state; and that if they are shown to be fraudulent, they are not to be held proof of any valid title whatever. This rule is applied in prize cases; and is just as applicable to the transactions of civil intercourse between nations in times of peace.

In the solemn treaties between nations it never can be presumed that either state intends to provide the means of perpetrating or protecting frauds; but all the provisions are to be construed as intended to be applied to bona fide transactions.

The seventeenth [***43] article of the treaty with Spain which provides for certain passports and certificates as evidence of property on board of the ships of both states, is, in its terms, applicable only to cases where either of the parties is engaged in war. This article required a certain form of passport to be agreed upon by the parties and annexed to the treaty. It never was annexed: and, therefore, in the case of The Amiable Isabella, 6 Wheaton, 1, it is held inoperative.

Supposing the African negroes on board the Amisted not to be slaves, but kidnapped, and free negroes, the treaty with Spain cannot be obligatory upon them; and the United States are bound to respect their rights, as much as those of Spanish subjects. The conflict of rights between the parties, under such circumstances, becomes positive and inevitable, and must be decided upon the invariable principles of justice and international law.

The treaty with Spain never could have been intended to take away the equal rights of all foreigners who should assert their claims to equal justice before the Courts of the United States; or to deprive such foreigners of the protection given to them by other treaties, or by the general laws of [***44] nations.

There is no ground to assert that the case of the negroes who were on board of the Amistad comes within the provisions of the act of Congress of 1799, or of any other of the prohibitory slave-trade acts. These negroes were never taken from Africa, or brought to the United States in contravention of these acts. When the Amistad arrived she was in possession of the negroes, asserting their freedom; and in no sense could possibly intend to import themselves into the United States as slaves, or for sale as slaves.

The carrying of the Amistad and her cargo into Connecticut by Lieutenant Gedney, and the officers and crew of the Washington, was a highly meritorious and useful service to the proprietors of the ship and cargo, and such, as by the general principles of the maritime law, is always deemed a just foundation for salvage. The rate allowed by the Court, (one-third) does not seem beyond the exercise of a sound discretion, under the very peculiar and embarrassing circumstances of the case.

COUNSEL: The case was argued for the United States, by Mr. Gilpin, the Attorney General, and by Mr. Baldwin and Mr. Adams, for the Appellees; Mr. Jones, on the part of Lieutenant Gedney [***45] and others, of the United States brig Washington, was not required by the Court to argue the claims to salvage.

Mr. Gilpin, the Attorney General, for the United States, reviewed the evidence, as set out in the record, of all the facts connected with the case, from the first clearance of the schooner Amistad, at Havana, on the 18th May, 1838, down to the 23d January, 1840, when the final decree of the District Court of the United States, for the District of Connecticut, was rendered.

The Attorney General proceeded to remark, that, on the 23d January, 1840, the case stood thus. The vessel, cargo, and negroes, were in possession of the Marshal, under process from the District Court, to answer to five separate claims; those of Lieutenant Gedney, and Messrs. Green and Fordham, for salvage; that of the United States, at the instance of the Spanish minister, for the vessel, cargo, and negroes, to be restored to the Spanish owners, in which claim those of Messrs. Ruiz and Montez were merged; that of the Spanish vice-consul, for the slave Antonio, to be restored to the Spanish owner; and that of Messrs. Tellincas, and Aspe and Laca, for the restoration of a part of the cargo belonging to [***46] them. The decree of the District Court found that the vessel, and the goods on board were the property of Spanish subjects, and that the passports under which the negroes were shipped at Havana, were signed by the Governor General of Cuba. It denied the claims of Lieutenant Gedney, and Messrs. Green and Fordham, to salvage on the slaves, but allowed the claims of the officers and crew of the Washington to salvage on the Amistad, and on the merchandise on board of that vessel. It also decreed that the residue of the goods, and the vessel, should be delivered to the Spanish minister, to be restored to the Spanish owners; and that the slave Antonio should be delivered to the Spanish vice-consul, for the same purpose. As to the negroes, claimed by Ruiz and Montez, it dismissed the claims of those persons, on the ground that they were included under that of the minister of Spain. The libel of the United States, claiming the delivery of the negroes to the Spanish minister, was dismissed, on the ground that they were not slaves, but were kidnapped and imported into Cuba; and that, at the time they were so imported, there was a law of Spain declaring persons so imported to be free. The [***47] alternative prayer of the United States, claiming the delivery of the negroes to be transported to Africa, was granted.

As soon as this decree was made, an appeal was taken by the United States to the Circuit Court, from the whole of it, except so far as it related to Antonio. At the succeeding term of the Circuit Court, the negroes moved that the appeal of the United States might be dismissed, on the ground that they had no interest in the negroes; and, also, on the ground that they have no right to prosecute claims to property in behalf of subjects of the Queen of Spain. That motion, however, was refused by the Circuit Court, which proceeded to affirm the decree of the District Court, on the libel of the United States. It is from this decree of the Circuit Court that the present appeal to the Supreme Court is prosecuted.

Was the decree of the Circuit Court correct?

The state of the facts, as found by the decree, and not denied, was this. The vessel, and the goods on board, were the property of Spanish subjects in Havana, on the 27th June, 1839. At that time slavery was recognised and in existence in the Spanish dominions. The negroes in question are certified at that time, [***48] in a document signed by the Governor General of Cuba, to be ladinos negroes—that is, slaves—the property of Spanish subjects. As such, permission is given by the Governor General, to their owners, to take them, by sea, to Puerto Principe, in the same island. The vessel with these slaves, thus certified, on board, and in charge of their alleged owners, regularly cleared and sailed from Havana, the documentary evidence aforesaid, and the papers of the vessel being also on board. During this voyage, the negroes rose, killed the captain, and took possession of the vessel. On the 26th August, the vessel, cargo, and negroes, were rescued and taken on the high seas, by a public officer of the United States, and brought into a port of the United States, where they await the decision of the judicial tribunals.

In this position of things, the minister of Spain demands that the vessel, cargo, and negroes, be restored, pursuant to the 9th article of the treaty of 27th October, 1795, which provides (1 Laws of the United States, 268) that "all ships and merchandise of what nature soever, which shall be rescued out of the hands of any pirates or robbers, on the high seas, shall be brought [***49] into some port of either state, and shall be delivered into the custody of the officers of that port, in order to be taken care of and restored entire to the true proprietor, as soon as due and sufficient proof shall be made concerning the property thereof."

The only inquiries, then, that present themselves, are,

1. Has "due and sufficient proof concerning the property thereof" been made?

2. If so, have the United States a right to interpose in the manner they have done, to obtain its restoration to the Spanish owners?

If these inquiries result in the affirmative, then the decree of the Circuit Court was erroneous, and ought to be reversed.

I. It is submitted that there has been due and sufficient proof concerning the property to authorize its restoration.

It is not denied that, under the laws of Spain, negroes may be held as slaves, as completely as they are in any of the states of this Union; nor will it be denied, if duly proved to be such, they are subject to restoration as much as other property, when coming under the provisions of this treaty. Now these negroes are declared, by the certificates of the Governor General, to be slaves, and the property of the Spanish subjects [***50] therein named. That officer (1 White's New Rec. 369. 371; 8 Peters, 310) is the highest functionary of the government in Cuba; his public acts are the highest evidence of any facts stated by him, within the scope of his authority. It is within the scope of his authority to declare what is property, and what are the rights of the subjects of Spain, within his jurisdiction, in regard to property.

Now, in the intercourse of nations, there is no rule better esablished than this, that full faith is to be given to such acts—to the authentic evidence of such acts. The question is not whether the act is right or wrong; it is, whether the scope of the been done, and whether it is an act within the scope of the authority. We are to inquire only whether the power existed, and whether it was exercised, and how it was exercised; not whether it was rightly or wrongly exercised.

The principle is universally admitted, that, wherever an authority is delegated to any public officer, to be exercised at his discretion, under his own judgment and upon his own responsibility, the acts done in the appropriate exercise of that authority, are binding as to the subject matter. Without such a rule [***51] there could be no peace or comity among nations; all harmony, all mutual respect would be destroyed; the Courts and tribunals of one country would become the judges of the local laws and property of others. Nor is it to be supposed that so important a principle would not be recognisd by Courts of justice. They have held, that, whether the act of the foreign functionary be executive, legislative, or judicial, it is, if exercised within its appropriate sphere, binding as to the subject-matter; and the authentic record of such act is full and complete evidence thereof. In the case of Marbury v. Madison, 1 Cranch, 170, this Court held, that a commission was conclusive evidence of an executive appointment; and that a party from whom it was withheld might obtain it through the process of a Court, as being such evidence of his rights. In the case of Thompson v. Tolmie, 2 Peters, 167, this Court sustained the binding and sufficient character of a decision, made by a competent tribunal, and not reversed, whether that decision was in itself right or wrong. In the case of The United States v. Arredondo, 6 Peters, 719, the whole doctrine on this subject is most forcibly stated. Indeed, nothing [***52] can be clearer than the principles thus laid down; nor can they apply more directly to any case than the present. Here is the authentic certificate or record of the highest officer known to the spanish law, declaring, in terms, that these negroes are the property of the several Spanish subjects. We have it countersigned by another of the principal officers. We have it executed and delivered, as the express evidence of property, to these persons. It is exactly the same as that deemed sufficient for the vessel and for the cargo. Would it not have been complete and positive evidence in the island of Cuba? If so, the principle laid down by this Court makes it such here.

But this general principle is strengthened by the particular circumstances of the case. Where property on board of a vessel is brought into a foreign port, the documentary evidence, whether it be a judicial decree, or the ship's papers, accompanied by possession, is the best evidence of ownership, and that to which Courts of justice invariably look. In the case of Bernardi v. Motteux, Douglas, 575, Lord Mansfield laid down the rule that a decree of a foreign Court was conclusive as to the right of property under [***53] it. In that of the Vigilantia, 1 Rob. 3. 11, the necessity or propriety of producing the ship's papers, as the first evidence of her character and property, and of ascertaining her national character from her passport, is expressly recognised. In that of the Cosmopolite, 3 Rob. 269, the title of the claimant, who was a Dane, to the vessel, was a decree of a French Court against an American vessel; the Court refused to inquire into the circumstances of the condemnation, but held the decree sufficient evidence for them. In that of the Sarah, 3 Rob. 166, the captors of a prize applied to be allowed to give proof of the property being owned by persons other than those stated in the ship's documents, but it was refused. In that of the Henrich and Maria, 4 Rob. 52, the very question was made, whether the Court would not look into the validity of a title, derived under a foreign Court of Admiralty, and it was refused.

These principles are fully sustained by our own Courts.

In the case of the Resolution, 2 Dall. 22, 23, possession of property on board of a vessel is held to be presumptive evidence of ownership; and the ship's papers, bills of lading, and other documents, are prima facie [***54] evidence of the facts they speak. It is on this evidence that vessels are generally acquitted or condemned. In that of the Ann Green, 1 Gall. 281. 284, it is laid down as the rule that the first and proper evidence in prize cases is the ship's papers; and that only in cases of doubt is further testimony to be received. The Court there say that as a general rule they would pronounce for the inadmissibility of such further evidence. So in that of the Diana, 2 Gall. 97, the general rule laid down is, that no claim is to be admitted in opposition to the ship's papers; the exceptions stand upon very particular grounds. In that of Ohl v. The Eagle Insurance Company, 4 Mason, 172, parol evidence was held not to be admissible to contradict a ship's papers. In that of M'Grath v. Candelero, Bee, 60, a decree of restitution in a foreign Court of Admiralty was held to be full evidence of the ownership, and such as was to be respected in all other countries. In that of Catlett v. The Pacific Insurance Company, Paine, 612, the register was held to be conclusive evidence of the national character of the vessel; and a similar rule was held to exist in regard to a pass, in the case of Barker [***55] v. The Phoenix Insurance Company.

Similar principles have been adopted in this Court.

The decree of a foreign Court of Admiralty, on a question of blockade, was allowed in the case of Croudson v. Leonard, 4 Cranch, 434, to be contradicted in the Court below; but this Court reversed that decision, and held it to be conclusive. In that of the Mary, 9 Cranch, 142, this Court sustained the proof of property founded on the register against a decree of a foreign Court of Admiralty. In that of the Pizarro, 2 Wheaton, 227, the Court look to the documentary evidence, as that to be relied on to prove ownership; and although the papers were not strictly correct, they still relied on them in preference to further extraneous proof. Add to all this the twelfth article of the treaty with Spain, (1 Laws of United States, 270,) which makes passports and certificates evidence of property; and the principle may be regarded as established beyond a question, that the regular documents are the best and primary evidence in regard to all property on board of vessels. This is indeed especially the case when they are merely coasting vessels, or such as are brought in on account of distress, shipwreck, [***56] or other accident. The injustice of requiring further evidence in such cases, is too apparent to need any argument on the subject. Nor is it a less settled rule of international law, that when a vessel puts in by reason of distress or any similar cause, she is not to be judged by the municipal law. The unjust results to which a different rule would lead are most apparent. Could we tolerate it, that if one of our own coasters was obliged to put into Cuba, and had regular coasting papers, the Courts of that country should look beyond them, as to proof of property?

If this point be established, is there any difference between property in slaves and other property? They existed as property at the time of the treaty in perhaps every nation of the globe; they still exist as property in Spain and the United States; they can be demanded as property in the states of this Union to which they fly, and where by the laws they would not, if domiciliated, be property. If, then, they are property, the rules laid down in regard to property extend to them. If they are found on board of a vessel, the evidence of property should be that which is recognised as the best in other casse of property [***57] —the vessel's papers, accompanied by possession. In the case of the Louis, 2 Dodson, 238, slaves are treated of, by Sir William Scott, in express terms, as property, and he directed that those taken unlawfully from a foreigner should be restored:

In the case of the Antelope, 10 Wheaton, 119, the decision in the case of the Louis is recognised, and the same principle was fully and completely acted upon. It was there conceded, (10 Wheaton, 124,) that possession on board of a vessel was evidence of property. In the case of Johnson v. Tompkins, 1 Baldwin, 577, it was held that, even where it was a question of freedom or slavery, the same rules of evidence prevailed as in other cases relative to the right of property. In the case of Choat v. Wright, 2 Devereux, 289, a sale of a slave accompanied by delivery is valid, though there be no bill of sale. And it is well settled, that a title to them is vested by the statute of limitations, as in other cases of property. 5 Cranch, 358. 361. 11 Wheaton, 361.

If, then, the same law exists in regard to property in slaves as in other things; and if documentary evidence, from the highest authority of the country where the property belonged, [***58] accompanied with possession, is produced; it follows that the title to the ownership of this property is as complete as is required by law.

But it is said that this evidence is insufficient, because it is in point of fact fraudulent and untrue. The ground of this assertion is, that the slaves were not property in Cuba, at the date of the document signed by the Governor General; because they had been lately introduced into that island from Africa, and persons so introduced were free. To this it is answered that, if it were so, this Court will not look beyond the authentic evidence under the official certificate of the Governor General; that, if it would, there is not such evidence as this Court can regard to be sufficient to overthrow the positive statement of that document; and that, if the evidence were even deemed sufficient to show the recent introduction of the negroes, it does not establish that they were free at the date of the certificate.

I. This Court will not look behind the certificate of the Governor General. It does not appear to be alleged that it is fraudulent in itself. It is found by the District Court to have been signed by him, and countersigned by the officer [***59] of the customs. It was issued by them in the appropriate exercise of their functions. It resembles an American register or coasting license. Now, all the authorities that have been cited show that these documents are received as the highest species of evidence, and that, even if there is error in the proceedings on which they are founded. The correction must be made by the tribunal from which it emanates. Where should we stop if we were to refuse to give faith to the documents of public officers? All national intercourse, all commerce must be at an end. If there is error in issuing these papers, the matter must be sent to the tribunals of Spain for correction.

II. But if this Court will look behind this paper; is the evidence sufficient to contradict it? The official declaration to be contradicted is certainly of a character not to be lightly set aside in the Courts of a foreign country. The question is not as to the impression we may derive from the evidence; but how far is it sufficient to justify us in declaring a fact in direct contradiction to such an official declaration. It is not evidence that could be received according to the established admiralty practice. Seamen [***60] (1 Peters, Ad. Dec. 211) on board of a vessel cannot be witnesses for one another in matters where they have a common interest. Again, the principal part of this evidence is not taken under oath. That of Dr. Madden, which is mainly relied upon, is chiefly hearsay; and is contradicted, in some of its most essential particulars, by that of other witnesses.

Would this Court be justified, on evidence such as this, in setting aside the admitted certificate of the Governor General? Would such evidence, in one of our own Courts, be deemed adequate to set aside a judicial proceeding, or an act of a public functionary, done in the due exercise of his office? How, then, can it be adequate to such an end, before the tribunals of a foreign country, when they pass upon the internal municipal acts of another government; and when the endeavour is made to set them aside, in a matter relating to their own property and people?

III. But admit this evidence to be competent and sufficient; admit these negroes were brought into Cuba a few weeks before the certificate was given; still, were they not slaves, under the Spanish laws? It is not denied that negroes imported from Africa into Cuba, might [***61] be slaves. If they are not, it is on account of some special law or decree. Has such a law been produced in the present case? The first document produced is the treaty with England, of 23d September, 1817. But that has no such effect. It promises, indeed, that Spain will take into consideration the means of preventing the slave trade, and it points out those means, so far as the trade on the coast of Africa is concerned. But it carefully limits the ascertainment of any infringement to two special tribunals; one at Sierra Leone, and the other at Havana. The next is the decree of December, 1817, which authorizes negroes, brought in against the treaty, to "be declared free." The treaty of 28th June, 1835, which is next adduced, is confined entirely to the slave trade on the coast of Africa, or the voyage from there. Now, it is evident that none of these documents show that these negroes were free in Cuba. They had not been "declared free" by any competent tribunal. Even had they been taken actually on board of a vessel engaged in the slave trade, they must have been adjudicated upon at one of the two special courts, and nowhere else. Can this Court, then, undertake to decide this [***62] question of property, when it has not even been decided by the Spanish Courts; and make such decision in the face of the certificate of the highest functionary of the island?

It is submitted, then, that if this Court does go behind the certificate of the Governor General, and look into the fact, whether or not these persons were slaves on the 18th June, 1839, yet there is no sufficient evidence on which they could adjudge it to be untrue. If this be so, the proof concerning the property is suffiicent to bring the case within the intention and provisions of the treaty.

The next question is, did the United States legally intervene to obtain the decree of the Court for the restoration of the property, in order that it might be delivered to the Spanish owners, according to the stipulations of the treaty? They did; because the property of foreigners, thus brought under the cognisance of the Courts, is, of right, deliverable to the public functionaries of the government to which such foreigners belong; because those functionaries have required the interposition of the United States on their behalf; and because the United States were authorized, on that request, to interpose, pursuant [***63] to their treaty obligations.

That the property of foreigners, under such circumstances may be delivered to the public functionaries, is so clearly established, by the decisions of this Court, that it is unnecessary to discuss the point. In the case (2 Mason, 411, 412. 463) of La Jeune Eugenie, there was a libel of the vessel, as in this case, and a claim interposed by the French consul, and also by the owners themselves. The Court there directed the delivery of the property to the public functionary. In that of the Divina Pastora, 4 Wheat. 52, the Spanish consul interposed. In that of the Antelope, 10 Wheat. 68, there where claims interposed, very much as in this case, by the captain as captor, and by the Vice Consuls of Spain and Portugal, for citizens of their respective countries; and by the United States. The Court directed their delivery, partly to the Consul of Spain, and partly to the United States. It is thus settled, that the public functionaries are entitled to intervene in such cases, on behalf of the citizens of their countries. In the present one, the Spanish minister did so intervene by applying to the United States to adopt, on his behalf, the necessary proceedings; [***64] and, upon his doing so, Ruiz and Montez withdrew their separate claims. The United States, on their part, acted as the treaty required. The executive is their agent in all such transactions, and on him devolved the obligation to see this property restored entire, if due proof concerning it was made. The form of proceeding was already established by procedent and by law. The course adopted was exactly that pursued in the case of M'Fadden v. The Exchange, 7 Cranch, 116, where a vessel was libelled in a port of the United States. Being a public vessel of a foreign sovereign, which the government was bound to protect, there intervened exactly in the same way. The libel was dismissed and the vessel restored to the custody of the public officers of France.

It is, therefore, equally clear, that the United States, in this instance, has pursued the course required by the laws of nations; and if the Court are satisfied, on the first point, that there is due proof concerning the property, then it ought to be delivered entire, so that it may be restored to the Spanish owners. If this be so, the Court below has erred, because it has not decreed any part of the property to be delivered entire, [***65] except the boy Antonio. From the vessel and cargo, it has deducted the salvage, diminishing them by that amount; and the negroes it has entirely refused to direct to be delivered.

Mr. Baldwin, for the defendants in error.

In preparing to address this honourable Court, on the questions arising upon this record, in behalf of the humble Africans whom I represent,—contending, as they are, for freedom and for life, with two powerful governments arrayed against the,—it has been to me a source of high gratification, in this unequal contest, that those questions will be heard and decided by a tribunal, not only elevated far above the influence of executive power and popular prejudice, but, from its very consitution, exempt from liability to those imputations to which a Court, less happily constituted, or composed only of members from one section of the Union, might, however unjustly, be exposed.

This case is not only one of deep interest in itself, as affecting the destiny of the unfortunate Africans, whom I represent, but it involves considerations deeply affecting out national character in the eyes of the whole civilized world, as well as questions of power on the part of the government [***66] of the United States, which are regarded with anxiety and alarm by a large portion of our citizens. It presents, for the first time, the question whether the government, which was established for the promotion of JUSTICE, which was founded on the great principles of the Revolution, as proclaimed in the Declaration of Independence, can, consistently with the genius of our institutions, become a party to proceedings for the enslavement of human beings cast upon our shores, and found in the condition of freemen within the territorial limits of a FREE AND SOVEREIGN STATE?

In the remarks I shall have occasion to make, it will be my design to appeal to no sectional prejudices, and to assume no positions in which I shall not hope to be sustained by intelligent minds from the south as well as from the north. Although I am in favour of the broadest liberty of inquiry and discussion,—happily secured by our Constitution to every citizen, subject only to his individual responsibility to the laws for its abuse; I have ever been of the opinion that the exercise of that liberty by citizens of one state, in regard to the institutions of another, should always be guided by discretion, and tempered [***67] with kindness.

Mr. Baldwin here proceeded to state all the facts of the case, and the proceedings in the District and Circuit Courts, in support of the motion to dismiss the appeal. As no decision was given by the Court on the motion, this part of the argument is, necessarily, omitted.

Mr. Baldwin continued: If the government of the United States could appear in any case as the representative of foreigners claiming property in the Court of Admiralty, it has no right to appear in their behalf to aid them in the recovery of fugitive slaves, even when domiciled in the country from which they escaped: much less the recent victims of the African slave trade, who have sought an asylum in one of the free states of the Union, without any wrongful act on our part, or for which, as in the case of the Antelope, we are in any way responsible.

The recently imported Africans of the Amistad, if they were ever slaves, which is denied, were in the actual condition of freedom when they came within the jurisdictional limits of the state of New York. They came there without any wrongful act on the part of any officer or citizen of the United States. They were in a state where, not only no law existed [***68] to make them slaves, but where, by an express statute, all persons, except fugitives, &c., from a sister state, are declared to be free.

They were under the protection of the laws of a state, which, in the language of the Supreme Court, in the case of Miln v. The City of New York, 11 Peters, 139, "has the same undeniable and unlimited jurisdiction over all persons and things within its territorial limits, as any foreign nation, when that jurisdiction is not surrendered or restrained by the Constitution of the United States."

The American people have never imposed it as a duty on the government of the United States, to become actors an attempt to reduce to slavery, men found in a state of freedom, by giving extra-territorial force to a foreign slave law. Such a duty would not only be repugnant to the feelings of a large portion of the citizens of the United States, but it would be wholly inconsistent with the fundamental principles of our government, and the purposes for which it was established, as well as with its policy in prohibiting the slave trade and giving freedom to its victims.

The recovery of slaves for their owners, whether foreign or domestic, is a matter with which [***69] the executive of the United States has no concern. The Constitution confers upon the government no power to establish or legalize the institution of slavery. It recognises it as existing in regard to persons held to service by the laws of the states which tolerate it; and contains a compact between the states, obliging them to respect the rights acquired under the slave laws of other states, in the cases specified in the Constitution. But it imposes no duty, and confers no power on the government of the United States to act in regard to it. So far as the compact extends, the Courts of the United States, whether sitting in a free state or a slave state, will give effect to it. Beyond that, all persons within the limits of a state are entitled to the protection of its laws.

If these Africans have been taken from the possession of their Spanish claimants, and wrongfully brought into the United States by our citizens, a question would have been presented similar to that which existed in the case of the Antelope. But when men have come here voluntarily, without any wrong on the part of the government or citizens of the United States, in withdrawing them from the jurisdiction of the [***70] Spanish laws, why should this government be required to become active in their restoration? They appear here freemen. They stand before out Courts on equal are presumed to be free. They stand before our Courts on equal ground with their claimants; and when the Courts, after an impartial hearing with all parties in interest before them, have pronounced them free, it is neither the duty nor the right of the executive of the United States, to interfere with the decision.

The question of the surrender of fugitive slaves to a foreign claimant, if the right exists at all, is left to the comity of the states which tolerate slavery. The government of the United States has nothing to do with it. In the letter of instructions addressed by Mr. Adams, when Secretary of State, to Messrs. Gallatin and Rush, dated November 2, 1818, in relation to a proposed arrangement with Great Britain, for a more active co-operation in the suppression of the slave trade, he assigns as a reason for rejecting the proposition for a mixed commission, "that the disposal of the negroes found on board the slave-trading vessels, which might be condemned by the sentence of the mixed Courts, cannot be carried into [***71] effect by the United States." "The condition of the blacks being in this Union regulated by the municipal laws of the separate states, the government of the United States can neither guarantee their liberty in the states where they could only be received as slaves, nor control them in the states where they would be recognised as free." Doc. 48, H. Rep. 2 sess. 16th Cong. p. 15.

It may comport with the interest or feelings of a slave state to surrender a fugitive slave to a foreigner, or at least to expel him from their borders. But the people of New England, except so far as they are bound by the compact, would cherish and protect him. To the extent of the compact we acknowledge our obligation, and have passed laws for its fulfilment. Beyond that our citizens would be unwilling to go.

A state has no power to surrender a fugitive criminal to a foreign government for punishment; because that is necessarily a matter of national concern. The fugitive is demanded for a national purpose. But the question of the surrender of fugitive slaves concerns individuals merely. They are demanded as property only, and for private purposes. It is, therefore, a proper subject for the action [***72] of the state, and not of the national authorities.

The surrender of neither is demandable of right, unless stipulated by treaty. See as to the surrender of fugitive criminals, 2 Brock. Rep. 493. 2 Sumner, 482. 14 Peters, 540. Doc. 199, H.R. 26 Cong. p. 53. 70. 10 Amer. State Pap. 151. 153. 433. 3 Hall's Law Jour. 135. An overture was once made by the government of the United States to negotiate a treaty with Great Britain for the mutual surrender of fugitive slaves. But it was instantly repelled by the british government. It may well be doubted whiether such a stipulation is within the treaty-making power under the Constitution of the United States. "The power to make treaties," says Chief Justice Taney, 14 Peters, 569, "is given in general terms,...and consequently it was designed to include all those subjects which in the ordinary intercourse of nations had usually been made subjects of negotiation and treaty; and which are consistent with the nature of our institutions, and the distribution of powers between the general and state governments." See Holmes v. Jennison, 14 Peters, 569. But, however this may be, the attempt to introduce it is evidence that, unless provided [***73] for by treaty, the obligation to surrender was not deemed to exist.

We deny that Ruiz and Montez, Spanish subjects, had a right to call on any officer or Court of the United States to use the force of the government, or the process of the law for the purpose of again enslaving those who have thus escaped from foreign slavery, and sought an asylum here. We deny that the seizure of these persons by Lieutenant Gedney for such a purpose was a legal or justifiable act.

How would it be—independently of the treaty between the United States and Spain—upon the principles of our government, of the common law, or of the law of nations?

If a foreign slave vessel, engaged in a traffic which by our laws is denounced as inhuman and piratical, should be captured by the slaves while on her voyage from Africa to Cuba, and they should succeed in reaching our shores, have the Constitution or laws of the United States imposed upon our judges, our naval officers, or our executive, the duty of seizing the unhappy fugitives and delivering them up to their oppressors? Did the people of the United States, whole government is based on the great principles of the Revolution, proclaimed in the Declaration [***74] of Independence, confer upon the federal, executive, or judicial tribunals, the power of making our nation assessories to such atrocious violations of human right?

Is there any principle of international law, or law of comity which requires it? Are our Courts bound, and if not, are they at liberty, to give effect here to the slave trade laws of a foreign nation; to laws affecting strangers, never domiciled there, when, to give them such effect would be to violate the natural rights of men?

These questions are answered in the negative by all the most approved writers on the laws of nations. 1 Burg. Confl. 741. Story, Confl. 92.

By the law of France, the slaves of their colonies, immediately on their arrival in France, become free. In the case of Forbes v. Cochrane, 2 Barn. and Cress. 463, this question is elaborately discussed and settled by the English Court of King's Bench.

By the law of the state of New York, a foreign slave escaping into that state becomes free. And the Courts of the United States, in acting upon the personal rights of men found within the jurisdiction of a free state, are bound to administer the laws as they would be administered by the state Courts, in [***75] all cases in which the laws of the state do not conflict with the laws or obligations of the United States. The United States as a nation have prohibited the slave trade as inhuman and piratical, and they have no law authorizing the enslaving of its victims. It is a maxim, to use the words of an eminent English judge, in the case of Forbes v. Cochrane, 2 Barn. and Cress., "that which is called comitas inter communitates, cannot prevail in any case, where it violates the law of our own country, the law of nature, or the law of God." 9 Eng. C.L.R. 149. And that the laws of a nation, proprio vigore, have no force beyond its own territories, except so far as it respects its own citizens, who owe it allegiance, is too familiarly settled to need the citation of authorities. See 9 Wheaton, 366. Apollon, 2 Mason, 151–158. The rules on this subject adopted in the English Court of Admiralty are the same which prevail in their Courts of common law, though they hae decided in the case of The Louis, 2 Dodson, 238, as the Supreme Court did in the case of the Antelope, 10 Wheaton, 66, that as the slave trade was not, at that time, prohibited by the law of nations, if a foreign slaver was captured [***76] by an English ship, it was a wrongful act, which it would be the duty of the Court of Admiralty to repair by restoring the possession. The principle of amoveas manus, adopted in these cases, has no application to the case of fugitives from slavery.

But it is claimed that if these Africans, though "recently imported into Cuba," were by the laws of Spain the property of Ruiz and Montez, the government of the United States is bound by the treaty to restore them; and that, therefore, the intervention of the executive in these proceedings is proper for that purpose. It has already, it is believed, been shown that even if the case were within the treaty, the intervention of the executive as a party before the judicial tribunals was unnecessary and improper, since the treaty provides for its own execution by the Courts, on the application of the parties in interest. And such a resort is expressly provided in the twentieth article of the treaty of 1794 with Great Britain, and in the twenty-sixth article of the treaty of 1801 with the French Republic, both of which are in other respects similar to the ninth article of the Spanish treaty, on which the Attorney General has principally relied.

[***77] The sixth article of the Spanish treaty has received a judicial construction in the case of the Santissima Trinidad, 7 Wheaton, 284, where it was decided that the obligation assumed in simply that of protecting belligerent vessels from capture within our jurisdiction. It can have no application therefore to a case like the present.

The ninth article of that treaty provides "that all ships and merchandise of what nature soever, which shall be rescued out of the hands of pirates or robbers, on the high seas, shall be brought into some port of either state, and shall be delivered to the custody of the officers of that port, in order to be taken care of, and restored entire to the true proprietors, as soon as due and sufficient proof shall be made concerning the property thereof."

To render this clause of the treaty applicable to the case under consideration, it must be assumed that under the term "merchandise" the contracting parties intended to include slaves; and that slaves, themselves the recent victims of piracy, who, by a successful revolt, have achieved their deliverance from slavery, on the high seas, and have availed themselves of the means of escape of which they have thus [***78] acquired the possession, are to be deemed "pirates and robbers," "from whose hands" such "merchandise has been rescued."

It is believed that such a construction of the words of the treaty is not in accordance with the rules of interpretation which ought to govern our Courts; and that when there is no special reference to human beings as property, who are not acknowledged as such by the law of comity of nations generally, but only by the municipal laws of the particular nations which tolerate slavery, it cannot be presumed that the contracting parties intended to include them under the general term "merchandise." As has already been remarked, it may well be doubted whether such a stipulation would be within the treaty-making power of the United States. It is to be remembered that the government of the United States is based on the principles promulgated in the Declaration of Independence by the Congress of 1776; "that all men are created equal; that they are endowed by their Creator with certain inalienable rights; that among these are life, liberty, and the pursuit of happiness; and that to secure these rights governments are instituted."

The convention which formed the Federal Constitution, [***79] though they recognised slavery as existing in regard to persons held to labour by the laws of the states which tolerated it, were careful to exclude from that instrument every expression that might be construed into an admission that there could be property in men. It appears by the report of the proceedings of the convention, (3 Madison Papers, 1428,) that the first clause of section 9, article 1, which provides for the imposition of a tax or duty on the importation of such persons as any of the states, then existing, might think proper to admit, &c., "not exceeding ten dollars for each person," was adopted in its present form, in consequence of the opposition by Roger Sherman and James Madison to the clause as it was originally reported, on the ground, "that it admitted that there could be property in men;" an idea which Mr. Madison said "he thought it wrong to admit in the Constitution." The words reported by the committee, and stricken out on this objection, were: "a tax or duty may be imposed on such migration or importation at a rate not exceeding the average of the duties laid upon imports." The Constitution as it now stands will be searched in vain for an expression recognising [***80] human beings as merchandise or legitimate subjects of commerce. In the case of New York v. Miln, 11 Peters, 104. 136, Judge Barbour, in giving the opinion of the Court, expressly declares, in reference to the power "to regulate commerce" conferred on Congress by the Constitution, that "persons are not the subjects of commerce." Judging from the public sentiment which prevailed at the time of the adoption of the Constitution, it is probable that the first act of the government in the exercise of its power to regulate commerce, would have been to prohibit the slave trade, if it had not been restrained until 1808, from prohibiting the importation of such persons as any of the states, then existing, should think proper to admit. But could Congress have passed an act authorizing the importation of slaves as articles of commerce, into any state in opposition to a law of the state, prohibiting their introduction? If they could, they may now force slavery into every state. For no state can prohibit the introduction of legitimate objects of foreign commerce, when authorized by Congress.

The United States must be regarded as comprehending free states as well as slave states: states which [***81] do not recognise slaves as property, as well as states which do so regard them. When all speak as a nation, general expressions ought to be construed to mean what all understand to be included in them; at all events, what may be included consistently with the law of nature.

The ninth article of the Spanish treaty was copied from the sixteenth article of the treaty with France, concluded in 1778, in the midst of the war of the Revolution, in which the great principles of liberty proclaimed in the Declaration of Independence were vindicated by our fathers.

By "merchandise rescued from pirates," the contracting parties must have had in view property, which it would be the duty of the public ships of the United States to rescue from its unlawful possessors. Because, if it is taken from those who are rightfully in possession, the capture would be wrongful, and it would be our duty to restore it. But is it a duty which our naval officers owe to a nation tolerating the slave trade, to subdue for their kidnappers the revolted victims of their cruelty? Could the people of the United States, consistently with their principles as a nation, have ever consented to a treaty stipulation which [***82] would impose such a duty on our naval officers? A duty which would drive every citizen of a free state from the service of his country? Has our government, which has been so cautious as not to oblige itself to surrender the most atrocious criminals, who have sought an asylum in the United States, bound itself, under the term "merchandise," to seize and surrender fugitive slaves?

The subject of the delivery of fugitives was under consideration before and during the negotiation of the Treaty of San Lorenzo; and was purposely omitted in the treaty. Sec. 10 Waite's State Papers, 151. 433. Our treaties with Tunis and Algiers contain similar expressions, in which both parties stipulate for the protection of the property of the subjects of each within the jurisdiction of the other. The Algerine regarded his Spanish captive as property; but was it ever supposed, that if an Algerine corsair should be seized by the captive slaves on board of her, it would be the duty of our naval officers, or our Courts of Admiralty, to recapture and restore them?

The phraseology of the entire article in the treaty, clearly shows that it was intended to apply only to inanimate things, or irrational animals; [***83] such as are universally regarded as property. It is "merchandise rescued from the hands of pirates and robbers on the high seas" that is to be restored. There is no provision for the surrender of the pirates themselves. And the reason is, because the article has reference only to those who are "hostes humani generis," whom it is lawful for, and the duty of all nations to capture and to punish. If these Africans were "pirates" or sea robbers, whom our naval officers might lawfully seize, it would be our duty to detain them for punishment; and then what would become of the "merchandise?"

But they were not pirates, nor in any sense hostes humani generis. Cinque, the master-spirit who guided them, had a single object in view. That object was—not piracy or robbery—but the deliverance of himself and his companions in suffering, from unlawful bondage. They owed no allegiance to Spain. They were on board of the Amistad by constraint. Their object was to free themselves from the fetters that bound them, in order that they might return to their kindred and their home. In so doing they were guilty of no crime, for which they could be held responsible as pirates. See Bee's Rep. [***84] 273. Suppose they had been impressed American seamen, who had regained their liberty in a similar manner, would they in that case have been deemed guilty of piracy and murder? Not in the opinion of Chief Justice Marshall. In his celebrated speech in justicfication of the surrender by President Adams of Nash under the British treaty, he says: "Had Thomas Nash been an impressed American, the homicide on board the Hermione would most certainly not have been murder. The act of impressing an American is an act of lawless violence. The confinement on board a vessel is a continuation of that violence, and an additional outrage. Death committed within the United States in resisting such violence, would not have been murder." Bee's Rep. 290.

The United States, as a nation, is to be regarded as a free state. And all men being presumptively free, when "merchandise" is spoken of in the treaty of a free state, it cannot be presumed that human beings are intended to be included as such. Hence, whenever our government have intended to speak of negroes as property, in their treaties, they have been specifically mentioned, as in the treaties with Great Britain, of 1783 and 1814. It was on [***85] the same principle, that Judge Drayton, of South Carolina, decided, in the case of Almeida, who had captured, during the last war, an English vessel with slaves, that the word "property" in the prize act, did not include negroes, and that they must be regarded as prisoners of war, and not sold or distributed merchandise. 5 Hall's Law Journal, 459.

And it was for the same reason, that it was deemed necessary in the Constitution, to insert an express stipulation in regard to fugitives from service. The law of comtiy would have obliged each state to protect and restore property belonging to a citizen of another, without such stipulation; but it would not have required the restoration of fugitive slaves from a sister state, unless they had been expressly mentioned.

In the interpretation of treaties we ought always to give such a construction to the words as is most consistent with the customary use of language; most suitable to the subject, and to the legitimate powers of the contracting parties; most conformable to the declared principles of the government; such a construction as will not lead to injustice to others, or in any way violate the laws of nature.

These are, in substance, [***86] the rules of interpretation as given by Vattel, v. ii. ch. 17. The construction claimed in behalf of the Spanish libellants, in the present case, is at war with them all.

It would be singular, indeed, if the tribunals of a government which has declared the slave-trade piracy, and has bound itself by a solemn treaty with Great Britain, in 1814, to make continued efforts "to promote its entire abolition, as a traffic irreconcilable with the principles of humanity and justice," should construe the general expressions of a treaty which since that period has been revised by the contracting parties, as obliging this nation to commit the injustice of treating as property the recent victims of this horrid traffic; more especially when it is borne in mind, that the government of Spain, anterior to the revision of the treaty in 1819, had formally notified our government that Africans were no longer the legitimate objects of trade; with a declaration that "His majesty felt confident that a measure so completely in harmony with the sentiments of this government, and of all the inhabitants of this republic, could not fail to be equally agreeable to the President." Doc. 48. 2 sess. 16 Cong. p. [***87] 8.

Would the people of the United States, in 1819, have assented to such a treaty? Would it not have furnished just ground of complaint by Great Britain, as a violation of the 10th article of the treaty of Ghant?

But even if the treaty in its terms were such as to oblige us to violate towards strangers the immutable laws of justice, it would, according of Vattel, impose no obligation. Vattel, c. 1, § 9; b. ii. c. 12, § 161; c. 17, § 311.

The law of nature and the law of nations, bind us as effectually to render justice to the African, as the treaty can to the Spaniard. Before a foreign tribunal, the parties litigating the question of freedom or slavery, stand on equal ground. And in a case like this, where it is admitted that the Africans were recently imported, and consequently never domiciled in Cuba, and owe no allegiance to its laws, their rights are to be determined by that law which is of universal obligation—the law of nature.

If, indeed, the vessel in which they sailed had been driven upon our coast by stress of weather or other unavoidable cause, and they had arrived here in the actual possession of their alleged owners, and had been slaves by the law of the [***88] country from which they sailed, and where they were domiciled, it would have been a very different question, whether the Courts of the United States could interfere to liberate them, as was done at Bermuda by the colonial tribunal, in the case of the Enterprise.

But in this case there has been no possession of these Africans by their claimants within our jurisdiction, of which they have been deprived, by the act of our government or its officers; and neither by the law of comity, or by force of the treaty, are the officers or Courts of the United States required, or by the principles of our government permitted to become actors in reducing them to slavery.

These preliminary questions have been made on account of the important principles involved in them, and not from any unwillingness to meet the question between the Africans and their claimants upon the facts in evidence, and on those alone, to vindicate their claims to freedom.

Suppose, then, the case to be properly here: and that Ruiz and Montez, unprejudiced by the decree of the Court below, were at liberty to take issue with the Africans upon their answer, and to call upon this Court to determine the question of liberty or [***89] property, how stands the case on the evidence before the Court?

The Africans, when found by Lieutenant Gedney, were in a free state, where all men are presumed to be free, and were in the actual condition of freemen. The burden of proof, therefore, rests on those who assert them to be slaves. 10 Wheaton, 66. 2 Mason, 459. When they call on the Courts of the United States to reduce to slavery men who are apparently free, they must show some law, having force in the place where they were taken, which makes them slaves, or that the claimants are entitled in our Courts to have some foreign law, obligatory on the Africans as well as on the claimants, enforced in respect to them; and that by such foreign law they are slaves.

It is not pretended that there was any law existing in the place where they were found, which made them slaves, but it is claimed that by the laws of Cuba they were slaves to Ruiz and Montez; and that those laws are to be here enforced. But before the laws of Cuba, if any such there be, can be applied to affect the personal status of individuals within a foreign jurisdiction, it is very clear that it must be shown that they were domiciled in Cuba.

It is admitted [***90] and proved in this case that these negroes are natives of Africa, and recently imported into Cuba. Their domicil of origin is consequently the place of their birth in Africa. And the presumption of law is, always, that the domicil of origin, is retained until the change is proved. 1 Burge's Conflict. 34. The burden of proving the change is cast on him who alleges it. 5 Vesey, 787.

The domicil of origin prevails until the party has not only acquired another, but has manifested and carried into execution an intention of abandoning his former domicil, and acquiring another, as his sole domicil. As it is the will or intention of the party which alone determines what is the real place of domicil which he has chosen, it follows that a former demicil is not abandoned by residence in another, if that residence be not voluntarily chosen. Those who are in exile, or in prison, as they are never presumed to have abandoned all hope of return, retain their former domicil. 1 Burg. 46. That these victims of fraud and piracy—husbands torn from their wives and families—children from their parents and kindred—neither intended to abandon the land of their nativity, nor had lost all [***91] hope of recovering it, sufficiently appears from the facts on this record. It cannot, surely, be claimed that a residence, under such circumstances, of these helpless beings for ten days in a slave barracoon, before they were transferred to the Amistad, changed their native domicil for that of Cuba.

It is not only incumbent on the claimants to prove that the Africans are domiciled in Cuba, and subject to its laws, but they must show that some law existed there by which "recently imported Africans" can be lawfully held in slavery. Such a law is not to be presumed, but the contrary. Comity would seem to require of us to presume that a traffic so abhorrent to the feelings of the whole civilized world is not lawful in Cuba. These respondents having been born free, and having been recently imported into Cuba, have a right to be every where regarded as free, until some law obligatory on them is produced authorizing their enslavement. Neither the law of nature nor the law of nations authorizes the slave-trade; although it was holden in the case of the Antelope, that the law of nations did not at that time actually prohibit it. If they are slaves, then, it must be by some positive law of [***92] Spain, existing at the time of their recent importation. No such law is exhibited. On the contrary, it is proved by the deposition of Dr. Madden, one of the British commissioners resident at Havana, that since the year 1820, there has been no such law in force there, either statute or common law.

But we do not rest the case here. We are willing to assume the burden of proof. On the 14th of May, 1818, the Spanish government, by their minister, announced to the government of the United States that the slave-trade was prohibited by Spain; and by express command of the King of Spain, Don Onis communicated to the President of the United States the treaty with Great Britain of September 23d, 1817, by which the King of Spain, moved partly by motives of humanity, and partly in consideration of four hundred thousand pounds sterling, paid to him by the British government for the accomplishment of so desirable an object, engaged that the slave-trade should be abolished throughout the dominions of Spain, on the 30th May, 1820. By the ordinance of the King of Spain of December, 1817, it is directed that every African imported into any of the colonies of Spain in violation of the treaty, shall [***93] be declared free in the first port at which he shall arrive.

By the treaty between Great Britain and Spain of the 28th of June, 1835, which is declared to be made for the purpose of "rendering the means taken for abolishing the inhuman traffic in slaves more effective," and to be in the spirit of the treaty contracted between both powers on the 23d of September, 1817, "the slave-trade is again declared on the part of Spain to be henceforward totally and finally abolished, in all parts of the world." And by the royal ordinance of November 2d, 1838, the Governor and the naval officers having command on the coast of Cuba, are stimulated to greater vigilance to suppress it.

Such, then, being the laws in force in all the dominions of Spain, and such the conceded facts in regard to the nativity and recent importation of these Africans, upon what plausible ground can it be claimed by the government of the United States, that they were slaves in the island of Cuba, and are here to be treated as property, and not as human beings?

The only evidence exhibited to prove them slaves, are the papers of the Amistad, giving to Jose Ruiz permission to transport forty-nine Ladinos belonging to him, [***94] from Havana to Puerto Principe; and a like permit to Pedro Montez, to transport three Ladinos. For one of the four Africans, claimed by Montez, (the boy Ka-le,) there is no permit at all.

It has been said in an official opinion by the late Attorney General, (Mr. Grundy,) that "as this vessel cleared out from one Spanish port to another Spanish port, with papers regularly authenticated by the proper officers at Havana, evidencing that these negroes were slaves, and that the destination of the vessel was to another Spanish port, the government of the United States would not be authorized to go into an investigation for the purpose of ascertaining whether the facts stated in those papers by the Spanish officers are true or not;"—"that if it were to permit itself to go behind the papers of the schooner Amistad, it would place itself in the embarrassing condition of judging upon Spanish laws, their force, effect, and application to the case under consideration." In support of this opinion, a reference is made to the opinion of this Court, in the case of Arredozdo, 6 Pet. 729, where it is stated to be "a universal principle, that where power or jurisdiction is delegated to any public [***95] officer or tribunal over a subject-matter, and its exercise is confided to his or their discretion, the acts so done are binding and valid as to the subject-matter; and individual rights will not be disturbed collaterally for any thing done in the exercise of that discretion within the authority conferred. The only questions which can arise between an individual claiming a right under the acts done, and the public, or any person denying its validity, are power in the officer, and fraud in the party."

The principle thus stated, was applicable to the case then before the Court, which related to the validity of a grant made by a public officer; but it does not tend to support the position for which it is cited in the present case. For, in the first place, there was no jurisdiction over these newly imported Africans, by the laws of Spain, to make them slaves, any more than if they had been white men. The ordinance of the king declared them free. Secondly, there was no intentional exercise of jurisdiction over them for such a purpose, by the officer who granted the permits; and, thirdly, the permits were fraudulently obtained, and fraudulently used by the parties claiming to take benefit [***96] of them. For the purposes for which they are attempted to be applied, the permits are as inoperative as would be a grant from a public officer, fraudulently obtained, where the state had no title to the thing granted, and the officer no authority to issue the grant. See 6 Peters, 730. 5 Wheat. 303.

But it is said, we have no right to place ourselves in the position of judging upon the Spanish laws. How can our Courts do otherwise, when Spanish subjects call upon them to enforce rights which, if they exist at all, must exist by force of Spanish laws? For what purpose did the government of Spain communicate to the government of the United States, the fact of the prohibition of the slave-trade, unless it was that it might be known and acted upon by our Courts? Suppose the permits to Ruiz and Montez had been granted for the express purpose of consigning to perpetual slavery, these recent victims of this prohibited trade, could the government of Spain now ask the government or the Courts of the United States, to give validity to the acts of a colonial officer, in direct violation of that prohibition; and thus make us aiders and abettors in what we know to be an atrocious wrong?

[***97] It may be admitted that, even after such an annunciation, our cruisers could not lawfully seize a Spanish slaver, cleared out as such by the Govenor of Cuba: but if the Africans on board of her could effect their own deliverance, and reach our shores, has not the government of Spain authorized us to treat them with hospitality as freemen? Could the Spanish minister, without offence, ask the government of the United States to seize these victims of fraud and felony, and treat them as property, because a colonial governor had thought proper to violate the ordinance of his king, in granting a permit to a slaver?

But in this case we make no charge upon the Governor of Cuba. A fraud upon him is proved to have been practised by Ruiz and Montez. He never undertook to assume jurisdiction over these Africans as slaves, or to decide any question in regard to them. He simply issued, on the application of Ruiz and Montez, passports for Ladino slaves from Havana to Puerto Principe. When under colour of those passports, they fraudulently put on board the Amistad, Bozals, who by the laws of Spain could not be slaves, we surely manifest no disrespect to the acts of the Governor, by giving efficacy [***98] to the laws of Spain, and denying to Ruiz and Montez the benefit of their fraud. The custom house license, to which the name of Espeleta in print was appended, was not a document given or intended to be used as evidence of property between Ruiz and Montez, and the Africans; any more than a permit from our customhouse would be to settle conflicting claims of ownership to the articles contained in the manifest. As between the government and the shippers, it would be evidence if the negroes described in the passport were actually put on board, and were, in truth, the property of Ruiz and Montez, that they were legally shipped; that the customhouse forms had been complied with; and nothing more.But in view of facts as they appear, and are admitted in the present case, the passports seem to have been obtained by Ruiz and Montez, only as a part of the necessary machinery for the completion of a slave voyage. The evidence tends strongly to prove that Ruiz, at least, was concerned in the importation of these Africans, and that the reshipment of them under colour of passports obtained for Ladinos, as the property of Ruiz and Montez, in connection with the false representation on the papers [***99] of the schooner, that they were "passengers for the government," was an artifice resorted to by these slave-traders, for the double purpose of evading the scrutiny of British cruisers, and legalizing the transfer of their victims to the place of their ultimate destination. It is a remarkable circumstance, that though more than a year has elapsed, since the decree of the District Court denying the title of Ruiz and Montez, and pronouncing the Africans free, not a particle of evidence has since been produced in support of their claims. And yet, strange as it may seem, during all this time, not only the sympathies of the Spanish minister, but the powerful aid of our own government have been enlisted in their behalf!

It was the purpose of the Reporter to insert the able and interesting argument of Mr. Adams, for the African appellees; and the publication of the "Reports" has been postponed in the hope of obtaining it, prepared by himself. It has not been received. As many of the points presented by Mr. Adams, in the discussion of the cause, were not considered by the Court essential to its decision: and were not taken notice of in the opinion of the Court, delivered by Mr. Justice [***100] STORY, the necessary omission of the argument is submitted to with less regret.

Mr. Gilpin, the Attoeny-General, in reply.

The judiciary act, which gives to this Court its powers, so far as they depend on the legislature, directs that, on an appeal from the decree of an inferior Court, this Court shall render such judgment as the Court below did, or should have rendered. It is to obtain from it such a decree in this case, that the United States present themselves here as appellants.

At the threshold of their application, the right so to present themselves is denied. They are to be turned away, as suitors having no claim to such interposition. The argument has gone a step further; it seems now to be contended, that their appearance in the Court below, which was not then objected to, is to be regarded as destitute of right, equally with their present appearance here. They are not even mere interlopers, seeking justice without warrant; they are dictators, in the form of supplicants, and their suggestions to the Court, and their application for its judgment, upon solemn and important questions of fact, are distorted by an ingenious logic which it is difficult to follow. Applications, [***101] made without the slightest expression of a wish, except to obtain that judgment, and in a form which, it might be supposed, would secure admission into any Court, are repudiated, under the harsh name of "executive interference." Yet in what single respect do the facts of this case sustain such allegations? How can it be justly said that there has been any "executive interference," not resulting from the adoption of that course which public duty made incumbent; and conducted in the manner, and in that manner only, which was required by that sense of public duty, from which, no officer, possessing a due regard for the obligations of his trust, will ever shrink?

In what situation is the case when it is first presented to the notice of the government of the United States? On nearly, if not exactly the same day that the Secretary of State receives from the minister of Spain an official communication, dated at New York, and stating the facts connected with the schooner L'Amistad, then just brought within the territory of the United States; stating also, that the vessel is a Spanish vessel, laden with merchandise, and with sundry negro slaves on board, accompanied with all the documents [***102] required by the laws of Spain, for navigating a vessel, and for proving ownership of property; and then making an application to the government of the United States to interpose, so that the property thus within our territory, might be restored to its owners pursuant to the treaty; and asserting also, that the negroes, who were guilty, as he contended, of a crime for which they ought to be punished, ought to be delivered up on that account, too, pursuant to the law of nations—on or about the same day, the letter of the District Attorney, which, though dated a day earlier, is written in Connecticut, also reaches the Department of State, conveying the information that this same property and these same negroes are already within the custody and authority of the judicial tribunals of the United States, by virtue of process, civil and criminal, issued by a judge of the United States, after solemn and deliberate inquiry. The vessel, the cargo, and the negroes had been all taken possession of by a warrant issued by the Court, "as property;" they were then, at that very time, in the custody, keeping, and possession of the Court, as property, without the slightest suggestion having been [***103] made by the executive branch of the government, or even a knowledge of the fact on its part; and when its interposition is formally solicited, its first information relative to the case received, it finds the subject of the demand already under the control of the judicial branch.

In this situation, the executive government, thus appealed to and thus informed, looks to its treaty stipulations, the most solemn and binding compacts that nations know among each other, and the obligations of which can never be treated lightly, so long as good faith forms the first duty of every community. Those stipulations entered into in 1795, (1 Laws of United States, 266,) provide, in the first place, (article 6,) that each party to the treaty, the United States and Spain, shall "endeavour, by all means in their power, to protect and defend all vessels and other effects belonging to the citizens or subjects of the other, which shall be within the extent of their jurisdiction." Again, in the eighth article, it is declared, that "in case the subjects or inhabitants of either country shall, with their shipping, be forced, through stress of weather, or any other urgent necessity for seeking shelter, to [***104] enter any port of the other, they shall enjoy all favour, protection, and help." Again, in the ninth article, it is provided, that "all ships and merchandise, of what nature soever, which shall be rescued out of the hands of any pirates or robbers on the high seas, shall be brought into some port of either state, and shall be delivered into the custody of the officers of that port, in order to be taken care of, and restored entire to the true proprietor, as soon as due and sufficient proof shall be made concerning the property thereof." In the sixteenth article it is further declared, that the liberty of navigation and commerce meant by the treaty, shall extend to all kinds of merchandise, excepting those only which are contraband, and they are expressly enumerated; and in the twenty-second article, the object of the treaty is declared to be "the extension of mutual commerce." When these stipulations were thus made, slaves were a notorious article of merchandise and traffic in each country; not only were they so in the United States, but there was a constitutional provision, prohibiting Congress from interfering to prevent their importation, as such, from abroad. This treaty, with [***105] these provisions thus solemnly and carefully framed, was renewed in 1819; was declared to be still in existence and force. It is declared, (7 Laws of United States, 624) that every one of the articles above quoted "remains confirmed." It stands exactly as it stood in 1795; and, in the year 1821, after both governments had abolished the slave-trade, the provisions adopted in 1795 are thus, as to "every clause and article thereof," so renewed, solemnly ratified, and confirmed by the President and Senate of the United States. No clause is introduced to vary the nature or character of the merchandise; none to lessen or change the obligations, as would have been the case, had any such change been contemplated; but the two treaties, having the final date of 1821, bear the character of a single instrument.

Now these are stipulations too clear to be misunderstood; too imperative to be wantonly neglected. Could we not ask of Spain the fulfilment of every one of them towards our own citizens? If so, were we not bound, at least, to see that, through some public functionary, or by some means in which nations fulfil mutual obligations, they were performed by us to the subjects of Spain whenever [***106] the casus foederis should arise?

Did it arise in this case? Here were unquestionably, as the representative of Spain believed and stated, a vessel and effects of subjects of that country within our jurisdiction; here was a vessel and merchandise rescued, as he alleged, from the hands of robbers, brought into one of our ports, and already in the custody of public officers.Did not a treaty stipulation require the United States to "endeavour by all means in their power to protect and defend this property?" Did not a treaty stipulation require us to "extend to them all favour, protection, and held?" Did not a treaty stipulation bind us to "restore, entire, the propety to the true proprietors, as soon as due and sufficient proof should be made concerning the same?" If not, then is there no force and meaning in language; and the words of solemn treaties are an idle breath, of which nations may be as regardless as of the passing wind.

The case then had arisen where it was the duty of the United States, as parties to this treaty, to interfere and see that its stipulations were performed. How were they to interfere? Certainly at the instance of the executive, through the medium of the judiciary, [***107] in whose custody and under whose control the property claimed already was. The questions incident to due and sufficient proof of property are clearly judicial questions; but when that property is already in the custody and under the jurisdiction of a Court, they are so from necessity, as it is desirable they always should be, from choice. This position, never denied, was eloquently urged by the counsel of these negroes when they first addressed the executive on the subject, (Cong. Doc. No. 185, p. 64,) and to that view they added the request that he "would submit the question for adjudication to the tribunals of the land."

He did so. He interposed at the instance of the Spanish minister to fulfil a treaty stipulation, by causing a suggestion to be filed in the Court which had already taken cognisance of the subject-matter, and which had the property in its custody. That suggestion stated the allegation of the Spanish minister, that this was property which ought to be restored under the treaty; prayed in effect an inquiry of the Court into that fact; and requested such a decree, after such inquiry, as might enable the United States as a nation to fulfil their treaty obligations [***108] to the Spanish nation. This has been called "executive interference" and "executive dictation." To answer such a charge in any other way than by appealing to the facts, would be to trespass on the patience of the Court.

As if such charges were felt to be insufficient, an attempt is made by argument to prove that the government of the United States had no right thus to interpose; no right to make this suggestion to the District Court. And why not? It is said, because there is no law giving this power, and it cannot be implied; because in a question of private property it must be left to the parties alone to prosecute their rights, and the parties in this case were already doing so for themselves; and because it was an interference and encroachment of the executive on the province of the Court, not sanctioned by any precedent. These are the grounds that have been taken, and it might be sufficient to say that although every one of them existed in as full force when the case was tried in the District Court, none of them were there taken; although every one of them was known before the plea and answer of the respondents, they started none of these objections.

After the decree and judgment [***109] of the Court below, it is too late to start them. But there is nothing in them, whenever made.

I. The executive government was bound to take the proper steps for having the treaty executed, and these were the proper steps. A treaty is the supreme law; the executive duty is especially to take care that the laws be faithfully executed; no branch of this duty is more usual or apparent than that which is executed in connection with the proceedings and decrees of Courts. What special assignment, by act of Congress, has been made of the executive duties in the fulfilment of laws through the decrees and judgments of the judiciary? Yet it is matter of daily occurrence. What gives the District Attorney a right to file his libel against a package of goods which the law says shall be forfeited on proof being made that they are falsely invoiced, any more than to file his libel against a vessel and her cargo, which a treaty (a still higher law) declares shall be restored on proof concerning the property thereof? In the one case it is the execution of a law, by an executive officer, through the medium or in connection with the Courts; in the other case it is the execution of a treaty in [***110] a similar manner. But in the latter the duty is, if possible, more imperative, since the execution of treaties being connected with public and foreign relations, is devolved upon the executive branch. These principles are clearly stated by this Court in the case of the Peggy, 1 Cranch, 103; and more fully in that of Williams v. The Suffolk Insurance Company, 13 Peters, 420.

As to its being a question of private property, which the parties might themselves prosecute, it is not perceived how this impairs the right, or even lessens the obligation of the United States to interfere, to the extent and in the manner they did, especially when solicitedby the minister representing these parties; they appeal on behalf, or at the instance of a foreign sovereignty in alliance with them, which assumes itself the rights and interests of the parties; those parties withdraw, as this record expressly shows, when they so appear; no act of theirs occurs after the interposition of the United States at the instance of the Spanish minister, and it is expressly stated that they so withdrew, because their claims were merged in that which was thus presented. This appearance of the United States is not, [***111] as has been argued, a substitution of themselves as parties in interest; it is a substitution under a treaty obligation; a substitution assumed in their public character to perform a public duty, by means of which the further prosecution of the individuals is (as the treaty intended it should be) rendered unnecessary. Besides, what is there to show that all the parties having an interest in this property were before the Court? It is nowhere so stated; and, if they were not, the objections totally fail.

How this proceeding is an interference by the executive with the Court; how it is an encroachment on the judicial department; how it is a dictation to the Court, or advice to it to do its duty, it is difficult to conceive; and therefore difficult to reply to such constructions of an act, analogous to the conduct of every proceeding in a Court, rendered necessary to or imperative upon the executive in the execution of the laws. If this libel, so definite in what it alleges and what it asks, founded on the official request of a public functionary, and intended to obtain the execution of a definite treaty obligation, be an infringement of judicial authority, it will be scarcely possible [***112] for a District Attorney, hereafter, to file an information, or present an indictment.

Nor is it, as is alleged, without precedent. In fact, every case of a libel filed by the United States, soliciting the examination and decree of a Court in rem, is a precedent, so far as any principle is concerned. But the cases of the Exchange, the Cassius, and the Eugenia, are not to be distinguished on any ground. They were cases of property in Court, under libels of private suitors; and United States interposed, under their obligations to foreign powers. That those obligations were general, not arising by special treaty provisions, makes the cases less strong. It is said, that the property in litigation, in those cases, was to be delivered to the sovereign; is this property less in that position, when it is asked for by the representative of the sovereign? It is said they were not delivered up as property; the Exchange and Cassius were so delivered: as public property of "the Emperor Napoleon," so stated in terms, and of the French republic. The Eugenia was delivered to the consul of France, that it might be proceeded against in rem, if desired. In the forms of proceeding by the United [***113] States, and in the decrees, every thing resembles what has been done or sought for in this case. But, in fact, every instance of interposition of foreign functionaries, consuls, and others, affords a precedent. They have no right of property. They are no parties in interest. They interpose in behalf of the citizen. Did not this Court, in the case of the Bello Corrunes, 6 Wheaton, 152, where the express point was made, and the interposition of the Spanish consul, on behalf of his fellow-citizens, was resisted, sustain his right, as a public functionary, although it was admitted he could show no special authority in the particular proceeding? So in the case of the Antelope, 10 Wheaton, 66, the consul was allowed to interpose for Spanish subjects, who were actually unknown. It will hardly be denied, that where the foreign functionary may thus come into our Courts, to prosecute for the party in interest, our own functionaries may do the same. As to the case of Nash, Bee, 266, it clearly sustains, so far as the course of proceeding, by means of the judiciary, is concerned, the right and duty of the executive thus to interpose. That was an application for the restoration of a criminal [***114] under treaty stipulations. The main question was, whether this surrender belonged exclusively to the executive, or was to be effected through the medium of the judiciary, and while Chief Justice Marshall sustained the authority of he executive, as founded on the casus faederis, he admitted that the aid of the judiciary might, in some cases, be called in. If this were so, as to persons, it is at least equally so, in regard to property. In respect to both, proof is to be made; without proof, neither the restoration of the one nor the other can be effected; that proof is appropriately made to and passed upon, by the judicial tribunals; but as the execution of the treaty stipulation is vested in the executive, if the case is proved to the satisfaction of the judiciary, its interposition, so far as is necessary to that end, forms a proper part of the judicial proceedings.

It seems clear, then, that these objections to the duty of the executive to interpose, where the property to be restored is in the custody of the Court, cannot be sustained either by principle or authority. And such appears to be the sentiment of the counsel for the appellees, from the zeal with which they have pressed [***115] another argument, to reach the same end. That argument is, that the United States could not interpose, because the Spanish minister never had asked for the restoration of the slaves as property; and, because, if he had, he had sought it solely from the executive department, and denied the jurisdiction of the Court. Now, suppose this were so, it would be a sufficient answer to say, that, independent of the request of the foreign functionary, the United States had a treaty obligation to perform, which they were bound to perform; and that, if a request in regard to its performance was made upon grounds not tenable, this did not release the United States from their obligation on grounds which, as they knew, did properly exist. But, in point of fact, the Spanish minister did, from the first, demand these negroes, as property belonging to Spanish subjects, which ought to be restored as property under the treaty of 1795. Passages have been culled from the letters of Mr. Calderon, and Mr. Argaiz, to show that their surrender as criminals was only sought for; but the correspondence, taken together, bears no such construction. It is true they were demanded as criminals; the alleged crime [***116] had been committed on Spanish subjects, and on board of a Spanish ship; by the law of nations and by the judgment of this Court, such a case was within Spanish jurisdiction. Whether a nation has a right, by the public law, under such circumstances, to require the extradition of the criminal, is a point on which jurists have differed; but most independent nations, if not all, have properly assumed and maintained the right to determine the question for themselves; denying the existence of any such obligation. To make the request, however, is a matter of constant occurrence; to sustain it by appeals to the law of nations, as conferring a right, is usual; we have in our own government asked for such extradition, at the very time we have denied the existence of the obligation. That the Spanish minister should, therefore, request the delivery of these persons as criminals; that he should sustain his request as one consonant to the law of nations, is not in the least a matter of surprise. But did that interfere with his demand for them also, as property? There is no reason why it should do so, and the correspondence shows that it did not, in point of fact.

The very first letter of Mr. [***117] Calderon, that of 6th September, 1839, quoted and commented upon by the counsel for the appellees, commences with a reference to the treaty stipulation, as one of the foundations and causes of his application. It is his imperious duty, he says, to claim an observance of the law of nations, and of the treaties existing between the United States and Spain. Then follow, throughout the letter, repeated references to the double character of the demand for the slaves; references which it seems scarcely possible to misconceive. He declares, officially declares, that the vessel, "previous to her departure, obtained her clearance from the custom-house, the necessary permit from the authorities for the transportation of the negroes, a passport, and all the other documents required by the laws of Spain for navigating a vessel, and for proving ownership of property; a circumstance particularly important," in his opinion.

So Mr. Argaiz, in his letter of the 26th November, 1839, evidently pursues the same double demand; that they should be surrendered under the treaty as property, and that they are also subject to delivery as criminals. If there were a doubt as to his meaning, it must be removed, [***118] by observing his course on the passage of the resolutions adopted unanimously by the American Senate, on the 15th of April last. Those resolutions declared:

1. That a ship or vessel on the high seas, in time of peace, engaged in a lawful voyage, is, according to the law of nations, under the exclusive jurisdiction of the state to which the flag belongs; as much so, as if constituting a part of its own domain.

2. That if such ship or vessel should be forced, by stress of weather, or other unavoidable cause, into the port and under the jurisdiction of a friendly power, she and her cargo, and persons on board, with their property, and all the rights belonging to their personal relations, as established by the laws of the state to which they belong, would be placed under the protection which the laws of nations extend to the unfortunate under such circumstances.

On the passage of these resolutions, so evidently referring to the slaves as property, adopted in relation to the slaves carried into Bermuda and there set free, Mr. Argaiz claimed, for the owners of the slaves on board the Amistad, the application of the same rules. To complete the chain of evidence derived from the correspondence, [***119] we have a letter addressed by him to the Secretary of State, on the first moment that the allegation of the request being for their delivery as criminals, was made official, by the motion of the appellees lately filed in this Court—we have a note to the Secretary of State, explicitly renewing his demand in the double relation.

It is evident, then, that there was a clear, distinct, and formal request, on the part of the Spanish minister, for the delivery of these negroes, by virtue of the treaty, as the property of Spanish subjects. This fact, it has been endeavoured to establish, from the correspondence, because it has been alleged that the executive of the United States has given a construction to the request of the Spanish minister, at variance with that stated in the libel of the District Attorney. As to any legal bearing on the case, it does not appear to be material. So far as the Courts of justice are concerned, no principle is better settled than that, in relation to the political operations of the government, the judiciary adopts the construction given to their own acts and those of foreign representatives, by the proper executive departments. The opinion of this Court [***120] to that effect, is apparent in the decisions, already cited in the cases of the Peggy and the Suffolk Insurance Co.; and when, in the case of Garcia v. Lee, the whole matter was reviewed, with special reference to the construction of treaties, it was solemnly and deliberately affirmed. That the Department of State regarded this request as one for the delivery of property, is evident, not merely from the libel of the District Attorney, but from the whole correspondence. To obtain a different view, we must, indeed, pick out sentences separate from their context, and give to particular phrases a meaning not consistent with the whole scope of the documents in which they are found.

But, as if the allegation, that the Spanish minister never required the restoration of these slaves as property, under the treaty, was not to be clearly established by the correspondence, it is endeavoured to be sustained by the fact, that he refused to submit to the judgment of the court, as definitive of the rights of Spain and her subjects, under the treaty. How this refusal changes the character of his demand on the one hand, or the proper mode of proceeding by the executive on the other, it is not easy [***121] to perceive. No nation looks, in its intercourse under a treaty with another, to any but the executive government. Every nation has a right to say with what act she will be satisfied as fulfilling a treaty stipulation, the other party to the treaty reserving the same right. Has not our executive over and over again demanded redress for acts sanctioned by decrees of foreign tribunals? Have we not sought that redress by applications made directly to their executives? Has it ever been heard, that the claims of American citizens for redress from foreign governments, are precluded, because foreign Courts have decided upon them? Such has not been the case in point of fact, and such is not the course authorized by the law, and adopted in the intercourse of nations. To say, therefore, that Spain would not recognise a decree of a Court, which should award her less than the treaty, in her opinion, stipulated she should receive, does not, as it must appear, affect, in any manner whatever, the rights under it, or the mode of proceeding to be adopted by our own executive. With the latter the course was plain. The matter was already before the judiciary, a component and independent branch [***122] of the government to which it appropriately belonged. Its action is calmly waited for, as affording the just and only basis of ultimate decision by the executive.

Viewed, then, on every ground of treaty obligation, of constitutional duty, of precedent, or of international intercourse, the interposition of the executive in the mode adopted, so far from being "unnecessary and improper," was one of duty and propriety, on receiving from the Spanish minister his official representation, and from the District Attorney the information that the matter was already in charge of the Court.

And now it may be asked, whether there is any thing in these facts to justify the censure so largely cast upon the executive for the course which it was deemed a duty to pursue; any thing that authorizes "its arraignment," to use the language of the counsel for the appellees, before the judicial tribunals, "for their judgment and censure?" Performing cautiously an international obligation; passing upon no rights private or public; submitting to the Courts of justice the facts made known officially to it; seeking the decrees of the legitimate tribunals; communicating to foreign functionaries, that by these [***123] decrees its course would be governed—it is these acts which are argued upon, as ground for censure and denunciation. With what justice may be well tested, by placing another government in the position of our own. Let us recollect that there is among nations as among men, a golden rule; let us do to them as we wish them to do to us; let us ask how we would have our own minister and representative in a foreign land to act by us, if we were thrown in like manner on a foreign shore—if a citizen of South Carolina, sailing to New Orleans with his slaves, were thus attacked, his associates killed, himself threatened with death, and carried for months in a vessel scarcely sea worthy, beneath a tropical sun. Should we blame the American minister who had asked the interposition of the Courts? Should we blame the foreign government that facilitated that interposition? Look at the case of the negroes carried to Bermuda; have we there—as we are now denounced for not doing—have we there gone as private suitors into the Courts, or have we sought redress, as nations seek it for their citizens?

The question of freedom or slavery was there brought, exactly as it was here, before the [***124] judicial tribunals, at the instance of persons who took up the cause of the slaves; the owners did not pursue their claims as a mere matter of private right; the government of the United States, through its minister, appealed to the executive government of Great Britain; sought redress from that quarter; and received it. The value of the slaves was paid, not to the individuals, but to our own government, who took their business upon themselves, exactly as the Spanish minister has assumed that of Ruiz and Montez.

Let us then be just; let us not demand one mode of proceeding for ourselves, and practise another towards those who have and equal right to claim similar conduct at our hands.

II. The Attorney General then proceeded to reply to the position of the counsel for the appellees, that whatever might be the right of the United States as parties to the proceedings in the District and Circuit Courts, they had yet no authority to appeal, in such a case, from the decrees of those Courts, to this tribunal, and that, therefore, the present appeal should be dismissed. As no decision was given by the Court on this point, and the argument in support of the motion, and on behalf of the [***125] appellees, has not been reported, that in reply, and in behalf of the United States, as appellants, is also necessarily omitted. The position contended for by the Attorney General was, that the case was before this Court—coram justice; and that the case itself, the parties to it, and the mode of bringing it up, were all in accordance with the law authorizing appeals. If so, he submitted, that this Court has jurisdiction of it, and will revise the decree that has been pronounced by the Circuit Court, which is all that was solicited. That the highest judicial tribunal should pronounce upon the facts set out in this record, was all that the executive could desire; they present questions that appropriately belong to the judiciary, as the basis of executive action; they relate to the rights of property, and the proofs concerning it; and when the decision of that co-ordinate branch of the government, to which the examination of such questions appropriately belongs, should be made, the course, of executive action would be plain.

III. The only question, then, that remains to be considered, is, was the decree erroneous?

The decree, as it stands, and as it now comes up for examination, [***126] is, that this vessel and her cargo shall be delivered up to the Spanish minister, for the Spanish owners, not entire, but after deducting one-thrid for salvage, to be given to Lieutenant Gedney and his associates; and that the negroes, except Antonio, shall be delivered to the President of the United States, to be sent to Africa, pursuant to the provisions of the act of 3d March, 1819, § 2. 2 Story's Laws, 1752. Now it is submitted, that this decree is erroneous, because the vessel, cargo, and negroes were all the property of Spanish subjects, rescued from robbers, and brought into a port of the United States, and due proof concerning the property in them was made; that, therefore, the decree should have been, that they be delivered to the Spanish owners, or to the Spanish minister, for the owners, according to the stipulations of the ninth article of the treaty of 1795.

The vessel and cargo are admitted to be merchandise or property, within the meaning of the treaty. Are slaves also property or merchandise, within its meaning? That they are not, has been very elaborately argued by the counsel for the appellees; yet, it is confidently submitted that, both by the laws of Spain and [***127] of the United States, slaves are property; and a fair construction of the treaty shows that it was intended to embrace every species of property recognised by the laws of the two contracting nations. We are asked for a law to this effect; a law establishing the existence of slavery in the Spanish dominions. It might be sufficient to say, that what is matter of notorious history will be recognised by this Court, without producing a statutory regulation; but the royal decree of 1817, which promulgates the abolition of the foreign slave trade, refers throughtout to the existence of slavery in the Spanish Indies, and this Court, in many of its adjudications, has recognised its existence.

If slaves then, were, property by the laws of Spain, it might be justly concluded that, even if they were not so recognised by the United States, still they are property within the meaning of the treaty, because the intention of the treaty was to protect the property of each nation. But, in fact, slaves were, and are, as clearly recognised by them to be property, as they ever were by Spain. Our citizens hold them as property; buy and sell them as property; legislate upon them as property. State after [***128] state has been received into this Union, with the solemn and deliberate assent of the national legislature, whose constitutions, previously submitted to and sanctioned by that legislature, recognise slaves as merchandise; to be held as such, carried as such from place to place, and bought and sold as such. It has been argued that this government, as a government, never has recognised property in slaves. To this it is answered, that if no other proof could be adduced, these acts of the national government are evidence that it has done so. The Constitution of the United States leaves to the states the regulation of their internal property, of which slaves were, at the time it was formed, a well known portion. It also guaranteed and protected the rights of the states to increase this property, up to the year 1808, by importation from abroad. How, then, can it be said, that this government, as a government, never has recognised this property? But, if slaves be not so regarded, by what authority did the general government demand indemnity for slaves set free in Bermuda by the British government? Is not this an act, recent in date and deliberate in conduct, showing the settled construction [***129] put upon slaves as property. Is not the resolution of the Senate—the unanimous resolution—a declaration that slaves, though liberated as persons, and so adjudged by a foreign Court, are, in fact, by the law of nations, property, if so allowed to be held in the country to which the owner belongs?

But it is contended that, although they may have been recognised as property by the two nations, they were not such property as was subject to restoration by the treaty. Now, to this it may be answered, in the first place, that every reason which can be suggested for the introduction of the treaty stipulations to protect and restore property, applies as fully to slaves as to any other. It is, in states where slavery exists, a valuable species of property; it is an object of traffic; it is transported from place to place. Can it be supposed, that the citizen of Virginia, sailing to New Orleans with his slaves, less needs the benefit of these treaty stipulations for them, than for any other property he may have on board, if he is carried into a port of Cuba, under any of the adverse circumstances for which the treaty was intended to provide? But, again; is not the treaty so broad [***130] and general in its terms, that one of the contracting parties has no right to make an exclusion of this property, without the assent of the other? The sixteenth article of the treaty says, it is to extend to "all kings" of merchandise, except that which is contraband. Was not a slave a kind of merchandise, then recognised as such by each nation, and allowed to be imported into each nation, by their respective laws?

The treaty of 1819, which was ratified in 1821, after the slave trade was abolished, but while slave property was held in both countries, renews this article as it stood in 1795. Is it possible to imagine that, if a new policy was to be adopted, there would not have been an express stipulation or change in regard to this, as there was in regard to other articles of the old treaty? If further proof were wanting, it would be found in the fact, that the executive authorities of both nations, at once and unequivocally, considered the terms of the treaty as extending to slave property. Independently of the authority which this decision on the political construction of a treaty will have with this Court, upon the principles it has laid down, it may be regarded as strong [***131] evidence of the intentions of the contracting parties; and when we see our own government and the Senate of the United States, seriously examining how far a similar case is one that falls within the class of international obligations, independent of treaty, we may give to its deliberate judgment, in the proper construction of this treaty, the highest weight.

The next inquiry is, whether the property in question was "rescued out of the hands of any pirates or robbers on the high seas, and brought into any port of the United States?" That the vessel was at anchor below low water mark when taken possession of, and consequently upon the high seas, as defined by the law of nations, is a fact not controverted; but it is objected that the negroes by whom she was held were not pirates or robbers in the sense of the treaty, and that if they were, its provisions could not apply to them, because they were themselves the persons who were rescued. That the acts committed by the negroes amount to piracy and robbery, seems too clear to be questioned. Piracy is an offence defined and ascertained by the law of nations; it is "forcible depredation on the sea, animo furandi." United States v. Smith, [***132] 5 Wheaton, 153. Every ingredient necessary to constitute a crime thus defined, is proved in the present case. It was the intention of the treaty, that whenever, by an act of piracy, a vessel and property were run away with—taken from the owners, who are citizens of the United States or Spain—it should, if it came into the possession of the other party, be kept by that party and restored entire. Slaves differ from other property, in the fact that they are persons as well as property; that they may be actors in the piracy; but it is not perceived how this act, of itself, changes the rights of the owners, where they exist and are recognised by law. If they are property, they are property rescued from pirates, and are to be restored, if brought by the necessary proof within the provisions of the treaty.

What are those provisions? That "due and sufficient proof must be made concerning the property thereof."

The first inquiry "concerning property," is its identity. Is there any doubt as to the identify of these slaves? There is clearly none. Are they negroes, in a country where slavery Spanish subjects? They are engroes, in a country where slavery exists, passing from one [***133] port of the Spanish dominions to another, in a regularly documented coasting vessel; and they are proved to be, at the time they leave Havana, in the actual possession of the persons claiming to be their owners. So far as all the prima facie evidence extends, derived from the circumstances of the case at that time, they may be regarded as slaves, as much as the negroes who accompany a planter between any two ports of the United States. This, then, is the first evidence of property—their actual existence in a state of slavery, and in the possession of their alleged owners, in a place where slavery is recognised, and exists by law.

In addition to this evidence derived from possession, Ruiz and Montez had, according to the statement of the Spanish minister, which was read by the counsel for the appellees, "all the documents required by the laws of Spain for proving ownership of property." They have a certificate, under the signature of the Governor General, countersigned or attested by the captain of the port, declaring that these negroes are the property of the Spanish citizens who are in possession of them. It has already been shown, by reference to the laws of Spain, that the [***134] powers of a Governor General in a Spanish colony are of a most plenary character. That his powers are judicial, was expressly recognised by this Court, in the case of Keene v. M'Donough, 8 Peters, 310. If such are the powers of this officer, and if this be a document established as emanating from him, it must be regarded as conclusive in a foreign country. The cases already cited, establish the two positions, that, as regards property on board of a vessel, the accompanying documents are the first and best evidence, especially when attended with possession; and that a decree, on judgment, or declaration of a foreign tribunal, made within the scope of its authority, is evidence, beyond which the Courts of another country will not look. These rules are essential to international intercourse. Could it be tolerated, that where vessels, on a coasting voyage, from one port of a country to another, are driven, without fault of their own, to take refuse in the harbour of another country, the authentic evidences of property in their own country are to be disregarded? That foreign Courts are to execute the municipal laws of another country, according to their construction of them? Can it [***135] be that the Courts of this country will refuse to recognise the evidence of property, which is recognised and deemed sufficient in the country to which that property belongs? We have unquestionable evidence, that such documents as these are regarded as adequate proofs of property in Cuba. But it is said this certificate is a mere passport, and no proof of property. To this it is replied, that it is recognised as the necessary and usual evidence of property, as appears by the testimony referred to. It is true it is a passport for Ruiz, but it is not a mere personal passport; it is one to take property with him, and it ascertains and describes that property.

But we are told it must be regarded as fraudulent by this Court; and the grounds on which this assertion is made, are the evidence adduced to show that these negroes have been imported into Cuba from Africa, since the treaty between Great Britain and Spain. Is this evidence legal and sufficient to authorize this Court to declare the particular fact for which it is vouched—that the negroes were imported into Cuba contrary to law? If it is sufficient for this, does such illegal importation make the negroes free men in he island [***136] of Cuba? If it does, will this Court declare the certificate to be null and void, or leave that act to the decision of the appropriate Spanish tribunals?

In the argument submitted on the part of the United States, in opening the case, the nature of this evidence has been commented upon. It is such chiefly as is not legal evidence in the Courts of the United States. Now, the question is not as to the impression derived from such evidence, but it is whether, on testimony not legally sufficient, the declaration of a competent foreign functionary will be set aside? As if there were doubt whether a Court of the United States would so do, the admissions of Ruiz, and of the Attorney of the United States are vouched. Yet it is apparent that these were admissions, not of facts known to themselves, but of impressions derived from evidence which is as much before this Court as it was before them. To neither one nor the other was the fact in question personally known. It was inferred by them from evidence now for the most part before this Court.

But, admitting the fact of the recent importation from Africa, still, nothing has been adduced to controvert the position, taken in opening, [***137] that the laws of Spain required, in such a case, and even in the case of negroes actually seized on board of a Spanish vessel on her voyage from Africa, a declaration by a Court expressly recognised by Spain, to establish their freedom. However much we may abhor the African slave trade, all nations have left to those in whose vessels it is carried on, the regulation and punishment of it. The extent to which Spain was willing to permit any other nation to interpose, where her vessels or her subjects were concerned, is carefully determined in this very treaty. The principal witness of the appellees expressly admits, that when negroes are landed, though in known violation of the treaty, it is a subject to be disposed of by the municipal law. Now, it is not pretended here, that, even if these negroes were unlawfully introduced, they have been declared free. Can, then, this Court adjudge that these negroes were free in the island of Cuba, even if the fact of their recent importation be proved? Much more, can they assume to do it, by putting their cosntruction on a treaty, not of the United States, but between two foreign nations; a treaty which those nations have the sole right to [***138] construe and act upon for themselves?

But, if satisfied that the Governor General has been imposed upon, and the documents fraudulently obtained, still, is the fraud to be punished and the error to be rectified in our Courts, or in those of Spain? What says Sir William Scott, in the case of the Louis, when asked what is to be done if a French ship laden with slaves, in violation of the laws of that country, is brought into an English port: "I answer," says he, "without hesitation, restore the possession which has been unlawfully divested; rescind the illegal act done by your own subject, and leave the foreigner to the justice of his own country." Can a rule more directly applicable to the present case be found? "The Courts of no country," says Chief Justice Marshall, in the case of the Antelope, "execute the penal laws of another." In the case of the Engenia, wehre a French vessel was liable to forfeiture under the laws of France, for violating the laws prohibiing the slave trade, Judge Story directed, not that she should be condemned in our own Courts, but that she should be sent to France. This, says he, "enables the foreign sovereign to exercise complete jurisdiction, if he [***139] shall prefer to have it remitted to his own Courts for adjudication." This, he afterwards adds, "makes our own country not a principal, but an auxiliary in enforcing the interdict of France, and subserves the great interests of universal justice."

Are not these the true principles which should govern nations in their intercourse with each other; principles sanctioned by great and venerated names? Are not these the principles by whcih we would require other nations to be governed, when our citizens are charged, in a foreign country, with a breach of our own muniticpal laws? And is it not productive of the same result? Do we doubt that the Courts and officers of Spain will justly administer her own laws? Will this Court act, on the presumption that the tribunals of a foreign and friendly nation will fail to pursue that course which humanity, justice, and the sacred obligations of their own laws demand? No nation has a right so to presume, in regard to another; and, notwithstanding the distrust that has been repeatedly expressed in the progress of this cause, in regard to the Spanish tribunals and the Spanish functionaries; yet a just respect towards another and a friendly nation; [***140] the common courtesy which will not suppose in advance, that it will intentionally do wrong; oblige us to believe, and warrant us in so doing, that if the laws of Spain have been violated; if its officers have been deceived; and if these negroes are really free; these facts will be there ascertained and acted upon, and we shall as "auxiliaries," not principals, best "subserve the cause of universal justice."

If this view be correct, and if the evidence is sufficient to prove the property of the Spanish subjects in the island of Cuba, the only question that remains to be considered is, whether the acts of the slaves during the voyage changed their condition. It has been argued strongly that they were free; that they were. "in the actual condition of freedom;" but how can that be maintained? If slaves by the laws of Spain, they were so on board of a Spanish vessel, as much as on her soil; and will it be asserted that the same acts in the island of Cuba would have made them free? This will hardly be contended. No nation recognising slavery, admits the sufficiency of forcible emancipation. In what respect were these slaves, if such by the laws of Spain, released from slavery by their [***141] own acts of aggression upon their masters, any more than a slave becomes free in Pennsylvania, who forcibly escapes from his owner in Virginia? For this Court to say that these acts constituted a release from slavery, would be to establish for another country municipal regulations in regard to her property; and, not that only, but to establish them directly in variance with our own laws, in analogous cases. If the negroes in this case were free, it was because they were not slaves when placed on board the Amistad, not because of the acts there committed by them.

It is submitted, then, that so far as this Court is concerned, there is sufficient evidence concerning this property, to warrant its restoration pursuant to the provisions of the treaty with Spain; and that, therefore, the judgment of the court below should be reversed, and a decree made by this Court for the entire restoration of the property.

OPINION BY: STORY

OPINION

[*587] [**851] Mr. Justice STORY delivered the opinion of the Court.

This is the case of an appeal from the decree of the Circuit Court of the District of Connecticut, sitting in admiralty. The leading facts, as they appear upon the transcript of the proceedings, [***142] are as follows: On the 27th of June, 1839, the schooner L'Amistad, being the property of Spanish subjects, cleared out from the port of Havana, in the island of Cuba, for Puerto Principe, in the same island. On board of the schooner were the captain, Ransom Ferrer, and Jose Ruiz, and Pedro Montez, all Spanish subjects. The former had with him a negro boy, named Antonio, claimed to be his slave. Jose Ruiz had with him forty-nine negroes, claimed by him as his slaves, and stated to be his property, in a certain pass or document, signed by the Governor General of Cuba. Pedro Montez had with him four other negroes, also claimed by him as his slaves, and stated to be his property, in a similar pass or document, also signed by the

Governor General [*588] of Cuba. On the voyage, and before the arrival of the vessel at her port of destination, the negroes rose, killed the captain, and took possession of her. On the 26th of August, the vessel was discovered by Lieutenant Gedney, of the United States brig Washington, at anchor on the high seas, at the distance of half a mile from the shore of Long Island. A part of the negroes were then on shore at Culloden Point, Long Island; who [***143] were seized by Lieutenant Gedney, and brought on board. The vessel, with the negroes and other persons on board, was brought by Lieutenant Gedney into the district of Connecticut, and there libeled for [**852] salvage in the District Court of the United States. A libel for salvage was also filed by Henry Green and Pelatiah Fordham, of Sag Harbour, Long Island. On the 18th of September, Ruiz and Montez filed claims and libels, in which they asserted their ownership of the negroes as their slaves, and of certain parts of the cargo, and prayed that the same might be "delivered to them, or to the representatives of her Catholic majesty, as might be most proper." On the 19th of September, the Attorney of the United states, for the district of Connecticut, filed an information or libel, setting forth, that the Spanish minister had officially presented to the proper department of the government of the United States, a claim for the restoration of the vessel, cargo, and slaves, as the property of Spanish subjects, which had arrived within the jurisdictional limits of the United States, and were taken possession of by the said public armed brig of the United States; under such circumstances [***144] as made it the duty of the United States to cause the same to be restored to the true proprietors, pursuant to the treaty between the United States and Spain: and praying the Court, on its being made legally to appear that the claim of the Spanish minister was well founded, to make such order for the disposal of the vessel, cargo, and slaves, as would best enable the United States to comply with their treaty stipulations. But if it should appear, that the negroes were persons transported from Africa, in violation of the laws of the United States, and brought within the United States contrary to the same laws; he then prayed the Court to make such order for their removal to the coast of Africa, pursuant to the laws of the United States, as it should deem fit.

[*589] On the 19th of November, the Attorney of the United States filed a second information or libel, similar to the first, with the exception of the second prayer above set forth in his former one. On the same day, Antonio G. Vega, the vice-consul of Spain, for the state of Connecticut, filed his libel, alleging that Antonio was a slave, the property of the representatives of Ramon Ferrer, and praying the Court to cause [***145] him to be delivered to the said vice-consul, that he might be returned by him to his lawful owner in the island of Cuba.

On the 7th of January, 1840, the negroes, Cinque and others, with the exception of Antonio, by their counsel, filed an answer, denying that they were slaves, or the property of Ruiz and Montez, or that the Court could, under the Constitution or laws of the United States, or under any treaty, exercise any jurisdiction over their persons, by reason of the premises; and praying that they might be dismissed. They specially set forth and insist in this answer, that they were native born Africans; born free, and still of right ought to be free and not slaves; that they were, on or about the 15th of April, 1839, unlawfully kidnapped, and forcibly and wrongfully carried on board a certain vessel on the coast of Africa, which was unlawfully engaged in the slave trade, and were unlawfully transported in the same vessel to the island of Cuba, for the purpose of being there unlawfully sold as slaves; that Ruiz and Montez, well knowing the premises, made a pretended purchase of them: that afterwards, on or about the 28th of June, 1839, Ruiz and Montez, confederating with Ferrer, [***146] (captain of the Amistad,) caused them, without law or right, to be placed on board of the Amistad, to be transported to some place unknown to them, and there to be enslaved for life; that, on the voyage, they rose on the master, and took possession of the vessel, intending to return therewith to their native country, or to seek an asylum in some free state; and the vessel arrived, about the 26th of August, 1839, off Montauk Point, near Long Island; a part of them were sent on shore, and were seized by Lieutenant Gedney, and carried on board; and all of them were afterwards brought by him into the district of Connecticut.

On the 7th of January, 1840, Jose Antonio Tellincas, and Messrs. Aspe and Laca, all Spanish subjects, residing in Cuba, filed their [*590] claims, as owners to certain portions of the goods found on board of the schooner L'Amistad.

On the same day, all the libellants and claimants, by their counsel, except Jose Ruiz and Pedro Montez, (whose libels and claims, as stated of record, respectively, were pursued by the Spanish minister, the same being merged in his claims,) appeared, and the negroes also appeared by their counsel; and the case was heard on the libels, [***147] claims, answers, and testimony of witnesses.

On the 23d day of January, 1840, the District Court made a decree. By that decree, the Court rejected the claim of Green and Fordham for salvage, but allowed salvage to Lieutenant Gedney and others, on the vessel and cargo, of one-third of the value thereof, but not on the negroes, Cinque and others; it allowed the claim of Tellincas, and Aspe and Laca with the exception of the above-mentioned salvage; it dismissed the libels and claims of Ruiz and Montez, with costs, as being included under the claim of the Spanish minister; it allowed the claim of the Spanish vice-consul for Antonio, on behalf of Ferrer's representatives; it rejected the claims of Ruiz and Montez for the delivery of the negroes, but admitted them for the cargo, with the exception of the above-mentioned salvage; it rejected the claim made by the Attorney of the United States on behalf of the Spanish minister, for the restoration of the negroes under the treaty; but it decreed that they should be delivered to the President of the United States, to be transported to Africa, pursuant to the act of 3d March, 1819.

From this decree the District Attorney, on behalf of the [***148] United States, appealed to the Circuit Court, except so far as related to the restoration of the slave Antonio. The claimants, Tellincas, and Aspe and Laca, also appealed from that part of the decree which awarded salvage on the property respectively claimed by them. No appeal was interposed by Ruiz or Montez, or on behalf of the representatives of the owners of the Amistad. The Circuit Court, by a mere pro forma decree, affirmed the decree of the District Court, reserving the question of salvage upon the claims of Tellincas, and Aspe and Laca. And from that decree the present appeal has been brought to this Court.

The cause has been very elaborately argued, as well upon the [*591] merits, as upon a [**853] motion on behalf of the appellees to dismiss the appeal. On the part of the United States, it has been contended, 1. That due and sufficient proof concerning the property has been made to authorize the restitution of the vessel, cargo, and negroes to the Spanish subjects on whose behalf they are claimed pursuant to the treaty with Spain, of the 27th of October, 1795. 2. That the United States had a right to intervene in the manner in which they have done, to obtain [***149] a decree for the restitution of the property, upon the application of the Spanish minister. These propositions have been strenuously denied on the other side. Other collateral and incidental points have been stated, upon which it is not necessary at this moment to dwell.

Before entering upon the discussion of the main points involved in this interesting and important controversy, it may be necessary to say a few words as to the actual posture of the case as it now stands before us. In the first place, then, the only parties now before the Court on one side, are the United States, intervening for the sole purpose of procuring restitution of the property as Spanish property, pursuant to the treaty, upon the grounds stated by the other parties claiming the property in their respective libels. The United States do not assert any property in themselves, or any violation of their own rights, or sovereignty, or laws, by the acts complained of. They do not insist that these negroes have been imported into the United States, in contravention of our own slave trade acts. They do not seek to have these negroes delivered up for the purpose of being transported to Cuba as pirates or robbers, [***150] or as fugitive criminals against the laws of Spain. They do not assert that the seizure, and bringing the vessel, and cargo, and negroes into port, by Lieutenant Gedney, for the purpose of adjudication, is a tortious act. They simply confine themselves to the right of the Spanish claimants to the restitution of their property, upon the facts asserted in their respective allegations.

In the next place, the parties before the Court on the other side as appellees, are Lieutenant Gedney, on his libel for salvage, and the negroes, (Cinque, and others,) asserting themselves, in their answer, not to be slaves, but free native Africans, kidnapped [*592] in their own country, and illegally transported by force from that country; and now entitled to maintain their freedom.

No question has been here made, as to the proprietary interests in the vessel and cargo. It is admitted that they belong to Spanish subjects, and that they ought to be restored. The only point on this head is, whether the restitution ought to be upon the payment of salvage or not? The main controversy is, whether these negroes are the property of Ruiz and Montez, and ought to be delivered up; and to this, accordingly, [***151] we shall first direct our attention.

It has been argued on behalf of the United States, that the Court are bound to deliver them up, according to the treaty of 1795, with Spain, which has in this particular been continued in full force, by the treaty of 1819, ratified in 1821. The sixth article of that treaty, seems to have had, principally, in view cases where the property of the subjects of either state had been taken possession of within the territorial jurisdiction of the other, during war. The eighth article provides for cases where the shipping of the inhabitants of either state are forced, through stress of weather, pursuit of pirates, or enemies, or any other urgent necessity, to seek shelter in the ports of the other. There may well be some doubt entertained, whether the present case, in its actual circumstances, falls within the purview of this article. But it does not seem necessary, for reasons hereafter stated, absolutely to decide it. The ninth article provides, "that all ships and merchandise, of what nature soever, which shall be rescued out of the hands of any pirates or robbers, on the high seas, shall be brought into some port of either state, and shall be [***152] delivered to the custody of the officers of that port, in order to be taken care of and restored entire to the true proprietor, as soon as due and sufficient proof shall be made concerning the property thereof." This is the article on which the main reliance is placed on behalf of the United States, for the restitution of these negroes. To bring the case within the article, it is essential to establish, First, That these negroes, under all the circumstances, fall within the description of merchandise, in the sense of the treaty. Secondly, That there has been a rescue of them on the high seas, out of the hands of the pirates and robbers; which, in the present case, can only be, by showing that they [*593] themselves are pirates and robbers; and, Thirdly, That Ruiz and Montez, the asserted proprietors, are the true proprietors, and have established their title by competent proof.

If these negroes were, at the time, lawfully held as slaves under the laws of Spain, and recognised by those laws as property capable of being lawfully bought and sold; we see no reason why they may not justly be deemed within the intent of the treaty, to be included under the denomination of merchandise, [***153] and, as such, ought to be restored to the claimants: for, upon that point, the laws of Spain would seem to furnish the proper rule of interpretation. But, admitting this, it is clear, in our opinion, that neither of the other essential facts and requisites has been established in proof; and the onus probandi of both lies upon the claimants to give rise to the causes foederis. It is plain beyond controversy, if we examine the evidence, that these negroes never were the lawful slaves of Ruiz or Montez, or of any other Spanish subjects. They are natives of Africa, and were kidnapped there, and were unlawfully transported to Cuba, in violation of the laws and treaties of Spain, and the most solemn edicts and declarations of that government. By those laws, and treaties, and edicts, the African slave trade is utterly abolished; the dealing in that trade is deemed a heinous crime; and the negroes thereby introduced into the dominions of Spain, are declared to be free. Ruiz and Montez are proved to have made the pretended purchase of these negroes, with a full knowledge of all the circumstances. And so cogent and irresistible is the evidence in this respect, that the District Attorney [***154] has admitted in open Court, upon the record, that these negroes were native Africans, and recently imported into Cuba, as alleged in their answers to the libels [**854] in the case. The supposed proprietary interest of Ruiz and Montez, is completely displaced, if we are at liberty to look at the evidence of the admissions of the District Attorney.

If, then, these negroes are not slaves, but are kidnapped Africans, who, by the laws of Spain itself, are entitled to their freedom, and were kidnapped and illegally carried to Cuba, and illegally detained and restrained on board of the Amistad; there is no pretence to say, that they are pirates or robbers. We may lament the dreadful acts, by which they asserted their liberty, and took possession of the Amistad, and endeavoured to regain their native [*594] country; but they cannot be deemed pirates or robbers in the sense of the law of nations, or the treaty with Spain, or the laws of Spain itself; at least so far as those laws have been brought to our knowledge. Nor do the libels of Ruiz or Montez assert them to be such.

This posture of the facts would seem, of itself, to put an end to the Whole inquiry upon the merits. But [***155] it is argued, on behalf of the United States, that the ship, and cargo, and negroes were duly documented as belonging to Spanish subjects, and this Court have no right to look behind these documents; that full faith and credit is to be given to them; and that they are to be held conclusive evidence in this cause, even although it should be established by the most satisfactory proofs, that they have been obtained by the grossest frauds and impositions upon the constituted authorities of Spain. To this argument we can, in no wise, assent. There is nothing in the treaty which justifies or sustains the argument. We do not here meddle with the point, whether there has been any connivance in this illegal traffic, on the part of any of the colonial authorities or subordinate officers of Cuba; because, in our view, such an examination is unnecessary, and ought not to be pursued, unless it were indispensable to public justice, although it has been strongly pressed at the bar. What we proceed upon is this, that although public documents of the government, accompanying property found on board of the private ships of a foreign nation, certainly are to be deemed prima facie evidence of the facts [***156] which they purport to state, yet they are always open to be impugned for fraud; and whether that fraud be in the original obtaining of these documents, or in the subsequent fraudulent and illegal use of them, when once it is satisfactorily established, it overthrows all their sanctity, and destroys them as proof. Fraud will vitiate any, even the most solemn transactions; and an asserted title to property, founded upon it, is utterly void. The very language of the ninth article of the treaty of 1795, requires the proprietor to make due and sufficient proof of his property. And how can that proof be deemed either due or sufficient, which is but a connected, and stained tissue of fraud? This is not a mere rule of municipal jurisprudence. Nothing is more clear in the law of nations, as an established rule to regulate their rights, and duties, [*595] and intercourse, than the doctrine, that the ship's papers are but prima facie evidence, and that, if they are shown to be fraudulent, they are not to be held proof of any valid title. This rule is familiarly applied, and, indeed, is of every-days occurrence in cases of prize, in the contests between belligerents and neutrals, as [***157] is apparent from numerous cases to be found in the Reports of this Court; and it is just as applicable to the transactions of civil intercourse between nations in times of peace. If a private ship, clothed with Spanish papers, should enter the ports of the United States, claiming the privileges, and immunities, and rights belonging to bona fide subjects of Spain, under our treaties or laws, and she should, in reality, belong to the subjects of another nation, which was not entitled to any such privileges, immunities, or rights, and the proprietors were seeking, by fraud, to cover their own illegal acts, under the flag of Spain; there can be no doubt, that it would be the duty of our Courts to strip off the disguise, and to look at the case according to its naked realities. In the solemn treaties between nations, it can never be presumed that either state intends to provide the means of perpetrating or protecting frauds; but all the provisions are to be construed as intended to be applied to bona fide transactions. The seventeenth article of the treaty with Spain, which provides for certain passports and certificates, as evidence of property on board of the ships of both states, [***158] is, in its terms, applicable only to cases where either of the parties is engaged in a war. This article required a certain form of passport to be agreed upon by the parties, and annexed to the treaty. It never was annexed; and, therefore, in the case of the Amiable Isabella, 6 Wheaton, 1, it was held inoperative.

It is also a most important consideration in the present case, which ought not to be lost sight of, that, supposing these African negroes not to be slaves, but kidnapped, and free negroes, the treaty with Spain cannot be obligatory upon them; and the United States are bound to respect their rights as much as those of Spanish subjects. The conflict of rights between the parties under such circumstances, becomes positive and inevitable, and must be decided upon the eternal principles of justice and international law. If the contest were about any goods on board of this ship, to which American citizens asserted a title, which was [*596] denied by the Spanish claimants, there could be no doubt of the right of such American citizens to litigate their claims before any competent American tribunal, notwithstanding the treaty with Spain. A fortiori, the doctrine must apply [***159] where human life and human liberty are in issue; and constitute the very essence of the controversy. The treaty with Spain never could have intended to take away the equal rights of all foreigners, who should contest their claims before any of our Courts, to equal justice; or to deprive such foreigners of the protection given them by other treaties, or by the general law of nations. Upon the merits of the case, then, there does not seem to us to be any ground for doubt, that these negroes ought to be deemed free; and that the Spanish treaty interposes no obstacle to the just assertion of their rights.

There is another consideration growing out of this part of the case, which necessarily rises in judgment. It is observable, that the United States, in their original claim, filed it in the alternative, to have the negroes, if slaves and Spanish property, restored to the proprietors; [**855] or, if not slaves, but negroes who had been transported from Africa, in violation of the laws of the United States, and brought into the United States contrary to the same laws, then the Court to pass an order to enable the United States to remove such persons to the coast of Africa, to be [***160] delivered there to such agent as may be authorized to receive and provide for them. At a subsequent period, this last alternative claim was not insisted on, and another claim was interposed, omitting it; from which the conclusion naturally arises that it was abandoned. The decree of the District Court, however, contained an order for the delivery of the negroes to the United States, to be transported to the coast of Africa, under the act of the 3d of March, 1819, ch. 224. The United States do not now insist upon any affirmance of this part of the decree; and, in our judgment, upon the admitted facts, there is no ground to assert that the case comes within the purview of the act of 1819, or of any other of our prohibitory slave trade acts. These negroes were never taken from Africa, or brought to the United States in contravention of those acts. When the Amistad arrived she was in possession of the negroes, asserting their freedom; and in no sense could they possibly intend to import themselves here, as [*597] slaves, or for sale as slaves. In this view of the matter, that part of the decree of the District Court is unmaintainable, and must be reversed.

The view which has [***161] been thus taken of this case, upon the merits, under the first point, renders it wholly unnecessary for us to give any opinion upon the other point, as to the right of the United States to intervene in this case in the manner already stated. We dismiss this, therefore, as well as several minor points made at the argument.

As to the claim of Lieutenant Gedney for the salvage service, it is understood that the United States do not now desire to interpose any obstacle to the allowance of it, if it is deemed reasonable by the Court. It was a highly meritorious and useful service to the proprietors of the ship and cargo; and such as, by the general principles of maritime law, is always deemed a just foundation for salvage. The rate allowed by the Court, does not seem to us to have been beyond the exercise of a sound discretion, under the very peculiar and embarrassing circumstances of the case.

Upon the whole, our opinion is, that the decree of the Circuit Court, affirming that of the District Court, ought to be affirmed, except so far as it directs the negroes to be delivered to the President, to be transported to Africa, in pursuance of the act of the 3d of March, 1819; and, as to [***162] this, it ought to be reversed: and that the said negroes be declared to be free, and be dismissed from the custody of the Court, and go without day.

DISSENT BY: BALDWIN

DISSENT

Mr. Jusitce BALDWIN dissented.

This cause came on to be heard on the transcript of the record from the Circuit Court of the United States, for the District of Connecticut, and was argued by counsel. On consideration whereof, it is the opinion of this Court, that there is error in that part of the decree of the Circuit Court, affirming the decree of the District Court, which ordered the said negroes to be delivered to the President of the United States, to be transported to Africa, in pursuance of the act of Congress, of the 3d of March, 1819; and that, as to that part, it ought to be reversed: and, in all other respects, that the said decree of the [*598] Circuit Court ought to be affirmed. It is therefore ordered adjudged, and decreed by this Court, that the decree of the said Circuit Court be, and the same is hereby, affirmed, except as to the part aforesaid, and as to that part, that it be reversed; and that the cause be remanded to the Circuit Court, with directions to enter, in lieu of that part, a decree, [***163] that the said negroes be, and are hereby, declared to be free, and that they be dismissed from the custody of the Court, and be discharged from the suit and go thereof quit without day.

APPENDIX D

LEXSEE 381 U.S. 479
GRISWOLD ET AL. v. CONNECTICUT
No. 496
SUPREME COURT OF THE UNITED STATES
381 U.S. 479; 85 S. Ct. 1678; 14 L. Ed. 2d 510; 1965 U.S. LEXIS 2282
March 29, 1965, Argued
June 7, 1965, Decided

PRIOR HISTORY: APPEAL FROM THE SUPREME COURT OF ERRORS OF CONNECTICUT.
DISPOSITION: *151 Conn. 544, 200 A. 2d 479*, reversed.

SUMMARY:

A Connecticut statute made the use of contraceptives a criminal offense. The executive and medical directors of the Planned Parenthood League of Connecticut were convicted in the Circuit Court for the Sixth Circuit in New Haven, Connecticut, on a charge of having violated the statute as accessories by giving information, instruction, and advice to married persons as to the means of preventing conception. The Appellate Division of the Circuit Court affirmed and its judgment was affirmed by the *Supreme Court of Errors of Connecticut. (151 Conn 544, 200 A2d 479.)*

On appeal, the Supreme Court of the United States reversed. In an opinion by Douglas, J., expressing the views of five members of the Court, it was held that (1) the defendants had standing to attack the statute, and (2) the statute was invalid as an unconstitutional invasion of the right of privacy of married persons.

Goldberg, J., with whom Warren, Ch.J., and Brennan, J., concurred, joined the opinion of the Court, elaborating in a separate opinion the view that the *Fourteenth Amendment* concept of liberty protects those personal rights that are fundamental, and is not confined to the specific terms of the *Bill of Rights*.

Harlan, J., concurred in the result, expressing the view that the statute violated basic values implicit in the concept of ordered liberty.

White, J., also concurred in the result, on the ground that the statute as applied to married couples deprived them of "liberty" without due process of law, as that concept is used in the *Fourteenth Amendment*.

Black and Stewart, JJ., dissented in separate opinions, each joining in the other's opinion. They expressed the view that the statute violated no provision of the Federal Constitution, Black, J., particularly emphasizing that there is no constitutional right of privacy.

COUNSEL: Thomas I. Emerson argued the cause for appellants. With him on the briefs was Catherine G. Roraback.

Joseph B. Clark argued the cause for appellee. With him on the brief was Julius Maretz.

Briefs of amici curiae, urging reversal, were filed by Whitney North Seymour and Eleanor M. Fox for Dr. John M. Adams et al.; by Morris L. Ernst, Harriet F. Pilpel and Nancy F. Wechsler for the Planned Parenthood Federation of America, Inc.; by Alfred L. Scanlon for the Catholic Council on Civil Liberties, and by Rhoda H. Karpatkin, Melvin L. Wulf and Jerome E. Caplan for the American Civil Liberties Union et al.

JUDGES: Warren, Black, Douglas, Clark, Harlan, Brennan, Stewart, White, Goldberg

OPINION BY: DOUGLAS

OPINION

[*480] [***512] [**1679] MR. JUSTICE DOUGLAS delivered the opinion of the Court.

Appellant Griswold is Executive Director of the Planned Parenthood League of Connecticut. Appellant Buxton is a licensed physician and a professor at the Yale Medical School who served as Medical Director for the League at its Center in New Haven—a center open and operating from November 1 to November 10, 1961, when appellants were arrested.

They gave information, instruction, and medical advice to *married persons* as to the means of preventing conception. They examined the wife and prescribed the best contraceptive device or material for her use. Fees were usually charged, although some couples were serviced free.

The statutes whose constitutionality is involved in this appeal are §§ 53-32 and *54-196* of the General Statutes of Connecticut (1958 rev.). The former provides:

"Any person who uses any drug, medicinal article or instrument for the purpose of preventing conception shall be fined not less than fifty dollars or imprisoned not less than sixty days nor more than one year or be both fined and imprisoned."

Section 54-196 provides:

"Any person who assists, abets, counsels, causes, hires or commands another to commit any offense may be prosecuted and punished as if he were the principal offender."

The appellants were found guilty as accessories and fined $ 100 each, against the claim that the accessory statute as so applied violated the *Fourteenth Amendment*. The Appellate Division of the Circuit Court affirmed. The Supreme Court of Errors affirmed that judgment. *151 Conn. 544, 200 A. 2d 479*. We noted probable jurisdiction. *379 U.S. 926*.

[*481] [***LEdHR1] [1] [***LEdHR2] [2]We think that appellants have standing to raise the constitutional rights of the married people with whom they had a professional relationship. *Tileston v. Ullman, 318 U.S. 44*, is different, for there the plaintiff seeking to represent others asked for a declaratory judgment. In that situation we thought that the requirements [***513] of standing should be strict, lest the standards of "case or controversy" in Article III of the Constitution become blurred. Here those doubts [**1680] are removed by reason of a criminal conviction for serving married couples in violation of an aiding-and-abetting statute. Certainly the accessory should have standing to assert that the offense which he is charged with assisting is not, or cannot constitutionally be, a crime.

This case is more akin to *Truax v. Raich, 239 U.S. 33*, where an employee was permitted to assert the rights of his employer; to *Pierce v. Society of Sisters, 268 U.S. 510*, where the owners of private schools were entitled to assert the rights of potential pupils and their parents; and to *Barrows v. Jackson, 346 U.S. 249*, where a white defendant, party to a racially restrictive covenant, who was being sued for damages by the covenantors because she had conveyed her property to Negroes, was allowed to raise the issue that enforcement of the covenant violated the rights of prospective Negro purchasers to equal protection, although no Negro was a party to the suit. And see *Meyer v. Nebraska, 262 U.S. 390*; *Adler v. Board of Education, 342 U.S. 485*; *NAACP v. Alabama, 357 U.S. 449*; *NAACP v. Button, 371 U.S. 415*. The rights of husband and wife, pressed here, are likely to be diluted or adversely affected unless those rights are considered in a suit involving those who have this kind of confidential relation to them.

[***LEdHR3] [3]Coming to the merits, we are met with a wide range of questions that implicate the *Due Process Clause of the Fourteenth Amendment*. Overtones of some arguments [*482] suggest that *Lochner v. New York, 198 U.S. 45*, should be our guide. But we decline that invitation as we did in *West Coast Hotel Co. v. Parrish, 300 U.S. 379*; *Olsen v. Nebraska, 313 U.S. 236*; *Lincoln Union v. Northwestern Co., 335 U.S. 525*; *Williamson v. Lee Optical Co., 348 U.S. 483*; *Giboney v. Empire Storage Co., 336 U.S. 490*. We do not sit as a super-legislature to determine the wisdom, need, and propriety of laws that touch economic problems, business affairs, or social conditions. This law, however, operates directly on an intimate relation of husband and wife and their physician's role in one aspect of that relation.

The association of people is not mentioned in the Constitution nor in the *Bill of Rights*. The right to educate a child in a school of the parents' choice—whether public or private or parochial—is also not mentioned. Nor is the right to study any particular subject or any foreign language. Yet the *First Amendment* has been construed to include certain of those rights.

[***LEdHR4] [4] [***LEdHR5] [5] [***LEdHR6] [6]By *Pierce v. Society of Sisters, supra*, the right to educate one's children as one chooses is made applicable to the States by the force of the *First* and *Fourteenth Amendments*. By *Meyer v. Nebraska, supra*, the same dignity is given the right to study the German language [***514] in a private school. In other words, the State may not, consistently with the spirit of the *First Amendment*, contract the spectrum of available knowledge. The right of freedom of speech and press includes not only the right to utter or to print, but the right to distribute, the right to receive, the right to read (*Martin v. Struthers, 319 U.S. 141, 143)* and freedom of inquiry, freedom of thought, and freedom to teach (see *Wieman v. Updegraff, 344 U.S. 183, 195)*—indeed the freedom of the entire university community. *Sweezy v. New Hampshire, 354 U.S. 234, 249-250, 261-263*; *Barenblatt v. United States, 360 U.S. 109, 112*; [**1681] *Baggett v. Bullitt, 377 U.S. 360, 369*. Without [*483] those peripheral rights the specific rights would be less secure. And so we reaffirm the principle of the *Pierce* and the *Meyer* cases.

[***LEdHR7] [7]

In *NAACP v. Alabama, 357 U.S. 449, 462*, we protected the "freedom to associate and privacy in one's associations," noting that freedom of association was a peripheral *First Amendment* right. Disclosure of membership lists of a constitutionally valid association, we held, was invalid "as entailing the likelihood of a substantial restraint upon the exercise by petitioner's members of their right to freedom of association." *Ibid*. In other words, the *First Amendment* has a penumbra where privacy is protected from governmental intrusion. In like context, we have protected forms of "association" that are not political in the customary sense but pertain to the social, legal, and economic benefit of the members. *NAACP v. Button, 371 U.S. 415, 430-431*. In *Schware v. Board of Bar Examiners, 353 U.S. 232*, we held it not permissible to bar a lawyer from practice, because he had once been a member of the Communist Party. The man's "association with that Party" was not shown to be "anything more than a political faith in a political party" (*id., at 244*) and was not action of a kind proving bad moral character. *Id., at 245-246*.

[***LEdHR8] [8] [***LEdHR9] [9]Those cases involved more than the "right of assembly"—a right that extends to all irrespective of their race or ideology. *De Jonge v. Oregon, 299 U.S. 353*. The right of "association," like the right of belief (*Board of Education v. Barnette, 319 U.S. 624*), is more than the right to attend a meeting; it includes the right to express one's attitudes or philosophies by membership in a group or by affiliation with it or by other lawful means. Association in that context is a form of expression of opinion; and while it is not expressly included in the *First Amendment* its existence is necessary in making the express guarantees fully meaningful.

[*484] [***LEdHR10] [10]The foregoing cases suggest that specific guarantees in the *Bill of Rights* have penumbras, formed by emanations from those guarantees that help give them life and substance. See *Poe v. Ullman, 367 U.S. 497, 516-522* (dissenting opinion). Various guarantees create zones of privacy. The right of association contained in the penumbra [***515] of the *First Amendment* is one, as we have seen. The *Third Amendment* in its prohibition against the quartering of soldiers "in any house" in time of peace without the consent of the owner is another facet of that privacy. The *Fourth Amendment* explicitly affirms the "right of the people to be secure in their persons, houses, papers, and effects, against unreasonable searches and seizures." The *Fifth Amendment* in its *Self-Incrimination Clause* enables the citizen to create a zone of privacy which government may not force him to surrender to his detriment. The *Ninth Amendment* provides: "The enumeration in the Constitution, of certain rights, shall not be construed to deny or disparage others retained by the people."

The *Fourth* and *Fifth Amendments* were described in *Boyd v. United States, 116 U.S. 616, 630*, as protection against all governmental invasions "of the sanctity of a man's home and the privacies of life." * We [**1682] recently referred [*485] in *Mapp v. Ohio, 367 U.S. 643, 656*, to the *Fourth Amendment* as creating a "right to privacy, no less important than any other right carefully and particularly reserved to the people." See Beaney, The Constitutional Right to Privacy, 1962 Sup. Ct. Rev. 212; Griswold, The Right to be Let Alone, 55 Nw. U. L. Rev. 216 (1960).

* The Court said in full about this right of privacy:
"The principles laid down in this opinion [by Lord Camden in *Entick* v. *Carrington*, 19 How. St. Tr. 1029] affect the very essence of constitutional liberty and security. They reach farther than the concrete form of the case then before the court, with its adventitious circumstances; they apply to all invasions on the part of the government and its employes of the sanctity of a man's home and the privacies of life. It is not the breaking of his doors, and the rummaging of his drawers, that constitutes the essence of the of-

fence; but it is the invasion of his indefeasible right of personal security, personal liberty and private property, where that right has never been forfeited by his conviction of some public offence, —it is the invasion of this sacred right which underlies and constitutes the essence of Lord Camden's judgment. Breaking into a house and opening boxes and drawers are circumstances of aggravation; but any forcible and compulsory extortion of a man's own testimony or of his private papers to be used as evidence to convict him of crime or to forfeit his goods, is within the condemnation of that judgment. In this regard the *Fourth* and *Fifth Amendments* run almost into each other." *116 U.S., at 630.*

We have had many controversies over these penumbral rights of "privacy and repose." See, *e. g., Breard v. Alexandria, 341 U.S. 622, 626, 644; Public Utilities Comm'n v. Pollak, 343 U.S. 451; Monroe v. Pape, 365 U.S. 167; Lanza v. New York, 370 U.S. 139; Frank v. Maryland, 359 U.S. 360; Skinner v. Oklahoma, 316 U.S. 535, 541.* These cases bear witness that the right of privacy which presses for recognition here is a legitimate one.

[***LEdHR11] [11] [***LEdHR12] [12]The present case, then, concerns a relationship lying within the zone of privacy created by several fundamental constitutional guarantees. And it concerns a law which, in forbidding the *use* of contraceptives rather than regulating their manufacture or sale, seeks to achieve its goals by means having a maximum destructive impact upon that relationship. Such a law cannot [***516] stand in light of the familiar principle, so often applied by this Court, that a "governmental purpose to control or prevent activities constitutionally subject to state regulation may not be achieved by means which sweep unnecessarily broadly and thereby invade the area of protected freedoms." *NAACP v. Alabama, 377 U.S. 288, 307.* Would we allow the police to search the sacred precincts of marital bedrooms for telltale signs of the use of contraceptives? The [*486] very idea is repulsive to the notions of privacy surrounding the marriage relationship.

We deal with a right of privacy older than the *Bill of Rights*—older than our political parties, older than our school system. Marriage is a coming together for better or for worse, hopefully enduring, and intimate to the degree of being sacred. It is an association that promotes a way of life, not causes; a harmony in living, not political faiths; a bilateral loyalty, not commercial or social projects. Yet it is an association for as noble a purpose as any involved in our prior decisions.

Reversed.

CONCUR BY: GOLDBERG; HARLAN; WHITE

CONCUR

MR. JUSTICE GOLDBERG, whom THE CHIEF JUSTICE and MR. JUSTICE BRENNAN join, concurring.

I agree with the Court that Connecticut's birth-control law unconstitutionally intrudes upon the right of marital privacy, and I join in its opinion and judgment. Although I have not accepted the view that "due process" as used in the *Fourteenth Amendment* incorporates all of the first eight Amendments (see my concurring opinion in *Pointer v. Texas, 380 U.S. 400, 410,* [**1683] and the dissenting opinion of MR. JUSTICE BRENNAN in *Cohen v. Hurley, 366 U.S. 117, 154)*, I do agree that the concept of liberty protects those personal rights that are fundamental, and is not confined to the specific terms of the *Bill of Rights*. My conclusion that the concept of liberty is not so restricted and that it embraces the right of marital privacy though that right is not mentioned explicitly in the Constitution[1] is supported both [***517] by numerous [*487] decisions of this Court, referred to in the Court's opinion, and by the language and history of the *Ninth Amendment*. In reaching the conclusion that the right of marital privacy is protected, as being within the protected penumbra of specific guarantees of the *Bill of Rights*, the Court refers to the *Ninth Amendment, ante*, at 484. I add these words to emphasize the relevance of that Amendment to the Court's holding.

1 My Brother STEWART dissents on the ground that he "can find no . . . general right of privacy in the *Bill of Rights*, in any other part of the Constitution, or in any case ever before decided by this Court." *Post*, at 530. He would require a more explicit guarantee than the one which the Court derives from several constitutional amendments. This Court, however, has never held that the *Bill of Rights* or the *Fourteenth Amendment* protects only those rights that the Constitution specifically mentions by name. See, e. g., *Bolling v. Sharpe, 347 U.S. 497; Aptheker v. Secretary of State, 378 U.S. 500; Kent v. Dulles, 357 U.S. 116; Carrington v. Rash, 380 U.S. 89, 96; Schware v. Board of Bar Examiners, 353 U.S. 232; NAACP v. Alabama, 360 U.S. 240; Pierce v. Society of Sisters, 268 U.S. 510; Meyer v. Nebraska, 262 U.S. 390*. To the contrary, this Court, for example, in *Bolling v. Sharpe, supra*, while recognizing that the *Fifth Amendment* does not contain the "explicit safeguard" of an *equal protection clause, id., at 499*, nevertheless derived an equal protection principle from that Amendment's Due Process Clause. And

in *Schware v. Board of Bar Examiners, supra*, the Court held that the *Fourteenth Amendment* protects from arbitrary state action the right to pursue an occupation, such as the practice of law.

The Court stated many years ago that the Due Process Clause protects those liberties that are "so rooted in the traditions and conscience of our people as to be ranked as fundamental." *Snyder v. Massachusetts, 291 U.S. 97, 105.* In *Gitlow v. New York, 268 U.S. 652, 666,* the Court said:

"For present purposes we may and do assume that freedom of speech and of the press—which are protected by the *First Amendment* from abridgment by Congress—are among the *fundamental* personal rights and 'liberties' protected by the *due process clause of the Fourteenth Amendment* from impairment by the States." (Emphasis added.)

[*488] And, in *Meyer v. Nebraska, 262 U.S. 390, 399,* the Court, referring to the *Fourteenth Amendment*, stated:

"While this Court has not attempted to define with exactness the liberty thus guaranteed, the term has received much consideration and some of the included things have been definitely stated. Without doubt, it denotes not merely freedom from bodily restraint but also [for example,] the right...to marry, establish a home and bring up children...."

This Court, in a series of decisions, has held that the *Fourteenth Amendment* absorbs and applies to the States those specifics of the first eight amendments which express fundamental personal [**1684] rights.[2] The language and history of the *Ninth Amendment* reveal that the Framers of the Constitution believed that there are additional fundamental rights, protected from governmental infringement, which exist alongside those fundamental rights specifically mentioned in the first eight constitutional amendments.

2 See, *e. g., Chicago, B. & Q. R. Co.* v. *Chicago, 166 U.S. 226; Gitlow v. New York, supra; Cantwell v. Connecticut, 310 U.S. 296; Wolf v. Colorado, 338 U.S. 25; Robinson v. California, 370 U.S. 660; Gideon v. Wainwright, 372 U.S. 335; Malloy v. Hogan, 378 U.S. 1; Pointer v. Texas, supra; Griffin v. California, 380 U.S. 609.*

The *Ninth Amendment* reads, "The enumeration in the Constitution, of certain rights, shall not be construed to deny or disparage others retained by the people." The Amendment is almost entirely the work of James Madison. It was introduced in Congress by him and passed the House and Senate with little or no debate and virtually no change in language. It was proffered to quiet expressed fears that a bill of specifically enumerated rights[3] could not be sufficiently broad to cover all essential [*489] rights and that the specific mention of certain rights [***518] would be interpreted as a denial that others were protected.[4]

3   Madison himself had previously pointed out the dangers of inaccuracy resulting from the fact that "no language is so copious as to supply words and phrases for every complex idea." The Federalist, No. 37 (Cooke ed. 1961), at 236.

4   Alexander Hamilton was opposed to a *bill of rights* on the ground that it was unnecessary because the Federal Government was a government of delegated powers and it was not granted the power to intrude upon fundamental personal rights. The Federalist, No. 84 (Cooke ed. 1961), at 578-579. He also argued, "I go further, and affirm that bills of rights, in the sense and in the extent in which they are contended for, are not only unnecessary in the proposed constitution, but would even be dangerous. They would contain various exceptions to powers which are not granted; and on this very account, would afford a colourable pretext to claim more than were granted. For why declare that things shall not be done which there is no power to do? Why for instance, should it be said, that the liberty of the press shall not be restrained, when no power is given by which restrictions may be imposed? I will not contend that such a provision would confer a regulating power; but it is evident that it would furnish, to men disposed to usurp, a plausible pretence for claiming that power." Id., at 579.

The *Ninth Amendment* and the *Tenth Amendment*, which provides, "The powers not delegated to the United States by the Constitution, nor prohibited by it to the States, are reserved to the States respectively, or to the people," were apparently also designed in part to meet the above-quoted argument of Hamilton.

In presenting the proposed Amendment, Madison said:

"It has been objected also against a *bill of rights*, that, by enumerating particular exceptions to the grant of power, it would disparage those rights which were not placed in that enumeration; and it might follow by implication, that those rights which were not singled out, were intended to be assigned into the hands of the General Government, and were consequently insecure. This is one of the most plausible arguments I have ever heard urged against the admission of a *bill of rights* into this system; but, I conceive, that it may be guarded against. I have attempted it, as gentlemen may see by turning to the [*490] last clause of the fourth resolution [the *Ninth Amendment*]." I Annals of Congress 439 (Gales and Seaton ed. 1834).

[**1685] Mr. Justice Story wrote of this argument against a *bill of rights* and the meaning of the *Ninth Amendment*:

"In regard to...[a] suggestion, that the affirmance of certain rights might disparage others, or might lead to argumentative implications in favor of other powers, it might be sufficient to say that such a course of reasoning could never be sustained upon any solid basis.... But a conclusive answer is, that such an attempt may be interdicted (as it has been) by a positive declaration in such a *bill of rights* that the enumeration of certain rights shall not be construed to deny or disparage others retained by the people." II Story, Commentaries on the Constitution of the United States 626-627 (5th ed. 1891).

He further stated, referring to the *Ninth Amendment*:

"This clause was manifestly introduced to prevent any perverse or ingenious misapplication of the well-known maxim, that an affirmation in particular cases implies a negation in all others; and, *e converso*, that a negation in particular cases implies an affirmation in all others." *Id., at 651.*

These statements of Madison and Story make clear that the Framers did not intend that the first eight amendments be construed to exhaust the basic and fundamental rights which the Constitution guaranteed to the people.[5]

5 The *Tenth Amendment* similarly made clear that the States and the people retained all those powers not expressly delegated to the Federal Government.

While [***519] this Court has had little occasion to interpret the *Ninth Amendment*, [6] "it cannot be presumed that any [*491] clause in the constitution is intended to be without effect." *Marbury v. Madison, 1 Cranch 137, 174.* In interpreting the Constitution, "real effect should be given to all the words it uses." *Myers v. United States, 272 U.S. 52, 151.* The *Ninth Amendment to the Constitution* may be regarded by some as a recent discovery and may be forgotten by others, but since 1791 it has been a basic part of the Constitution which we are sworn to uphold. To hold that a right so basic and fundamental and so deep-rooted in our society as the right of privacy in marriage may be infringed because that right is not guaranteed in so many words by the first eight amendments to the Constitution is to ignore the *Ninth Amendment* and to give it no effect whatsoever. Moreover, a judicial construction that this fundamental right is not protected by the Constitution because [**1686] it is not mentioned in explicit terms by one of the first eight amendments or elsewhere in the Constitution would violate the *Ninth Amendment*, which specifically states that [*492] "the enumeration in the Constitution, of certain rights, shall not be *construed* to deny or disparage others retained by the people." (Emphasis added.)

6 This Amendment has been referred to as "The Forgotten *Ninth Amendment*," in a book with that title by Bennett B.

Patterson (1955). Other commentary on the *Ninth Amendment* includes Redlich, Are There "Certain Rights...Retained by the People"? 37 N. Y. U. L. Rev. 787 (1962), and Kelsey, The *Ninth Amendment of the Federal Constitution*, 11 Ind. L. J. 309 (1936). As far as I am aware, until today this Court has referred to the *Ninth Amendment* only in *United Public Workers v. Mitchell, 330 U.S. 75, 94-95*; *Tennessee Electric Power Co. v. TVA, 306 U.S. 118, 143-144*; and *Ashwander v. TVA, 297 U.S. 288, 330-331*. See also *Calder v. Bull*, 3 Dall. 386, 388; *Loan Assn. v. Topeka, 20 Wall. 655, 662-663*.

In *United Public Workers v. Mitchell, supra, at 94-95*, the Court stated: "We accept appellants' contention that the nature of political rights reserved to the people by the *Ninth* and *Tenth Amendments* [is] involved. The right claimed as inviolate may be stated as the right of a citizen to act as a party official or worker to further his own political views. Thus we have a measure of interference by the Hatch Act and the Rules with what otherwise would be the freedom of the civil servant under the *First, Ninth* and *Tenth Amendments*. And, if we look upon due process as a guarantee of freedom in those fields, there is a corresponding impairment of that right under the *Fifth Amendment*."

A dissenting opinion suggests that my interpretation of the *Ninth Amendment* somehow "broaden[s] the powers of this Court." *Post*, at 520. With all due respect, I believe that it misses the import of what I am saying. I do not take the position of my Brother BLACK in his dissent in *Adamson v. California, 332 U.S. 46, 68*, that the entire *Bill of Rights* is incorporated in the *Fourteenth Amendment*, and I do not mean to imply that the *Ninth Amendment* is applied against the States by the Fourteenth. Nor do I mean to state that the *Ninth Amendment* constitutes an independent source of rights protected from infringement by either the States or the Federal Government. Rather, the *Ninth Amendment* shows a belief of the Constitution's authors that fundamental rights exist that are not expressly enumerated in the first eight amendments and an intent that the list of rights included there not be [***520] deemed exhaustive. As any student of this Court's opinions knows, this Court has held, often unanimously, that the *Fifth* and *Fourteenth Amendments* protect certain fundamental personal liberties from abridgment by the Federal Government or the States. See, *e.g., Bolling v. Sharpe, 347 U.S. 497*; *Aptheker v. Secretary of State, 378 U.S. 500*; *Kent v. Dulles, 357 U.S. 116*; *Cantwell v. Connecticut, 310 U.S. 296*; *NAACP v. Alabama, 357 U.S. 449*; *Gideon v. Wainwright, 372 U.S. 335*; *New York Times Co. v. Sullivan, 376 U.S. 254*. The *Ninth Amendment* simply shows the intent of the Constitution's authors that other fundamental personal rights should not be denied such protection or disparaged in any other way simply because they are not specifically listed in the first eight constitutional amendments. I do not see how this broadens the authority [*493] of the Court; rather it serves to support what this Court has been doing in protecting fundamental rights.

Nor am I turning somersaults with history in arguing that the *Ninth Amendment* is relevant in a case dealing with a *State's* infringement of a fundamental right. While the *Ninth Amendment*—and indeed the entire *Bill of Rights*—originally concerned restrictions upon *federal* power, the subsequently enacted *Fourteenth Amendment* prohibits the States as well from abridging fundamental personal liberties. And, the *Ninth Amendment*, in indicating that not all such liberties are specifically mentioned in the first eight amendments, is surely relevant in showing the existence of other fundamental personal rights, now protected from state, as well as federal, infringement. In sum, the *Ninth Amendment* simply lends strong support to the view that the "liberty" protected by the *Fifth* and *Fourteenth Amendments* from infringement by the Federal Government or the States is not restricted to rights specifically mentioned in the first eight amendments. Cf. *United Public Workers v. Mitchell, 330 U.S. 75, 94-95.*

In determining which rights are fundamental, judges are not left at large to decide cases in light of their personal and private notions. Rather, they must look to the "traditions and [collective] conscience of our people" to determine whether a principle is "so rooted [there]...as to be ranked as fundamental." *Snyder v. Massachusetts, 291 U.S. 97, 105.* The inquiry is whether a right involved "is of such a character that it cannot be denied without violating those 'fundamental principles of liberty and justice [**1687] which lie at the base of all our civil and political institutions'...." *Powell v. Alabama, 287 U.S. 45, 67.* "Liberty" also "gains content from the emanations of...specific [constitutional] guarantees" and "from experience with the requirements of a free society." *Poe* [*494] *v. Ullman, 367 U.S. 497, 517* (dissenting opinion of MR. JUSTICE DOUGLAS).[7]

7 In light of the tests enunciated in these cases it cannot be said that a judge's responsibility to determine whether a right is basic and fundamental in this sense vests him with unrestricted personal discretion. In fact, a hesitancy to allow too broad a discretion was a substantial reason leading me to conclude in *Pointer v. Texas, supra, at 413-414,* that those rights absorbed by the *Fourteenth Amendment* and applied to the States because they are fundamental apply with equal force and to the same extent against both federal and state governments. In *Pointer* I said that the contrary view would require "this Court to make the ex-

tremely subjective and excessively discretionary determination as to whether a practice, forbidden the Federal Government by a fundamental constitutional guarantee, is, as viewed in the factual circumstances surrounding each individual case, sufficiently repugnant to the notion of due process as to be forbidden the States." *Id., at 413.*

I [***521] agree fully with the Court that, applying these tests, the right of privacy is a fundamental personal right, emanating "from the totality of the constitutional scheme under which we live." *Id., at 521.* Mr. Justice Brandeis, dissenting in *Olmstead v. United States, 277 U.S. 438, 478,* comprehensively summarized the principles underlying the Constitution's guarantees of privacy:

"The protection guaranteed by the [Fourth and Fifth] Amendments is much broader in scope. The makers of our Constitution undertook to secure conditions favorable to the pursuit of happiness. They recognized the significance of man's spiritual nature, of his feelings and of his intellect. They knew that only a part of the pain, pleasure and satisfactions of life are to be found in material things. They sought to protect Americans in their beliefs, their thoughts, their emotions and their sensations. They conferred, as against the Government, the right to be let alone—the most comprehensive of rights and the right most valued by civilized men."

[*495] The Connecticut statutes here involved deal with a particularly important and sensitive area of privacy—that of the marital relation and the marital home. This Court recognized in *Meyer v. Nebraska, supra,* that the right "to marry, establish a home and bring up children" was an essential part of the liberty guaranteed by the *Fourteenth Amendment. 262 U.S., at 399.* In *Pierce v. Society of Sisters, 268 U.S. 510,* the Court held unconstitutional an Oregon Act which forbade parents from sending their children to private schools because such an act "unreasonably interferes with the liberty of parents and guardians to direct the upbringing and education of children under their control." *268 U.S., at 534-535.* As this Court said in *Prince v. Massachusetts, 321 U.S. 158, at 166,* the *Meyer* and *Pierce* decisions "have respected the private realm of family life which the state cannot enter."

I agree with MR. JUSTICE HARLAN'S statement in his dissenting opinion in *Poe v. Ullman, 367 U.S. 497, 551-552*: "Certainly the safeguarding of the home does not follow merely from the sanctity of property rights. The home derives its pre-eminence as the seat of family life. And the integrity of that life is something so fundamental that it has been found to draw to its protection the principles of more than one explicitly granted [**1688] Constitutional right.... Of this whole 'private realm of family life' it is difficult to imagine what is more private or more intimate than a husband and wife's marital relations."

[***522] The entire fabric of the Constitution and the purposes that clearly underlie its specific guarantees demonstrate that the rights to marital privacy and to marry and raise a family are of similar order and magnitude as the fundamental rights specifically protected.

Although the Constitution does not speak in so many words of the right of privacy in marriage, I cannot believe that it offers these fundamental rights no protection. The fact that no particular provision of the Constitution [*496] explicitly forbids the State from disrupting the traditional relation of the family—a relation as old and as fundamental as our entire civilization—surely does not show that the Government was meant to have the power to do so. Rather, as the *Ninth Amendment* expressly recognizes, there are fundamental personal rights such as this one, which are protected from abridgment by the Government though not specifically mentioned in the Constitution.

My Brother STEWART, while characterizing the Connecticut birth control law as "an uncommonly silly law," *post*, at 527, would nevertheless let it stand on the ground that it is not for the courts to "'substitute their social and economic beliefs for the judgment of legislative bodies, who are elected to pass laws.'" *Post*, at 528. Elsewhere, I have stated that "while I quite agree with Mr. Justice Brandeis that...'a...State may...serve as a laboratory; and try novel social and economic experiments,' *New State Ice Co. v. Liebmann, 285 U.S. 262, 280, 311* (dissenting opinion), I do not believe that this includes the power to experiment with the fundamental liberties of citizens...."[8] The vice of the dissenters' views is that it would permit such experimentation by the States in the area of the fundamental personal rights of its citizens. I cannot agree that the Constitution grants such power either to the States or to the Federal Government.

8 *Pointer v. Texas, supra, at 413.* See also the discussion of my Brother DOUGLAS, *Poe v. Ullman, supra, at 517-518* (dissenting opinion).

The logic of the dissents would sanction federal or state legislation that seems to me even more plainly unconstitutional than the statute before us. Surely the Government, absent a showing of a compelling subordinating state interest, could not decree that all husbands and wives must be sterilized after two children have been born [*497] to them. Yet by their reasoning such an invasion of marital privacy would not be subject to constitutional challenge because, while it might be "silly," no provision of the Constitution specifically prevents the Government from curtailing the marital right to bear children and raise a family. While it may shock some of my Brethren that the Court today holds that the Constitution protects the right of marital privacy, in my view it is far more shocking to believe that the personal liberty guaranteed by the Constitution does not include protection against such totalitarian limitation of family size, which is at complete variance with our constitutional concepts. Yet, if upon a showing of a slender basis of rationality, a law outlawing voluntary birth control by married persons is valid, then, by the same reasoning, a law requiring compulsory birth control also would seem to [***523] be valid. In my view, however, both types of law would unjustifiably intrude upon rights of marital privacy which are constitutionally protected.

In a long series of cases this Court has held that where fundamental personal liberties are involved, they may not be [**1689] abridged by the States simply on a showing that a regulatory statute has some rational relationship to the effectuation of a proper state purpose. "Where there is a significant encroachment upon personal liberty, the State may prevail only upon showing a subordinating interest which is compelling," *Bates v. Little Rock, 361 U.S. 516, 524*. The law must be shown "necessary, and not merely rationally related, to the accomplishment of a permissible state policy." *McLaughlin v. Florida, 379 U.S. 184, 196*. See *Schneider v. Irvington, 308 U.S. 147, 161*.

Although the Connecticut birth-control law obviously encroaches upon a fundamental personal liberty, the State does not show that the law serves any "subordinating [state] interest which is compelling" or that it is "necessary...[*498] to the accomplishment of a permissible state policy." The State, at most, argues that there is some rational relation between this statute and what is admittedly a legitimate subject of state concern—the discouraging of extra-marital relations. It says that preventing the use of birth-control devices by married persons helps prevent the indulgence by some in such extra-marital relations. The rationality of this justification is dubious, particularly in light of the admitted widespread availability to all persons in the State of Connecticut, unmarried as well as married, of birth-control devices for the prevention of disease, as distinguished from the prevention of conception, see *Tileston v. Ullman, 129 Conn. 84, 26 A. 2d 582*. But, in any event, it is clear that the state interest in safeguarding marital fidelity can be served by a more discriminately tailored statute, which does not, like the present one, sweep unnecessarily broadly, reaching far beyond the evil sought to be dealt with and intruding upon the privacy of all married couples. See *Aptheker v. Secretary of State, 378 U.S. 500, 514*; *NAACP v. Alabama, 377 U.S. 288, 307-308*; *McLaughlin v. Florida, supra, at 196*. Here, as elsewhere, "precision of regulation must be the touchstone in an area so closely touching our most precious freedoms."

NAACP v. Button, 371 U.S. 415, 438. The State of Connecticut does have statutes, the constitutionality of which is beyond doubt, which prohibit adultery and fornication. *See* Conn. Gen. Stat. §§ 53-218, 53-219 *et seq*. These statutes demonstrate that means for achieving the same basic purpose of protecting marital fidelity are available to Connecticut without the need to "invade the area of protected freedoms." *NAACP v. Alabama, supra, at 307*. See *McLaughlin v. Florida, supra, at 196*.

Finally, it should be said of the Court's holding today that it in no way interferes with a State's proper regulation [*499] of sexual promiscuity or misconduct. As my Brother HARLAN so well stated in his dissenting opinion in *Poe v. Ullman, supra, at 553*.

"Adultery, homosexuality and the like are sexual intimacies which the [***524] State forbids...but the intimacy of husband and wife is necessarily an essential and accepted feature of the institution of marriage, an institution which the State not only must allow, but which always and in every age it has fostered and protected. It is one thing when the State exerts its power either to forbid extra-marital sexuality...or to say who may marry, but it is quite another when, having acknowledged a marriage and the intimacies inherent in it, it undertakes to regulate by means of the criminal law the details of that intimacy."

[**1690] In sum, I believe that the right of privacy in the marital relation is fundamental and basic—a personal right "retained by the people" within the meaning of the *Ninth Amendment*. Connecticut cannot constitutionally abridge this fundamental right, which is protected by the *Fourteenth Amendment* from infringement by the States. I agree with the Court that petitioners' convictions must therefore be reversed.

MR. JUSTICE HARLAN, concurring in the judgment.

I fully agree with the judgment of reversal, but find myself unable to join the Court's opinion. The reason is that it seems to me to evince an approach to this case very much like that taken by my Brothers BLACK and STEWART in dissent, namely: the *Due Process Clause of the Fourteenth Amendment* does not touch this Connecticut statute unless the enactment is found to violate some right assured by the letter or penumbra of the *Bill of Rights*.

[*500] In other words, what I find implicit in the Court's opinion is that the "incorporation" doctrine may be used to *restrict* the reach of *Fourteenth Amendment* Due Process. For me this is just as unacceptable constitutional doctrine as is the use of the "incorporation" approach to *impose* upon the States all the requirements of the *Bill of Rights* as found in the provisions of the first eight amendments and in the decisions of this Court

interpreting them. See, *e. g.*, my concurring opinions in *Pointer v. Texas, 380 U.S. 400, 408*, and *Griffin v. California, 380 U.S. 609, 615*, and my dissenting opinion in *Poe v. Ullman, 367 U.S. 497, 522, at pp. 539-545*.

In my view, the proper constitutional inquiry in this case is whether this Connecticut statute infringes the *Due Process Clause of the Fourteenth Amendment* because the enactment violates basic values "implicit in the concept of ordered liberty," *Palko v. Connecticut, 302 U.S. 319, 325*. For reasons stated at length in my dissenting opinion in *Poe v. Ullman, supra*, I believe that it does. While the relevant inquiry may be aided by resort to one or more of the provisions of the *Bill of Rights*, it is not dependent on them or any of their radiations. The *Due Process Clause of the Fourteenth Amendment* stands, in my opinion, on its own bottom.

A further observation seems in order respecting the justification of my Brothers BLACK and STEWART for their "incorporation" approach to this case. Their approach does not rest on historical reasons, which are of course wholly lacking (*see* Fairman, Does the *Fourteenth Amendment* Incorporate the *Bill of Rights?* The Original Understanding, 2 Stan. L. Rev. 5 (1949)), but on the thesis that by limiting the content of the [***525] *Due Process Clause of the Fourteenth Amendment* to the protection of rights which can be found elsewhere in the Constitution, in this instance in the *Bill of Rights*, judges will thus be confined to "interpretation" of specific constitutional [*501] provisions, and will thereby be restrained from introducing their own notions of constitutional right and wrong into the "vague contours of the Due Process Clause." *Rochin v. California, 342 U.S. 165, 170.*

While I could not more heartily agree that judicial "self restraint" is an indispensable ingredient of sound constitutional adjudication, I do submit that the formula suggested for achieving it is more hollow than real. "Specific" provisions of the Constitution, no less than "due process," lend themselves as readily to "personal" interpretations by judges whose constitutional outlook is simply to keep the Constitution in supposed "tune with the times" (*post*, p. 522). Need one go further than to recall last Term's reapportionment cases, *Wesberry v. Sanders*, [**1691] *376 U.S. 1*, and *Reynolds v. Sims, 377 U.S. 533*, where a majority of the Court "interpreted" "by the People" (Art. I, § 2) and "equal protection" (*Amdt. 14*) to command "one person, one vote," an interpretation that was made in the face of irrefutable and still unanswered history to the contrary? See my dissenting opinions in those cases, *376 U.S., at 20; 377 U.S., at 589*.

Judicial self-restraint will not, I suggest, be brought about in the "due process" area by the historically unfounded incorporation formula long advanced by my Brother BLACK, and now in part espoused by my Brother

STEWART. It will be achieved in this area, as in other constitutional areas, only by continual insistence upon respect for the teachings of history, solid recognition of the basic values that underlie our society, and wise appreciation of the great roles that the doctrines of federalism and separation of powers have played in establishing and preserving American freedoms. See *Adamson v. California, 332 U.S. 46, 59* (Mr. Justice Frankfurter, concurring). Adherence to these principles will not, of course, obviate all constitutional differences of opinion among judges, nor should it. Their continued recognition [*502] will, however, go farther toward keeping most judges from roaming at large in the constitutional field than will the interpolation into the Constitution of an artificial and largely illusory restriction on the content of the Due Process Clause.*

* Indeed, my Brother BLACK, in arguing his thesis, is forced to lay aside a host of cases in which the Court has recognized fundamental rights in the *Fourteenth Amendment* without specific reliance upon the *Bill of Rights. Post*, p. 512, n. 4.

MR. JUSTICE WHITE, concurring in the judgment.

In my view this Connecticut law as applied to married couples deprives them of "liberty" without due process of law, as that concept is used in the *Fourteenth Amendment*. I therefore concur in the judgment of the Court reversing these convictions under Connecticut's aiding and abetting statute.

It would be unduly repetitious, and belaboring the obvious, to expound on the impact of this statute on the liberty guaranteed by the *Fourteenth* [***526] *Amendment* against arbitrary or capricious denials or on the nature of this liberty. Suffice it to say that this is not the first time this Court has had occasion to articulate that the liberty entitled to protection under the *Fourteenth Amendment* includes the right "to marry, establish a home and bring up children," *Meyer v. Nebraska, 262 U.S. 390, 399,* and "the liberty...to direct the upbringing and education of children," *Pierce v. Society of Sisters, 268 U.S. 510, 534-535,* and that these are among "the basic civil rights of man." *Skinner v. Oklahoma, 316 U.S. 535, 541.* These decisions affirm that there is a "realm of family life which the state cannot enter" without substantial justification. *Prince v. Massachusetts, 321 U.S. 158, 166.* Surely the right invoked in this case, to be free of regulation of the intimacies of [*503] the marriage relationship, "come[s] to this Court with a momentum for respect lacking when appeal is made to liberties which derive merely from shifting economic arrangements." *Kovacs v. Cooper, 336 U.S. 77, 95* (opinion of Frankfurter, J.).

The Connecticut anti-contraceptive statute deals rather substantially with [**1692] this relationship. For it forbids all married persons the right to use birth-control devices, regardless of whether their use is dictated by considerations of family planning, *Trubek v. Ullman, 147 Conn. 633, 165 A. 2d 158*, health, or indeed even of life itself. *Buxton v. Ullman, 147 Conn. 48, 156 A. 2d 508*. The anti-use statute, together with the general aiding and abetting statute, prohibits doctors from affording advice to married persons on proper and effective methods of birth control. *Tileston v. Ullman, 129 Conn. 84, 26 A. 2d 582*. And the clear effect of these statutes, as enforced, is to deny disadvantaged citizens of Connecticut, those without either adequate knowledge or resources to obtain private counseling, access to medical assistance and up-to-date information in respect to proper methods of birth control. *State v. Nelson, 126 Conn. 412, 11 A. 2d 856*; *State v. Griswold, 151 Conn. 544, 200 A. 2d 479*. In my view, a statute with these effects bears a substantial burden of justification when attacked under the Fourteenth Amendment. *Yick Wo v. Hopkins, 118 U.S. 356*; *Skinner v. Oklahoma, 316 U.S. 535*; *Schware v. Board of Bar Examiners, 353 U.S. 232*; *McLaughlin v. Florida, 379 U.S. 184, 192*.

An examination of the justification offered, however, cannot be avoided by saying that the Connecticut anti-use statute invades a protected area of privacy and association or that it demeans the marriage relationship. The nature of the right invaded is pertinent, to be sure, for statutes regulating sensitive areas of liberty do, under [*504] the cases of this Court, require "strict scrutiny," *Skinner v. Oklahoma, 316 U.S. 535, 541*, and "must be viewed in the light of less drastic means for achieving the same basic purpose." *Shelton v. Tucker, 364 U.S. 479, 488*. [***527] "Where there is a significant encroachment upon personal liberty, the State may prevail only upon showing a subordinating interest which is compelling." *Bates v. Little Rock, 361 U.S. 516, 524*. See also *McLaughlin v. Florida, 379 U.S. 184*. But such statutes, if reasonably necessary for the effectuation of a legitimate and substantial state interest, and not arbitrary or capricious in application, are not invalid under the Due Process Clause. *Zemel v. Rusk, 381 U.S. 1.* *

> * Dissenting opinions assert that the liberty guaranteed by the Due Process Clause is limited to a guarantee against unduly vague statutes and against procedural unfairness at trial. Under this view the Court is without authority to ascertain whether a challenged statute, or its application, has a permissible purpose and whether the manner of regulation bears a rational or justifying relationship to this purpose. A long line of cases makes very clear that this has not been the view of this Court. *Dent v. West Virginia, 129 U.S. 114*; *Jacobson v. Massachusetts, 197 U.S. 11*; *Douglas v. Noble, 261 U.S. 165*; *Meyer v. Nebraska, 262 U.S. 390*; *Pierce v. Society*

of Sisters, 268 U.S. 510; *Schware v. Board of Bar Examiners, 353 U.S. 232*; *Aptheker v. Secretary of State, 378 U.S. 500*; *Zemel v. Rusk, 381 U.S. 1.*

The traditional due process test was well articulated, and applied, in *Schware v. Board of Bar Examiners, supra*, a case which placed no reliance on the specific guarantees of the *Bill of Rights*. "A State cannot exclude a person from the practice of law or from any other occupation in a manner or for reasons that contravene the Due Process or *Equal Protection Clause of the Fourteenth Amendment. Dent v. West Virginia, 129 U.S. 114.* Cf. *Slochower v. Board of Education, 350 U.S. 551*; *Wieman v. Updegraff, 344 U.S. 183.* And see *Ex parte Secombe, 19 How. 9, 13*. A State can require high standards of qualification, such as good moral character or proficiency in its law, before it admits an applicant to the bar, but any qualification must have a rational connection with the applicant's fitness or capacity to practice law. *Douglas v. Noble, 261 U.S. 165*; *Cummings v. Missouri, 4 Wall. 277, 319-320*. Cf. *Nebbia v. New York, 291 U.S. 502*. Obviously an applicant could not be excluded merely because he was a Republican or a Negro or a member of a particular church. Even in applying permissible standards, officers of a State cannot exclude an applicant when there is no basis for their finding that he fails to meet these standards, or when their action is invidiously discriminatory." *353 U.S., at 238-239.* Cf. *Martin v. Walton, 368 U.S. 25, 26* (DOUGLAS, J., dissenting).

[*505] [**1693] As I read the opinions of the Connecticut courts and the argument of Connecticut in this Court, the State claims but one justification for its anti-use statute. Cf. *Allied Stores of Ohio v. Bowers, 358 U.S. 522, 530*; *Martin v. Walton, 368 U.S. 25, 28* (DOUGLAS, J., dissenting). There is no serious contention that Connecticut thinks the use of artificial or external methods of contraception immoral or unwise in itself, or that the anti-use statute is founded upon any policy of promoting population expansion. Rather, the statute is said to serve the State's policy against all forms of promiscuous or illicit sexual relationships, be they premarital or extramarital, concededly a permissible and legitimate legislative goal.

Without taking issue with the premise that the fear of conception operates as a deterrent to such relationships in addition to the criminal proscriptions Connecticut has [***528] against such conduct, I wholly fail to see how the ban on the use of contraceptives by married couples in any way reinforces the State's ban on illicit sexual relationships. See *Schware v. Board of Bar Examiners, 353 U.S. 232, 239*. Connecticut does not bar the importation or possession of contraceptive devices; they are not considered contraband material under state law, *State v. Certain Contraceptive Materials, 126 Conn. 428, 11 A. 2d 863*, and their availability in that State is not seriously disputed. The only way Connecticut seeks to limit or control the availability of such devices is through its general aiding and abetting statute whose operation in this context has [*506] been quite obviously ineffective and whose most serious use has been against birth-control clinics rendering advice to married, rather than unmarried, persons. Cf. *Yick Wo v. Hopkins, 118 U.S. 356*. Indeed, after over 80 years of the State's proscription of use, the legality of the sale of such devices to prevent disease has never been expressly passed upon, although it appears that sales have long occurred and have only infrequently been challenged. This "undeviating policy...throughout all the long years...bespeaks more than prosecutorial paralysis." *Poe v. Ullman, 367 U.S. 497, 502*. Moreover, it would appear that the sale of contraceptives to prevent disease is plainly legal under Connecticut law.

In these circumstances one is rather hard pressed to explain how the ban on use by married persons in any way prevents use of such devices by persons engaging in illicit sexual relations and thereby contributes to the State's policy against such relationships. Neither the state courts nor the State before the bar of this Court has tendered such an explanation. It is purely fanciful to believe that the broad proscription on use facilitates discovery of use by persons engaging in a prohibited relationship or for some other reason makes such use more unlikely and thus can be supported by any sort of administrative consideration. Perhaps the theory is that the flat ban on use prevents married people from possessing contraceptives and without the ready availability of such devices for use in the marital relationship, there [**1694] will be no or less temptation to use them in extramarital ones. This reasoning rests on the premise that married people will comply with the ban in regard to their marital relationship, notwithstanding total nonenforcement in this context and apparent nonenforcibility, but will not comply with criminal statutes prohibiting extramarital affairs and the anti-use statute in respect to illicit sexual relationships, a premise whose validity has not been [*507] demonstrated and whose intrinsic validity is not very evident. At most the broad ban is of marginal utility to the declared objective. A statute limiting its prohibition on use to persons engaging in the prohibited relationship would serve the end posited by Connecticut in the same way, and with the same effectiveness, or ineffectiveness, as the broad anti-use statute under attack in this case. I find nothing in this record justifying the sweeping scope of this statute, with its telling effect on the freedoms of married persons, and therefore conclude that it deprives such persons of liberty without due process of law.

DISSENT BY: BLACK; STEWART

DISSENT

[***529] MR. JUSTICE BLACK, with whom MR. JUSTICE STEWART joins, dissenting.

I agree with my Brother STEWART'S dissenting opinion. And like him I do not to any extent whatever base my view that this Connecticut law is constitutional on a belief that the law is wise or that its policy is a good one. In order that there may be no room at all to doubt why I vote as I do, I feel constrained to add that the law is every bit as offensive to me as it is to my Brethren of the majority and my Brothers HARLAN, WHITE and GOLDBERG who, reciting reasons why it is offensive to them, hold it unconstitutional. There is no single one of the graphic and eloquent strictures and criticisms fired at the policy of this Connecticut law either by the Court's opinion or by those of my concurring Brethren to which I cannot subscribe—except their conclusion that the evil qualities they see in the law make it unconstitutional.

Had the doctor defendant here, or even the nondoctor defendant, been convicted for doing nothing more than expressing opinions to persons coming to the clinic that certain contraceptive devices, medicines or practices would do them good and would be desirable, or for telling people how devices could be used, I can think of no reasons at this time why their expressions of views would not be [*508] protected by the *First* and *Fourteenth Amendments*, which guarantee freedom of speech. Cf. *Brotherhood of Railroad Trainmen v. Virginia ex rel. Virginia State Bar, 377 U.S. 1*; *NAACP v. Button, 371 U.S. 415*. But speech is one thing; conduct and physical activities are quite another. See, *e. g., Cox v. Louisiana, 379 U.S. 536, 554-555*; *Cox v. Louisiana, 379 U.S. 559, 563-564; id., 575-584* (concurring opinion); *Giboney v. Empire Storage & Ice Co., 336 U.S. 490*; cf. *Reynolds v. United States, 98 U.S. 145, 163-164*. The two defendants here were active participants in an organization which gave physical examinations to women, advised them what kind of contraceptive devices or medicines would most likely be satisfactory for them, and then supplied the devices themselves, all for a graduated scale of fees, based on the family income. Thus these defendants admittedly engaged with others in a planned course of conduct to help people violate the Connecticut law. Merely because some speech was used in carrying on that conduct—just as in ordinary life some speech accompanies most kinds of conduct—we are not in my view justified in holding that the *First Amendment* forbids the State to punish their conduct. Strongly as I desire to protect all *First Amendment* freedoms, I am unable to stretch the

Amendment [**1695] so as to afford protection to the conduct of these defendants in violating the Connecticut law. What would be the constitutional fate of the law if hereafter applied to punish nothing but speech is, as I have said, quite another matter.

The Court talks about a constitutional "right of privacy" as though there is some constitutional provision or provisions forbidding any law ever to be passed which might abridge the "privacy" of individuals. But there is not. There are, of course, guarantees in certain specific constitutional provisions which are [***530] designed in part to protect privacy at certain times and places with respect to certain activities. Such, for example, is the *Fourth* [*509] *Amendment's* guarantee against "unreasonable searches and seizures." But I think it belittles that Amendment to talk about it as though it protects nothing but "privacy." To treat it that way is to give it a niggardly interpretation, not the kind of liberal reading I think any *Bill of Rights* provision should be given. The average man would very likely not have his feelings soothed any more by having his property seized openly than by having it seized privately and by stealth. He simply wants his property left alone. And a person can be just as much, if not more, irritated, annoyed and injured by an unceremonious public arrest by a policeman as he is by a seizure in the privacy of his office or home.

One of the most effective ways of diluting or expanding a constitutionally guaranteed right is to substitute for the crucial word or words of a constitutional guarantee another word or words, more or less flexible and more or less restricted in meaning. This fact is well illustrated by the use of the term "right of privacy" as a comprehensive substitute for the *Fourth Amendment's* guarantee against "unreasonable searches and seizures." "Privacy" is a broad, abstract and ambiguous concept which can easily be shrunken in meaning but which can also, on the other hand, easily be interpreted as a constitutional ban against many things other than searches and seizures. I have expressed the view many times that *First Amendment* freedoms, for example, have suffered from a failure of the courts to stick to the simple language of the *First Amendment* in construing it, instead of invoking multitudes of words substituted for those the Framers used. See, *e. g., New York Times Co.* v. *Sullivan, 376 U.S. 254, 293* (concurring opinion); cases collected in *City of El Paso v. Simmons, 379 U.S. 497, 517, n. 1* (dissenting opinion); Black, The *Bill of Rights*, 35 N. Y. U. L. Rev. 865. For these reasons I get nowhere in this case by talk about a constitutional "right of privacy" as an emanation from [*510] one or more constitutional provisions.[1] I like [**1696] my privacy as well [***531] as the next one, but I am nevertheless compelled to admit that government has a right to invade it unless prohibited by some specific constitutional provision. For these reasons I cannot agree with the Court's judgment and the reasons it gives for holding this Connecticut law unconstitutional.

1 The phrase "right to privacy" appears first to have gained currency from an article written by Messrs. Warren and (later Mr. Justice) Brandeis in 1890 which urged that States should give some form of tort relief to persons whose private affairs were exploited by others. The Right to Privacy, 4 Harv. L. Rev. 193. Largely as a result of this article, some States have passed statutes creating such a cause of action, and in others state courts have done the same thing by exercising their powers as courts of common law. See generally 41 Am. Jur. 926-927. Thus the Supreme Court of Georgia, in granting a cause of action for damages to a man whose picture had been used in a newspaper advertisement without his consent, said that "A right of privacy in matters purely private is...derived from natural law" and that "The conclusion reached by us seems to be...thoroughly in accord with natural justice, with the principles of the law of every civilized nation, and especially with the elastic principles of the common law...." *Pavesich v. New England Life Ins. Co., 122 Ga. 190, 194, 218, 50 S. E. 68, 70, 80.* Observing that "the right of privacy...presses for recognition here," today this Court, which I did not understand to have power to sit as a court of common law, now appears to be exalting a phrase which Warren and Brandeis used in discussing grounds for tort relief, to the level of a constitutional rule which prevents state legislatures from passing any law deemed by this Court to interfere with "privacy."

This brings me to the arguments made by my Brothers HARLAN, WHITE and GOLDBERG for invalidating the Connecticut law. Brothers HARLAN[2] and WHITE would invalidate it by reliance on the *Due Process Clause of the Fourteenth Amendment*, but Brother GOLDBERG, while agreeing with Brother HARLAN, relies also on the *Ninth Amendment*. I have no doubt that the Connecticut law could be applied in such a way as to abridge freedom of [*511] speech and press and therefore violate the *First* and *Fourteenth Amendments*. My disagreement with the Court's opinion holding that there is such a violation here is a narrow one, relating to the application of the *First Amendment* to the facts and circumstances of this particular case. But my disagreement with Brothers HARLAN, WHITE and GOLDBERG is more basic. I think that if properly construed neither the Due Process Clause nor the *Ninth Amendment*, nor both together, could under any circumstances be a proper basis for invalidating the Connecticut law. I discuss the due process and *Ninth Amendment* arguments together because on analysis they turn out to be the same thing—merely using different words to claim for this Court and the federal judiciary power to invalidate any legislative act which the judges find irrational, unreasonable or offensive.

    2 Brother HARLAN's views are spelled out at greater length in his dissenting opinion in *Poe v. Ullman, 367 U.S. 497, 539-555.*

The due process argument which my Brothers HARLAN and WHITE adopt here is based, as their opinions indicate, on the premise that this Court is vested with power to invalidate all state laws that it considers to be arbitrary, capricious, unreasonable, or oppressive, or on this Court's belief that a particular state law under scrutiny has no "rational or justifying" purpose, or is offensive to a "sense of fairness and justice."[3] If these formulas based on "natural justice," or others which mean the same thing,[4] are to prevail, they require [**1697] judges to determine [*512] what is or is not constitutional on [***532] the basis of their own appraisal of what laws are unwise or unnecessary. The power to make such decisions is of course that of a legislative body. Surely it has to be admitted that no provision of the Constitution specifically gives such blanket power to courts to exercise such a supervisory veto over the wisdom and value of legislative policies and to hold unconstitutional those laws which they believe unwise or dangerous. I readily admit that no legislative body, state or national, should pass laws that can justly be given any [*513] of the invidious labels invoked as constitutional excuses to strike down state laws. But perhaps it is not too much to say that no legislative body ever does pass laws without believing that they will accomplish a sane, rational, wise and justifiable purpose. While I completely subscribe to the holding of *Marbury v. Madison, 1 Cranch 137,* and subsequent cases, that our Court has constitutional power to strike down statutes, state or federal, that violate commands of the Federal Constitution, I do not believe that we are granted power by the Due Process Clause or any other constitutional provision or provisions to measure constitutionality by our belief that legislation is arbitrary, capricious or unreasonable, or accomplishes no justifiable purpose, or is offensive to our own notions of "civilized standards of conduct."[5] [***533] Such an appraisal of the wisdom of legislation is an attribute of the power to make laws, not of the power to interpret them. The use by federal courts of such a formula or doctrine or whatnot to veto federal or state laws simply takes away from Congress and States the power to make laws based on their own judgment of fairness and wisdom and transfers that power to this Court for ultimate determination—a power which was specifically [**1698] denied to federal courts by the convention that framed the Constitution.[6]

3   Indeed, Brother WHITE appears to have gone beyond past pronouncements of the natural law due process theory, which at least said that the Court should exercise this unlimited power to declare state acts unconstitutional with "restraint." He now says that, instead of being presumed constitutional (see *Munn v. Illinois*, 94 U.S. 113, 123; compare *Adkins v. Children's Hospital*, 261 U.S. 525, 544), the statute here "bears a substantial burden of justification when attacked under the *Fourteenth Amendment*."

4   A collection of the catchwords and catch phrases invoked by judges who would strike down under the *Fourteenth Amendment* laws which offend their notions of natural justice would fill many pages. Thus it has been said that this Court can forbid state action which "shocks the conscience," *Rochin v. California*, 342 U.S. 165, 172, sufficiently to "shock itself into the protective arms of the Constitution," *Irvine v. California*, 347 U.S. 128, 138 (concurring opinion). It has been urged that States may not run counter to the "decencies of civilized conduct," *Rochin, supra, at 173*, or "some principle of justice so rooted in the traditions and conscience of our people as to be ranked as fundamental," *Snyder v. Massachusetts*, 291 U.S. 97, 105, or to "those canons of decency and fairness which express the notions of justice of English-speaking peoples," *Malinski v. New York*, 324 U.S. 401, 417 (concurring opinion), or to "the community's sense of fair play and decency," *Rochin, supra, at 173*. It has been said that we must decide whether a state law is "fair, reasonable and appropriate," or is rather "an unreasonable, unnecessary and arbitrary interference with the right of the individual to his personal liberty or to enter into . . . contracts," *Lochner v. New York*, 198 U.S. 45, 56. States, under this philosophy, cannot act in conflict with "deeply rooted feelings of the community," *Haley v. Ohio*, 332 U.S. 596, 604 (separate opinion), or with "fundamental notions of fairness and justice," *id.*, 607. See also, *e. g.*, *Wolf v. Colorado*, 338 U.S. 25, 27 ("rights . . . basic to our free society"); *Hebert v. Louisiana*, 272 U.S. 312, 316 ("fundamental principles of liberty and justice"); *Adkins v. Children's Hospital*, 261 U.S. 525, 561 ("arbitrary restraint of . . . liberties"); *Betts v. Brady*, 316 U.S. 455, 462 ("denial of fundamental fairness, shocking to the universal sense of justice"); *Poe v. Ullman*, 367 U.S. 497, 539 (dissenting opinion) ("intolerable and unjustifiable"). Perhaps the clearest, frankest and briefest explanation of how this due process approach works is the statement in another case handed down today that this Court is to invoke the Due Process

Clause to strike down state procedures or laws which it can "not tolerate." *Linkletter v. Walker, post*, p. 618, at 631.

5 *See* Hand, The *Bill of Rights* (1958) 70:

"Judges are seldom content merely to annul the particular solution before them; they do not, indeed they may not, say that taking all things into consideration, the legislators' solution is too strong for the judicial stomach. On the contrary they wrap up their veto in a protective veil of adjectives such as 'arbitrary,' 'artificial,' 'normal,' 'reasonable,' 'inherent,' 'fundamental,' or 'essential,' whose office usually, though quite innocently, is to disguise what they are doing and impute to it a derivation far more impressive than their personal preferences, which are all that in fact lie behind the decision." See also *Rochin v. California, 342 U.S. 165, 174* (concurring opinion). But see *Linkletter v. Walker, supra*, n. 4, at 631.

6 This Court held in *Marbury v. Madison, 1 Cranch 137*, that this Court has power to invalidate laws on the ground that they exceed the constitutional power of Congress or violate some specific prohibition of the Constitution. See also *Fletcher v. Peck, 6 Cranch 87*. But the Constitutional Convention did on at least two occasions reject proposals which would have given the federal judiciary a part in recommending laws or in vetoing as bad or unwise the legislation passed by the Congress. Edmund Randolph of Virginia proposed that the President

"...and a convenient number of the National Judiciary, ought to compose a council of revision with authority to examine every act of the National Legislature before it shall operate, & every act of a particular Legislature before a Negative thereon shall be final; and that the dissent of the said Council shall amount to a rejection, unless the Act of the National Legislature be again passed, or that of a particular Legislature be again negatived by [original word illegible] of the members of each branch." 1 The Records of the Federal Convention of 1787 (Farrand ed. 1911) 21.

In support of a plan of this kind James Wilson of Pennsylvania argued that:

". . . It had been said that the Judges, as expositors of the Laws would have an opportunity of defending their constitutional rights. There was weight in this observation; but this power of the Judges did not go far enough. Laws may be unjust, may be unwise, may be dangerous, may be destructive; and yet not be so unconstitutional as to justify the Judges in refusing to give them effect. Let them have a share in the Revisionary power, and they will have an opportunity of taking notice of these characters of a law, and of counteracting, by the weight of their opinions the improper views of the Legislature." 2 *id., at* 73.

Nathaniel Gorham of Massachusetts "did not see the advantage of employing the Judges in this way. As Judges they are not to be presumed to possess any peculiar knowledge of the mere policy of public measures." *Ibid*.

Elbridge Gerry of Massachusetts likewise opposed the proposal for a council of revision:

"...He relied for his part on the Representatives of the people as the guardians of their Rights & interests. It [the proposal] was making the Expositors of the Laws, the Legislators which ought never to be done." *Id., at* 75.

And at another point:

"Mr. Gerry doubts whether the Judiciary ought to form a part of it [the proposed council of revision], as they will have a sufficient check agst. encroachments on their own department by their exposition of the laws, which involved a power of deciding on their Constitutionality.... It was quite foreign from the nature of ye. office to make them judges of the policy of public measures." 1 *Id.*, at 97-98.

Madison supported the proposal on the ground that "a Check [on the legislature] is necessary." *Id., at 108*. John Dickinson of Delaware opposed it on the ground that "the Judges must interpret the Laws they ought not to be legislators." *Ibid*. The proposal for a council of revision was defeated.

The following proposal was also advanced:

"To assist the President in conducting the Public affairs there shall be a Council of State composed of the following officers --
1. The Chief Justice of the Supreme Court, who shall from time to time recommend such alterations of and additions to the laws of the U.S. as may in his opinion be necessary to the due administration of Justice, and such as may promote useful learning and inculcate sound morality throughout the Union...." 2 *id., at 342*.
This proposal too was rejected.

[*514] Of the cases on which my Brothers WHITE and GOLDBERG rely so heavily, undoubtedly the reasoning of two of them supports their result here—as would that of a number of others which they do not bother to name, *e. g.,* [*515] *Lochner v. New York,* 198 U.S. 45, [***534] *Coppage v. Kansas,* 236 U.S. 1, *Jay Burns Baking Co.* v. *Bryan,* 264 U.S. 504, and *Adkins*

v. Children's Hospital, 261 U.S. 525. The two they do cite and quote from, *Meyer v. Nebraska, 262 U.S. 390*, and *Pierce v. Society of Sisters, 268 U.S. 510*, were both decided in opinions [**1699] by Mr. Justice McReynolds which elaborated the same natural law due process philosophy found in *Lochner v. New York, supra*, one of the cases on which he relied in *Meyer*, along with such other long-discredited decisions as, *e. g., Adams v. Tanner, 244 U.S. 590*, and *Adkins v. Children's Hospital, supra*. *Meyer* held unconstitutional, as an "arbitrary" and unreasonable interference with the right of a teacher to carry on his occupation and of parents to hire him, a [*516] state law forbidding the teaching of modern foreign languages to young children in the schools. [7] And in *Pierce*, relying principally on *Meyer*, Mr. Justice McReynolds said that a state law requiring that all children attend public schools interfered unconstitutionally with the property rights of private school corporations because it was an "arbitrary, unreasonable and unlawful interference" which threatened "destruction of their business and property." *268 U.S., at 536*. Without expressing an opinion as to whether either of those cases reached a correct result in light of our later decisions applying the *First Amendment* to the States through the Fourteenth,[8] I merely point out that the reasoning stated in *Meyer* and *Pierce* was the same natural law due process philosophy which many later opinions repudiated, and which I cannot accept. Brothers WHITE and GOLDBERG also cite other cases, such as *NAACP v. Button, 371 U.S. 415, Shelton v. Tucker, 364 U.S. 479*, and *Schneider v. State, 308 U.S. 147*, which held that States in regulating conduct could not, consistently with the *First Amendment* as applied to them by the Fourteenth, pass unnecessarily broad laws which might indirectly infringe on *First Amendment* freedoms.[9] See *Brotherhood of Railroad Trainmen v. Virginia ex rel.* [*517] *Virginia State Bar, 377 U.S. 1, 7-8*.[10] Brothers WHITE and GOLDBERG [***535] [**1700] now apparently would start from this requirement that laws be narrowly drafted so as not to curtail free speech and assembly, and extend it limitlessly to require States to justify any law restricting "liberty" as my Brethren define "liberty." This would mean at the [*518] very least, I suppose, that every state criminal statute—since it must inevitably curtail "liberty" to some extent—would be suspect, and would have to be justified to this Court.[11]

    7 In *Meyer*, in the very same sentence quoted in part by my Brethren in which he asserted that the Due Process Clause gave an abstract and inviolable right "to marry, establish a home and bring up children," Mr. Justice McReynolds also asserted the heretofore discredited doctrine that the Due Process Clause prevented States from interfering with "the right of the individual to

contract." *262 U.S., at 399*.

8 Compare *Poe v. Ullman, 367 U.S., at 543-544* (HARLAN, J., dissenting).

9 The Court has also said that in view of the *Fourteenth Amendment's* major purpose of eliminating state-enforced racial discrimination, this Court will scrutinize carefully any law embodying a racial classification to make sure that it does not deny equal protection of the laws. See *McLaughlin v. Florida, 379 U.S. 184*.

10 None of the other cases decided in the past 25 years which Brothers WHITE and GOLDBERG cite can justly be read as holding that judges have power to use a natural law due process formula to strike down all state laws which they think are unwise, dangerous, or irrational. *Prince v. Massachusetts, 321 U.S. 158, upheld* a state law forbidding minors from selling publications on the streets. *Kent v. Dulles, 357 U.S. 116*, recognized the power of Congress to restrict travel outside the country so long as it accorded persons the procedural safeguards of due process and did not violate any other specific constitutional provision. *Schware v. Board of Bar Examiners, 353 U.S. 232*, held simply that a State could not, consistently with due process, refuse a lawyer a license to practice law on the basis of a finding that he was morally unfit when there was no evidence in the record, *353 U.S., at 246-247*, to support such a finding. Compare *Thompson v. City of Louisville, 362 U.S. 199*, in which the Court relied in part on *Schware*. See also *Konigsberg v. State Bar, 353 U.S. 252*. And *Bolling v. Sharpe, 347 U.S. 497*, merely recognized what had been the understanding from the beginning of the country, an understanding shared by many of the draftsmen of the *Fourteenth Amendment*, that the whole *Bill of Rights*, including the *Due Process Clause of the Fifth Amendment*, was a guarantee that all persons would receive equal treatment under the law. Compare *Chambers v. Florida, 309 U.S. 227, 240-241*. With one exception, the other modern cases relied on by my Brethren were decided either solely under the *Equal Protection Clause of the Fourteenth Amendment* or under the *First Amendment*, made applicable to the States by the Fourteenth, some of the latter group involving the right of association which this Court has held to be a part of the rights of speech, press and assembly guaranteed by the *First Amendment*. As for *Aptheker v. Secretary of State, 378 U.S. 500*, I am compelled to say that if that decision was written or intended to bring about the abrupt and drastic reversal in the course of constitutional adjudication which is now attributed to it, the

change was certainly made in a very quiet and unprovocative manner, without any attempt to justify it.

11   Compare *Adkins v. Children's Hospital,* 261 U.S. 525, 568 (Holmes, J., dissenting):
"The earlier decisions upon the same words [the Due Process Clause] in the *Fourteenth Amendment* began within our memory and went no farther than an unpretentious assertion of the liberty to follow the ordinary callings. Later that innocuous generality was expanded into the dogma, Liberty of Contract. Contract is not specially mentioned in the text that we have to construe. It is merely an example of doing what you want to do, embodied in the word liberty. But pretty much all law consists in forbidding men to do some things that they want to do, and contract is no more exempt from law than other acts."

My Brother GOLDBERG has adopted the recent discovery[12] that the *Ninth Amendment* as well as the Due Process [***536] Clause can be used by this Court as authority to strike down all state legislation which this Court thinks [*519] violates "fundamental principles of liberty and justice," or is contrary to the "traditions and [collective] conscience of our people." He also states, without proof satisfactory to me, that in making decisions on this basis judges will not consider "their personal and private notions." One may ask how they can avoid considering them. Our Court certainly has no machinery with which to take a Gallup Poll.[13] And [**1701] the scientific miracles of this age have not yet produced a gadget which the Court can use to determine what traditions are rooted in the "[collective] conscience of our people." Moreover, one would certainly have to look far beyond the language of the *Ninth Amendment*[14] to find that the Framers vested in this Court any such awesome veto powers over lawmaking, either by the States or by the Congress. Nor does anything in the history of the Amendment offer any support for such a shocking doctrine. The whole history of the adoption of the Constitution and *Bill of Rights* points the other way, and the very material quoted by my Brother GOLDBERG shows that the *Ninth Amendment* was intended to protect against the idea that "by enumerating particular exceptions to the grant of power" to the Federal Government, "those rights which were not singled out, were intended to be assigned into the hands of the General Government [the United States], and were consequently [*520] insecure."[15] That Amendment was passed, not to broaden the powers of this Court or any other department of "the General Government," but, as every student of history knows, to assure the people that the Constitution in all its provisions was intended to limit the Federal Government to the powers granted expressly or by necessary implication. If any broad, unlimited power to hold laws unconstitutional because they offend what this Court conceives to be the "[collective] conscience of our people" is vested in this Court by the *Ninth Amendment*, the *Fourteenth Amendment*, or any other provision of the Constitution, it was not given by the Framers, but rather has been bestowed on the Court by the Court. This fact is perhaps responsible for the peculiar phenomenon that for a period of a century and a half no serious suggestion [***537] was ever made that the *Ninth Amendment*, enacted to protect state powers against federal invasion, could be used as a weapon of federal power to prevent state legislatures from passing laws they consider appropriate to govern local affairs. Use of any such broad, unbounded judicial authority would make of this Court's members a day-to-day constitutional convention.

12 *See* Patterson, The Forgotten *Ninth Amendment* (1955). Mr. Patterson urges that the *Ninth Amendment* be used to protect unspecified "natural and inalienable rights." P. 4. The Introduction by Roscoe Pound states that "there is a marked revival of natural law ideas throughout the world. Interest in the *Ninth Amendment* is a symptom of that revival." P. iii.

In Redlich, Are There "Certain Rights...Retained by the People"?, 37 N. Y. U. L. Rev. 787, Professor Redlich, in advocating reliance on the *Ninth* and *Tenth Amendments* to invalidate the Connecticut law before us, frankly states:

"But for one who feels that the marriage relationship should be beyond the reach of a state law forbidding the use of contraceptives, the birth control case poses a troublesome and challenging problem of constitutional interpretation. He may find himself saying, 'The law is unconstitutional—but why?' There are two possible paths to travel in finding the answer. One is to revert to a frankly flexible due process concept even on matters that do not involve specific constitutional prohibitions. The other is to attempt to evolve a new constitutional framework within which to meet this and similar problems which are likely to arise." *Id.*, at 798.

13 Of course one cannot be oblivious to the fact that Mr. Gallup has already published the results of a poll which he says show that 46% of the people in this country believe schools should teach about birth control. Washington Post, May 21, 1965, p. 2, col. 1. I can hardly believe, however, that Brother GOLDBERG would view 46% of the persons polled as so overwhelming a proportion that this Court may now rely on it to declare that the

Connecticut law infringes "fundamental" rights, and overrule the long-standing view of the people of Connecticut expressed through their elected representatives.

14 *U.S. Const., Amend. IX*, provides:

"The enumeration in the Constitution, of certain rights, shall not be construed to deny or disparage others retained by the people."

15 1 Annals of Congress 439. See also II Story, Commentaries on the Constitution of the United States (5th ed. 1891): "This clause was manifestly introduced to prevent any perverse or ingenious misapplication of the well-known maxim, that an affirmation in particular cases implies a negation in all others; and, *e converso*, that a negation in particular cases implies an affirmation in all others. The maxim, rightly understood, is perfectly sound and safe; but it has often been strangely forced from its natural meaning into the support of the most dangerous political heresies." *Id., at 651* (footnote omitted).

I repeat so as not to be misunderstood that this Court does have power, which it should exercise, to hold laws unconstitutional where they are forbidden by the Federal Constitution. My point is that there is no provision [*521] of the Constitution which either expressly or impliedly vests power in this Court to sit as a supervisory agency over acts of duly constituted legislative bodies and set aside their laws because of the Court's belief that the legislative policies adopted are unreasonable, unwise, arbitrary, capricious or irrational. The adoption of such a loose, flexible, uncontrolled standard for holding laws unconstitutional, if ever it is finally achieved, will amount to [**1702] a great unconstitutional shift of power to the courts which I believe and am constrained to say will be bad for the courts and worse for the country. Subjecting federal and state laws to such an unrestrained and unrestrainable judicial control as to the wisdom of legislative enactments would, I fear, jeopardize the separation of governmental powers that the Framers set up and at the same time threaten to take away much of the power of States to govern themselves which the Constitution plainly intended them to have.16

16 Justice Holmes in one of his last dissents, written in reply to Mr. Justice McReynolds' opinion for the Court in *Baldwin v. Missouri, 281 U.S. 586*, solemnly warned against a due process formula apparently approved by my concurring Brethren today. He said:

"I have not yet adequately expressed the more than anxiety that I feel at the ever increasing scope given to the *Fourteenth Amendment* in cutting down what I believe to be the constitutional rights of the States. As the decisions now stand, I see hardly any limit but the sky to the invalidating of those rights if they happen to strike a majority of this Court as for any reason undesirable. I cannot believe that the Amendment was intended to give us *carte blanche* to embody our economic or moral beliefs in its prohibitions. Yet I can think of no narrower reason that seems to me to justify the present and the earlier decisions to which I have referred. Of course the words 'due process of law,' if taken in their literal meaning, have no application to this case; and while it is too late to deny that they have been given a much more extended and artificial signification, still we ought to remember the great caution shown by the Constitution in limiting the power of the States, and should be slow to construe the clause in the *Fourteenth Amendment* as committing to the Court, with no guide but the Court's own discretion, the validity of whatever laws the States may pass." *281 U.S., at 595. See* 2 Holmes-Pollock Letters (Howe ed. 1941) 267-268.

[*522] I realize that many good and able men have eloquently spoken and written, sometimes in rhapsodical strains, about the duty of this Court to keep the Constitution in tune with the times. The idea is that the Constitution must be changed from time to time and that this Court is charged with a duty to make those changes. For myself, I must with all deference reject that philosophy. The Constitution makers knew the need for change and provided for it. Amendments suggested by the people's elected representatives can be submitted to the people or their selected agents for ratification. That method of change was good for our Fathers, and being somewhat old-fashioned I must add it is good enough for me. And so, I cannot rely on the Due Process Clause or [***538] the *Ninth Amendment* or any mysterious and uncertain natural law concept as a reason for striking down this state law. The Due Process Clause with an "arbitrary and capricious" or "shocking to the conscience" formula was liberally used by this Court to strike down economic legislation in the early decades of this century, threatening, many people thought, the tranquility and stability of the Nation. See, *e. g., Lochner v. New York, 198 U.S. 45.* That formula, based on subjective considerations of "natural justice," is no less dangerous when used to enforce this Court's views about personal rights than those about economic rights. I had thought that we had laid that formula, as a means for striking down state legislation, to rest once and for all in cases like *West Coast Hotel Co. v. Parrish, 300 U.S. 379*; *Olsen v. Nebraska ex rel. Western Reference & Bond Assn., 313 U.S. 236,* and many other [*523] opinions.[17] See also *Lochner v. New York, 198 U.S. 45,* 74 [**1703] (Holmes, J., dissenting).

17   E. g., in *Day-Brite Lighting, Inc. v. Missouri, 342 U.S. 421, 423*, this Court held that "Our recent decisions make plain that we do not sit as a superlegislature to weigh the wisdom of legislation nor to decide whether the policy which it expresses offends the public welfare."

Compare *Gardner v. Massachusetts, 305 U.S. 559*, which the Court today apparently overrules, which held that a challenge under the Federal Constitution to a state law forbidding the sale or furnishing of contraceptives did not raise a substantial federal question.

In *Ferguson v. Skrupa, 372 U.S. 726, 730*, this Court two years ago said in an opinion joined by all the Justices but one[18] that

"The doctrine that prevailed in *Lochner, Coppage, Adkins, Burns*, and like cases—that due process authorizes courts to hold laws unconstitutional when they believe the legislature has acted unwisely—has long since been discarded. We have returned to the original constitutional proposition that courts do not substitute their social and economic beliefs for the judgment of legislative bodies, who are elected to pass laws."

And only six weeks ago, without even bothering to hear argument, this Court overruled *Tyson & Brother v. Banton, 273 U.S. 418*, which had held state laws regulating ticket brokers to be a denial of due process of law.[19] *Gold* [*524] *v. DiCarlo, 380 U.S. 520*. I find April's holding hard to square with what my concurring Brethren urge today. They would reinstate the *Lochner, Coppage, Adkins, Burns* line of cases, cases from which this Court recoiled after the 1930's, and which had been I thought totally discredited until [***539] now. Apparently my Brethren have less quarrel with state economic regulations than former Justices of their persuasion had. But any limitation upon their using the natural law due process philosophy to strike down any state law, dealing with any activity whatever, will obviously be only self-imposed.[20]

18   Brother HARLAN, who has consistently stated his belief in the power of courts to strike down laws which they consider arbitrary or unreasonable, see, *e. g., Poe v. Ullman, 367 U.S. 497, 539-555* (dissenting opinion), did not join the Court's opinion in *Ferguson v. Skrupa*.

19   Justice Holmes, dissenting in *Tyson*, said:

"I think the proper course is to recognize that a state legislature can do whatever it sees fit to do unless it is restrained by some express prohibition in the Constitution of the United States or of the State, and that Courts should be careful not to extend such prohibitions beyond their obvious meaning by reading into them conceptions of public policy that the particular Court may happen to entertain." *273 U.S., at 446.*

20   Compare *Nicchia v. New York, 254 U.S. 228, 231,* upholding a New York dog-licensing statute on the ground that it did not "deprive dog owners of liberty without due process of law." And as I said concurring in *Rochin v. California, 342 U.S. 165, 175,* "I believe that faithful adherence to the specific guarantees in the *Bill of Rights* insures a more permanent protection of individual liberty than that which can be afforded by the nebulous standards" urged by my concurring Brethren today.

In 1798, when this Court was asked to hold another Connecticut law unconstitutional, Justice Iredell said:

"It has been the policy of all the *American* states, which have, individually, framed their state constitutions since the revolution, and of the people of the *United States,* when they framed the Federal Constitution, to define with precision the objects of the legislative power, and to restrain its exercise within marked and settled boundaries. If any act of Congress, or of the Legislature of a state, violates those constitutional provisions, it is unquestionably void; though, I admit, that as the authority to declare it void is of a delicate and awful nature, the Court will [**1704] never resort to that authority, but in a clear and urgent case. If, on the other hand, the Legislature of the Union, or the Legislature of any member of the Union, shall pass a law, within the [*525] general scope of their constitutional power, the Court cannot pronounce it to be void, merely because it is, in their judgment, contrary to the principles of natural justice. The ideas of natural justice are regulated by no fixed standard: the ablest and the purest men have differed upon the subject; and all that the Court could properly say, in such an event, would be, that the Legislature (possessed of an equal right of opinion) had passed an act which, in the opinion of the judges, was inconsistent with the abstract principles of natural justice." *Calder v. Bull,* 3 Dall. 386, 399 (emphasis in original).

I would adhere to that constitutional philosophy in passing on this Connecticut law today. I am not persuaded to deviate from the view which I stated in 1947 in *Adamson v. California, 332 U.S. 46, 90-92* (dissenting opinion):

"Since *Marbury v. Madison, 1 Cranch 137,* was decided, the practice has been firmly established, for better or worse, that courts can strike down legislative enactments which violate the Constitution. This process, of course, involves interpretation, and since words can have many meanings, interpretation obviously may result in contraction or extension of the original purpose of a constitutional provision, thereby affecting policy. But to pass upon the constitutionality of statutes by looking to the particular standards enumerated in the *Bill of Rights* and other parts of the Constitution is one thing; to invalidate statutes because of application of 'natural law' deemed to be above and undefined by the Constitution is another. 'In the one instance, courts proceeding within clearly marked constitutional boundaries seek to execute policies written into [***540] the Constitution: in the other, they roam at will in the limitless [*526] area of their own beliefs as to reasonableness and actually select policies, a responsibility which the Constitution entrusts to the legislative representatives of the people.' *Federal Power Commission v. Pipeline Co., 315 U.S. 575, 599, 601, n. 4.*"21 (Footnotes omitted.)

The late Judge Learned Hand, after emphasizing his view that judges should not [**1705] use the due process formula suggested in the concurring opinions today or any other formula like it to invalidate legislation offensive to their "personal preferences,"22 made the statement, with which I fully agree, that:

"For myself it would be most irksome to be ruled by a bevy of Platonic Guardians, even if I [*527] knew how to choose them, which I assuredly do not."23

So far as I am concerned, Connecticut's law as applied here is not forbidden by any provision of the Federal Constitution as that Constitution was written, and I would therefore affirm.

21 *Gideon v. Wainwright, 372 U.S. 335*, and similar cases applying specific *Bill of Rights* provisions to the States do not in my view stand for the proposition that this Court can rely on its own concept of "ordered liberty" or "shocking the conscience" or natural law to decide what laws it will permit state legislatures to enact. *Gideon* in applying to state prosecutions the *Sixth Amendment's* guarantee of right to counsel followed *Palko v. Connecticut, 302 U.S. 319*, which had held that specific provisions of the *Bill of Rights*, rather than the *Bill of Rights* as a whole, would be selectively applied to the States. While expressing my own belief (not shared by MR. JUSTICE STEWART) that all the provisions of the *Bill of Rights* were made applicable to the States by the *Fourteenth Amendment*, in my dissent in *Adamson v. California, 332 U.S. 46, 89*, I also said:

"If the choice must be between the selective process of the *Palko* decision applying some of the *Bill of Rights* to the States, or the *Twining* rule applying none of them, I would choose the *Palko* selective process."

Gideon and similar cases merely followed the *Palko* rule, which in *Adamson* I agreed to follow if necessary to make *Bill of Rights* safeguards applicable to the States. See also *Pointer v. Texas, 380 U.S. 400*; *Malloy v. Hogan, 378 U.S. 1*.

22 Hand, The *Bill of Rights* (1958) 70. See note 5, *supra*. See generally *id., at 35-45*.

23 *Id., at 73*. While Judge Hand condemned as unjustified the invalidation of state laws under the natural law due process formula, see *id., at 35-45*, he also expressed the view that this Court in a number of cases had gone too far in holding legislation to be in violation of specific guarantees of the *Bill of Rights*. Although I agree with his criticism of use of the due process formula, I do not agree with all the views he expressed about construing the specific guarantees of the *Bill of Rights*.

MR. JUSTICE STEWART, whom MR. JUSTICE BLACK joins, dissenting.

Since 1879 Connecticut has had on its books a law which forbids the use of contraceptives by anyone. I think this is an uncommonly silly law. As a practical matter, the law is obviously unenforceable, except in the oblique context of the present case. As a philosophical matter, I believe the use of contraceptives in the relationship of marriage should be left to personal and private choice, based upon each individual's moral, ethical, and religious beliefs. As a matter of social policy, I think professional counsel about methods of birth control should be available to all, so that each individual's choice can be meaningfully made. But we are not asked in this case to say whether we think this law is unwise, or even asinine. We are asked to [***541] hold that it violates the United States Constitution. And that I cannot do.

In the course of its opinion the Court refers to no less than six Amendments to the Constitution: the First, the Third, the Fourth, the Fifth, the Ninth, and the Fourteenth. [*528] But the Court does not say which of these Amendments, if any, it thinks is infringed by this Connecticut law.

We *are* told that the *Due Process Clause of the Fourteenth Amendment* is not, as such, the "guide" in this case. With that much I agree. There is no claim that this law, duly enacted by the Connecticut Legislature, is unconstitutionally vague. There is no claim that the appellants were denied any of the elements of procedural due process at their trial, so as to make their convictions constitutionally invalid. And, as the Court says, the day has long passed since the Due Process Clause was regarded as a proper instrument for determining "the wisdom, need, and propriety" of state laws. Compare *Lochner v. New York, 198 U.S. 45*, with *Ferguson v. Skrupa, 372 U.S.*

726. My Brothers HARLAN and WHITE to the contrary, "we have returned to the original constitutional proposition that courts do not substitute their social and economic beliefs for the judgment of legislative bodies, who are elected to pass laws." *Ferguson v. Skrupa, supra, at 730.*

As to the *First, Third, Fourth,* and *Fifth Amendments,* I can find nothing in any of them to invalidate this Connecticut law, even assuming that all those Amendments are fully applicable against the States.[1] It has [*529] not even been argued [**1706] that this is a law "respecting an establishment of religion, or prohibiting the free exercise thereof."[2] And surely, unless the solemn process of constitutional adjudication is to descend to the level of a play on words, there is not involved here any abridgment of "the freedom of speech, or of the press; or the right of the people peaceably to assemble, and to petition the Government for a redress of grievances."[3] No soldier has been quartered in any house.[4] There has been no search, and no seizure.[5] Nobody has been compelled [***542] to be a witness against himself.[6]

1   The Amendments in question were, as everyone knows, originally adopted as limitations upon the power of the newly created Federal Government, not as limitations upon the powers of the individual States. But the Court has held that many of the provisions of the first eight amendments are fully embraced by the *Fourteenth Amendment* as limitations upon state action, and some members of the Court have held the view that the adoption of the *Fourteenth Amendment* made every provision of the first eight amendments fully applicable against the States. See *Adamson v. California, 332 U.S. 46, 68* (dissenting opinion of MR. JUSTICE BLACK).

2   *U.S. Constitution, Amendment I.* To be sure, the injunction contained in the Connecticut statute coincides with the doctrine of certain religious faiths. But if that were enough to invalidate a law under the provisions of the *First Amendment* relating to religion, then most criminal laws would be invalidated. See, *e. g.,* the Ten Commandments. The Bible, Exodus 20:2-17 (King James).

3   *U.S. Constitution, Amendment I.* If all the appellants had done was to advise people that they thought the use of contraceptives was desirable, or even to counsel their use, the appellants would, of course, have a substantial *First Amendment* claim. But their activities went far beyond mere advocacy. They prescribed specific contraceptive devices and furnished patients with the prescribed contraceptive materials.

4   *U.S. Constitution, Amendment III.*

5 *U.S. Constitution, Amendment IV.*
6 *U.S. Constitution, Amendment V.*

The Court also quotes the *Ninth Amendment*, and my Brother GOLDBERG's concurring opinion relies heavily upon it. But to say that the *Ninth Amendment* has anything to do with this case is to turn somersaults with history. The *Ninth Amendment*, like its companion the Tenth, which this Court held "states but a truism that all is retained which has not been surrendered," *United States v. Darby, 312 U.S. 100, 124,* was framed by James Madison and adopted by the States simply to make clear that the adoption of the *Bill of Rights* did not alter the plan that [*530] the *Federal* Government was to be a government of express and limited powers, and that all rights and powers not delegated to it were retained by the people and the individual States. Until today no member of this Court has ever suggested that the *Ninth Amendment* meant anything else, and the idea that a federal court could ever use the *Ninth Amendment* to annul a law passed by the elected representatives of the people of the State of Connecticut would have caused James Madison no little wonder.

What provision of the Constitution, then, does make this state law invalid? The Court says it is the right of privacy "created by several fundamental constitutional guarantees." With all deference, I can find no such general right of privacy in the *Bill of Rights*, in any other part of the Constitution, or in any case ever before decided by this Court.[7]

7 Cases like *Shelton v. Tucker, 364 U.S. 479* and *Bates v. Little Rock, 361 U.S. 516,* relied upon in the concurring opinions today, dealt with true *First Amendment* rights of association and are wholly inapposite here. See also, *e.g., NAACP v. Alabama, 357 U.S. 449; Edwards v. South Carolina, 372 U.S. 229.* Our decision in *McLaughlin v. Florida, 379 U.S. 184,* is equally far afield. That case held invalid under the *Equal Protection Clause*, a state criminal law which discriminated against Negroes.

The Court does not say how far the new constitutional right of privacy announced today extends. See, *e.g.,* Mueller, Legal Regulation of Sexual Conduct, at 127; Ploscowe, Sex and the Law, at 189. I suppose, however, that even after today a State can constitutionally still punish at least some offenses which are not committed in public.

At [**1707] the oral argument in this case we were told that the Connecticut law does not "conform to current community standards." But it is not the function of this Court to decide cases on the basis of community standards. We are here to decide cases "agreeably to the Constitution and laws of the United States." It is the essence of judicial [*531] duty to subordinate our own personal views, our own ideas of what legislation is wise and what is not. If, as I should surely hope, the law before us does not reflect the standards of the people of Connecticut, the people of Connecticut can freely exercise their true *Ninth* and *Tenth Amendment* rights to persuade their elected representatives to repeal it. That is the constitutional way to take this law off the books.[8]

8 See *Reynolds v. Sims, 377 U.S. 533, 562.* The Connecticut House of Representatives recently passed a bill (House Bill No. 2462) repealing the birth control law. The State Senate has apparently not yet acted on the measure, and today is relieved of that responsibility by the Court. New Haven Journal-Courier, Wed., May 19, 1965, p. 1, col. 4, and p. 13, col. 7.

APPENDIX E

STATE OF CONNECTICUT V. LONNIE MCLUCAS

[NO NUMBER IN ORIGINAL]

SUPREME COURT OF CONNECTICUT

172 CONN. 542; 375 A.2D 1014; 1977 CONN. LEXIS 926

DECEMBER 10, 1976, ARGUED
MARCH 15, 1977, DECIDED

PRIOR HISTORY: Indictment charging the defendant with the crime of kidnapping resulting in death, and information charging the defendant with the crimes of conspiracy to commit kidnapping, conspiracy to commit murder, and binding with intent to commit a crime, brought to the Superior Court in New Haven County and tried to the jury before *Mulvey, J.;* verdict and judgment of guilty of conspiracy to commit murder and appeal by the defendant.
The appellant filed a motion for reargument which was denied.

DISPOSITION: *No error.*

COUNSEL: *Michael P. Koskoff,* with whom were *Lucy V. Katz* and, on the brief, *Theodore I. Koskoff* and *John D. Jessep,* for the appellant (defendant). *Ernest J. Diette, Jr.,* assistant state's attorney, with whom, on the brief, was *Arnold Markle,* state's attorney, for the appellee (state).

JUDGES: House, C. J., Loiselle, Bogdanski, Longo and Barber, Js.

OPINION BY: BARBER

OPINION

The defendant was charged with the following violations of the General Statutes (Rev. to 1968): by indictment with the crime of kidnapping resulting in death in violation of General Statutes § 53-27, and by information with the crimes of conspiracy to commit kidnapping in violation of § 53-27, conspiracy to commit murder in violation of § 54-197, and with the crime of binding with intent to commit crime in violation of § 53-19.

A jury found the defendant guilty of conspiracy to commit the crime of murder and not guilty of the other crimes. The defendant has appealed from the judgment rendered, assigning as error a number of rulings by the trial court.

A brief statement of some of the background facts, not disputed by the parties, will put the issues in proper perspective. The charges against the defendant, Lonnie McLucas, all arose out of events culminating in the death of Alex Rackley. The defendant and others had established a branch of the Black Panther Party in New Haven. The conspiracy to murder Rackley was alleged to have developed during the period of May 18 through May 21, 1969, and was alleged to have included several members and affiliates of the Black Panther Party in New Haven. Those charged included the national party chairman, Bobby Seale, who was indicted for participation in the murder and was alleged to have given the order that Rackley be killed. The state contended that Rackley was tortured and killed because he was suspected of being a police informer. A number of those charged with being involved in the murder entered guilty pleas. Two pleaded guilty to second degree murder, two pleaded guilty to conspiracy to commit murder, three pleaded guilty to aggravated assault, and one pleaded guilty to conspiracy to commit kidnapping. All charges against Bobby Seale were dismissed after a lengthy trial ended in a hung jury. The defendant was tried alone after being denied a joint trial with several other defendants. It is undisputed that Rackley was "disciplined" by torture and then was bound and driven to a swamp in Middlefield. During the trial, the defendant described his participation in the events and admitted that after Rackley had been taken to a wooded area and had been shot once, he, McLucas, was given the gun and fired a second shot. The defendant's defense for his actions was predicated on the claim of an overwhelming fear of, and coercion by, another alleged participant, George Sams, whom the defendant sought to portray as a madman. The state contended that Rackley was tortured and killed not because of pressure from one individual, Sams, but because he was suspected of being a police informer within the Black Panther Party.

The court made a finding on each of the rulings involved in this appeal, which finding includes such facts as were considered incidental to each of the respective rulings.

I

Prior to the trial, the defendant moved to suppress as evidence a tape recorder, tape recordings, and a .45-caliber pistol, which had been seized from an apartment at 365 Orchard Street in New Haven. The motion was denied without prejudice to the defendant's right to renew it at the time of trial. There was subsequently a full hearing on the motion at the time of trial. The defendant claimed that he had standing to challenge the search on the basis of his membership on the central staff of the Black Panther Party. The court concluded that the defendant did not have standing to challenge the search and seizure in that he was not on the premises at the time of the seizure and had no possessory interest in either the premises or the articles seized. "[T]here is no standing to contest a search and seizure where...the defendants: (a) were not on the premises at the time of the contested search and seizure; (b) alleged no proprietary or possessory interest in the premises; and (c) were not charged with an offense that includes, as an essential element of the offense charged, possession of the seized evidence at the time of the contested search and seizure." *Brown v. United States, 411 U.S. 223, 229, 93 S. Ct. 1565, 36 L. Ed. 2d 208.* A person may have a possessory interest in the premises searched even though he has no title to the premises. *Mancusi v. DeForte, 392 U.S. 364, 367-68, 88 S. Ct. 2120, 20 L. Ed. 2d 1154; Jones v. United States, 362 U.S. 257, 265, 80 S. Ct. 725, 4 L. Ed. 2d 697; State v. Darwin, 161 Conn. 413, 419, 288 A.2d 422.* The defendant had the burden of establishing the facts necessary to demonstrate a basis for standing to attack the search and seizure. *See Combs v. United States, 408 U.S. 224, 227, 92 S. Ct. 2284, 33 L. Ed. 2d 308.* It has been made clear that capacity to claim the protection of the fourth amendment depends not upon a property right in the premises searched but upon whether the area was one in which there was a reasonable expectation of freedom from governmental intrusion. *Mancusi v. DeForte, supra, 368; Katz v. United States, 389 U.S. 347, 352, 88 S. Ct. 507, 19 L. Ed. 2d 576.* It is evident that the defendant was not charged with an offense that had as an essential element the possession of seized evidence at the time of the search and seizure. *See Brown v. United States, supra.* In addition, it appears from the finding that the defendant was not at the apartment when the police entered and the seizure occurred, and the articles neither belonged to the defendant nor were they in his custody at the time they were seized.

In this case, the critical issue on the defendant's motion to suppress as evidence the property seized is whether, in light of all the circumstances, the defendant had a possessory interest in the searched premises at 365 Orchard Street such that those premises constituted an area in which the defendant had a "reasonable expectation of freedom from governmental intrusion." *Mancusi v. DeForte, supra.* In *Mancusi,* the defendant union official was found to have standing to object to the seizure of certain union records. The papers were taken from an office which was used for union purposes and which the defendant shared with several other union officials. It was stipulated that he spent a considerable amount of time in that office, and that he had custody of the papers at the moment of their seizure. He was present in the office during the seizure, and protested the taking of the papers. In marked contrast, it appears from the finding in the present case that Warren Kimbro was the person who resided in, and paid the rent for, the apartment at 365 Orchard Street; that the defendant did not live in this apartment, had no proprietary interest in it, and had only stayed overnight there once; that the defendant had no possessory interest in the articles seized; that the Black Panther group in New Haven held meetings at Warren Kimbro's apartment; and that the apartment was mainly a residence and only sometimes used for office purposes by the Black Panther group. In further contrast to the situation in *Mancusi*, in the present case there was no stipulation or finding that the defendant had custody of the items at the moment of seizure. The defendant's reliance on *State v. Darwin, 161 Conn. 413, 288 A.2d 422*, is also misplaced. In that case, we held (p. 420) that a husband had standing to challenge a search and seizure involving his wife's automobile because "[t]o hold...that a vehicle titularly owned by a wife is not also owned by the husband for purposes of search and seizure would seem to be an improper stretching of technicalities." Such a situation is clearly distinguishable from the remote connection, which the defendant had with the premises in question here. The conclusions of the trial court set forth in the finding must stand if they are legally and logically consistent with the subordinate facts found unless they involve the application of some erroneous rule of law material to the case. *State v. Bowen, 167 Conn. 526, 531, 356 A.2d 162*; *Consiglio v. Warden, 160 Conn. 151, 157, 276 A.2d 773*. We have examined the subordinate facts in the finding relating to this issue and are of the opinion both that they support the conclusions reached and that those conclusions involve no erroneous rule of law.

II

The defendant moved to suppress statements made by him to officers in Salt Lake City, Utah, before voluntarily returning to this state, and a statement made by him to Sergeant Vincent J. DeRosa in New Haven on June 11, 1969. There was a full hearing on the motion to suppress statements at the time of trial. A detailed recital of all the facts contained in the voluminous finding would unduly lengthen this opinion, but we do include the following summary of the facts found by the court: On June 6, 1969, the Salt Lake City office of the Federal Bureau of Investigation (hereinafter referred to as the F.B.I.) had received a call from the F.B.I.'s New York office that two individuals for whom the New York office had fugitive warrants would possibly stop at the Western Union office in Salt

Lake City. The bureau had a fugitive warrant for the defendant who arrived at the Western Union office on June 6, 1969. The defendant was taken into custody and advised of his rights. At the F.B.I. office in Salt Lake City, he was charged with unlawful flight to avoid prosecution and was informed of the Connecticut warrant charging him with conspiracy, murder, kidnapping and other crimes. The defendant signed a formal, written statement of his rights, which statement included a waiver of his right to an attorney. It was explained to the defendant that he did not have to sign the form. Thereafter, Lynn G. Twede, an agent for the F.B.I., interviewed the defendant briefly before he was taken to be presented before a United States commissioner. The defendant indicated to Twede that he (the defendant) knew who had killed Alex Rackley and that he could produce witnesses, but he wanted assurances that he would not have to testify.

Sergeant DeRosa first saw the defendant in Salt Lake City on June 8, 1969. At that time the defendant signed a form containing the "Miranda" warnings and indicated that he understood them. At the time, and in the presence of Sergeants DeRosa and Nicholas Pastore of the New Haven police department, and two agents of the F.B.I., the defendant further indicated that he would be willing to talk about the investigation of the case. It does not appear what conversation subsequently took place on June 8, 1969. On June 9, 1969, the defendant was at the Salt Lake County courthouse with a lawyer. Sergeant DeRosa had not known on the previous day that an attorney had been appointed for the defendant. After conferring with his attorney, the defendant waived extradition and left Salt Lake City by airplane on June 10, 1969, with Sergeants DeRosa and Pastore. It does not appear what statements relative to the case under investigation were made by the defendant during the course of the plane trip. Sergeant DeRosa did show the defendant photographs of some of the people involved in the investigation and disclosed parts of statements which had been taken from others and which might tend to incriminate him. The defendant was arraigned in the Superior Court in New Haven on June 11, 1969. The clerk of the court informed the defendant of his rights but did not tell the defendant that if he could not afford an attorney one would be appointed for him. After the defendant was arraigned on June 11, 1969, he was given two warnings of his constitutional rights. The second warning forms a part of a statement that was reduced to typewritten form.

The defendant waived extradition, entered this state voluntarily, and was put to plea in this case. No question was raised as to the defendant's arrest in Salt Lake City prior to voluntarily returning to this jurisdiction, and none was ever made to the trial court. The defendant, however, issued subpoenas to the F.B.I., seeking information on the legality of his arrest, when the motion for suppression was being heard. Those subpoenas were quashed on motion of the assistant United States attorney.

The court concluded that the defendant in all stages of the proceeding on June 11, 1969, had his constitutional rights explained to him and that he voluntarily, knowingly and intelligently waived those rights. The court further concluded that the tape of the defendant's interview on June 11, 1969, and the taped statement of such interview were voluntarily given and should be admitted as evidence, and that the motion to quash the subpoenas, which was made by the United States, should be granted on the basis of *5 U.S.C. § 552 (b) (7)*.

In attacking the admission of statements made to officers in Salt Lake City, the defendant contends that such statements made by him while in custody should have been suppressed because an attorney had been appointed to represent him by a United States commissioner. The difficulties with the defendant's argument are that he does not particularize what statements are involved and he misplaces his reliance on the case of *Miranda v. Arizona, 384 U.S. 436, 86 S. Ct. 1602, 16 L. Ed. 2d 694*. The *Miranda* case holds that no effective waiver of right to counsel during interrogation can be recognized unless specifically made after the person interrogated has been apprised of his rights by being given the "Miranda" warnings. Despite the defendant's assertion, it does not hold that "[o]nce a criminal defendant is represented by counsel, he cannot waive any of his so-called 'Miranda' rights without his attorney's aid and advice." *See United States v. Hall, 523 F.2d 665, 668 n.4* (2d Cir.); *United States v. Diggs, 497 F.2d 391, 393* (2d Cir.); *Moore v. Wolff, 495 F.2d 35, 36-37* (8th Cir.); *United States v. Cobbs, 481 F.2d 196, 199* (3d Cir.); *United States v. Barone, 467 F.2d 247, 249* (2d Cir.). As stated in *Moore v. Wolff, supra, 37*: "If an accused can voluntarily, knowingly, and intelligently waive his right to counsel before one has been appointed, there seems no compelling reason to hold that he may not voluntarily, knowingly, and intelligently waive his right to have counsel present at an interrogation after counsel has been appointed. Of course, the Government will have a heavy burden to show that the waiver was knowingly and intelligently made, *Miranda v. Arizona,[384 U.S. 436, 475, 86 S. Ct. 1602, 16 L. Ed. 2d 694]* but we perceive no compelling reason to adopt the per se rule advocated by petitioner." In similar circumstances, the court held that "[s]ince there was no coercion or deception and . . . [the defendant] waived his right to counsel, the [F.B.I.] agents were not required, before taking his voluntary statement, to seek out the attorney who had been appointed." *United States v. Hall, supra*. This is not a case where the defendant waived his right to counsel without full knowledge of the crimes of which he was suspected. See *United States v. Diggs, supra, 393 n.3*. There is no showing that the defendant ever requested that an attorney be present or indicated a desire to remain silent. *See State v. Moscone, 171 Conn. 500, 370 A.2d 1030*. In the present case the facts establish beyond any doubt that the state's burden was discharged and that the defendant's waiver was voluntarily, knowingly and intelligently made.

In attacking the admission of the statement made to Sergeant DeRosa in New Haven on June 11, 1969, the defendant contends that it was tainted by a possible illegal arrest of the defendant by the F.B.I. in Salt Lake City. "The defendant suspected that his arrest might have been aided by the use of illegal electronic surveillance. The defendant argues that in the case of an illegal arrest the statement given by him on June 11, 1969, was the "fruit of the poisonous tree" and should have been suppressed. *See Wong Sun v. United States, 371 U.S. 471, 487-88, 83 S. Ct. 407, 9 L. Ed. 2d 441*. In attempting to pursue his suspicion that electronic eavesdropping had been involved in his arrest, the defendant issued two subpoenas directed to several F.B.I. agents, seeking to compel them to appear and bring certain electronic surveillance documents. The first subpoena sought information as to whether the F.B.I. had received information regarding the defendant's presence in Salt Lake City through electronic surveillance or wiretapping of the Jersey City Black Panther office or from an informant or from disclosure by Western Union. The second subpoena had to do with wiretapping devices, if any, of Warren Kimbro's apartment at 365 Orchard Street, New Haven, although the defendant did not claim that there were any wiretapping devices there. The court granted the motion to quash of the assistant United States attorney on the basis of *5 U.S.C. § 552 (b) (7)*. At the time of trial, *5 U.S.C. § 552* established the guidelines for public access to information held by a federal agency, while *5 U.S.C. § 552 (b) (7)* exempted from the general disclosure requirements "investigatory files compiled for law enforcement purposes except to the extent available by law to a party other than an agency." In his brief, the defendant apparently seeks to come within the exception of *5 U.S.C. § 552 (b) (7)* for disclosure of matter "available by law to a party" by his discussion of *18 U.S.C. § 2518 (8) (d)*, which provides for notice of electronic surveillance to "persons named in the [wiretap] order or the application, and such other parties to intercepted communications as the judge may determine." The defendant did not actually claim that there were any wiretapping devices at Warren Kimbro's apartment, and the rest of his allegations are equally speculative. Federal wiretapping legislation at the time of trial provided that an "aggrieved person" could move to suppress "the contents of any intercepted wire or oral communication, or evidence derived therefrom" on the ground of its unlawful interception; *18 U.S.C. § 2518 (10) (a)*; and defined such an aggrieved person as one "who was a party to any intercepted wire or oral communication or a person against whom the interception was directed." *18 U.S.C. § 2510 (11)*. In assessing claims of suspected illegal electronic surveillance, courts have looked for a relatively precise showing of the facts which reasonably have led a person to believe he has been subjected to undisclosed electronic surveillance, and have disapproved of speculative claims which lack sufficient precision and substantiation. See, e.g., *United States v. See, 505 F.2d 845, 856* (5th Cir.), affidavits vague and conclusory to the point of being a fishing expedition; *United States v. Alter, 482 F.2d 1016, 1026* (9th Cir.); *Cohen v. United States, 378 F.2d 751, 761* (9th Cir.); *People v. Cruz, 34 N.Y.2d 362, 314 N.E.2d 39*. The defendant's contention that he would be a party entitled by law to access to the F.B.I.'s investigative material and wiretap data because *18 U.S.C. § 2518 (8) (d)* "mandates eventual wiretap notice" appears rather tenuous. [1]

> 1 See State v. DeMartin, 171 Conn. 524, 534, 370 A.2d 1038, which contains a detailed history and discussion of present federal and state statutes relating to electronic surveillance.

The defendant also argues that he was denied his Sixth Amendment right to have compulsory process for obtaining witnesses in his favor by the fact that F.B.I. agent Twede testified for the state while the defendant was prevented, by the quashing of his subpoenas, from compelling certain other F.B.I. agents to appear and bring electronic surveillance documents. The defendant relies entirely on *Washington v. Texas, 388 U.S. 14, 87 S. Ct. 1920, 18 L. Ed. 2d 1019*, for his contention that the sixth amendment mandated that he have access to the alleged wiretap information under these circumstances. In *Washington v. Texas, supra,* the United States Supreme Court (p. 22) found that the federal constitution was violated by two Texas statutes which allowed a participant in a crime to testify for the prosecution but not for a defendant coparticipant and thereby established "arbitrary rules that prevent whole categories of defense witnesses from testifying on the basis of a priori categories that presume them unworthy of belief." Such a situation is certainly distinguishable from the facts of the present case. The defendant was nowhere deliberately prevented from presenting his version of the facts. There was no statute or rule making the testimony of F.B.I. agents available to, and competent evidence for, the state but not for the defendant. The quashing of the defendant's subpoenas had to do with the conjectural nature of his claims rather than with any discriminatory and arbitrary statutory scheme.

The issue of whether the court erred in quashing the subpoenas would not be dispositive of whether the defendant's statement to

Sergeant DeRosa was admissible. This is because even were we to assume [2] the illegality of the defendant's arrest in Salt Lake City this would not end our inquiry under the "poisonous tree" doctrine of *Wong Sun v. United States, 371 U.S. 471, 487-88, 83 S. Ct. 407, 9 L. Ed. 2d 441*. In his brief, the defendant has relied heavily on the wiretap question and his inability to probe the legality of his original arrest. Under the facts of this case, however, the central and dispositive issue is, rather, the voluntariness of the defendant's statement and whether such voluntariness is sufficient to sever any causal relationship between any prior illegality and the statement. "We need not hold that all evidence is 'fruit of the poisonous tree' simply because it would not have come to light but for the illegal actions of the police. Rather, the more apt question in such a case is 'whether, granting establishment of the primary illegality, the evidence...has been come at by exploitation of that illegality or instead by means sufficiently distinguishable to be purged of the primary taint.' [Citation omitted.]" *Wong Sun v. United States, supra*. The question of whether a statement is sufficiently voluntary under *Wong Sun* to be deemed independent of any prior illegality must be resolved upon the facts of each case. No single fact is dispositive, and the burden of showing the admissibility of the statement rests upon the state. *Brown v. Illinois, 422 U.S. 590, 603-604, 95 S. Ct. 2254, 45 L. Ed. 2d 416*. The *Miranda* warnings are an important factor in determining the voluntariness of the statement, and other relevant factors are the temporal proximity of the arrest and the statement, the presence of intervening circumstances and, particularly, the purpose and flagrancy of the official misconduct. *Ibid*. In the present case, the claimed illegality is that an illegal search (a wiretap) occurred in which information was obtained as to the location of the defendant for whom the authorities already had a valid arrest warrant. Days and not two hours as in *Brown v. Illinois, supra*, separated the initial arrest on June 6, 1969, Sergeant DeRosa's first meeting with the defendant on June 8, 1969, and the defendant's statement to DeRosa on June 11, 1969, which was the object of the motion to suppress. The defendant had repeatedly been given his *Miranda* warnings and had indicated that he understood them and still wished to waive his rights. It appears from the finding that it was the defendant who sought to initiate a bargaining process by indicating that he had information regarding Rackley's murder but wanted assurances that he would not have to testify. *See United States v. Mullens, 536 F.2d 997, 1000* (2d Cir.). The defendant was fully aware of the charges facing him, and there is no intimation that the defendant did not fully understand the consequences of his actions. *Ibid*. As the United States Supreme Court has recently emphasized, in finding that a defendant's consent to a police search of his automobile was voluntary, "[t]here is no indication in this record that [the defendant] was a newcomer to the law, mentally deficient, or unable in the face of custodial arrest to exercise a free choice." *United States v. Watson, 423 U.S. 411, 424-25, 96 S. Ct. 820, 46 L. Ed. 2d 598*. There is no indication in the finding that any promises were made or that there were "more subtle forms of coercion that might flaw his judgment." *Id., 424*. The fact of custody alone "has never been enough in itself to demonstrate a coerced confession or consent to search." *Ibid*. Although *United States v. Watson, supra*, involved a legal arrest and, therefore, a lesser burden of proof on the state because there was no taint of illegality to purge; see *State v. Traub, 151 Conn. 246, 249, 196 A.2d 755*, cert. denied, *377 U.S. 960, 84 S. Ct. 1637, 12 L. Ed. 2d 503*; the same factors are relevant in determining the voluntariness of the defendant's statement in the present case. Above all, there was no suggestion whatsoever in this case that "[t]he illegality...had a quality of purposefulness. The impropriety of the arrest was obvious...The manner in which [the] arrest was effected gives the appearance of having been calculated to cause surprise, fright, and confusion." *Brown v. Illinois, supra, 605*. Nor was any police overreaching or overt act or threat of force proved or claimed. See *United States v. Watson, supra, 424*; *United States v. Mullens, supra*. In short, there was ample evidence on which the court could base its conclusion that the defendant's statement was completely voluntary, "an act of free will unaffected by the initial illegality." *Brown v. Illinois, supra*; see *State v. Traub, supra*. The court therefore did not err in admitting the defendant's statement to Sergeant DeRosa.

    2 This assumption, however, appears remote in light of the recent decision in *United States v. Donovan*, 429 U.S. 413, 97 S. Ct. 658, 50 L. Ed. 2d 652.

III

Prior to the trial the state moved to sever the trial of the defendant from that of others alleged to be involved in the death of Alex Rackley. Over the defendant's opposition the court granted the state's motion. Subsequently, the defendant moved that he be tried after the other defendants or, in the alternative, together with the others, and, finally, that immunity be granted to certain witnesses. Those motions were denied. The defendant assigns as error the action of the trial court on those motions. The defendant argues (1) that he had a right to be tried together with the others, (2) that he could waive the right to be tried separately, and (3) that the court should have granted his request for immunity of the witnesses facing charges arising out of the same subject matter.

Ordinarily it is the defendant who moves for a separate trial and when he does so the determination of the motion is within the discretion of the court. *State v. Holup, 167 Conn. 240, 244, 355 A.2d 119*; *State v. Klein, 97 Conn. 321, 324, 116 A. 596.* "[C]ases arise where the defenses of the different parties are antagonistic, or where evidence will be introduced against one which will not be admissible against others. Where from the nature of the case it appears that a joint trial will probably be prejudicial to the rights of one or more of the parties, a separate trial should be granted when properly requested." *State v. Brauneis, 84 Conn. 222, 226, 79 A. 70.* A motion for a separate trial can be determined only on the basis of whether at the time "it appears that a joint trial will probably result in substantial injustice." *State v. Castelli, 92 Conn. 58, 63, 101 A. 476; State v. Holup, supra, 245.* A similar test should be applied when the prosecutor makes the motion for a separate trial. See ABA, Standards Relating to Joinder and Severance (1968) § 2.3 (b). At the time of trial our rules of practice permitted joinder of defendants, subject to the power of the court to order separate trials. Practice Book § 532. [3]

[3] Our new rules of criminal procedure (effective October 1, 1976) provide that each defendant shall be charged in a separate indictment or information; Practice Book § 2036; and that upon order two or more indictments or informations against different defendants may be tried together. Practice Book § 2240.

The state based its motion on (1) the fact that it had a statement from the defendant and that the statement could not be used in a trial involving several defendants together because of the rule enunciated in *Bruton v. United States, 391 U.S. 123, 88 S. Ct. 1620, 20 L. Ed. 2d 476*; (2) the defendant had been informed against individually by indictment and substituted information; and (3) the defendant was not on the Orchard Street premises at the time that the arrests and searches incident to said arrests were made there and that, therefore, he would have a different status from the others insofar as standing regarding a motion to suppress was concerned.

The *Bruton* case holds that the introduction into evidence in a joint trial of a confession implicating the defendant and made by a codefendant who does not testify is improper and cannot be cured by jury instructions. See *State v. Hunt, 154 Conn. 517, 227 A.2d 69*, vacated and remanded, *392 U.S. 304, 88 S. Ct. 2063, 20 L. Ed. 2d 1110*, for further consideration in the light of *Bruton v. United States, supra,* and *Roberts v. Russell, 392 U.S. 293, 88 S. Ct. 1921, 20 L. Ed. 2d 1100*. The defendant argues that he did testify at the trial and at all times intended to do so. The short answer to this argument is that at the time the motion was heard there was no sure way of knowing whether the defendant would take the witness stand and expose himself to cross-examination. Under the circumstances the court did not abuse its discretion in granting a separate trial on the ground that the defendant had made a confession incriminating other codefendants. *State v. Klein, supra, 324*; see *State v. Castelli, supra.* It is unnecessary to consider the further grounds for a separate trial except to note that they had a tendency to bolster the state's first ground for a separate trial.

The defendant asserts that the right to be tried separately from one's codefendants is a right which belongs to an accused and can be waived. Of course there is no constitutional or absolute right to a separate trial. 5 Wharton, *Criminal Law and Procedure* (Anderson) §§ 1943, 1944; see annot., 59 A.L.R.2d 841. Assuming the ability of an accused in a proper case to waive a right to a separate trial, that right does not necessarily carry with it the right to insist upon the opposite of that right, in this case a joint trial. See *Singer v. United States, 380 U.S. 24, 34-35, 85 S. Ct. 783, 13 L. Ed. 2d 630.*

The defendant further contends that once the court had granted the motion for a separate trial, it should have granted the defendant's requests for immunity of witnesses facing charges arising out of the same subject matter. We have recently considered the issue of immunity and have held that there is no authority for a court in this state to grant immunity to an accused's witnesses, and *General Statutes § 54-47a* does not apply. *State v. Simms, 170 Conn. 206, 210-11, 365 A.2d 821.* As in *Simms*, the defendant in this case has failed to cite any case that supports his claim. We find no merit to the defendant's claim.

IV

The defendant next claims that the court erred in excluding the testimony of three witnesses regarding the character, mental stability, prior violent and erratic behavior, and reputation for truthfulness of George Sams. Sams was an accomplice in the Alex Rackley murder who testified as a state's witness against the defendant at trial after having pleaded guilty to second degree murder prior to trial. The defendant claims alternatively that the evidence had relevance either on the question of Sams' credibility or on the defense of his own state of mind based on the alleged duress caused by Sams. The testimony proffered by the defendant's witnesses concerned how others perceived Sams, with no attempt to show that the defendant personally was aware of Sams' alleged reputation and prior acts of violence at the time the defendant himself was participating in the murder conspiracy culminating in the death of Rackley. Thus, such testimony would have been irrelevant to the issue of the defendant's own alleged fear of Sams. The defendant testified at trial that he only knew "a little" about Sams, which was that Sams had been expelled from the Black Panther Party because of a stabbing incident. The defense was in fact allowed to present testimony regarding Sams' erratic behavior, his reputation for mental instability, his violence and his reputation for veracity. In addition, a psychiatrist appointed to determine Sams' competency to testify was used as a defense witness on the question of Sams' mental stability and propensity for violence during the events leading up to Rackley's murder. The court did not err in excluding the testimony of the other witnesses concerning their knowledge of Sams' reputation for mental instability and violent behavior and his previous acts of violence. The trial court has broad discretion in determining the relevancy of evidence. *State v. Mullings*, 166 Conn. 268, 279, 348 A.2d 645; *State v. Lombardo*, 163 Conn. 241, 243, 304 A.2d 36; *Johnson v. Newell*, 160 Conn. 269, 277, 278 A.2d 776. There was no abuse of this discretion on the facts presented here. It was error for the court to refuse to permit the three witnesses to testify to Sams' reputation for veracity. See *Creer v. Active Auto Exchange, Inc.*, 99 Conn. 266, 278, 121 A. 888; Holden & Daly, Connecticut Evidence § 125 b (3); McCormick, Evidence (2d Ed.) § 44. The court realized its error and attempted to cure it by admitting the testimony of a fourth witness as to Sams' reputation for truthfulness in the community, and the witness testified that Sams had no reputation for truthfulness and had a reputation for being a "crazy liar." Sams himself testified that he was sometimes called "Crazy George" or "Madman George." "In order to constitute reversible error...the rulings must have been both wrong and harmful." *State v. Tropiano*, 158 Conn. 412, 427, 262 A.2d 147, cert. denied, *398 U.S. 949, 90 S. Ct. 1866, 26 L. Ed. 2d 288*. Under the circumstances, the error in excluding the testimony of the other three witnesses was harmless.

V

Prior to trial the defendant moved to dismiss the indictment on the ground that the grand jury was unconstitutionally selected. Subsequently the defendant challenged the jury array and moved to dismiss the jury panel on the ground that it was unconstitutionally and unlawfully selected. Both motions were denied. The defendant, conceding in his brief that recent decisions of this court are controlling on both motions and will result in affirmance of the trial court's rulings, does not further brief those motions. See *State v. Brown*, 169 Conn. 692, 696, 364 A.2d 186 (jury array); *State v. Hart*, 169 Conn. 428, 433, 363 A.2d 80 (jury array); *State v. Townsend*, 167 Conn. 539, 545, 356 A.2d 125 (jury array); *State v. Cobbs*, 164 Conn. 402, 406-15, 324 A.2d 234 (grand jury), cert. denied, *414 U.S. 861, 94 S. Ct. 77, 38 L. Ed. 2d 112*. We agree that those recent cases are sufficient authority to support the action of the court denying the defendant's motions challenging the selection of the grand jury and the jury array.

VI

Finally the defendant assigns error in the denial of his motion to dismiss on the ground that the state's attorneys are appointed by the judges of the Superior Court and that such relationship results in a violation of the constitutional doctrine of separation of powers as well as in a denial of due process of law. In his brief, the defendant states that he does not brief this assignment of error in view of the court's holding in *State v. Moynahan, 164 Conn. 560, 567, 325 A.2d 199*, cert. denied, *414 U.S. 976, 94 S. Ct. 291, 38 L. Ed. 2d 219*. There is no merit to the defendant's claim relating to the denial of his motion to dismiss because of the method of appointing state's attorneys. *State v. Moynahan, supra.*

There is no error.

In this opinion the other judges concurred.

Bibliography

1. THE DEVIL COMES TO CONNECTICUT: CONNECTICUT WITCH TRIALS IN THE SEVENTEENTH CENTURY

ARTICLES

Beach, Randall. "'Hang the Witch!' Was A Cry Heard All Too Often in Connecticut." *New Haven Register*, May 20, 2007.

Campbell, Susan. "Colonial Witch Hysteria Recalled." *Hartford Courant*, May 27, 2007.

Drake, Frederick C. "Witchcraft in the American Colonies, 1647-1662." *American Quarterly* 20, no. 4 (Winter 1968): 694-725.

"Salem May Pardon Accused Witches of 1692." *Boston Globe*, November, 1, 2004.

BOOKS

Demos, John Putnam. *Entertaining Satan*. New York: Oxford University Press, 1982.

Godbeer, Richard. *Escaping Salem: The Other Witch Hunt of 1692*. New York: Oxford University Press, 2005.

Hall, David D. *Witch Hunting in Seventeenth-Century New England: A Documentary History 1658-1693*. New York: Duke University Press, 1999.

Karlsen, Carol F. *The Devil in the Shape of a Woman: Witchcraft in Colonial New England*. New York: W. W. Norton & Company, 1998.

Tomlinson, R.G. *Witchcraft Trials of Connecticut*. Hartford: Connecticut Research, Inc., 1978.

ONLINE

"Famous American Trials: Salem Witchcraft Trials 1692." http://www.law.umkc.edu/faculty/projects/ftrials/salem/SALEM.HTM.

Norman-Eady, Sandra and Jennifer Bernier. "Connecticut Witch Trials and Posthumous Pardons." *Old Research Report*, December 2006. www.cga.ct.gov/2006/rpt/2006-R-0718.htm.

Ransom, Rebecca. "From Washington, a Witch's Tale." *Litchfield County Times*, October 26, 2006. http://www.countytimes.com/site/index.cfm?newsid=17382096&BRD=2303&PAG=461&dept_id=478976&rfi=8.

"Studies: United States History: The Witches of Salem." U.S. Department of State: Country, http://countrystudies.us/united-states/history-19.htm.

OTHER

Marcus, Ronald. "Elizabeth Clawson, Thou Deservest to Dye." Stamford: Stamford Historical Society, 1976.

Pagliuco, Linda G. "Before Salem: Witch Trials in Seventeenth Century Connecticut. Public Records of the Colony of Connecticut, 1636-1665." Hartford: Hartford Brown & Parsons, 1850. Preservation photocopy 2001, Connecticut State Library.

"Records of the Particular Court of Connecticut 1639-1663." Hartford: Connecticut Historical Society and the Society of Colonial Wars in the State of Connecticut, 1928.

Appendix A: MacKenzie, Ruth. "Connecticut Justice and Mercy." 39 Conn. B. J., Vol. 4, 558-573 (December 1965).

2. TEACHING TOLERANCE: PRUDENCE CRANDALL AND HER SCHOOL FOR "YOUNG LADIES AND LITTLE MISSES OF COLOR"

ARTICLES

"Advertisement and Notice Regarding the Opening of a "High School for Young Colored Ladies and Misses," *The Liberator*, March 2, 1833. Reprinted by the Gilder Lehrman Center for the Study of Slavery.

May, Samuel J. "Some Recollections of Our Antislavery Conflict." Boston: Fields, Osgood & Co., 1869. Reprinted by the Gilder Lehrman Center for the Study of Slavery.

"Prudence Crandall's Obituary." *Cleveland Gazette*, February 8, 1890.

Judson, Andrew. "Appeal to the American Colonization Society." *Fruits of Colonization*, March 22, 1833. Reprinted by the Gilder Lehrman Center for the Study of Slavery.

Judson, Andrew. "Argument of Andrew T. Judson in the case of the State of Connecticut v. Prudence Crandall." Delivered before the Supreme Court of Errors of the State of Connecticut, July 1834. Reprinted by the Gilder Lehrman Center for the Study of Slavery.

Judson, Andrew. "Remarks to the Jury on the Trial of the Case State v. P. Crandall, Superior Court, October Term, 1833, Windham County." Hartford: John Russell, Printer, 1833. Reprinted by the Gilder Lehrman Center for the Study of Slavery.

BOOKS

Strane, Susan. *A Whole-Souled Woman: Prudence Crandall and the Education of Black Women.* New York: W. W. Norton & Co., Inc., 1990.

Welch, Marvis Olive. *Prudence Crandall: A Biography.* New Hartford, Connecticut: Jason Publishers, 1983.

Yates, Elizabeth. *Prudence Crandall: Woman of Courage.* New York: E. P. Dutton & Co., Inc., 1955.

OTHER

McCain, Diana Ross. *To All On Equal Terms: The Life and Legacy of Prudence Crandall.* Connecticut: Prudence Crandall Museum, 2004.

"Prudence Crandall's Trials." Pamphlet of the Prudence Crandall Museum.

Appendix B: www.yale.edu/glc/crandall/12.htm.

3. A MUTINOUS LANDING IN UNSUSPECTING NEW HAVEN: THE AMISTAD TRIAL

ARTICLE

Lang, Joel. "New Chapter for Amistad." *Hartford Courant*, June 20, 2007.

BOOKS

Jones, Howard. *Mutiny on the Amistad*. New York: Oxford University Press, 1987.

Myers, Walter Dean. *Amistad: A Long Road to Freedom*. New York: Puffin, 1998.

Zeinert, Karen. *The Amistad Slave Revolt and American Abolition*. North Haven, Connecticut: Linnet Books, 1997.

COURT CASES

United States v. The Libellants and Claimants of the Schooner Amistad, 40 U.S. 518 (1841).

ONLINE

The following resources were accessed via Mystic Seaport's "Exploring *Amistad*" Web site.

"African Captives in Court." *Colored American*, September 28, 1939. http://*Amistad*.mysticseaport.org/library/news/col.am/*Amistad*.library.fmp?-database=*Amistad*.library.fmp&-layout=html&response=%2fsearch%2fframeset.lasso&-operator=eq&recnum=302&-token.frames=on&-search.

"Argument Of John Quincy Adams, Before The Supreme Court Of The United States, In The Case Of The United States, Appellants, Vs. Cinqué, And Others, Africans, Captured In The Schooner *Amistad*, By Lieut. Gedney." Delivered On The February 24, 1841 and March 1, 1841. http://*Amistad*.Mysticseaport.Org/Library/Court/Supreme/1841.Jqa.Argument.1.html.

"Argument Of Roger S. Baldwin, Of New Haven, Before The Supreme Court Of The United States, In The Case Of The United States, Appellants, Vs. Cinqué, And Others, Africans Of The *Amistad*." New York: S. W. Benedict, 1841. http://*Amistad*.mysticseaport.org/library/court/supreme/1841.baldwin.argument.html.

"From our Washington Correspondent, U.S. Representatives' Hall, Washington, D.C. March 1, 1841." *Colored American*, March 6, 1841. http://*Amistad*.mysticseaport.org/library/news/col.am/*Amistad*.library.fmp?-database=*Amistad*.library.fmp&-layout=html&-response=%

2fsearch%2fframeset.lasso&-operator=eq&recnum=332&-token. frames=on&-search.

"Deposition of Dr. Richard R. Madden, November 20, 1839, U.S. District Court, Connecticut." http://*Amistad*.mysticseaport.org/library/court/district/*Amistad*.library.fmp?-database=*Amistad*.library.fmp&-layout=html&-response=%2fsearch%2fframeset.lasso&-operator=eq&recnum=530&-token.frames=on&-search.

"Final Records, Petition for the Sale of the *Amistad*, September 17, 1840, U.S. Circuit Court, Connecticut." http://*Amistad*.mysticseaport.org/library/court/appellate/1840.9.17.requestsale.html.

"Letter from Cinqué." *The African Repository & Colonial Journal*, Vol. XVII, no. 23, December 1, 1841. http://*Amistad*.mysticseaport.org/library/news/afrep.coljrnl/1841.12.01.Cinqué.html.

"Mr. Forsyth to Mr. Calderon, 16th September, 1839." U.S. Congress. *Africans Taken in the Amistad*. 26th Congress., 1st sess., 1840. H. Doc. 185. http://*Amistad*.mysticseaport.org/library/diplomacy/doc.185.11.html.

"Mr. Calderon to Mr. Forsyth, 6th September, 1839, and translation." U.S. Congress. House. *Africans Taken in the Amistad*. 26th Congress., 1st sess., 1840.H. Doc. 185. http://*Amistad*.mysticseaport.org/library/diplomacy/doc.185.10.html.

"Newspaper Accounts." *New London Gazette*, August 26, 1839. UMKC Law Amistad Project. http://www.law.umkc.edu/faculty/projects/ftrials/Amistad/AMI_NEWS.HTM.

"Peale's Museum and Portrait Gallery." *New York Commercial Advertiser*, June 16, 1840. http://*Amistad*.mysticseaport.org/library/news/nyca/1840.06.16.pealemusm.html.

"Public Statutes At Large of the United States Of America From The Organization Of The Government In 1789 To March 3, 1845." http://*Amistad*.mysticseaport.org/library/govt.papers/legis/1807.act.barsslavetrade.html.

"Rough draft of Andrew Judson's jurisdiction ruling, January 1840." Andrew T. Judson Papers, Coll. 247, box 1/6, Manuscripts Collection, Mystic Seaport Museum. http://*Amistad*.mysticseaport.org/library/court/district/*Amistad*.library.fmp?-database=*Amistad*.library.fmp&-layout=html&-response=%2fsearch%2fframeset.lasso&-operator=eq&recnum=519&-token.frames=on&-search.

"Ruiz and Montez." *New York Commercial Advertiser*, October 18, 1839. http://*Amistad*.mysticseaport.org/library/news/nyca/1839.10.18.ruizandmontez.html.

"Sale of the *Amistad*." *Intelligencer*, October 27, 1840 http://*Amistad*.mysticseaport.org/library/news/intelligencer/*Amistad*.library.fmp?-database=*Amistad*.library.fmp&-layout=html&-response=%2fsearch%2fframeset.lasso&-operator=eq&recnum=498&-token.frames=on&-search.

"Testimony of Antonio, January 9, 1840, U.S. District Court, Connecticut." http://*Amistad*.mysticseaport.org/library/court/district/*Amistad*.library.fmp?-database=*Amistad*.library.fmp&-layout=html&-response=%2fsearch%2fframeset.lasso&-operator=eq&recnum=510&-token.frames=on&-search.

"Testimony of Cinqué, January 8, 1840, U.S. District Court, Connecticut." http://*Amistad*.mysticseaport.org/library/court/district/*Amistad*.library.fmp?-database=*Amistad*.library.fmp&-layout=html&-response=%2fsearch%2fframeset.lasso&-operator=eq&recnum=512&-token.frames=on&-search.

"Testimony of Fuliwa, January 8, 1840, U.S. District Court, Connecticut." http://*Amistad*.mysticseaport.org/library/court/district/*Amistad*.library.fmp?-database=*Amistad*.library.fmp&-layout=html&-response=%2fsearch%2fframeset.lasso&-operator=eq&recnum=514&-token.frames=on&-search.

"Testimony of Henry Green, November 19, 1839, U.S. District Court, Connecticut." http://*Amistad*.mysticseaport.org/library/court/district/*Amistad*.library.fmp?-database=*Amistad*.library.fmp&-layout=html&-response=%2fsearch%2fframeset.lasso&-operator=eq&recnum=515&-token.frames=on&-search.

"Testimony of James Covey January 7, 1840, U.S. District Court, Connecticut." http://*Amistad*.mysticseaport.org/library/court/district/*Amistad*.library.fmp?-database=*Amistad*.library.fmp&-layout=html&-response=%2fsearch%2fframeset.lasso&-operator=eq&recnum=473&-token.frames=on&-search.

"The *Amistad* Circuit Court Trial." *New York Commercial Advertiser*, September 23, 1839. http://www.law.umkc.edu/faculty/projects/ftrials/*Amistad*/Ami_trialrep.html.

"The Long, Low, Black Schooner." *New York Journal of Commerce*, September 2, 1839. http://*Amistad*.mysticseaport.org/library/news/nyjc/*Amistad*.library.fmp?-database=*Amistad*.library.fmp&-layout=html&-response=%2fsearch%2fframeset.lasso&-operator=eq&recnum=186&-token.frames=on&-search.

"Timeline: Legal Path of the *Amistad* Case: 1839–1845." http://*Amistad*.mysticseaport.org/timeline/courttimeline.html.

Appendix C: www.law.cornell.edu/background/amistad/opinion.html.

4. PRIVACY IN THE BEDROOM: *GRISWOLD V. CONNECTICUT*

Articles

"Letters From the People, A Problem For Mrs. Sanger." *Hartford Courant*, February 18, 1923.

"Wants State to Have Birth Control Clinics." *Hartford Courant*, February 12, 1923.

Hunter, Marjorie. "High Court Hears Birth-Curb Case." *New York Times*, March 30, 1965.

"New Haven Police Shut Birth Clinic." *New York Times*, November 11, 1961.

Books

Duffy, Jill and Mersky, Roy, eds. *A Documentary History of the Legal Aspects of Abortion in the United States: Griswold v. Connecticut*. Littleton, Colorado: Fred B. Rothman & Co., 2001.

Garrow, David. *Liberty and Sexuality: The Right to Privacy and the Making of Roe v. Wade*. California: University of California Press, 1998.

Hoffer, Peter Charles and N.E.H. Hull. *Roe v. Wade: The Abortion Rights Controversy in American History*. Kansas: University Press of Kansas, 2001.

Johnson, John. *Griswold v. Connecticut: Birth Control and the Constitutional Right to Privacy*. Kansas: University Press of Kansas, 2005.

Wawrose, Susan. *Griswold v. Connecticut: Contraception and the Right of Privacy*. Danbury, Connecticut: Franklin Watts, 1996.

Court Cases

Buxton v. Ullman, 147 Conn. 48 (1959).
Griswold v. Connecticut, 381 U.S. 479 (1965).
Poe v. Ullman, 367 U.S. 497, 509 (1961).
State v. Nelson, 7 Conn. Supp. 262 (1939).
State v. Nelson, 126 Conn. 412 (1940).
Tileston v. Ullman, 129 Conn. 84, 88-89 (1942).
Tileston v. Ullman, 318 U.S. 44 (1943).
United States v. One Package, 86 F.2d 737 (2d Cir. 1936).

Online

"Connecticut Women's Hall of Fame: Catherine Roraback." http://www.cwhf.org/hall/roraback/roraback.htm.

"Consortium in Connecticut." *Time Magazine*, March 10, 1961. http://www.time.com/time/magazine/article/0,9171,826939,00.html.

"Important Dates in the Reproductive Rights Movement." Planned Parenthood, http://www.ppct.org/who/importantdates.html.

Fowler "Chick" Vincent Harper, Author of the Right to Privacy, Class of 1921, Ohio Northern College of Law." http://www.law.onu.edu/about/fowlerharper.html.

Other

Connecticut Bar Foundation James W. Cooper Fellows Oral History of Connecticut Women in the Legal Profession Project, Catherine Roraback Interviews May 4, 2004 and September 14, 2004.

Appendix D: http://caselaw.findlaw.com.

5. THE CIRCUS COMES TO NEW HAVEN: THE TRIAL OF THE BLACK PANTHERS

Articles

"2 Top Panthers Jailed for Contempt." *New York Times*, April 15, 1970, p. 32.

"2 Women Panthers in Rackley Case Freed on Probation." *New York Times*, October 3, 1970, p. 57.

"A Panther Admits He Killed Another." *New York Times*, January 17, 1970, p. 1.

"A Panther Pleads Guilty to Assault in Rackley Case." *New York Times*, September 24, 1970, p. 29.

"Bail Hearings End for Five Panthers." *New York Times*, December 5, 1969, p. 28.

"Black Panther Chief Seized in Berkley in Torture-Slaying." *New York Times*, August 20, 1969, p. 15.

"Black Panther Pleads Guilty in Slayings." *New York Times*, December 2, 1969, p. 59.

"Black Panther Wanted in State Starts Return." *Hartford Courant*, June 11, 1969, p. 13.

"Canadians Hold Figure in Slaying." *Hartford Courant*, August 9, 1969, p. 2.

"Charges False Seale Declares." *New York Times*, September 30, 1970, p. 35.

"Court Orders Bail for Woman Panther." *New York Times*, June 11, 1970, p. 24.

"Damage Estimated at $100,000 after Harvard Riot." *New York Times*, April 17, 1970, p. 35.

"New Haven Judge Ends Panther Case." *New York Times*, November 20, 1971, p. 35.

"New Haven Judge Releases Panther." *New York Times*, August 6, 1970, p. 24.

"New Haven Panther Free on Probation." *New York Times*, October 24, 1970, p. 18.

"New Recess is Taken in Bobby Seale Case." *New York Times*, April 6, 1971, p. 13.

"Ninth Suspect Arrested in Black Panther Slaying." *Hartford Courant*, May 29, 1969 p. 2.

"North Carolinian Sought in Black Panther Slaying." *Hartford Courant*, May 31, 1969, p. 4.

"Panther Challenge to Jury Law Concluded in New Haven Court." *New York Times*, October 18, 1970, p. 60.

"Panther Lawyers in New Haven Subpoena Newspaper Records." *New York Times*, May 31, 1970, p. 27.

"Panther Sentenced in Rackley Slaying." *New York Times*, September 11, 1970, p. 46.

"Panthers Seeking Tests on Witnesses." *New York Times*, July 8, 1970, p. 28.

"Policeman Denies Panthers' Charge." *New York Times*, Feb. 8, 1970, p. 20.

"Rights Violated Seale Suit Says." *New York Times*, October 9, 1970, p. 41.

"Ruling in Connecticut." *New York Times*, July 30, 1971, p. 30.

"Seale is Main Drawing Card for Panther Rally in New Haven." *New York Times*, May 1, 1970, p. 41.

"Seale Jury Plea Spurned, Trial Will Begin Tuesday." *New York Times*, November 13, 1970, p. 40.

"Seale Jury Seated after 4 Months of Question 1,035." *New York Times*, March 12, 1971, p. 43.

"Seale Motion Denied." *New York Times*, October 22, 1970, p. 42.

"Seale Trial Fails to Add New Jurors." *New York Times*, December 12, 1970, p. 35.

"Shortage of Jurors Delays Seale Trial." *New York Times*, April 1, 1971, p. 33.

"Two Panthers Win Delay in Colorado." *New York Times*, December 14, 1969, p. 64.

"Witness Tells Court that Seale ordered Black Panther Killed." *New York Times*, April 23, 1970, p. 1.

Bergan, John. "Panthers Indicted on Murder Charge." *Hartford Courant*, June 25, 1969, p. 1.

Bigart, Homer. "New Haven Police Set Off Tear Gas at Panther Rally." *New York Times*, May 2, 1970, p. 1.

Bigart, Homer. "Panther Motions Denied by Court." *New York Times*, May 6, 1970, p. 44.

Bigart, Homer. "US Troops Flown in for Panther Rally." *New York Times*, May 1, 1970, p. 1.

Darnton, John. "8 Black Panthers Seized in Torture Murder Case." *New York Times*, May 23, 1969, p. 24.

Darnton, John. "New Haven is Looking with Foreboding to the Murder Trial of Bobby Seale, the Black Panther Leader." *New York Times*, March 22, 1970, p. 57.

Darnton, John. "Panthers' Apologies Free Two Jailed for New Haven Contempt." *New York Times*, April 22, 1970, p. 1.

Darnton, John. "Seale, Under Guard, Shows Up in New Haven Court in Slaying." *New York Times*, March 19, 1970, p. 36.

Darnton, John. "Sherriff Testifies at Seale Hearing." *New York Times*, April 24, 1970, p. 23.

Davies, Lawrence. "Panther Chief Held in Murder Case." *New York Times*, Aug. 21, 1969, p. 32.

Epps, Garrett. "The Trial of Bobby Seale." *The Harvard Crimson*, June 11, 1970.

Lelyveld, Joseph. "Arguments End in Panther Trial." *New York Times*, August 26, 1970, p. 38.

Lelyveld, Joseph. "Defense Begins Case in Panther Trial." *New York Times*, August 13, 1970, p. 17.

Lelyveld, Joseph. "FBI Agent Testifies Panther Told of Shooting Murder Victim." *New York Times*, July 22, 1970, p. 26.

Lelyveld, Joseph. "Former Panther Tells of Dispute." *New York Times*, August 8, 1970, p. 19.

Lelyveld, Joseph. "Jury Reports Split on McLucas, but Judge Orders it to Continue." *New York Times*, August 31, 1970, p. 1.

Lelyveld, Joseph. "Kimbro Describes Panther Slaying." *New York Times*, July 24, 1970, p. 17.

Lelyveld, Joseph. "Kunstler is on Stand in New Haven Panther Trial." *New York Times*, August 14, 1970, p. 22.

Lelyveld, Joseph. "McLucas Guilty of Plotting in Panther Murder Case." *New York Times*, September 1, 1970, p. 1.

Lelyveld, Joseph. "McLucas is Given 12-15 Year Term." *New York Times*, September 19, 1970, p. 1.

Lelyveld, Joseph. "McLucas Testifies at Panther Trial." *New York Times*, August 20, 1970, p. 1.

Lelyveld, Joseph. "New Haven Panther Trial Opens; State Will Not Seek Death." *New York Times*, June 17, 1970, p. 28.

Lelyveld, Joseph. "New Haven Panther Trial Sees Color Slides of Torture Victim." *New York Times*, July 15, 1970, p. 45.

Lelyveld, Joseph. "New Haven Panther Trial Told About Murder Night." *New York Times*, July 16, 1970, p. 21.

Lelyveld, Joseph. "Panther Testifies He 'Assumed' Party Leaders Ordered Murder." *New York Times*, July 28, 1970, p. 34.

Lelyveld, Joseph. "Prosecution Rests in Panther Trial in New Haven." *New York Times*, August 12, 1970, p. 29.

Lelyveld, Joseph. "Sams Takes Stand in Panther Trial." *New York Times*, August 7, 1970, p. 1.

Lelyveld, Joseph. "Seale Reportedly Visited Panthers Before Slaying." *New York Times*, August 15, 1970, p. 25.

Lelyveld, Joseph. "Seale Testifies at Panther Trial." *New York Times*, August 22, 1970, p. 1.

Lelyveld, Joseph. "Seale Trial Opens in Quiet Setting." *New York Times*, November 18, 1970, p. 49.

Lelyveld, Joseph. "Torture is Described at Panther Trial in New Haven." *New York Times*, July 18, 1970, p. 17.

Lelyveld, Joseph. "Woman Testifies in New Haven that McLucas Wept after Rackley's Murder." *New York Times*, August 19, 1970, p. 24.

Oelsner, Lesley. "A Seale Witness Shifts Testimony." *New York Times*, April 15, 1971, p. 51.

Oelsner, Lesley. "Charges Dropped in Seale Case." *New York Times*, May 26, 1971, p. 1.

Oelsner, Lesley. "Deadlock by Jury Results in Seale-Huggins Mistrial." *New York Times*, May 25, 1971, p. 1.

Oelsner, Lesley. "Defense Finishes in Seale Case." *New York Times*, May 14, 1971, p. 21.

Oelsner, Lesley. "Defense Witness Testifies Sams Sought to "Get Even" with Seale." *New York Times*, May 6, 1971, p. 18.

Oelsner, Lesley. "Judge Rules Rackley Case Raid Legal." *New York Times*, March 31, 1971, p. 24.

Oelsner, Lesley. "Lawyers Sum Up in the Seale Case." *New York Times*, May 19, 1971, p. 41.

Oelsner, Lesley. "Mrs. Huggins, on Witness Stand, Protests Innocence." *New York Times*, May 12, 1971, p. 87.

Oelsner, Lesley. "Pictures Shown to Seale Jurors." *New York Times*, April 17, 1971, p. 23.

Oelsner, Lesley. "Sams and Kimbro are Sentenced to Life in Panther Killing." *New York Times*, June 24, 1971, p. 33.

Oelsner, Lesley. "Sams Denounces Seale and Garry." *New York Times*, April 24, 1971, p. 27.

Oelsner, Lesley. "Sams Testified Seale Ordered Panthers to Murder Rackley." *New York Times*, April 23, 1971, p. 15.

Oelsner, Lesley. "Seale is Linked to Slain Panther." *New York Times*, April 14, 1971, p. 57.

Oelsner, Lesley. "Seale is Praised as Peaceful Man." *New York Times*, May 7, 1971, p. 49.

Oelsner, Lesley. "Seale Loses Bid to Fight Tapes' Use." *New York Times*, March 26, 1971, p. 79.

Oelsner, Lesley. "The Seale Jurors." *New York Times*, May 28, 1971, p. 34.

Oelsner, Lesley. "Torture of Rackley Described At Trial." *New York Times*, March 25, 1971, p. 28.

Oelsner, Lesley. "Witness Links Seale to House where Murder Victim was Held." *New York Times*, April 22, 1971, p. 32.

Oelsner, Lesley. "Witness puts Seale's Co-Defendant in Murder Victim's Room." *New York Times*, March 19, 1971, p. 27.

Simon, Stan. "Markle Ends Silence on Trial. *Hartford Courant*, May 27, 1971, p. 1.

Treaster, Joseph B. "2 Panthers Plead Guilty in Rackley Slaying." *New York Times*, September 26, 1970, p. 18.

Treaster, Joseph B. "A Panther Case Nearing its End." *New York Times*, October 27, 1971, p. 29.

Treaster, Joseph B. "Judge Says Yale Perils Fair Trial." *New York Times*, April 26, 1970, p. 45.

Treaster, Joseph B. "Seale in Connecticut for Murder Trial." *New York Times*, March 14, 1970, p. 35.

Vasquez, Juan. "Seale Trial Gets First Two Jurors." *New York Times*, November 20, 1970, p. 48.

Books

Ashe, Robert. *Halifax Champion: Black Power in Gloves*. Halifax: Formac Publishing Limited, 2005.

Bass, Paul and Douglas Rae. *Murder in the Model City: The Black Panthers, Yale, and the Redemption of a Killer*. New York: Basic Books, 2006.

Seale, Bobby. *Seize the Time, The Story of the Black Panther Party and Huey P. Newton*, Black Classic Press, 1991.

Court Cases

Bobby Seale and Ericka Huggins v. John R. Manson, Commissioner of Corrections of the State of Connecticut, 326 F. Supp. 1375, May 5, 1971.

Online

"Black Panther Party Community Programs, 1966–1982." Black Panther Party Research Project. http://www.stanford.edu/group/blackpanthers/programs.shtml.

"Black Panther Party Time Line." University of California at Berkeley Library. http://www.lib.berkeley.edu/MRC/pacificapanthers.html.

"Ericka Huggins: Women's Leadership for Human Rights: From the Black Panther Party to Contemporary Feminism and Spirituality." Speak Out! http://www.speakoutnow.org/userdata_display.php?modin=50&uid=1568.

"Huey P. Newton." Biography Resource Center, Africawithin.com. http://africawithin.com/bios/huey_newton.htm.

"Robert George Seale." Biography Resource Center, Africawithin.com. http://africawithin.com/bios/bobby_seale.htm.

Westcott, Kathryn. "Marching for Freedom." BBC News Online, August 23, 2003. http://news.bbc.co.uk/2/hi/americas/3150657.stm.

Other

Connecticut Bar Foundation James W. Cooper Fellows Oral History of Connecticut Women in the Legal Profession Project, Catherine Roraback Interviews May 4, 2004 and September 14, 2004.

Newton, Huey P., and Bobby Seale. "Black Panther 10 Point Program." Dr. Huey P. Newton Foundation Inc.

Newton, Huey P. "Executive Mandate Number 1." Dr. Huey P. Newton Foundation, Inc.

Remarks of President Kingman Brewster at Yale College Faculty Meeting, April 23, 1970, Records Documenting the May Day Rally and Yale (RU 86). Manuscripts and Archives, Yale University Library.

Reporter Notes, WYBC, Yale University, Records (RU 59). Manuscripts and Archives, Yale University Library.

Transcript of Confiscated Tapes, WYBC, Yale University, Records (RU 59). Manuscripts and Archives, Yale University Library.

Appendix E: http://66.161.141.176/cgibin/texis/web/caselaw/+AewSWKD2eoxbnmeN62weozZxwwxFqEwApWmWhr6B96w3w+tr_mKnVV39IFqqgR/svindex.html?doc=1.

6. DESEGREGATING HARTFORD PUBLIC SCHOOLS: *SHEFF V. O'NEILL*

Articles

"City May Join Efforts to Overturn Sheff Ruling." *Hartford Courant*, May 6, 1995.

"Sheff at a Tortoise Pace." *Hartford Courant*, August 8, 2004.

"Sheff Panel Recommendations." *Hartford Courant*, January 23, 1997.

"Supreme Court to Hear Desegregation Case." *Hartford Courant*, May 3, 1995.

Frahm, Robert and Matthew Daly. "6 Sheff Panel Appointments Fail to Address Concerns." *Hartford Courant*, August 9, 1996.

Frahm, Robert and Rachel Gottlieb. "State Expects To Fall Short on Sheff." *Hartford Courant*, August 4, 2004.

Frahm, Robert and Rick Green. "Plaintiffs Rest in Sheff Case." *Hartford Courant*, January 29, 1993.

Frahm, Robert. "A Losing Battle, So Far." *Hartford Courant*, June 13, 2007.

Frahm, Robert. "Broad-Based Panel to Advise Lawmakers on Sheff Remedy." *Hartford Courant*, July 26, 1996.

Frahm, Robert. "Court Orders Desegregation." *Hartford Courant*, July 10, 1996.

Frahm, Robert. "Final Arguments Prepared in Segregation Case." *Hartford Courant*, December 5, 1998.

Frahm, Robert. "Hammer Requests Help in Rewriting Sheff Case." *Hartford Courant*, June 7, 1995.

Frahm, Robert. "Hammer's Sheff Findings Support State." *Hartford Courant*, June 28, 1995.

Frahm, Robert. "In Sheff, a Truce, Then a Deal." *Hartford Courant*, January 26, 2003.

Frahm, Robert. "Judge Given More Time to Review Sheff Case." *Hartford Courant*, June 14, 1995.

Frahm, Robert. "Justices Go to Heart of Sheff Case; Does Constitution Require Racial Diversity in Schools?" *Hartford Courant*, September 29, 1995.

Frahm, Robert. "Legislators Approve Sheff Settlement." *Hartford Courant*, February 26, 2003.

Frahm, Robert. "Missing Children." *Hartford Courant*, April 1, 2007.

Frahm, Robert. "Plan Shifts School Aid." *Hartford Courant*, April 24, 2002.

Frahm, Robert. "Poll: Sharp splits on school integration." *Hartford Courant*, February 14, 1993.

Frahm, Robert. "Racial Balance Remains an Issue." *Hartford Courant*, April 15, 2002.

Frahm, Robert. "Sheff Case Returns to Court." *Hartford Courant*, July 6, 2007.

Frahm, Robert. "Sheff Judge Asks for Proposals." *Hartford Courant*, May 4, 2002.

Frahm, Robert. "Sheff Panel Lacks Focus at First Try." *Hartford Courant*, August 29, 1996.

Frahm, Robert. "Sheff Plaintiffs Back to Prod Desegregation." *Hartford Courant*, December 29, 2000.

Frahm, Robert. "Sheff Plaintiffs Not Satisfied." *Hartford Courant*, August 3, 2004.

Frahm, Robert. "State Revising Its Response to Sheff." *Hartford Courant*, June 7, 2007.

Frahm, Robert. "Witness in Sheff Case Faults State for Lack of Desegregation Goals." *Hartford Courant*, September 10, 1998.

Frank, Rachel Gottlieb. "Desegregation by Order?" *Hartford Courant*, January 4, 2008.

Frank, Rachel Gottlieb. "Judge Sends Sheff Deal Back." *Hartford Courant*, January 25, 2008.

Frank, Rachel Gottlieb. "Tougher Hand with Suburbs." *Hartford Courant*, November 14, 2007.

Gottlieb, Rachel. "Extra Push Needed by State?" *Hartford Courant*, November 7, 2007.

Gottlieb, Rachel. "Lawyer Says Integration Effort Lags." *Hartford Courant*, October 18, 2003.

Gottlieb, Rachel. "Sides Seek Sheff Pact." *Hartford Courant*, July 13, 2002.

Gottlieb, Rachel. "Spotty Sheff Enforcement." *Hartford Courant*, November 9, 2007.

Gottlieb, Rachel. "State Fares Well in Sheff Hearing." *Hartford Courant*, June 21, 2005.

Gottlieb, Rachel. "State Promises Magnet School Help." *Hartford Courant*, August 12, 2004.

Green, Rick and Liz Halloran. "Sheff Lawsuit Supporters Protest in City." *Hartford Courant*, April 18, 1995.

Green, Rick. "Plaintiffs React To Verdict: Dejected, But Determined." *Hartford Courant*, April 13, 1995.

Green, Rick. "Poll: 6 In 10 Support Sheff Case Ruling." *Hartford Courant*, April 28, 1995.

Green, Rick. "Ruling In Sheff Case Won't Be Appealed." *Hartford Courant*, March 24, 1999.

Green, Rick. "Sheff Case Goes Back to Court." *Hartford Courant*, March 6, 1998.

Green, Rick. "State Defends Efforts To Integrate Schools." *Hartford Courant*, September 12, 1998.

Green, Rick. "State Focuses on Magnet Schools." *Hartford Courant*, February 27, 2001.

Green, Rick. "State Sees Gains on Integration." *Hartford Courant*, February 4, 1993.

Johnson, Kirk. "Connecticut Schools Get a Voluntary Racial Plan." *New York Times*, April 6, 1989

Johnson, Kirk. "Schools Need Race Balance, Weicker Says." *New York Times*, January 7, 1993.

Johnson, Kirk. "Suit in Connecticut Challenges Schools as Racially Divided." *New York Times*, April 28, 1989

Judson, George. "Expert on Demographics Testifies at Hartford Trial." *New York Times*, February 3, 1993.

Judson, George. "First Student Testifies in Suit to Integrate Hartford Schools." *New York Times*, January 13, 1993.

Judson, George. "Hartford Schools Molded by Racial Isolation." *New York Times*, February 13, 1993.

Judson, George. "Merge City and Suburban Schools, Lawsuit Urges." *New York Times*, December 17, 1992.

Judson, George. "School Segregation Case Too Knotty, Lawyers Say." *New York Times*, November 22, 1991.

Kauffman, Matthew. "Sheff Appeal to End Up in High Court." *Hartford Courant*, April 13, 1995.

Keating, Christopher. "Legislature: Sheff On Hold." *Hartford Courant*, July 21, 2007.

Keating, Christopher. "Rowland Says He's Sorry." *Hartford Courant*, April 21, 1995.

Libov, Charlotte. "A Young Crusader Fights for Integration." *New York Times*, July 22, 1990.

Libov, Charlotte. "Racial Report on Schools: The Fallout." *New York Times*, January 31, 1988.

Libov, Charlotte. "State Readies Court Reply to Desegregation Suit." *New York Times*, August 13, 1989.

Mahony, Edmund. "Perez May Step Into Sheff Case." *Hartford Courant*, January 29, 2006.

Sheridan, Chris. "Ruling in Landmark School Case; Desegregation Lawsuit Fails; Judge Finds No Fault On State's Part." *Hartford Courant*, April 13, 1995.

Sheridan, Chris. "Sheff Put On Fast Track; Order Would Clear Way For Justices To Review Case In Fall." *Hartford Courant*, May 12, 1995.

Simpson, Stan. "A Decade of Half Measures." *Hartford Courant*, July 23, 2006.

Court Cases

Brown v. Board of Education, 347 U.S. 483 (1954).
Green v. County School Board of New Kent County, 391 U.S. 430 (1968).
Sheff v. O'Neill, 13 Conn. L. Rptr. 553 (1995).
Sheff v. O'Neill, 238 Conn. 1, (1996).
Spencer v. Kugler, 326 F.Supp. 1235 (1971), aff'd 404 U.S. 1027 (1972).

Online

Connecticut Attorney General's Office, Press Release, *Sheff v. O'Neill* Ruling, March 3, 1999, accessed at http://www.ct.gov/ag/cwp/view.asp?A=1774&Q=282854.

Holladay, Jennifer, compiler, *Brown v. Board*: Timeline of School Integration in the U.S., http://www.tolerance.org/teach/magazine/features.jsp?ar=487, updated 2007.

Thomas J. Dodd Research Center Materials

Affidavit of John Allison, *Sheff v. O'Neill*, September 19, 1991, Connecticut Civil Liberties Union Collection, Archives and Special Collections at the Thomas J. Dodd Research Center, University of Connecticut Libraries.

Affidavit of Hernan Lafontaine, *Sheff v. O'Neill*, September 19, 1991, Connecticut Civil Liberties Union Collection, Archives and Special Collections at the Thomas J. Dodd Research Center, University of Connecticut Libraries.

Complaint, *Sheff v. O'Neill*, April 26, 1989, Connecticut Civil Liberties Union Collection, Archives and Special Collections at the Thomas J. Dodd Research Center, University of Connecticut Libraries.

Defendants-Appellees' Preliminary Statement of Issues, *Sheff v. O'Neill*, May 10, 1995, Connecticut Civil Liberties Union Collection, Archives and Special Collections at the Thomas J. Dodd Research Center, University of Connecticut Libraries.

Defendants' Post Trial Brief, *Sheff v. O'Neill*, June 28, 1993, Connecticut Civil Liberties Union Collection, Folder 241, Archives and Special Collections at the Thomas J. Dodd Research Center, University of Connecticut Libraries.

Defendants' Pretrial Memorandum, *Sheff v. O'Neill*, November 16, 1992, Connecticut Civil Liberties Union Collection, Folder 230, Archives and Special Collections at the Thomas J. Dodd Research Center, University of Connecticut Libraries.

Defendants' Response To Plaintiffs' List Of Trial Exhibits, *Sheff v. O'Neill*, November 23, 1992, Connecticut Civil Liberties Union Collection, Folder 234, Archives and Special Collections at the Thomas J. Dodd Research Center, University of Connecticut Libraries.

Memorandum of Decision on the Defendant's Motion to Strike, *Sheff v. O'Neill*, May 18, 1990, Connecticut Civil Liberties Union Collection, Archives and Special Collections at the Thomas J. Dodd Research Center, University of Connecticut Libraries.

Memorandum of Law in Support of Defendants' Motion for Summary Judgment, *Sheff v. O'Neill*, July 8, 1991, Connecticut Civil Liberties Union Collection, Folder 242, Archives and Special Collections at the Thomas J. Dodd Research Center, University of Connecticut Libraries.

Memorandum of Decision on the Defendant's Motion for Summary Judgment, *Sheff v. O'Neill*, February 24, 1992, Connecticut Civil Liberties Union Collection, Archives and Special Collections at the Thomas J. Dodd Research Center, University of Connecticut Libraries.

Motion to Expedite the Appeal, *Sheff v. O'Neill*, May 10, 1995, Connecticut Civil Liberties Union Collection, Archives and Special Collections at the Thomas J. Dodd Research Center, University of Connecticut Libraries.

Motion for Summary Judgment, *Sheff v. O'Neill*, July 8, 1991, Connecticut Civil Liberties Union Collection, Folder 229, Archives and Special Collections at the Thomas J. Dodd Research Center, University of Connecticut Libraries.

Order, State of Connecticut Supreme Court, *Sheff v. O'Neill*, August 8, 1995, Connecticut Civil Liberties Union Collection, Folder 268, Archives and Special Collections at the Thomas J. Dodd Research Center, University of Connecticut Libraries.

Plaintiff's Pretrial Memorandum, *Sheff v. O'Neill*, November 16, 1992, Connecticut Civil Liberties Union Collection, Archives and Special Collections at the Thomas J. Dodd Research Center, University of Connecticut Libraries.

Plaintiff's Memorandum of Law in Opposition to Respondents' Motion for Summary Judgment, *Sheff v. O'Neill*, September 20, 1991, Connecticut Civil Liberties Union Collection, Archives and Special Collections at the Thomas J. Dodd Research Center, University of Connecticut Libraries.

Preliminary Statement of the Issues, *Sheff v. O'Neill*, April 27, 1995, Connecticut Civil Liberties Union Collection, Archives and Special Collections at the Thomas J. Dodd Research Center, University of Connecticut Libraries.

OTHER

Constitution of The State of Connecticut

Dougherty, Jack, Jesse Wanzer, and Christina Ramsay. "Missing the Goal: A Visual Guide to *Sheff v. O'Neill* School Desegregation," June 2007, Trinity College, October 15, 2007, citing CT State Department of Education (CSDE). Revised October 2007.

House Resolution No. 4, Resolution Approving the Settlement Agreement in *Sheff v. O'Neill*.

Interview, Milo Sheff, March 1, 2008.

Office of Legislative Research Report, Panel Recommendations, 97-R-0175, January 23, 1997.

Public Act 93-263, An Act Improving Educational Quality and Diversity, June 28, 1993.

Public Act 97-290, An Act Enhancing Educational Choices and Opportunities, June 26, 1997.

Senate Resolution 005, 2008, Resolution Approving the Settlement Agreement in *Sheff v. O'Neill*.

Special Act 97-4, An Act Concerning the Hartford Public Schools, April 18, 1997.

Stipulation and Order, *Sheff v. O'Neill*, January 22, 2003.

ABOUT THE AUTHOR

REGINA FORKER, an honor student at the University of Connecticut School of Law, has worked as a summer associate with Brown Paindiris & Scott LLP in Glastonbury, CT, and Updike Kelly & Spellacy PC in Hartford, CT. In 2007, she was accepted into the University of Connecticut's Intellectual Property Certificate Program and recently gave a speech at a conference of the World Intellectual Property Organization in Geneva, Switzerland. She is in her second semester as student associate with the Intellectual Property and Entrepreneurship Clinic at the law school, counseling small business clients. *Controversial Court Cases in Connecticut, Part I* is the first in a two-part series with the second book currently in production.